THE

HAND OF GOD IN HISTORY;

OR,

DIVINE PROVIDENCE HISTORICALLY ILLUSTRATED

IN

THE EXTENSION AND ESTABLISHMENT

OF

Christianity.

BY HOLLIS READ, A.M.

UTHOR OF THE CHRISTIAN BRAHMUN, AND LATE MISSIONARY OF
THE AMERICAN BOARD.

"THAT ALL THE PEOPLE OF THE EARTH MIGHT KNOW THE HAND OF THE LORD,
THAT IT IS MIGHTY."—*Josh.* iv. 94

HARTFORD:

H. E. ROBINS AND CO

STEREOTYPED BY
RICHARD H. HOERG,
HARTFORD, CONN

GOD
IN
HISTORY.

HENRY E. ROBINS & CO. HARTFORD.

PREFACE.

"THE history of the world is gradually losing itself in the history of the church." "The full history of the world is a history of redemption." "In no period of the history of redemption, not even when preparing the fullness of time for the Messiah's advent, has the providence of God been more marked than of late years, in its bearing on the extension of the Redeemer's kingdom." "The providence of God, in respect to this work," says another, "would form one of the most interesting chapters in the history of his government." "To the casual observer of Providence, to the ordinary reader of this world's history, the whole appears like a chaos of incidents, no thread, no system, no line of connection running through it. One course of events is seen here, and another there. Kingdoms rise on the stage one after another, and become great and powerful, and then pass away and are forgotten. And the history of the church seems scarcely less a chaos than that of the world. Changes are continually going on within it and around it, and these apparently without much order."

Yet all is not a chaos. The Christian student, with his eye devoutly fixed on the Hand of God, looks out upon the world, and back on the wide field of its history, and takes altogether a different view. What before seemed so chaotic and disorderly, now puts on the appearance of system and form. All is animated by one soul, and that soul is Providence.

The writer of the following pages believes his subject *timely*. Perhaps as never before, the minds of the most sagacious writers of our age are watching with profound and pious interest the progress of human events. The aim of the author has been to make the work *historical*, at least so abounding in narrative, anecdote, biography, and in the delineations of men and things in real life, as to commend it to the general reader; and at the same time to reveal at every step the Hand of God overruling the events of history, to subserve his one great end: an attempt to contribute a mite to rescue history from the melancholy abuse under which it has lain almost to the present time. History, when rightly written, is but a record of providence; and he who would read history rightly, must read it with his eye constantly fixed on the hand of God. Every change, every revolution in human affairs, is, in the mind of God, a movement to the consummation of the great work of redemption. There is no doubt at the present time, a growing tendency so to write and so to understand history. And if the writer has contributed any thing to advance a consummation so devoutly to be wished, he will feel that he has not labored in vain.

In the preparation of the following pages, the writer has felt his mind constantly burdened with the magnitude of the subject. It has seemed too mighty to grapple with, and painfully conscious has he been of his inability to do it justice. Originating as it did, in the perplexity he felt, as a friend of Christian missions, in the inadequacy of any means now employed, or likely soon to be employed, to secure the evangelization of the world, and in the many fluctuations of the mis sionary enterprise, he has been led to trace out the *Divine* agency, which has, in every age of Christianity, been employed to carry forward the work. With his eye fixed on the hand of God, as engaged to consummate his plans of mercy through the cross, he has for the last seven years made his reading of history subservient to the work which he now ventures to offer to the public; hoping he has struck out a course, and gathered a mass and variety of facts in illustration of his position, which, while it shall do something to magnify in the minds of his people the power and grace of God, to confirm their hopes, and give confidence in the sure and final triumph of the gospel, shall contribute something to aid abler pens to consummate what he has begun.

Hartford, *May*, 1849.

SOME OF THE AUTHORS CONSULTED.

Hallam's MIDDLE AGES.

Robertson's CHARLES V., and his ANCIENT INDIA.

Guizot's HISTORY OF CIVILIZATION.

W. C. Taylor's NATURAL HISTORY OF SOCIETY.

GIBBON'S ROME.

Prescott's FERDINAND AND ISABELLA.

Bancroft's HISTORY OF UNITED STATES.

D'Aubigne's HISTORY OF THE REFORMATION.

Edwards' HISTORY OF REDEMPTION.

Titler's UNIVERSAL HISTORY.

AMERICAN ENCYCLOPEDIA.

Mosheim's CHURCH HISTORY

Gessler's CHURCH HISTORY

Hume's HISTORY OF ENGLAND.

Allison's MODERN EUROPE.

Mills' MOHAMMEDANISM.

Foster's MOHAMMEDANISM UNVEILED.

Milman's CHURCH HISTORY.

Harris' GREAT COMMISSION.

Smith's and Choules' HISTORY OF MISSIONS.

Moffatt's SOUTH AFRICA.

Williams' MISSIONARY ENTERPRISES.

MISSIONARY HERALD — REPORTS OF BENEVOLENT
    SOCIETIES.

Dr. Duff's INDIA, AND INDIA MISSIONS.

Dr. Grant's NESTORIANS, AND THE LOST TRIBES

Prof. Tholock—Dr. Baird—Bishop Wilson.

Lorimer's PROTESTANT CHURCH OF FRANCE.

Bingham's SANDWICH ISLANDS.

CONTENTS.

Page.

PREFACE. 3

CHAPTER I.

INTRODUCTION. General illustrations of Providential Agency: Joseph—Moses—Esther—Daniel. History an exponent of Providence. Ezekiel's wheel. John's sealed Book. Pentecost. Persecution about Stephen—about Paul. Dispersion of the Jews. The Roman Empire. Introduction of the Gospel into Abyssinia—Iberia—Britain—Bulgaria. Our plan. Christianity progressive. 11

CHAPTER II.

ART OF PRINTING—Paper-making—Mariner's Compass. The Discovery of America, at precisely the right time: a new field for Christianity. First settlement. Romanists. None but Puritan seed takes deep root here. Character of the first settlers. Geographical position. Capabilities and resources of America. Language, Intelligence, Political supremacy. Coal. Steam. A cloud. 31

CHAPTER III.

THE REFORMATION.—General remarks—state of Europe and the world. The crusades—their cause and effect. Revival of Greek literature in Europe. The Arabs. Daring spirit of inquiry. Bold spirit of adventure. Columbus. The Cabots. Charles V. Henry VIII. Francis I. Leo X. Rise of liberty. Feudalism. Distribution of political power. 63

CHAPTER IV.

THE REFORMATION. Europe clamors for reform. Causes. Abuses. Boniface VIII. The Great Schism. Infallibility. Bad moral character of Popes—Alexander VI. Leo X. Elector of Saxony. Early Reformers. Waldenses—Nestorians. The Reformation a necessary effect—a child of Providence. Martin Luther; his origin, early education, history. Finds the Bible. His conversion. Luther the preacher—the Theological Professor—at Rome. "Pilate's staircase." Compelled to be a Reformer. His coadjutors. Opposition. Results. 69

CHAPTER V.

Page.

JAPHETH *in the tents of Shem:* or, the Hand of God, as seen in the opening a way to India by the way of the Cape of Good Hope. The posterity of Japheth. The Portuguese empire in the East—its extent and extinction. Designs of Providence in opening India to Europe—not silks and satins, but to illustrate the evil of Idolatry, and the inefficacy of false religions and philosophy to reform men. The power of true religion. · · · · · · · · · · · · · · · · · 85

CHAPTER VI.

GOD IN HISTORY. The Church safe. Expulsion of the Moors from Spain. Transfer of India to Protestant hands. Philip II. and Holland. Spanish Invincible Armada. The bloody Mary of England. Dr. Cole and Elizabeth Edmonds. Cromwell and Hampden to sail for America. Return of the Waldenses and Henry Arnaud. Gunpowder plot. Cromwell's usurpation. Revolution of 1688. James II. and Louis XIV. Peter the Great. Rare constellation of great men. · · · · · · 109

CHAPTER VII

GOD IN MODERN MISSIONS.—Their early history. Benevolent societies The Moravians.—English Baptist's society. Birmah Missions. David Bogue and the London Missionary Society. Captain James Wilson and the South Sea Mission. The tradition of the *unseen God.*—Success. Destruction of Idols.—Gospel brought to Rurutu—Aitutaki—Rarotonga—Mangaia—Navigator's Islands. · · · 122

CHAPTER VIII.

MODERN MISSIONS continued.—Henry Obookiah and the Sandwich Islands. Vancouver and the Council. Dr. Vanderkemp and South Africa. Africaner. Hand of God in the Origin of Benevolent Societies. Remarkable preservation of Missionaries. · 136

CHAPTER IX.

THE WESLEYAN REFORMATION; its origin and leaders; its rapid growth and wide extension; its great moral results. · · · · · · · · · · · · · · · · 156

CHAPTER X.

HAND OF GOD in facilities and resources by which to spread Christianity. The supremacy of England and America: prevalence of the English language, and European manners, habits and dress. Modern improvements; facilities for locomotion. Isthmus of Suez and Darien. Commercial relations. Post-Office. · · 170

CHAPTER XI.

HAND OF GOD in facilities and resources. General peace. Progress of knowledge, civilization and freedom. The three great obstacles essentially removed, Paganism, the Papacy, and Mohammedanism. · · · · · · · · · · · · · · · 190

CHAPTER XII.

Page.

THE FIELD PREPARED. General Remarks;—First, PAPAL COUNTRIES, or Europe; their condition now, and fifty years ago. France—the Revolution—Napoleon. 1845, an epoch—present condition of Europe. Character of her monarchs. Catholic countries;—Spain and Rome—Austria—France, an open field. France and Rome. Geneva. Benevolent and reforming societies. Religion in high places. Mind awake. Liberty. Condition of Romanism and Protestantism.   - - - - 210

CHAPTER XIII.

CONTINUED. Second, PAGAN COUNTRIES. Paganism in its dotage. Fifty years ago scarcely a tribe of Pagans accessible. 1793, another epoch. Pagan nations, how accessible. Facilities. War. The effective force in the field. Resources of Providence in laborers, education, and the press. Toleration. Success. Kirshnuggar. South India. - - - - - - - - - - - - - - - - - - 235

CHAPTER XIV.

THE FIELD PREPARED. Islands of the Pacific. Native agency. Liberality of native Churches. Outpouring of the Spirit and answers to Prayer. The first Monday of January. Timing of things. England in India—her influence. Success, a cumulative force for progress. The world at the feet of the Church. - - - - - 253

CHAPTER XV.

MOHAMMEDAN COUNTRIES AND MOHAMMEDANISM. The design, origin, character success, extent of Islamism. Mohammed a Reformer—not an Impostor. Whence the power and permanency of Mohammedanism ? Promise to Ishmael —hope for him. The power of Islam on the wane. Turks the watch-dogs of Providence, to hold in check the Beast and the Dragon. Turkish reforms— Toleration—Innovations—A pleasing reflection. - - - - - - - - - - - - 269

CHAPTER XVI.

HAND OF GOD IN THE TURKISH EMPIRE. The Turkish Government and Christianity. Mr. Dwight's communication. Change of the last fifty years. Destruction of the Janizaries. Greek Revolution. Reform. Death of Mahmoud. The Charter of Gul Khaneh. Religious Liberty. Persecution arrested. Steam Navigation in Turkey. Providential incidents. Protestant Governments and Turkey. Their present Embassadors. Foreign Protestant Residents. Late exemption from the plague. - 288

CHAPTER XVII.

Page.

AFRICA, the land of paradoxes—Hope for Africa. Elements of renovation—Anglo-Saxon influence—Colonizing—The Slave Trade and Slavery—Commerce. A moral machinery—education, the Press, a preached Gospel. Free Government. African Education and Civilization Society. The Arabic Press. African languages. - 304

CHAPTER XVIII.

THE ARMENIANS—their history, number, location. Dispersion and preservation of the Armenians. The American Mission; Asaad Shidiak; exile of Hohannes The great Revival. The Persecution, and what God has brought out of it. - - 327

CHAPTER XIX.

THE JEWS. Providential features of their present condition, indicating their preparedness to receive the Gospel. - - - - - - - - - - - - - - - - - - 346

CHAPTER XX.

THE NESTORIANS—their country, number, history. The Ten lost Tribes. Early conversion to Christianity. Their missionary character. The American Mission among them. Dr. Grant and the Koordish mountains. The massacre. The great Revival—extends into the mountains. The untamed mountaineer. A bright day dawning. - 365

CHAPTER XXI.

EUROPE IN 1848. The Mission of Puritanism—in Europe. The failure of the reformation. Divorce of Church and State. The *moral* element in Government. Progress of liberty in Europe; religious Liberty. Causes of the late European movement. The downfall of Louis Philippe. What the end shall be. - - - - 379

CHAPTER XXII.

REMARKABLE PROVIDENCES—small beginnings and great results. Abraham. Joseph. Moses. David. Ruth. Ptolemy's map. Printing. The Mayflower. Bunyan. John Newton. The old marine. The poor Choctaw boy. The linen seller. Russian Bible Society. The little girl's tears, and Bible Societies. Conclusion. - 397

A LIST of some of the Authors consulted. - - - - - - - - - - - - - - - 417

Overflowing of the Nile.   Page 11.

HAND OF GOD IN HISTORY.

CHAPTER I.

Introduction. General illustrations of Providential Agency : Joseph—Moses—Esther—Daniel. History an exponent of Providence. Ezekiel's wheel. John's sealed Book. Pentecost. Persecution about Stephen—about Paul. Dispersion of the Jews. The Roman Empire. Introduction of the Gospel into Abyssinia—Iberia—Britain—Bulgaria. Our plan. Christianity progressive.

" *Behold, how great a matter a little fire kindleth.*"—James, ii. 5.

A YOUNG shepherd boy, as he tends his father's flocks on the hills of Palestine, dreams a dream. No strange event this, and, accustomed as he was to gaze on the starry concave, not strange that he should dream of the sun, moon and stars—or that it should have been interpreted of his future greatness, or that his brethren should on this account hate him—or that Joseph should be sold a slave into Egypt. Here seemed an end of the whole matter. The exiled youth would soon wear out in bondage, unknown and unwept ; a disconsolate father go down to the grave mourning, and the posterity of Jacob cultivate their fields, and watch their flocks, forgetful that this outrage to humanity ever disgraced the annals of their family history. But not so the mind of God. Joseph is enslaved—accused of crime—thrown into prison. Yet in that dark cell is nourished the germ of hope to the church of the living God. Israel should grow up on the banks of the Nile, and spread his boughs to the river, and his branches to the sea. The eye of God was here steadily fixed on the advancement of his church.

Again, something is seen floating amidst the flags of the river of Egypt. A servant woman is ordered to bring it. It is an ark of rushes. Thousands of Hebrew children had perished uncared for; but now, as by accident, one is found and introduced into the palace of the king and to the court. He is educated in all the learning of the Egyptians, and schooled in the discipline needful to make him a legislator and a military leader. With what care did God watch that little rush bark, and with what consummate skill order every event, till he had reared up Moses, and fitted him to act a more prominent part in the advancement of his cause than any mortal had acted before.

Or, an obscure female is born in Persia. At an early age she is left an orphan. An uncle adopts her, and hopes she may yet solace his declining years. She is beautiful, lovely, modest—yet nothing points her out to any enviable station above the thousands of the daughters of Persia. To all human forethought she would live and die unknown as she was born. But the church of God is scattered throughout the hundred and twenty and seven provinces of Persia. Esther is a daughter of the captivity; and God would raise up some guardian spirit to save his people from an impending danger, and honor them in the sight of the heathen. The palace of Shushan, and the gorgeous court of the Shah, shall stand in awe of Esther's God. By a singular train of circumstances the obscure orphan is brought to the notice of the king—finds favor, and is called to share with him the honors of his throne. And what deliverances she wrought for her people—how she brought them out from their long obscurity, and gave them notoriety and enlargement, and prepared the way for their restoration to their native land and to the Holy Hill of Zion, is known to all who have traced the hand of Providence in this portion of Sacred History.

Again, a youth of nineteen years is carried captive to Babylon. But there was nothing singular in this. Thousands of every age and rank had been forced away from their native hills and valleys of Palestine, the victims of unsuccessful war. But the time had come when God would proclaim his name and his rightful claims to sovereignty from the high battlements of the greatest of earthly potentates. Again he would magnify his church in the sight of all nations. Hence Daniel's captivity—hence that youthful saint prayed and exemplified an enlightened, unbending piety, till the king and his court, the nobles and the people, publicly acknowledged the *God* of *Daniel*, and "blessed the Most High, and praised and honored him that liveth forever, whose dominion is an everlasting dominion, and his kingdom is from generation to generation."

"Providence is the light of history and the soul of the world." "God is in history, and all history has a unity because God is in it." "The work of Redemption is the sum of all God's providences."

In the following pages, an attempt is made to present, within prescribed limits, *an historical illustration of the Hand of God as displayed in the extension and establishment of Christianity.* And the author will compass his end in proportion as he may contribute any thing to a right apprehension of history—of the divine purposes in the vicissitudes and revolutions of human affairs, discerning in the records of all true history the one great end,

> " For which all nature stands,
> And stars their courses move."

All veritable history is but an exponent of Providence, and it cannot but interest the mind of intelligent piety, to trace the hand of God in all the changes and revolutions of our world's history. All are made beautifully to subserve the interests of the church; all tend to the furtherance of *the one* great purpose of the Divine mind; the glory of God in the redemption of man. He that would rightly study history must keep his eye constantly fixed on the great scheme of human salvation. History, however, has been written with no such intent. "The first thing that it should have shown is the last thing that it has shown. The relation of all events to God's grand design is by most historians quite overlooked." All past history is but the unravelling of God's eternal plan respecting our race. The whole course of human events is made finally to subserve this one great purpose. The philosophy of history can be learned only in the laboratory of heaven—with the eye fixed on the Hand that

2

moves the world, and the spirit in harmony with the great Spirit that animates the universe.

It is only when we see God—Christ—redemption, in history, that we read it in the light of truth. "This is the golden thread that passes through its entire web, and gives it its strength, its lustre and consistency."

With beautiful propriety the Prophet Ezekiel prefaces his predictions with a striking delineation of Divine Providence. Or rather God prepares the prophet's mind to become the vehicle of the most extraordinary series of predictions concerning his people, by a vision emblematical of Providence. It came under the similitude of a "wheel," or a sphere made of a "wheel in the middle of a wheel."

A whirlwind and a cloud appear in the north, illumined with a brightness as of fire. Out of the midst of the cloud appears the likeness of four *living creatures;* each has four faces; four wings, and hands under their wings; straight feet like the ox; and the four faces are severally like the face of a man, of a lion, of an ox and an eagle, denoting wisdom, strength, swiftness and obedience. Their wings are raised and joined one to another, and when they move they move "straight forward," as directed by the Spirit, and they turn not as they go. These may be taken to represent the *ministers* of Providence—angels, with ready wing to obey the behests of Heaven—intent on their errands of mercy or of wrath—turning neither to the right hand or the left, subject to no mistakes, hindered by no obstructions—and all their movements directed by one great Mind. "Whither the Spirit was to go, they went; they run and return as the appearance of a flash of lightning."

By the side of these was a wheel or sphere, composed of a "wheel within a wheel." This may be regarded as an emblem of Divine Providence. The wheel had *four faces*—looked every way, moved every way; was connected with the living creatures, and moved in perfect harmony with them; *was full of eyes*—never moved blindly or by chance; its operations, though endlessly diversified in detail, were harmonious in action and one in their end, for all were guided by one great, controlling

Agent. The wheels had a regular, uniformly onward movement—no turning aside or turning back; and so enormous were they in circumference that their "height was dreadful."

And such is God's Providence—a scheme for carrying out purposes high as heaven, and lasting as eternity—vast, profound in the conception, sublime in result. and, like God himself, omniscient, omnipresent and omnipotent. God is the soul of Providence.

The general appearance of this singular mechanism was *like unto the color of a beryl*—azure—ocean-like. Providence like the ocean!—an apt and beautiful allusion. The ocean, broken only here and there by a few large patches of land sitting, as it were, on its heaving bosom, stretches from pole to pole, and from equator to equator; is all-pervading, never at rest, irresistible. It ebbs and flows; has its calms and tempests, its depressions and elevations. Whether lashed into fury by the storm, or sleeping tranquilly on its coral bed, it is accomplishing its destined end. It washes every land; its vapors suffuse the entire atmosphere; its waters, filtered through the earth, are brought to our door, and distributed through every hill and valley.

Common and useful as the ocean is, we are but partially acquainted with its utility, and so boundless is it that human vision can take in but a mere speck of its whole surface. We stand on its shore, or sit on some little floating speck on its bosom, and, save a little lake or pond that heaves in restless throes about us, the ocean itself lies beyond the field of our vision, shut out by the azure curtain of the encircling sky.

And such is Providence—a deep, unfathomable deep—none but the omniscient eye can fathom it—none but infinite Wisdom can scan its secret recesses; so boundless, everywhere active, all-influential, that none but the infinite Mind can survey and comprehend its wonder-working operations; so mighty, all-controlling, irresistible, that nothing short of omnipotence can guide it. Like the sea, Providence has its flows and ebbs, its calms and tempests, its depressions and elevations. At one time we ride on the swelling bosom of prosperity. The tide of life runs

high and strong. The sunbeams of health and joy glisten
in our tranquil waters, and we scarcely fear a disturbing
change. Again the tide sets back upon us. Disappointment, poverty, sickness, bodily or mental affliction, throw
life and all its enjoyments in the ebb. We are tossed on
the crested billow, or lie struggling beneath the overwhelming wave. Like the sea, Providence is not only
the minister of the Divine mercy, but of the Divine displeasure, executing judgments on the froward and disobe-
dient : a minister of discipline, too, casting into the furnace of affliction, that it may bring out the soul seven
times purified. We can see but little of its boundless
surface, or sound but little of its unfathomable depths.

"And I saw in the right hand of him that sat on the
throne a book written within and on the back side, sealed
with seven seals. And I saw a strong angel proclaiming
with a loud voice, Who is able to open the book and to
loose the seals thereof? And no man in heaven, nor in
earth, neither under the earth, was able to open the book.
And I wept. And one of the elders said unto me, Weep
not : behold, the Lion of the tribe of Judah, the Root of
David, hath prevailed to open the book, and to loose the
seven seals thereof." This book was an ancient roll,
composed of seven distinct parts—(the number *seven* denoting universality ;) so rolled as to leave an end of each
on the outside, which was sealed with a separate seal.
The book was written within—reserved in the keeping
of Him that sitteth on the throne—held in the right hand
of Omnipotence—the understanding and unfolding of its
secrets was committed only to the Son, the Lion of the
tribe of Judah. None could "look thereon," or take it
from the right hand of Him that sitteth on the throne,
but the Lamb that stood in the "midst of the throne."

This is another apt and beautiful emblem of Divine
Providence. As mediatorial King, the Lord Jesus Christ
undertakes the unrolling of this mysterious scroll—the
unfolding of the eternal purposes of Jehovah—the controlling of all events, and the ordering and overruling of
all the vicissitudes and revolutions in human affairs, to
the carrying out of the Divine purposes. It was a book
of seven chapters, some of which are divided into sections

as marked by the seven trumpets, the seven thunders and the seven vials of the seven last plagues.

The Lamb takes the book—becomes the executor of the Divine will in his purposes of mercy to man : " Lo! I come in the volume of the book as it is written of me, I delight to do thy will, O my God." " And when he had taken the book," and thereby engaged to execute the magnificent scheme of the Divine Mind, the four living creatures and the four and twenty elders fell down before the Lamb, having harps, and golden vials full of odors, which are the prayers of saints. And they sung a new song, saying, thou art worthy to take the book, and to open the seals thereof."

Then follows, in awful succession, scene after scene in the sublime drama, till John had witnessed, in shadowy outline, as in a moving panorama before him, the great events, political and ecclesiastical, which should transpire in coming time—reaching forward to the end of the present dispensation or the full establishment of Messiah's kingdom. Holding in his hand the book of God's purposes, the Lamb rides forth, King and Conqueror, in the chariot of God's providences. In a word, the solution of the dark sayings of this book—the evolving of the Divine purposes concerning the scheme of grace, is to be sought *in the progress and final triumph of Immanuel's kingdom.*

Whoever will read the history of the world and of the church of God, with his eye fixed on the providential agency which everywhere overrules the events of the one to the furtherance and well-being of the other, will see all history illuminated by a light, and animated by a spirit, of which the mere chronicler of historical events knows nothing. He will feel that history has a sacred philosophy—that he is standing in the council chamber of eternity, reading the annals of infinite Wisdom and Mercy, as blended and developed in the great work of human redemption. He will see in all history such a shaping of every event as finally to further the cause of truth. Events apparently contradictory often stand in the relation of cause and effect. A Pharaoh and a Nebuchadnezzar, an Alexander and a Nero, a Domitian and a Bor-

gia, Henry the VIII. and Napoleon, men world-renowned,
yet oftentimes prodigies of wickedness, are in every age
made the instruments and the agents to work out the
scheme of His operations who maketh the wrath of man
to praise him. "Howbeit they mean not so."

The Lord's portion is his people; Jacob is the lot of
his inheritance. He found him in a desert land and in a
waste, howling wilder   ; he led him about, he instructed him, he kept h.   as the apple of his eye. As
an eagle stirreth up her nest, fluttereth over her young,
spreadeth abroad her wings, taketh them, beareth them
on her wings; so the Lord alone did lead him. He has
engraven him on the palms of his hands. By some anom-
aly of nature a mother may forget her sucking child, but
God will not forget his inheritance in Jacob. The earth
changes; the sea changes; change is the order of all ter-
restrial things. They appear and pass away, and we
scarcely know they have been. But not so with the
church of God. As He lives so she shall live.

The Lord went before them by day in a pillar of cloud
to lead them, and by night in a pillar of fire to give them
light; a beautiful emblem of a superintending Providence
over his church. And "he has never taken away the
pillar of cloud by day or the pillar of fire by night." By
his sleepless energy he has prepared the way before them,
and led them by his own right hand. For their sakes he
has made and unmade kings—formed and dissolved empires—cast down and discomfited enemies, and raised up
friends.

It shall be our delightful task to trace the footsteps of
Providence in the extension and establishment of the
church. While much has been done for the spread of
the true religion by *missionary* effort, much more has been
done through *the direct agency of Providence*. Illustrations crowd upon us unsought: a few of which, as isolated cases, shall be allowed to fill up our first chapter.

1. Peter and the Pentecost. I do not here refer directly to the extraordinary outpouring of the spirit on
that day, or to the great number of converts, but to the remarkable *concurrence of circumstances*, which made that
a radiat'ng point of the newly risen Sun of Righteousness

.o most of the nations of the earth. Had not the Parthians and the Medes, the Arabians and the dwellers in Mesopotamia—*devout men out of every nation under heaven*, been there, the influence of that occasion had been confined within a narrow province. But as the event was, the gospel flew as on the wings of the wind, through all the countries represented in Peter's assembly on that memorable day. And as the apostles afterwards traversed those same regions, they found the glad tidings of Pentecost had gone before them as pioneers to their success, and harbingers of peace to welcome the more perfect establishment of Messiah's kingdom. All this was purely providential—a conjunction of circumstances to bring about results which should be felt over the whole known world.

2. *The persecution which arose about Stephen.* Its immediate and obvious result was a cruel persecution against the whole church, scattering abroad the disciples through all the neighboring nations. The ultimate and more glorious result—the *providential* aspect and design, was that they should, wherever dispersed, *go preaching the gospel.* The converts of Pentecost now need to be reinforced, strengthened and encouraged; and they who had sat longer at the feet of the apostles, and learned the way of life more perfectly, were sent to strengthen the things that were ready to perish. Where was the smoking flax they fanned it to a flame; where the flickering lamp, they replenished it from the horn of salvation. And the gospel, too, was by this means introduced and established in other regions. They that had long sit in the land of the shadow of death, light shined on them.

3. Paul's being carried prisoner to Rome. Rome was the imperial city, the metropolis of the world. Judea, the cradle of Christianity, was, on the other hand, but an insignificant province; the Jews, a hated people, and the founder of Christianity, was contemned as a crucified malefactor. But Jesus of Nazareth shall be known and honored at Rome. Her seven hills shall be as the seven golden candlesticks to send the light of truth abroad. But with man this was impossible. There were Christians in Rome; yet Rome was a proud, pagan city. The

church and her envoys were equally in bad repute. Her
excellencies were unknown, and her beauties, as dimly
seen through the fogs of ignorance and prejudice, were
unappreciated. But the religion of Calvary shall be
honored at Rome—there shall be a church in the "household of Cæsar." That great pagan empire shall yield to
the cross, and her proud capital shall be the radiating
point of light.

It is fit, then, that the prince of the apostles should go
there—that his puissant arm should wield the sword of
the Spirit amidst those giant powers of darkness—that
his voice should be heard in the forum, and his eloquence
plead in the palace of Cæsar. But how can this be?
God had a way—*Paul* must be arrested in the midst of
his successful mission in Asia Minor. This seemed a
sore evil—no one could supply his place there. But the
great Husbandman had need of him in another part of
his vineyard. He must be arrested—brought before a
Roman tribunal—be accused—allowed an *appeal* to Cæsar—and to *Cæsar he must go.*

But he goes, though in chains, the embassador of
heaven, the messenger of Christianity, to the capital of the
empire, and to the palace of the monarch. He goes at
the expense of a pagan government, in a government
ship, under governmental protection, and for the express
purpose of making a *defence* which shall lay a necessity
on him to preach Christ and him crucified before the imperial court.

All this is providential. On this highest summit of
earthly power, Paul kindled a fire whose light soon shone
to the remotest bounds of the Roman empire.

4. *The dispersion of the Jews* was another providential
interposition which contributed immensely to the wide
and rapid spread of the gospel. Jerusalem had been divinely appointed the radiating point of Christianity. The
gospel must *first* be preached at Jerusalem; then to the
mongrel tribes of Samaria; and thence, chiefly through
the instrumentality of Jews, to the remotest parts of
the earth. But the Jews were a people proverbially
averse to mingling with other nations; and how shall *they*
become the messengers of salvation to a perishing world?

Rome. Page 20.

A signal providence here interposed: Jerusalem is besieged by a Roman army; her mighty ramparts are broken down; her palaces demolished; her gorgeous temple laid in ruins. The nation is disbanded, and the Jewish church is no more. The fold broken up, the sheep are scattered. They spread themselves over the plains of Asia, even to the confines of the Chinese sea. They wander over the hills, and settle down in the valleys of Europe; nor does the broad Atlantic arrest their progress to the new world. Wherever dispersed, they bear testimony to the truth of Christianity. Whether in Kamskatka or on the torrid sands of Africa, on the Columbia or the Ganges, the Jew is everywhere a Jew— and the *peculiarities* which make him such, make him everywhere a preacher of righteousness. The bare fact of his dispersion was a living and palpable illustration of God's truth. If not a direct preacher of righteousness, he was at least verifying the predictions of a long line of prophets, and confirming the testimony of all former ages. Nothing so abundantly favored the propagation of the gospel as the dispersion of the Jews: "Through their fall salvation is come to the Gentiles." Their rejection was the *occasion* and the means of a wider and a richer diffusion of the gospel.

Indeed, at every step of the progress of Christianity we meet a wonder-working Providence opening and preparing the way for the kingdom of God among the nations of the earth.

5. *The extent and character of the Roman Empire*, at this time, affords another notable instance. In the construction of that vast empire, God had, for near forty centuries, been preparing a stupendous machinery for the triumph of the truth over the superstition and ignorance, the learning and philosophy of the whole earth. It was the grand concentration of all that was good, and much that was bad, in the great monarchies which had gone before it. It was, indeed, a magnificent structure; in extent, covering nearly the whole known world, and in political, intellectual, and moral height, overtopping all that had gone before it. The mighty monarchies which had gone before, were schools and vast workshops in which

to prepare materials out of which to build Rome. In polit
ical wisdom and the science of government, in the arts and
sciences, in civilization and refinement, Rome drew much
from the ever instructive past. In point of religion, too,
she had gained much. Having adopted the mythologies
of her predecessors, the lapse of time had shown her their
inefficacy and nothingness; and, consequently, long before the coming of Christ, *the state of religion* was little
more than the ridicule of the philosopher, the policy of
the magistrate, and the mere habit of superstition with
the populace; and, of consequence, in a state as favorable as may well be conceived for the introduction and
rapid spread of a new religion.

Such, in a word, was the character, the extent, and
facilities of communication possessed by the Roman Empire, as admirably to fit her to act the conspicuous part
in the spread of the gospel for which Providence had
prepared her.

A nod from the Roman throne made the world tremble.
What started with a Roman influence reached the boundaries of that vast empire.* When, therefore, Paul
brought the religion of Jesus into the forum and the palace, into the schools of philosophy, and the chief places
of learning, a blow was struck which vibrated through
every nerve of that vast body politic. And we need not
be surprised at the triumphant declaration of the great
apostle to the Gentiles, that, in less than half a century
after the resurrection, "verily their sound had gone into
all the earth, and their words to the ends of the world."

The universality and consolidation of the Roman Empire remarkably favored such a result. Narrow nation-
alities had fallen. Rome was the world. When Christianity became the national religion, it, in a sense, became
the religion of the world. The observant reader of Gib-

---

* Of the peculiar facilities afforded by the Roman Empire for the universal spread of
the gospel, take, for an example, her *national roads* and *posts*. From Rome to Scotland
on the west, and to Jerusalem on the east, a distance of four thousand Roman miles—
and from the imperial capital through the heart of every province, there extended a
national road by which even the remotest provinces were accessible. This furnished
facilities before unknown for the communication of knowledge and the propagation of
Christianity. To open and improve the facilities for intercommunication, is among the
first measures for effecting, or for advancing the civilization of any country. Modern
Europe received its first lessons here from the Saracens of the twelfth and following
centuries.

bon cannot have overlooked the singular fact, that not
only every new conquest added new dominion to Christianity, but every *defeat*.   The conquerors of Rome almost invariably embraced the religion of the conquered.
The strong arm of Jehovah made the Roman monarchy
a mighty engine in the advancement of his truth.

Under its benign auspices the Saviour was born.   Augustus Cæsar, the first Roman Emperor, began his reign
about twenty-four years before this event.   The Roman
Empire had now just reached its culminating point.
Augustus was the emperor of the *heathen world*.   Never
before had Satan's kingdom attained to so gigantic a
height in point of power, wealth, and learning.   This
was consummated but a year before the birth of Christ.
Augustus having subdued his last enemy, the world was
hushed into universal peace—a befitting time for the advent of the Prince of Peace.   The church was, at that
time, brought exceedingly low—her enemies raised to the
greatest height of glory and power—the four winds of
heaven were stayed, and God's anointed came.

Thus did God magnify the power of his church, and
display the omnipotency of his truth, by bringing them
in near connection with the prince of the power of the
air when he was at the point of his greatest glory, and
then overruling the honor and might of the enemy, to the
furtherance of his own eternal scheme of mercy.   The
great worldly aggrandizement of the Roman Empire was,
in a remarkable degree, made to subserve the rising cause
of Christianity.

6. Unroll the map of history where you please, and
you will meet, portrayed before you, the wonder-working
Hand stretched out to protect his people, and to overrule
men and events to the praise of his name, and the furtherance of his gracious plans.

The emperor, Antoninus, a persecutor of the Christian
church, is warring with a barbarous people in Germany.
His army is perishing with heat and thirst, and the enemy
near.   Being informed of a Christian legion in his army,
who were said to obtain what they desired by their
prayers, the emperor commanded them to call on their
God for assistance.   The entire legion fell on their knees

and besought the Lord for rain. Suddenly the sky was overcast—a terrific storm of thunder and lightning burst on their enemies. They were panic-struck and completely routed, while a copious shower afforded the imperial troops ample refreshment. The heart of the emperor is turned to favor the new sect. The Christian's God and the gospel is known and honored in the high places of imperial Rome.

A similar purpose was achieved at a later period by the conversion of the emperor Philip.

There is light in Rome, while yet the British Isle is covered with pagan darkness. Caractacus, with his family and his father Brennus, is carried prisoner of war to Rome. They embrace the Christian faith, and, after seven years, return to their native island, accompanied by three Christian preachers, one a Jew, who introduced the religion of Calvary, in the first century. The mission, sent at a later period by Gregory the great, was a child of the same Providence. Walking, one day, in the market-place, he saw some fine youths, of florid complexion, bound with cords and exposed to sale as slaves. Deeply interested in their behalf, he inquired whence they came. Being informed they were natives of Britain, and pagans, he gave his spirit no rest till a mission had been dispatched to that idolatrous island.

When, in the reign of the emperor Philip, the church had rest, and her ministers had quiet and comfort at home, and the apostolic and missionary spirit was declining, yet a wide and effectual door was open to the heathen—Providence had a resource little thought of: *Barbarian invaders carry away among their captives several Christian bishops,* who, contrary to their expectations, are forced to become missionaries and preachers in foreign lands, and are the instruments of the conversion of many, who had otherwise died in the region and shadow of death.

In a little town on the gulf of Nicomedia lived an obscure inn-keeper. Constantius, a Roman embassador, returning from the court of Persia, lodges in the inn—becomes enamored of Helena, the inn-keeper's daughter—marries her, and the son of their union they call *Constantine.* Constantius becomes a distinguished Roman general, and is at length honored with the purple—divorces Helena, the wife of obscure parentage, and leaves her son to humiliation and disgrace. But he was a chosen vessel. He signalized his valor in war, and in peace showed himself worthy to be the son of a Roman Empe- ror. His father dies, and the army constrain him to ac- cept the imperial crown. On his way to Rome he en- counters his formidable rivals. Rallying for battle, he sees (he says,) in the air a CROSS, on which was written, BY THIS CONQUER. He becomes a Christian—makes a cross the standard of his army, under which he fought and conquered. He becomes the patron of the Christian church, and the royal defender of the faith.

By exalting to the imperial dignity a decidedly Chris- tian prince, God makes bare his arm more conspicuously in the eyes of the nations.

The church had been withering under ten cruel perse- cutions. Long, dark, and fearful had been her night The morning dawned; she hailed Constantine as her de- liverer. "The four winds of the earth" were restrained that they should "not blow on the earth, nor on the sea, nor on any green tree." The church had rest. Nothing that imperial power and princely munificence could do was wanting, to abolish idolatry, to erect churches, and to extend the dominions of Christianity. The Goths and Germans, the Iberians and Armenians, the refined Per- sian and the rude Abyssinian, the dwellers in India and Ethiopia, received, under the gracious reign of Constan- tine, the embassadors of peace and pardon, and were gath- ered into the fold of the good Shepherd.

The danger now lay on the side of prosperity—and on this rock the newly launched vessel struck. Neverthe- less, her extension and unparalleled prosperity was an act of a wise and gracious Providence in the elevation of this Christian prince.

Nothing can be more intensely interesting than the phasis of Providence at this particular epoch. While the gigantic fabric of pagan Rome is falling to decay— while the huge image of her greatness and glory is crum- bling to ruins, another kingdom is rising in all the beauty and vigor of youth, deriving strength from every opposi-

3

tion, towering above every human difficulty, bidding defiance to the gorgeous array of Roman power and Roman
paganism, and soon waving the triumphant banner of the
cross over the ruins of imperial Rome. A mighty hand
was at work, as surely and irresistibly undermining, and
removing out of the way, the huge colossus of Rome, as he
was, with the same onward and resistless step, rearing up
that kingdom which should never end.

There seemed inwrought, in the mind of the Roman
army and the Roman world, the impression that Constantine was a signal instrument, in the hands of God, to establish the empire of Christianity throughout the earth—
that "his commission was no less special than that of
Moses, Joshua, or Gideon."

A Tyrian merchant, in the 4th century, visits Abyssinia with two lads. Meropius is attacked by the natives,
and murdered. The boys, Frumentius and Edesius, are
spared, presented to the king, and taken under his patronage. In due time Frumentius is made prime minister, and uses the advantages of his station to introduce
Christianity. A church is established in that pagan land,
of which he is afterwards constituted Bishop. And, what
is a matter of no little interest, Christianity has lived in
that country till the present day, a bulwark against the
assaults of the Moslems, or the stratagems and cruelties
of popery. How great a matter a little fire kindleth!

The *Iberians*, a pagan people bordering on the Black
sea, take captive in war a Christian female of great piety.
They soon learn to respect, then to revere her holy deportment—and the more, on account of some remarkable
answers to her prayers. Hence she was brought to the
notice of the king, which led, eventually, to the conversion of the king and queen, and to the introduction by them
of Christian teachers to instruct their people. Thus another portion of the great desert was inclosed in the garden of the Lord, through the gracious interposition of an
Almighty Providence.

Again, the sister of the king of the Bulgarians, a Scla-
vonic people, is, in the ninth century, carried captive to
Constantinople—hears and embraces the truth of the gospel; returning home, spares no pains to turn her brother,

the king, from the vanity of his idols; but apparently to no effect, till a pestilence invades his dominions, when he is persuaded to pray to the God of the Christians. The plague is removed—the king embraces Christianity, and sends to Constantinople for missionaries to teach his people :—and another nation is added to the territory of Christianity.

Thus did the "vine brought out of Egypt," which had taken deep root on the hills of Judah, spread its branches eastward and westward, till its songs of praise were sung on the Ganges and the Chinese sea, and echoed back from the mountain-tops of the farthest known west. In all its leading features, in all its grand aggressive movements and rich acquisitions, we trace the mighty, overruling hand of Providence. Christian *missions* did but *follow*, at a respectful distance, this magnificent agency of Heaven. Missions overcame their thousands, providential interpositions their tens of thousands. He that sat upon the white horse, who is called Faithful and True, whose name is the word of God, rode forth victoriously to the conquest of the world. The Christian church is the favorite child of an ever-watchful Providence.

In the further prosecution of the subject, the agency of Providence will be illustrated by means of a variety of historical events, connected, directly or indirectly, with the history of the church: such as the art of printing and paper-making. The invention of the mariner's compass. The discovery and first settlement of America. The opening to Christian nations of India and the East by the Cape of Good Hope. The reformation of the sixteenth century. The expulsion of the Moors from Spain. Transfer of India to protestant hands. The destruction of the Spanish invincible armada. Philip II., and Holland. The gun-powder plot. The usurpation of Cromwell. The hand of God in the origin and progress of modern missions. And the present condition of the world as prepared by Providence for the universal spread of the gospel.

Such a view of history, it is believed, will magnify in the reader's mind the *great moral enterprise* which God, through his providence, is achieving in our world; and conduct to the conclusion that *Christianity has, from the beginning, had an onward progress*

She has seen days of darkness, of persecution, of ap
parent retrogression, and sometimes has seemed almost
extinct. She has had her nights, long and gloomy—her
winters, protracted and dreary. But is the night less
conducive to man's comfort and prosperity, or the earth's
fertility, than the day? In the morning man goes forth,
in the dew of his youth, fresh to his labor; and the earth,
smiling through pearl-drop tears, appears in fresher beauty
and vigor than before. Or is the winter a blank—or a
retrograde move in nature? It is a vicissitude that has
its uses in the economy of the great whole, no less salutary
and promotive of the great good, than the freshness of
spring, or the maturity of summer, or the full sheaf of
autumn.

The dark days of the church have been days of *prep
aration*. When eclipsed as to worldly prosperity—when
crushed beneath the foot of despotism, or bleeding from
the hand of persecution, she has been gathering strength
and preparing for a new display of her beauties, and for
a wider extension of her territories. A thousand years
with the Lord is but as one day. Time is but a moment to
eternity. The few generations of depression in Egypt,
when the people of God were learning obedience, and
gathering strength for their first exhibition as a nation
and a church, was but a brief season to prepare for their
future prosperity and glory. The night of a thousand
years which preceded the morning of the glorious Reformation, and the more glorious events which were to follow,
was no more than the necessary preparatory season for
that onward movement of the church. A complete revolution was to transpire in the political affairs of the
world—the ecclesiastical world was to be turned upside
down—and the social relations of man to be changed.
A thousand years was not a long time in which to effect
such changes—changes, every one of which looked forward to the extension and establishment of the church.

The kingdom of heaven is like unto *leaven* which a
woman took and hid in three measures of meal, till the
whole was leavened. It matters not in what part of the
meal it is put, or that the quantity of leaven is small, or
that it is lost sight of in the mass. It works and fer-

ments, and pervades the whole mass. Yet no marked *effect* is visible till the process is complete.

Such is the process and the progress of Christianity. The apostles cast the leaven into the corrupt mass of humanity. The fermentation began and has never ceased, and shall never cease till the whole immense mass of this corrupt world shall be leavened. It has been a steady, silent, irresistible process—always onward, though not always visible, and sometimes, seemingly, retrograde. It is pervading the whole lump, yet no marked effect shall appear till the process shall be complete. Kingdoms rise and fall—moral earthquakes shake the earth—commotions, unaccountable and terrific, follow on the heels of commotions—the leaven of Christianity seems lost in the fearful and general fermentation—the sun is darkened, the moon is covered in sackcloth, the stars fall from heaven—all human affairs are thrown into perturbation, and Christianity is, from time to time, scouted from the habitations of men; yet all this is but the silent, invisible, onward, restless workings of the leaven cast over the world from the hill of Calvary. Every revolution, every commotion, war, oppression, persecution, famine, pestilence, the wrath of man, and the rage of the elements, are, under the mighty hand of God, but parts of the great fermenting process, which the world is undergoing from the leaven of Christianity.

Seasons of unpropitious appearances are, oftentimes, seasons of the most decided advancement—especially are they seasons of preparation for some onward and glorious progress. Above all these contending elements of human strife, sits serenely the Majesty of Heaven, guiding them all to the furtherance of his cause.

We may very justly regard the present advanced condition of the world, in the science of government, in philosophy and general learning, in social, national and scientific improvements, in the arts, in morality and religion, as a state of things providentially induced, to prepare the world for that yet more advanced condition which we denominate the millennium. We believe the world must, morally, socially, and politically, undergo very great changes before it will become a fit habitation for

3*

that Christianity which shall bless the earth in the days of her millennial glory. But these changes are not the work of a generation, but of centuries. And where is the century, or the year in any century, in which this work has not been going forward—and going forward as fast as, in the nature of things, and in consistency with the mode of the Divine working, could be?

The science of government is, necessarily, a science of slow progress. An entire century scarcely affords time for a single experiment; and this experiment may be a failure, or, at most, may develop but a little progress towards the right. Half a score of centuries is but a moderate period in which to gather up the fragments of good which may have resulted from a series of experiments of this kind, and to form them into one. Modern liberty, though yet scarcely advanced beyond the gristle, is the growth of more than a thousand years. Indeed, she lay in embryo nearly that period before she saw daylight.

And so it is in the formation and growth of other great features which shall characterize the period of Christianity's consummation on earth. Human improvement is the growth of centuries.

It was needful, too, that, first of all, the *disease*, to be removed by the healing waters of Bethesda, should be *known*, and its evil be fully developed—that sin should have time to mature and bring forth its bitter fruits, and exhibit its hatefulness and ruin—that Satan should be allowed first to show what *he* can make of this earth and its resources, before the rightful Proprietor shall come, and by his all-pervading providence reduce confusion to order, bring light out of darkness, and good out of evil.

Are we not right, then, in the suggestion that Christianity has, from the beginning, had an *onward progress?* When seemingly overwhelmed in the commotions of political revolutions—when seemingly crushed beneath the ponderous foot of persecution, her real progress has not been arrested. These have been as the grinding of the corn, peparing it for the action of the *leaven*—the breaking to pieces, and the removing out of the way, the things that shall be removed, and the establishing of those things which shall abide forever

CHAPTER II.

Art of Printing—Paper-making—Mariner's Compass. The Discovery of America, at precisely the right time : a new field for Christianity. First settlement. Romanists. None but Puritan seed takes deep root here. Character of the first settlers. Geographical position. Capabilities and resources of America. Language, Intelligence Political supremacy. Coal. Steam. A cloud.

" *Thou hast brought a vine out of Egypt ; thou hast cast out the heathen and planted it. Thou preparedst room before it, and didst cause it to take deep root, and it filled the land. The hills were covered with the shadow of it, and the boughs thereof were like the goodly cedars. She sent out her boughs unto the sea, and her branches unto the river.*"—Psalms, lxxx. 8—11.

THE next great event by which Providence most signally lengthened the cords and strengthened the stakes of his spiritual Israel, was the DISCOVERY OF AMERICA.

While this will be allowed to engross our attention in the present chapter, I must briefly notice a few preliminary steps by which Providence has wrought, and is still working, wonders in carrying on the work of human redemption. I refer to the *invention of the art of printing, of paper-making, and the mariner's compass*, and to the rise of correct views of astronomy.

These, in the hands of God, have wrought marvels in the extension and establishment of the true religion.

When, in the evolutions of time, the period had arrived that God would employ the agency of the press to extend and perpetuate his truth, the first crude idea of the process of printing is, divinely no doubt, suggested to a human mind. And how natural, yet purely providential it was.

A man of Harlem, a town in Holland, four centuries ago, **(1430,)** named Laurentius or Lawrence Koster, is amusing himself in cutting some letters on the smooth bark of a tree. It occurs to him to transfer an impression of these letters on paper. He thus impressed two or three lines as a specimen for the amusement of his children. Here was the whole art. An apparently accidental circumstance gave him the needed *hint*—from which his mind was sent out on the adventurous wings of invention—contriving a suitable ink—cutting whole pages of letters on blocks of wood, and transferring them thence on paper.

Other minds were now put on the same track, and soon the theory of printing was so far made a practical art, that copies of the Bible were multiplied with such facility that the entire book was offered for sale, in Paris, for sixty crowns. The number and uniformity of the copies excited no small agitation and astonishment. The vender was thought a magician, and, but for his timely escape, would have been executed for witchcraft.

There is not, perhaps, in the hands of Providence another so powerful an engine as the press for diffusing a knowledge of God and his law, and for carrying out the Divine purposes of mercy towards our world. Books are mighty things, whether for good or evil. And the art which multiplies and perpetuates books by tens of thousands daily, is an art of vast efficiency—capable of doing more to enlighten, reform, and bless the world, than any other. In *this* view, we cannot too devoutly admire the providential agency in the invention of the art of printing. But what is more especially to our present purpose is the fact, that the invention of an art of such importance in extending the boundaries of truth and *perpetuating its conquests*, should be made at this *identical time*, (at the period of the general revival of learning in Europe and throughout Christendom,) and that the precious grant should be made to *Christianity*—and not only be early confided to Christian hands, no doubt pre-eminently for the propagation of religion, but the same Providence has kept it, even to the present day, almost exclusively the companion and handmaid of Christianity. And if we contemplate the power of the press, not only in the present and the past, but in the yet more important part it is destined to act in the spread of gospel truth, we shall

admire anew the wonder-working hand; God working
all things after the counsel of his own will.

The influence of the art of printing, upon the condition
of the world, can scarcely be exaggerated or exhausted;
"its influence upon all arts and all science—upon every
physical, intellectual and moral resource—every social
and religious interest—upon the intelligence and freedom,
the refinement and happiness of mankind—upon all mind
and all matter."

A few years before the invention of the art of printing,
the same inventive Providence gave birth to the *science
of navigation*. There was navigation before, but till the
discovery of the *polarity* of the magnet and the application of its properties, navigation was a mere coasting
affair.

The discovery was as simple as providential: some
curious persons are amusing themselves by making
swim, in a basin of water, a loadstone suspended on a
piece of cork. When left at liberty they observe it
points to the north. The discovery of this simple fact
soon threw a new aspect over the whole world. Oceans,
hitherto unknown and pathless, became a highway for
the nations. Nations hitherto isolated, were brought
into neighborhood. The wide realms of the ocean were
now subjected to the dominion of man. Without this
discovery the mariner had been still feeling his way along
his native shore, afraid to launch out beyond the length
of his line; America had probably remained unknown,
the islands of the sea undiscovered; and all the world
has gained, and vastly more that it shall gain from international communication, from commerce, from immensely
increased facilities for advancing learning, civilization,
freedom, the science of government and religion, would
be wanting. Without the mariner's compass, the work
of the missionary and the Bible would be confined within
the narrow limits of a coasting voyage or a land journey.

When, therefore, the time approached that God would
advance, by mightier strides than before, the work of
civilization and Christianity, he discovered the nations
one to another, through the agency of the mariner's
compass; and put into the hands of his people the thou-

sand facilities which have followed in the wake of this one providential discovery.

But I proceed to the topic which is chiefly to occupy the present chapter.

The Hand of God as discernible in the discovery and first settlement of America.

The time had arrived when God would give enlargement to Zion. For this purpose he had reserved a large and noble continent—a land fitted, by its mighty rivers and lofty mountains, its vast prairies and inexhaustible mineral productions, to be a theatre for more extensive and grand developments of the scheme of redemption than had ever yet transpired. The old world had ceased to be a fit arena on which the divine purposes connected with the church should be carried out. Despotism had so choaked the rising germ of liberty, that no fair hope remained that she should there ever come to any considerable maturity. Ecclesiastical domination had so monopolized and trampled down religious rights and freedom, that it seemed vain to expect that religion, pure and undefiled, should, on such a soil, flourish, spreading her branches in all her native beauty and grandeur, and bringing forth her golden fruits. So sickly has she already become, that she could not stand, except as propped up by the civil power ; and so impotent as too often to be the sport of every changing wind of politics. And the institutions of *caste*—the usurpations of privileged orders, had so disorganized the natural order of society, so broken up social relations which God and nature approved, and introduced in their stead the most unnatural divisions in society, as to make the social institutions of Europe unsuited to that free and rapid progress of the truth which the divine purpose now contemplated. These had become thorns and briars to the rising growth of genuine piety. Religion can thrive and expand itself in all its native luxuriance, only in the atmosphere of political freedom and religious tolerance, and where social rights are not systematically invaded, and social intercourse trammeled by aristocratic pride. It is the nature of our religion to bind heart to heart, to make all one in Christ. Free, unbounded, disinterested benevolence is its genius.

It is a kingdom above all the kingdoms of the earth, incorporating its subjects into a society of its own peculiar kind. They acknowledge one Lord, one faith, one baptism by the Holy Ghost.

If social relations had become so deranged, or unnaturally modified in the old world as no longer to afford a congenial soil to the growth of Christianity; if the prevailing customs, maxims, principles, and habits of thinking, had become such as to preclude the expectation that religion would there flourish in all her loveliness and vigor; and if Despotism, religious and civil, stood up in array against its onward march and speedy victory, we see reason why God should transplant his choice vine into a soil unoccupied by such noxious plants, and more favorable to its growth and security. Such a soil was found in America, unoccupied, and where "the vine brought out of Egypt" might take deep root, "that the hills might be covered with the shadow of it, and the boughs thereof be like the goodly cedars; that she should send out her boughs unto the sea, and her branches unto the river."

Here, somewhat analogous to the re-commencement of religious institutions after the flood, the church was, as it were, re-established; here, again, an opportunity afforded to remove the "hay, wood and stubble," on which the former building had been reared, and to build anew on the foundation of the prophets and apostles, Jesus Christ being the chief corner-stone.

Contemplate, then, the discovery of America, as one of those leading acts of Providence for the propagation and establishment of the truth. When God would enlarge the theatre on which to display the riches of his grace, he caused a spirit of bold adventure to move upon the face of the stagnant waters of Europe, which found no rest till it brought forth a new world. I am not here to dilate on the glory of this discovery, or the magnitude of many of its results. It had *political and commercial* bearings more magnificent than could then have been conceived, or than are at this late period understood by us. These, however, were no more than the incidental advantages of the main design of this event. America was now added to the known domains of the world, *to make room for the church,* and to become in its turn a fountain, from which should go forth streams of salvation to the ends of the earth. This I conceive to be *the design* of Providence in this discovery.

The particulars which here demand our attention, are the *time* of the discovery; the *manner* of the first settlement of this country; the *character* of the first colonists and the *geographical position and capabilities* of America. These all distinctly indicate the hand of God, and our future destinies in reference to the church.

1. The discovery of this country happened *at the precise time* when the exigencies of the church demanded a new and enlarged field for her better protection, and for the more glorious development of her excellencies. When America had become sufficiently known and prepared to receive her precious charge, the reformation had done its work, and yet the church was but partially emancipated from the bondage of papal corruption. The reformed church of England and of Europe was, at that period, as far advanced, perhaps, towards the primitive simplicity and purity of the gospel, as could reasonably be expected on the *soil* where the principles of the reformation were laboring to take root. That soil was already pre-occupied and overrun with a growth hostile to those principles. Though manumitted from the dark cells and galling chains of Romanism, religion found herself but ill at ease in her new relations. She was still laced tight in the stays of forms and liturgies, and compelled to move stiffly about among mitred heads and princely dignitaries—to wear the gewgaws of honor, or shine in the baubles of vanity. Though hailed once more as the daughter of liberty, she neither breathed freely, nor moved untrammeled, nor, unencumbered, stretched forth her hand to wield mightily the sword of the spirit, to overcome principalities and powers, and to dispense her celestial gifts, till man shall be happy and the world free.

It was at such a time that the " woman, clothed with the sun, and the moon under her feet, and upon her head a crown of twelve stars," having long, and in various ways, been persecuted by the great red dragon, of ' seven heads and ten horns, and seven crowns on his heads," had given to her the two wings of a great eagle, that she might fly into the *wilderness*, where she had a place prepared of God, that they should feed her there a thousand, two hundred and three score days.   And here, free, strong, lofty as the eagle, (our national banner,) she lives, and breathes, and moves, stable as our everlasting hills, extensively diffused as our far-reaching rivers, and free as our mountain air.   Once it were enough that a persecuted church should find refuge in the straightened valleys of Piedmont and Languedock ; now she must have the valleys of the Connecticut, the Hudson, the Ohio, the Mississippi, and all the lofty hills and the rich vales that stretch out, in their varied beauty and luxuriance, from the Atlantic to the Pacific.

Thus did God open an asylum for his oppressed people precisely at the time they needed it.*   And thus, with a mighty hand, did he establish his church in this new world.

2. There were, too, many things connected with *the first settlement* of this country, which indicate the grand design of Providence in its discovery.   Follow his footsteps for a moment and you will see it.

The leading design was, no doubt, a *religious* one—else why should the King of nations, who setteth up one and pulleth down another, have given preference to those arrangements which show religion and his church to have been the chief objects of his regard and agency. That it was so, a few facts will testify :

It is known that the first discoverers of this continent were *Roman Catholics*.   America was taken possession of and made subject to Catholic governments.   Bearing in mind this fact, you will, with the greater pleasure, follow the wonder-working Hand which overturned and overturned till this once Roman Catholic country has been wrested, piece-meal, (as the wants of the reformed religion have required,) from the domination of Rome and the ghostly tyranny of the Pope, and given into the hands of Protestants, and made the strong hold of the

---

* "The Mahammedans," says M. Oelsner, " would have discovered America even centuries before Columbus, had not their fleet been wrecked in a tempest, after clearing the straits of Gibraltar. -*Foster, vol. II. p.* 237.

doctrines of the reformation. Near.y the whole of North
America has already been transferred. Nor is this all.
It was not enough that it should become a *Protestant*
country. It should grow up into a nation under the *still
more* benign influences of Protestantism reformed. New
England was to be the nursery, and Puritanism the spirit
that should pervade this new world.

And what a singular train of providences brought about
so important, yet so unlikely an event. Nothing seemed
more probable at one time, than that FRANCE would be
the owner of New England—that these hills and valleys,
now so healthful in moral vigor, would have languished
under the crucifix and the mitred priest, and groaned
beneath the heavy rod of the Roman pontiff. And New
England might have been as notorious as a fountain of
abominations and papal sorceries, as she now is as a
radiating point of light, and intellectual and spiritual life.
But mark the hand of God here.

New England was early an object of desire with the
French. As early as the year 1605, De Mont "explored
and claimed for France, the rivers, the coasts and bays
of New England." But the decree had gone out that the
beast of Rome should never pollute this land of promise,
and it could not be revoked. The hostile savages first
prevent their settlement. Yet they yield not their purpose. Thrice in the following year was the attempt
renewed, and twice were they driven back by adverse
winds, and the third time wrecked at sea. Again did
Pourtrincourt attempt the same enterprise, but was, in
like manner, compelled to abandon the project. It was
not so written. This was the land of promise which God
would give to the people of his own choice. Hither he
would transplant the "vine" which he had brought out
of Egypt. Here it should take root and send out its
boughs unto the sea, and its branches unto the river.*

At a still later period, a French armament of forty ships
of war, under the Duke D'Anville, was destined for the
destruction of New England. It sailed from Chebucto,
in Nova Scotia, for this purpose. In the meantime, the

---

* Bancroft's History of United States.

pious people, apprised of their danger, had appointed a day of fasting and prayer, to be observed in all the churches. While Mr. Prince was officiating in Old South Church, Boston, on this fast day, and praying most fervently that the dreaded calamity might be averted, a sudden gust of wind arose (the day, till then, had been perfectly clear,) so violently, as to cause the clattering of the windows. The reverend gentleman paused in his prayer, and looking around on the congregation with a countenance of hope, he again commenced, and with great devotional ardor, supplicated the Almighty to cause that wind to frustrate the object of their enemies. A tempest ensued, in which the greater part of the French fleet was wrecked. The duke and his principal general committed suicide—many died with disease, and thousands were drowned. A small remnant returned to France, without health, and spiritless, and the enterprise was abandoned forever.

It is worthy of remark, how God made *room* for his people before he brought them here. He drove out the heathen before them. A pestilence raged just before the arrival of the Pilgrims, which swept off vast numbers of the Indians. And the newly arrived were preserved from absolute starvation by the *very corn* which the Indians had buried for their winter's provisions.

And here we may note another providence : none but *Puritan* feet should tread this virgin soil, and occupy the portion God had chosen for his own heritage. Before the arrival of the Pilgrims, a grant had been given and a colony established in New England, called new Plymouth. But this did not prosper. A new and modified patent was then granted to Lord Lenox and the Marquis of Buckingham. But no permanent settlement was made. The hierarchy of England should not have the possession. They to whom the Court of Heaven had granted it, had not yet come. It was reserved for the Puritans. Here should be nurtured, in the cradle of hardships, and perils from the savages, and from the wilderness, and sufferings manifold and grievous, a spirit which should nerve the moral muscles of the soul, and rear up a soldiery of

the cross made of sturdier stuff, and animated by a purer
spirit than the world had before known.

"Had New England," says the historian of those times,
"been colonized immediately on the discovery of the
American continent, the old English institutions would
have been planted under the powerful influence of the
Roman Catholic religion. Had the settlement been made
under Elizabeth, it would have been before the activity
of the popular mind in religion had conducted to a corresponding activity of mind in politics. The Pilgrims
were Englishmen, protestants, exiles for religion, men
disciplined by misfortune, cultivated by opportunities of
extensive observation, equal in rank as in rights, and
bound by no code but that which was imposed by
religion, or might be created by the public will."

"America opened as a field of adventure just at the
the time when mind began to assume its independence,
and religion its vitality."

This continent seemed signalized from the first as the
asylum of *freedom*. Nothing else would thrive here.
Ecclesiastical domination and political despotism were
often transplanted hither, and nourished by all the kindly
influences of wealth and nobility; they basked for a time
in the sunshine of the court and the king, yet they were
exotics, and never thrived. While it was yet the spring-
time of Puritanism, its institutions taking root and sending up its thrifty germs, and giving promise of a sturdy
growth, those strange vines already begun to look sear,
and give no doubtful tokens of a stinted existence and a
premature decay. Read the records of the first settlement of several of the colonies to this country—especially
one in Massachusetts and another in Virginia, where
strenuous attempts were made to introduce the peculiar
institutions of the old world, and you will not fail to
observe the singular fact that all such attempts were abortive. Providence had decreed this should be the land of
toleration and freedom. The colonies which were not
founded on such principles, either failed of success, or did
not prosper till leavened with the good leaven of Puritanism—clearly indicating that Providence designed this to
be a theatre for the more perfect development of his

grace to man. It was Religion that built up the first
nation in this wilderness, and it is only our *moral* pre-
eminence and prospects that distinguish us from other
nations.*

3. *The character of the first colonists.* There is perhaps nothing in which the hand of God is so conspicuous
towards America, as in the *selection of the materials* with
which to rear the superstructure of religion and government in this new world. God had been preparing these
materials nearly three centuries. Wickliff was the father
of the Puritans; and from him followed a succession of
dauntless advocates for the emancipation of the human
mind from the power of despotism. The mighty spirits
that rose at the time of the reformation were but the
pupils of their predecessors. The principles so boldly
proclaimed by Luther, and so logically and judiciously
sustained by Calvin, were the principles, matured and
more fully developed, of Huss and Jerome—of many a
revolving mind in England and on the continent. Puritanism is the reformation reformed. The principles
which led to the settlement of New England, and which
pervaded her colonies, and became the only principles on
which Heaven would smile throughout this wide continent, are but the principles of the reformation matured
and advanced. Those extraordinary characters, who,
for religion's sake, braved dangers incredible, endured
sacrifices that seemed not endurable, and periled all
things in these western wilds, were Heaven's chosen
agents, to prepare a new and a wider field for the display
of what Christianity *can* do to bless the world. Europe
had been sifted, and her finest wheat taken to sow in this
American soil. Her hills and dales had been again and
again ransacked, to collect the choice few who should
found a new state, and plant a new church. The Pilgrims
were the best men, selected from the best portion of the
best nation on the face of the earth. May we not, then,
indulge the delightful hope that God has purposes of yet

* The first colony in North America, save Mexico, was a Protestant colony, planted
by Caspar de Coligni, as a city of Refuge for Protestants. It was destroyed expressly
as Protestant. Thus was North America baptized by Jesuit priests with Protestant
blood; yet despite all the machinations of Rome, God has confirmed the covenant and
made this land the asylum and home of Protestantism.—*Bancroft, vol. I., pp.* 61, 73.

more moral grandeur to fulfill, in connection with this country?

Indeed, this idea seems to have been coupled with the earliest conceptions in the mind of Columbus, concerning an American continent. That great navigator is said to have been a diligent and devout student of the prophecies, and was actuated, in no small degree, in his adventures westward, "by the hopes he cherished of extending here the kingdom of Christ." And in the mind of his royal patroness, (Isabella of Arragon,) the conversion of the heathen to Christianity, was an object "paramount to all the rest."*

It was a signal providence that prepared such materials in the heart of England and in the bosom of the English church, preserved them and proved them in the furnace of affliction, while in their own land, and during their exile in Holland, and in their journeyings on the deep, and, finally, collected them on the iron bound coasts of New England, and formed them into one living temple, fitly joined together, furnished and beautified as a *model* building for generations yet to come.

The longer the world stands, the more profoundly will be revered the character of our Pilgrim fathers, and the more religiously shall we admire the Divine agency which so controlled events, that one of the first settlements in the new world should be composed of *such characters*, and should so soon gain a pre-eminence over all the other colonies, and so soon, too, and in all after time, exercise a controlling influence on the destinies of the whole country and of the world. For the institutions of this country, both civil and religious, were cast in the mould of Puritanism. Had any other of the colonies been allowed to stand in this relation to the whole, how different would have been the cast of American liberty and religion! As it was, men of the most unbending integrity and untiring industry; men humble and unobtrusive, yet courageous and immovable at the post of duty; yielding when wrong, yet inflexible when right; plain and frugal, yet intelligent and liberal; men who

* Prescott's Ferdinand and Isabella, vol. II. p. 496.

had been nurtured in the school of persecution, and suffered the loss of all things, that they might breathe the
uncontaminated air of freedom; men who hated oppression, abhorred ignorance and vice—who were, in their
very souls, *republicans* and *Christians*—these were the
men, chosen out by sovereign Wisdom, to control the
destinies of the new world. And they have done it.
The enterprise and intelligence, the undying love of
liberty, the religious spirit—I may say, the population of
our puritan colonies, have spread themselves over the
whole continent. And what is worthy of special remark,
these only prosper in our country. You look in vain
over the wide expanse of our territory to find thrift and
prosperity, temporal or spiritual, except under the
auspices of a Puritan influence. Who people our wide
western domains, and plant there the institutions of learning and religion? Who found our colleges and seminaries, publish our books, teach our youth, sustain our
benevolent enterprises, and go to pagan lands to make
wretchedness smile, and ignorance speak wisdom? By
whose skill and industry rolls the railroad car over the
length and breadth of our land, and whiten the ocean with
canvas? *Who*, if not the sons of the Pilgrims, nerved
with the spirit of the Pilgrims? Tell me in what proportion, in any section of our country, the people are leavened
with the leaven imported in the May-flower, and I can
tell you in what proportion they are an enterprising,
prosperous, moral and religious people. *Time* shall
expire, before the immeasurable influences of Puritanism
on the destinies of our country and the world shall cease
to act.

Massachusetts and Mexico furnish a forcible illustration of our idea. Mexico was colonized just one hundred
years before Massachusetts. Her first settlers were the
noblest spirits of Spain in her Augustan age; the epoch
of Cervantes, Cortes, Pizaro, Columbus, Gonzalvo de
Cordova, Cardinal Ximenes, and the great and good Isabella. Massachusetts was settled by the poor Pilgrims
of Plymouth, who carried with them nothing but their
own hardy virtues and indomitable energy. Mexico, with
a rich soil, and adapted to the production of every thing

which grows out of the earth, and possessing every metal used by man—Massachusetts, with a sterile soil and un-congenial climate, and no single article of transportation but ice and rock. How have these blessings, profusely given by Providence, been improved on the one hand, and obstacles overcome on the other? What is now the respective condition of the two countries? In produc-tive industry, wide-spread diffusion of knowledge, public institutions of every kind, general happiness and continu-ally increasing prosperity; in letters, arts, morals, re-ligion,—in every thing which makes a people great, there is not in the world, and there never was in the world, such a commonwealth as Massachusetts. And Mexico—what is she?*

But who ordered all the circumstances which brought about an event so unexpected, yet so influential as *such a settlement of America*? And for what purpose—if not that he might here plant the glory of Lebanon and the excellency of Carmel and Sharon? Here he "prepared room before it, and caused it to take deep root."

4. Again, we discover the wonder-working hand of Providence in the *geographical position and resources* of our country, as indicating her future destinies in refer-ence to the church and the world.

There is much worthy of notice in our *geographical position*. This gives us peculiar advantages. We are separated, by the expanse of a wide ocean, from every principal nation on the face of the earth. We may live at peace with all. The old world may be convulsed—Europe and Asia be deluged in blood, yet not a clarion of war be heard west of the Atlantic, or a river tinged in all our wide domains. Here we may live safe from all those upheavings of revolution, which have, and which will continue to overturn and overturn, till the great fountains of error and despotism be broken up, and free institutions be planted on their ruins. Here we may direct all our energies, mental, physical, or moral, to the consummating of those stupendous plans of Providence in reference to this country. Far removed from the

* See Waddy Thompson's Mexico.

lands where errors in religion and politics had become stereotyped in habit, and interwoven in the very warp and woof of social relations, we lack no opportunity in which to try the great experiment of Liberty. Such are our local advantages—such our institutions, that we may, unlike the people of any other nation, advance learning, establish and propagate religion, and subserve the general interests of the church. Religion exists here untrammeled, free as the air we breathe, or the water we drink. This makes our nation more suitable than any other to become a fountain from which shall go out streams of salvation to the ends of the earth.

But a yet more remarkable feature is to be found in the *capabilities* of our country, to become a mighty instrument in the hands of God for the universal spread of Christianity.

I have referred to our facilities in free institutions, and freedom from the trammels of ecclesiastical organizations. The American church, if she will go forth in the vigor and simplicity of herself, would be like a young man prepared to run a race. She is admirably constituted to be Heaven's almoner to the nations. Pure Christianity is republican. The American soil is peculiarly adapted to produce that enterprise, freedom and simplicity, suited to extend religion and its thousand blessings to the ends of the earth. No church in the world is so constituted that it may put forth so great a moral power. We have only to employ the rare facilities of our position, to make us the most efficient instrument in the conversion of the world.

But I referred more especially to the *resources* here prepared by Providence, for the accomplishment of the work in question—resources in territory, in soil, in population *prospectively*; in wealth and language; in learning and enterprise; and in the *power of steam*.

The present territory of the United States is equal to that of all Europe, exclusive of Russia. It is more than six times larger than Great Britain and France together; and as large as China and Hindoostan united.

And if we admit that our soil is not surpassed in fertility by any other, or our climate in salubrity, there

seems nothing to hinder America becoming as populous
as any other portion of the world.   Suppose it to reach
the present ratio of population in Europe—110 to the
square mile—and there would teem on our vast territories a population of 220 millions.   Or should the density
equal that of China—150 to the square mile—our population would be 300 millions.   That the soil of the United
States is capable of supporting this number there can be no
doubt.   A European writer of credit has asserted that the
"resources of the American continent, if fully developed,
would afford sustenance to 3,600 millions of inhabitants,
or four times the present population of the globe"—and
that the actual population will not fall short of 2,000
millions—giving to the United States 270 millions.

   Nor is this merely what *may* be.   The present rapid
increase of our population is actually swelling our numbers into these enormous dimensions.   " And what is
more surprising," says the writer just quoted, "there is
every probability that this prodigious population will be
in existence within three or four centuries.   The imagination is lost in contemplating a state of things which will
make so great and rapid a change in the condition of the
world.   We almost fancy it a dream ; yet the result is
based on principles quite as certain as those which govern
men in their ordinary pursuits."*

   Our population is found to double every 23 years—say.
for safety's sake, 25 years—and we have to look forward
only 100 years, and our present ratio of increase gives us
288 millions ; or 125 years, and we have on our soil 576
millions ; or 150 years, and we number more than the
present population of the globe.   Indeed, to take the
result of 100 years (288 millions) as the ultimatum of
increase to which the resources of our soil will allow our
population to advance, and what a host have we here for
the moral conquest of the world.   And suppose this enormous population to be what, under the peculiar smiles of
Heaven, they ought to be ; and what, in the singular
dealings of God, they were designed to be ; and what,
under the quickening and transforming power of the

---

* De Toqueville.

Holy Ghost, they would be, and how grand their prospective influence on the regeneration of the world! Portray in your mind a nation of 288 millions, imbued with the principles of Puritan integrity, enterprise, decision, self-denial, and benevolence; her civil institutions so modeled as to leave Religion free as our mountain air, to invigorate the plants of virtue her ;, or to waft its blessings over the arid sands of Africa, or the snow-top mountains of Tartary; her social relations unshackled by the iron chains of custom and caste; her religion no longer laced in the stays of needless rites, liturgies, prelacy, or state interference; the public mind enlightened by an efficient system of common education; or you may, if you please, contemplate our nation as peculiarly fitted to bring to bear on the nations the *power of the press*, or to facilitate the world's deliverance by the unlimited scope of our navigation—from whatever point you look, you will find, in this land of the Pilgrims, resources laid up in store, by which Providence may, in his own set time, revolutionize the world.

What means this curtailing of distances—this facility of intercourse between the remotest points of our own country and of the world, if He that worketh all things after the counsel of his own will, be not about to use it for the furtherance of the cause which is as the apple of his eye? If the introduction of the Greek classics into Europe, drew aside the veil of the dark ages, and the invention of paper-making and of printing perpetuated the advantages of the Reformation, may we not expect that the application of the *power of steam* is destined to subserve a scarcely less important end, in the conversion of the world?

To appreciate the force of this, we need to contemplate in the same view, three collateral facts: *the extensive prevalence of the English language*, and its treasures of religious knowledge; the present *supremacy*, on the political arena, of *the nations who speak this language;* and the singular distribution of these immense deposits of *coal*, which are to supply the power to print and distribute books, and to convey them, by whom "knowledge shall increase," over the broad world.

Ours is the language of the arts and sciences, of trade and commerce, of civilization and religious liberty. It is the language of Protestantism—I had almost said, of piety. It is a store-house of the varied knowledge which brings a nation within the pale of civilization and Christianity. As a vehicle of our institutions and principles of civil and religious liberty, it is "belting the earth," push ing east and west, and extending over the five great geographical divisions of the world, giving no doubtful presage that, with its extraordinary resources for ameliorating the condition of man, it will soon become universal. Already it is the language of the Bible. More copies of the sacred Scriptures have been published in the English language, than in all other tongues combined. And the annual issues in this language, at the present time, beyond all doubt, far surpass those of all the world besides. So prevalent is this language already become, as to betoken that it may soon become the language of international communication for the world.* This fact, connected with the next, that *the two nations speaking this language have, within a few years past, gained the most extraordinary ascendancy*, holding in their hands nearly all the maritime commerce and naval power of the world, giving tone to national opinion and feeling, and sitting as arbiters among the nations, dictating terms of peace and war, and extending their empire over the nations of the East, holds out a glorious presage of the part *America* is destined to act in the subjugation of the world to Christ. I say *America*, believing that

> " *Westward* the star of empire takes its way ;
> The four first acts already past,
> A *fifth* shall close the drama of the day.
> Time's noblest offspring is the last."

If it be a fact (and history proves it,) that wealth,

---

* The New York Observer recently acknowledged the receipt of the following foreign papers published in English :
Three published at Hong Kong and Canton, China.
Ten or twelve in Hindoostan and the British East Indies.
Four in Rome, (Italy,) and about the Mediterranean.
Four in Liberia and South Africa.
Twelve or thirteen in Australia and the Sandwich Islands.
Four in Oregon, California and Northern Mexico.
Six or seven in Southern Mexico.

power, science, literature, all follow in the train of numbers, general intelligence and freedom, we may expect that America will ere long become the metropolis of civilization, and the grand depository of the vast resources which Providence has prepared for the salvation of the world. The same causes which transferred the "sceptre of civilization" and the crown of knowledge from the banks of the Nile and the Euphrates, must, at no distant day, bear them onward to the valley of the Mississippi.

But we must not overlook our *third* fact: the singular distribution of *coal deposits.*

Coal, like the English language, like freedom, general intelligence, or piety, is *protestant.* In vain do you search the world over to find any considerable deposit of this agent, except where the English language is spoken, or where the protestant religion is professed. Hence the *power of steam*—as the power of the press and of common education, three mighty transformers of nations—has been given to the people of God for the noblest of purposes.

"Steam," says the London Quarterly, "is the acknowledged new element of advancement by which this age is distinguished from all which have preceded it. By its magic power, distance is set at nought; and the productions of the antipodes are brought rapidly together. Coal must, therefore, henceforth be the motor and metor of all commercial nations. Without it no modern people can become great, either in manufactures or the *naval art.*"

As an illustration of this, if the digression may be allowed, the mighty transformations that are this day taking place in the countries about the Mediterranean, especially among the Turks, where lives the presiding genius of Moslemism, might be adduced. The paddle wheels of European intelligence and enterprise, are there daily breaking up the stagnant waters of oriental superstition, ignorance and despotism. Not a steamer plows the waters from the pillars of Hercules to the sea of Japan, that goes not as a herald of civilization and Christianity to those benighted nations.

And another fact: the English Steam Navigation

5

Company is furrowing the broad Pacific amidst its thousand Islands, and along the western main of America. And, what is yet more in point, extensive beds of coal have been found on the western coasts of both North and South America, and also on the Atlantic side of the Isthmus of Panama; deposits stored away by the hand of the Great Disposer, ready, at the time of need, to generate a power that shall, at Heaven's bidding, convert the whole Pacific into one great highway for the nations to pass over.*

Yet, while indulging these pleasant anticipations, I have not lost sight of the cloud that at present darkens our atmosphere. When I speak of the tremendous power of the press for good, I am aware of its abuse. When I speak of American enterprise and zeal, I am not unmindful that we can scarcely, for any length of time, prosecute any good cause without making it a hobby, and riding it so far and so fast, as to cripple it for life, if not to kill it. We are not always satisfied in pursuing plans of benevolence and reform, till we have driven ourselves, and all about us, into a swamp from which we can neither extricate ourselves nor be extricated. And when I speak of the stern principles which originated the first settlement of this country, and of the admirable institutions of our forefathers, and of our high pretensions to freedom, intelligence and piety, I bear in mind that we have proved ourselves unworthy our noble inheritance, and recreant to our good professions. But I am attempting to look beyond the cloud, which at present intercepts our vision, to those better things reserved for the second Israel. Despotism and anarchy may cover our land with a temporary gloom. So gross, indeed, have been our national sins, and so heaven-provoking our ingratitude, and our perversion of heaven's richest gifts, that we may experience the divine rebuke, sore as death, yet the counsels of God shall not come to nought. He shall not, in vain, prepare such munitions of war, and provide such vast

---

* The late discovery of immense beds of coal on Vancouver's Island deserves a more special notice. In the new contemplated route to the Indies, across the American continent and the Pacific, we are beginning to see the *reasons* why these vast deposits were placed there, and *why* they are brought to light just at this time.

resources for his work, and then not make them effectual
in the subjugation of the world to his beloved Son.

In the review of this subject, the mind naturally recurs
to the great Disposer of events—what a display here of
his sovereignty—of his power, wisdom and goodness—
how incomprehensible his plans—how inflexible his determination to sustain and carry forward his cause—how
infinitely foolish is all resistance. Such reflections are
befitting as we read the providential history of our country. Yet we ought here especially to bear in mind,

1. *To what a rich inheritance we are born.* One of
Heaven's richest blessings, is a religious parentage. This
is a patrimony more precious than fine gold. Our national parentage was eminently religious. The difference between a people starting into existence from barbarism and ignorance, or amidst all the propitious
circumstances which smiled on the first settlement of
this country, is vast beyond calculation. We were born
to a rich inheritance—to an undying love of liberty—to
toleration—to a high state of intelligence—to the sternest
principles of morality—to the unwavering practice of
virtue. We ought, therefore, to be the most religious,
free, happy, benevolent people on the face of the earth.

2. *Our responsibilities and duties correspond with our
privileges.* God expects much of us. He has made us
a full fountain, that we may send forth copious streams to
fertilize the desert around. He has embodied in our
nation a moral power, and put into our hands a machinery, which, if kept in operation, will not fail to make
its power felt to the ends of the earth, till all nations shall
be subjugated to Prince Immanuel.

3. America is the land of magnificent *experiments*—the
land in which should be developed new principles and
forms of government—a new social condition, and an
advanced condition of the church—popular government,
equal rights and a free church. Columbus added a new
province to the world, new territory for civilization and
religion to expand upon—and new domains on which
should flourish a freer government and purer church than
was practicable in the old world. Here God is solving
certain great problems: can the church support herself?

Can a people govern themselves?   Can society exist
without caste ?   In the great republic of North America,
these experiments, which, in the old world, have resulted
in so indifferent success, have been in successful progress
three quarters of a century, and we hazard little, it is
believed, in predicting their complete success.   In no
country have the ends for which governments are constituted, been better realized, or the designs of religion
been more nobly carried out, yet the power of governing
lies in the hands of the people, and the support and
extension of religion is dependent on free contributions.

4. *The tremendous guilt of our dereliction in duty.*
After all that God has done to make us *such* a nation—
such a one as he has need of to win over the nations to
himself, if we hold ourselves aloof from his great plans
of mercy towards our world, and refuse the honor he
would confer upon us, in making us the instruments of his
will, we must expect he will withdraw from us the light
of his countenance, and choose others more worthy of
his favor.   How ought we, then, to fear lest we displease
God by our apathy, and be left to drink the cup of his
indignation for our manifold sins.

5. The immense immigration to our country at the
present time, is filling a page in the providential history
of America, not to be overlooked.   Had such immigra-
tions taken place at any former period of our history, they
would have ruined us.   Every receding wave of the Atlantic, returns freighted with a new cargo of foreign population.   This heterogeneous mass now amounts to near
half a million annually.   At no former period could our
young and forming institutions have sustained the shock
of so huge a mass.   What would have crushed the sap-
ling, may not harm the sturdy oak.   Perhaps we cannot
meet unharmed the shock now : certainly not, unless our
institutions are founded deep and firm in the basis of
everlasting truth, and stand as a rock amidst the rolling
waves.   We do, however, indulge the hope that such is
now the maturity and stability of our civil and religious
institutions, that we may, with safety to ourselves, and
great benefit to the surplus population of the old world,
open wide our arms and receive them to our bosom.

And now that we are prepared to receive them, oppression, famine, pestilence and revolution, conjoin to eject immense masses from Europe to seek an asylum in this new world.

We cannot here too profoundly admire the wisdom of that Providence, which has hitherto delayed the full tide of immigration till we were able to bear it. What fearful responsibilities has God laid upon us! What wisdom and virtue is needed in our national counsels; what faith, and holiness, and prayer, in the church! Millions of the papal world are, like an overwhelming tide, rolling in upon us, to be enlightened, elevated, Christianized, and taught the privileges and prerogatives of freemen—to say nothing here of the three millions of instruments placed in our hands by a system of unrighteous bondage, to "sharpen, polish, and prepare for the subjugation of another continent to the Prince of Peace."

CHAPTER III.

The Reformation.—General remarks—state of Europe and the world. The Crusades—their cause and effect. Revival of Greek literature in Europe. The Arabs. Daring spirit of inquiry. Bold spirit of adventure. Columbus. The Cabots. Charles V. Henry VIII. Francis I. Leo X. Rise of liberty. Feudalism. Distribution of political power.

" *All the inhabitants of the earth are reputed as nothing ; and he doeth according to his will in the army of heaven, and among the inhabitants of the earth, and none can stay his hand, or say unto him, What doest thou?*"—Daniel, iv. 35.

So spake the monarch of Chaldea after he had been brought by a most signal interposition of Divine Providence, to "bless the Most High, and to praise and honor Him that liveth forever"—another illustrious instance of the sovereignty of Providence in the extension of the true religion. God spake and it was done—He looked on the throne of the potent monarch, and it trembled, he touched the towering hills of Babylon's pride and power, and they vanished like smoke. The name of the God of Israel was proclaimed from the throne, from the palace and the court, and wafted on by princes, nobles, and people, throughout the vast dominions of the Chaldean empire.

So God has always shaped the destinies of nations, to suit the prosperity of his church; turning the hearts of kings, princes, and people, to favor Zion as her need require, or blotting out of existence the nation that should dare to raise its hand against the Lord's anointed ones. It is awfully grand to contemplate the exactitude with which the declaration has been verified: "I will bless them that bless thee, and curse him that curseth thee." And it is a remarkable fact, that no people or nation, since the call of Abraham, have lifted their hand to oppress or maltreat the true church, and not, in their turn, fallen under the ban of the Divine displeasure. Did Laban prosper after he defrauded Jacob of his wages? Did the Egyptians prosper after they began to afflict the people of God? Was it well with the Moabites, who refused to let Israel pass, or to relieve their necessities with bread and water? Where now are those mighty empires who once presumed to raise the arm of oppression against Israel? Egypt, Moab, Ammon, the nations of Palestine— proud Babylon, imperial Rome? So shall it be with the King's enemies. Has Spain ever prospered since she drew the sword of persecution against the seed of Jacob? Has the white flag of peace since waved a truce to Heaven's indignation? Where are those kingdoms, that, during the bloody reign of the Beast, devoured fifty millions of the saints of the Most High?—burning, torturing, impaling, butchering, without mercy, the unoffending children of God?

On the other hand, how was it with *Abimelech*, who proffered his generous hospitality to the patriarch Abraham? How with the Egyptians, while they favored the heirs of promise? And how went the world with Obed-

edom while the ark of the Lord found a resting place in
his house?

How have the mighty wheels of Providence rolled on,
crushing beneath them all that opposeth, and bearing
aloft, far above the stormy atmosphere of earth, the precious interests of Zion! How have the *inhabitants of the
earth*, the great, the noble, the wise, been *reputed as
nothing*, while the sovereign Lord *has done according to
his will in the army of heaven, and among the inhabitants
of the earth, and none can stay his hand or say to him,
What doest thou?*

The next event selected by which to illustrate our general subject, is *the Reformation of the sixteenth century.*
This is another of those great instrumentalities, cradled
in the fifteenth century, which Providence employed, on
the breaking away of the darkness of the dark ages, for
the honor and enlargement of his church.

We should view this extraordinary event from three
points: Its causes and preliminary steps: The great
transaction itself: Some of its general results.

No attempt will be made to furnish a history of the
Reformation, or to gauge the vast dimensions of its influence on the world. I present it only as a magnificent
scheme of Providence for the advancement of his church.

1. *Causes and preliminary steps.* That we may have
some just idea of the origin and real character of the Reformation, we shall needs take a brief survey of the civil,
moral and religious condition of Europe and of the
world, previous to this notable event.

You cannot, without astonishment, read the history of
those times. It would seem as if man had then yielded
up the native dignity of manhood, and consented to pros-
titute the nobility of immortal mind to the meanest purposes of ignorance, superstition, and crime. The history
of the dark ages may be written in a word—it was an
INTELLECTUAL THRALDOM. The lamp of intelligence had
been extinguished amidst the floods of barbarism, which
swept, wave after wave, over the Romish church and
empire. Hence that general corruption of religion which
disgraced the church, and made the church disgrace the
world—hence the vile brood of superstitions which over-

ran and spoiled the fair heritage of God, and the disgust
ing combinations of vice and crime which invaded the
very temple of the church, not sparing the altar.

Religion finds no rest in the bosom of ignorance.
Cradle her there, and she pines and dies; or, rather, instead of being the bird of paradise, fledged with angels'
wings, and borne aloft with the eagle's strength, and
plumed with a seraph's beauty, she becomes the loathsome
reptile of superstition, without form or comeliness, without soul or spirit.

A night of a thousand years had brooded over the
earth. It was long and tempestuous, as if the light of
moral day were extinguished forever, and the king of
darkness had begun his final reign. Only here and there,
over the wide expanse, glimmered the light of science,
and the lamp of religion burnt but dimly amidst the general desolation. Despotism, religious and civil, crushed
the energies of the immortal mind, and iniquity, like a
flood deep and broad, submerged all Europe. Nearly all
the learning that did exist, was confined to the clergy;
and yet they were so profoundly ignorant as to afford a
subject of universal reproach and ridicule. In a council
held in 992, it was asserted there was scarcely a person
in Rome itself who knew the first elements of letters. In
Spain, not one priest in a thousand could address a common letter of salutation to a friend. In England, not a
priest south of the Thames understood the common
prayers, or could translate a sentence of Latin into his
mother tongue. Learning was almost extinct. Its flickering lamp scarcely emitted a ray of light.

And, as might be expected, this long and dreary night
of ignorance generated a loathsome brood of superstitions. Controversies were settled by *ordeal*. The accused person was made to prove his innocence by holding, with impunity, red-hot iron, or plunging the arm into
boiling fluids, or walking, unharmed, on burning coals, or
on red-hot plowshares. Nothing can surpass the wild fa-
naticims of that period. To such a height did the
phrenzy for a crusade to the Holy Land rise, that in one
instance, (1211,) an army of ninety thousand, mostly
children, and commanded by a child, set out from Ger

many for the purpose of recovering the Holy Land from
Infidels.   Again we meet with the "Brethren of the white
caps," dealing out vengeance and blood, in honor of the
peaceful Lady of Loretto.   Next arises a *Jehu*, who
thinks he can in no way serve God so acceptably as by
leading an immense rabble on a crusade against the
clergy, monasteries. and the Jews, plundering, massacre-
ing, butchering wherever they went; and all this, of
course, for religion's sake.   And as yet more characteristic of those times, and of the misguided zeal of unen-
lightened piety, rose the *Flagellants.*   This religious con-
tagion, not, as usual, confined to the populace, spread
among every rank, age, and sex.   Immense crowds
marched, two by two, in procession along the streets and
public roads, mingling groans and dolorous hymns with
the sounds of leathern whips, which they applied without
mercy to their own naked backs.   The *Bianchi* wandered from city to city, and from province to province,
bearing before them a huge crucifix, and with their faces
covered and bent towards the ground, crying, "*misericordia*," "*misericordia;*" and what is not to be overlooked in these phrenzied religionists as identifying them
with modern fanatics, a prominent article in their creed
was, that all who did not join their craft and act as ab-
surdly as themselves, were branded as heretics and enemies.
   The legendary tales of those days are too absurd to repeat, and, to save humanity a blush, we fain hope they
did not gain any very general credence, even in those
degenerate times.   They show how faint the light of intellect may shine, and how groveling man may become.
   I mention but one more instance, which more strikingly
illustrates the extreme debasement into which the human
mind had fallen, and the hopeless corruption of the
church.   I allude to *indulgences.*   The doctrine of penance had long been taught in the church.   Salvation
was of *works.*   But it did not sufficiently subserve the
interests of a mercenary priesthood, that the poor delin-
quent should go through five, ten, or twenty years of
penance, or submit to some barbarous austerity.   An ex-

pedient was devised, more agreeable to the penitent, more profitable to the priest.

It was at length discovered that the sacrifice of Christ did much more than to reconcile God to man. It accumulated an inexhaustible *treasury of merit* in the church, left at the disposal of the Pope! and that this accumulation is increased by the supererogatory merits of the saints, the reward of works over and above the obligations of duty.

It now only remained to label every sin with its *price*, and to add purgatory to the dominions of the Pope. Then the proclamation:—perjury, robbery, murder, incest, any thing you please! if you will pay the price. Mendicants, friars, priests, bishops, now traverse the country, proclaiming an eternal amnesty with heaven, provided the Pope's coffers be filled, and his hirelings be well paid. Money now became the key which alone could open heaven and none could shut, or shut hell and none could open. The most scandalous sins which, according to the orthodoxy of more ancient Romanism, would have cost years of penance, might now be committed for a few shillings. This was an *improvement* of the thirteenth century!

The influence of this system on public morals cannot be mistaken. Virtue was scouted from the earth—at least she sought a hiding place in the caves and dens of obscurity. And no marvel that the clergy were indecently idle, haughty, avaricious, and dissolute; and the common people sunk in turpitude still lower. Churches were filled with relics, the pulpit occupied by worthless priests, and the world, to all appearance, abandoned to the empire of sin.

Nor was the *civil* condition of the world more promising. Despotism had bound all nations fast in iron chains, and there was none to deliver. The Papacy in the west, and Moslemism in the east, had hushed to sleep the last throbbings of liberty. The Pope set his iron heel on the necks of kings, and made emperors hold his stirrup while he mounted his horse. The dark curtain of despotism was drawn around the world; yet, during the long and dismal night, ever and anon a gleam of light breaks above the horizon—a morning star amidst the sable drapery of the East. Expectant piety hopes the day is breaking; and knowledge, long benighted, and freedom, sorely oppressed, inspire the hope of speedy relief. But in a moment, all is overcast. A cloud, darker than before, gathers about the eastern sky.

The first considerable event that moved these stagnant waters of ignorance and sin, was the quixotic expeditions of European nations to the East, called the *Crusades*. To the dormant mind of Europe, these were as if a burning mountain were cast into the sea. They produced some light, more smoke, and much convulsion. They broke the spell of slavery, which had for more than six centuries manacled the human mind. Here was struck the death blow to mental despotism—here the work of emancipation begun, though in its details, strength and beauty, it was not completed for some centuries. Now men begun again to launch forth on the untried ocean of thought; and, unskilled as they were, and unfurnished with chart, rudder, and compass, no wonder some foundered. But we must look upon this great drama a little more particularly.

Deluded by the idea that the end of the world was near, and burning with enthusiasm to deliver from the profane tread of infidels the land where the Prince of Life lived, taught, suffered, and died, and where still was the Holy Sepulchre ; and, indignant at the recital of the oppressions and cruelties inflicted on Christian pilgrims, all Europe was roused to raise the banners of the cross, and march to the rescue of the holy hill of Zion, and in vindication of the Holy Virgin. All sorts of motives, ambition, avarice, love of adventure ; the promise of exemption from debts, taxes, and punishment for crimes ; religious zeal and bigotry, and the confident hope of heaven, stirred up the people of all ranks, ages, and sexes, to embark their lives and fortunes in these holy expeditions. Princes hoped to enlarge the boundaries of their empire, and add new stars to their crowns ; priests and popes hoped to reach farther and to extend wider the arms of their ghostly dominion ; and all classes hoped, by some means, to further their own interests, or minister to their gratifi-

cation. Six millions of souls, following the ignis-fatuus
of an overheated imagination, were, from time to time,
led out of Europe to mark their pathway to the East with
blood, or to whiten the hills and valleys of Palestine with
their bones.

Though visionary in the extreme, and prodigal of life
and treasure, and unsuccessful in their professed object,
yet, from all this confusion came order, from all this darkness, light, and from the most miserable combination of
evil, was educed a lasting good. The fountains of the
great deep were now broken up, the stagnations of ignorance and corruption which had for centuries choked and
poisoned all that attempted to live, and breathe, and
move in them, began to heave and give signs of such
coming commotion as must, ere long, purify their putrid
waters.

A spirit of enterprise from this time nerved the arm of
every nation in Europe. A highway was opened to the
nations of the East. The barbarity and ignorance of Europe were brought into comparison with the greater intelligence, wealth, and civilization of Asia. The boundaries of men's ideas were greatly enlarged. They saw in
the advanced condition of the Orientals, the advantages
which the arts and sciences, industry and civilization,
give a people. In these they discovered the main spring
of national greatness, and of social and individual comfort and prosperity. They formed new commercial relations; acquired new ideas of agriculture—the handicrafts
of industry were plied to minister to the new demands
which an acquaintance with the East had created. They
lost, too, amidst Asiatic associations, many of the superstitions and prejudices which had so long kept the mind
of Europe in bondage, and acquired new views in all the
economy of life. And strange, if, on their return, they
did not profit by the new habits and information they had
acquired.

Here we date the early dawn of the day that should
soon rise upon the nations. Ever and anon the darkness
broke away, and light gleamed above the horizon.
Learning began to revive; colleges and universities were
founded; an acquaintance with the East had introduced

Arabs in Costume—Pyramids in the distance.   Page 62.

into Europe the Greek classics, which fixed a new era in
its literature, as well as worked wonders in the progress
of its civilization.   For the Greek language had, for centuries, been the language of history, of the arts and sciences, of civilization and religion.   Philo and Josephus
chose to embalm the chronicles of their times in the
Grecian tongue, that they might thus speak to more of
the world's population than in any other language.   And
when Socrates and Aristotle reasoned and wrote in their
mother tongue, they reasoned and wrote for the civilization and elevation of Europe, fifteen centuries afterwards.
And when Alexander pushed his conquests eastward, and
settled Greek colonies near the confines of India, (in
Bactria,) he opened the way, through Christian churches
planted in Bactria, for the introduction of the gospel, centuries after, in Tartary and China.

The introduction of Greek literature into Europe did
much to draw aside the veil of the dark ages.   By this
means the society, the ethics, the improvements of ancient Greece, were now disinterred from the dust of ages,
and transmitted, reanimated and nourished on the soil of
modern Europe.

And what, in the history of Providence, should not be
here overlooked, the Arabs, the determined foes of Christianity, were used as the instruments of preserving and
transmitting that knowledge which, finally, became the
regenerator of Europe.   They were made to subserve
the purposes of the truth, up to a certain point, when the
privilege was transferred to worthier hands.   At the
period of which I am speaking, it seemed altogether probable that learning and the arts, the power of knowledge
and the press, would be transmitted to future ages
through the followers of the false prophet.   For it was
through them that learning revived, and the inventions
and discoveries, which so effectually wield the destinies
of the world, were divulged.

In less than a century after the Saracens first turned
their hostile spears against their foreign enemies, (the
Greeks, at the battle of Muta, in 630,) their empire ex-
ceeded in extent the greatest monarchies of ancient
times.   The successors of the prophet were the most

powerful and absolute sovereigns on the earth. Their
caliphs exercised a most unlimited and undefined prerogative—reigned over numerous nations, from Gibralter to the Chinese sea, two hundred days' journey from
east to west. And, what is no less extraordinary, within
about the same period, after the barbarous act of Omar,
which consigned to the flames the splendid library of
Alexandria, (640,) the world became indebted to the Saracens in respect to literature and science—though it was
nearly two centuries more before they attained to their
Augustan age.

The court of the caliph became the resort of poets,
philosophers, and mathematicians, from every country,
and from every creed. Literary relics of the conquered
countries were brought to the foot of the throne—hundreds of camels were seen entering Bagdad, loaded with
volumes of Greek, Hebrew, and Persian literature, translated by the most skillful interpreters into the Arabic language. Masters, instructors, translators, commentators,
formed the court at Bagdad. Schools, academies, and
libraries were established in every considerable town, and
colleges were munificently endowed. It was the glory of
every city to collect treasures of literature and science
throughout the Moslem dominions, whether in Asia, Africa, or Europe. Grammar, eloquence and poetry were
cultivated with great care. So were metaphysics, philosophy, political economy, geography, astronomy, and the
natural sciences. Botany and chemistry were cultivated
with ardor and success. The Arabs particularly excelled
in architecture. The revenue of kingdoms were ex-
pended in public buildings and fine arts; painting, sculp-
ture, and music, shared largely in their regards. And in
nothing did they more excel than in agriculture and
metallurgy. They were the depositories of science in the
dark ages, and the restorers of letters to Europe.

Had not this course of things been arrested—had not
a mandate from the skies uttered the decree, that the
Arabian should no longer rule in the empire of letters, how
different would have been the destiny of our race! Instead of the full-orbed day of the Sun of Righteouness,
casting his benignant rays on our seminaries of learning,

they would have grown up under the pale and sickly hues of the crescent. The power of science and the arts, printing and paper-making, the mariner's compass and the spirit of foreign discovery, and the power of steam, (all Arabian in their origin,) would have been devoted .o the propagation and establishment of Mohammedanism. The press had been a monopoly of the Arabian imposture; and the Ganges and Euphrates, the Red sea and the Caspian, illumined only by the moon-light of Islam, would have been the channels through which the world's commerce would have flowed into Mohammedan emporiums.

But He that controlleth all events, would not have it so. These mighty engines of reformation and advancement should nerve the arm of truth; the press be the handmaid of Christianity, to establish and embalm its doctrines and precepts on the enduring page; and the control which men should gain over the elements, to facilitate labor, contract distances, and bring out the resources of nature, be the handmaid of the Cross. Otherwise, Christianity had been the twin sister of barbarism; and Moslemism and Idolatry had been nurtured under the favoring influences of learning, civilization, and the art of printing. It is worthy of remark, that the press, up to the present day, has been confined almost exclusively within the precincts of Christianity.

And not only has Providence so interposed as to consign to the hands of civilization and Christianity, almost the exclusive monopoly of the press, but, under the guidance of the same unerring Wisdom, the *future* literature, as well as the society and government of the Gentile nations, is likely to descend to them through the purest Christianity. While science and literature are cultivated and honored by Christian nations, they are stationary or retrograde among Pagans and Mohammedans. This is giving Christianity immense advantages. For nearly the entire supply of books, schools, and the means of education, are furnished through Christian missions. Almost the only book of the convert from heathenism, is the Bible, or a religious book. Who but the Christian missionary, form alphabets, construct grammars and dictionaries for Pagan nations, and thus form the basis of their

literature, and guide their untutored minds in all matters
of education, government and religion ?   In these things,
how admirable the orderings of Providence.   Christianity
at once takes possession of the strong holds of society,
and gives promise of permanency.   For there is all the
difference of civilization and barbarism, of religion and infidelity, in the kind of literature a people have.   If supplied by the enlightened mind, the pure heart, and the
liberal hand of Christianity, it will be as a fountain of
living waters.

Another providential feature of the period now under
review, was *a spirit of bold inquiry*.

As the time for the world's emancipation from the
thraldom of the dark ages drew near, there was a singular boldness for overstepping the wonted boundaries of
thought.   Ignorance and superstition had so narrowed
the compass of men's ideas, that it had become a crime,
—at least a heresy, for one to *think further* than his fathers had done.   It is exceedingly interesting to trace the
progress of the human mind from the eleventh to the sixteenth century.   The inundation of the Roman empire, by
northern barbarians, as completely extinguished the lamp
of learning, as the light of religion.   The dark ages were
the winter season of the human mind.   Though not
annihilated, its activities were repressed, and it lay in a
torpid state, awaiting its resuscitation on the return of
spring.   There seemed written on the furled banners of
the returning crusaders, " Lo, the winter is past."   Mind
was uncaged.   The holy wars had given to its domains
an enchanting extension.   The social sphere was enlarged, and, on every side, an opening field for all sorts
of activity.

Mind was now roused from its long sleep.   Popery
and despotism could not much longer enslave it.   There
now arose, for the carrying out of providential schemes,
great and glorious, a class of bold thinkers, who quailed
not before the thunders of the Vatican, nor recoiled to
investigate maxims, doctrines or practices, because venerable for age, or disdained truth, because fresh with nov-
elty.

Years before Columbus launched his adventurous bark

on the pathless Atlantic, or Martin Luther shook the
foundations of Rome, there was a rousing up of the dor
mant mind of Europe, and a bold demand for *truth.*
Fiction, romance, legends of saints, cloisters and ghosts
could no longer suffice.   Schools of learning,—the minds
of the first scholars in Christendom were seized with an
unwonted mania for investigation.   And not only the
universities and chief seminaries of learning, but the
same spirit had crept into tribunals of justice, and halls
of legislation, had looked into the windows of palaces,
and seized on the minds of nobles and princes.   Not only
divines of the most profound erudition, but philosophers
and eminent scholars of noble blood, as Reuchlin and
Ulrich de Hutten, employed all their learning and wit to
free the church and the world from the bondage of ignorance and superstition.

And, as coeval and co-extensive with this spirit of inquiry, Providence created an unaccountable *spirit for bold
adventure*, which equally presaged some notable revolution near.   The flames of a restless ambition burned.
There was an irrepressible desire of *enterprise.*   The bold
and adventurous spirit of Columbus, of the Cabots, of
Amerigo Vespucci, of Charles V., Francis I., Henry VIII.,
Leo X., was widely diffused through Europe.   Spain,
Portugal, Genoa, France and England, were struggling,
who should first whiten an unknown sea with their canvas, or reach farthest the arms of conquest.   Dormant energies were aroused.   *Discovery* was the mania
of the day.   And no wonder that an expectation, bordering on certainty, was entertained, that some great change
was at hand.

Nor were the movements of Providence less conspicuous at this time, on the *great political arena.*   The wide
domains of Christendom were crushed beneath the foot
of the Pope.   But the decree had gone out that the power
of despotism should be broken.

Modern liberty, paradoxical as it may seem, is the offspring of *Feudalism.*   As a strange, yet comely vine, it
sprung up and grew for a time in the rugged villas of
feudal barons.   The process was this: The feudal
system broke into pieces the before unbroken empire of

6*

despotism; and though the feudal lords were despots
in their little domains, yet each clan or tribe was independent one of another, and the germ of a half-civilized,
half-barbarous liberty, was all this time taking root in a
rugged soil, ready to be transplanted where it should
grow more stately and gracefully, and bear a better and
more abundant fruit. When this tree, or rather *shrub*,
had flourished as long as it could on feudal ground, the
Hand that ever protects all on earth, which pleases Him,
broke down the system that first gave it birth, yet saved
his chosen plant from the common ruin.

The crusades struck the death-blow to the feudal system, and opened the way in Europe for the successful
struggle of Liberty. This was the grand *transition* state
from Despotism to Monarchy.

In England, Liberty, long oppressed and abused, rose
amidst the troubled waters of King John's tyranny, and
they called her Magna Charta,—the keystone of English liberty, the bulwark of constitutional law. This noble monument of indignant popular freedom against
royal usurpation, bears date 1215.

Next, the light of smothered liberty is seen gleaming
up over the sable empire of Spain. It rises in Arragon
as early as 1283. An instrument called the "General
Privilege," is granted by Peter III., in response to the popular clamor for liberty, containing a series of provisions
against arbitrary power, more full and satisfactory, as a
basis of liberty, than the great Charter of England. And
had we time to trace the connection, we might institute
the inquiry, how far might this rising genius of liberty
in Arragon have infused its spirit into Columbus and
his adventurous cotemporaries, and induced the patronage
he received from the throne? Or what connection had
this with the conquest of Grenada, and the expulsion of
the Moors? Or with the discovery of the great East by
the Cape of Good Hope?—three nearly simultaneous
events, and each big with the destiny of the Church and
the world.

The same leaven is at work in *Germany*. The Emperor becomes elective; checks are imposed on his power,
all matters of moment are referred to the States Gen-

eral. Switzerland achieves her freedom in the beginning
of the fourteenth century. Indeed, "free cities," small re-
publics, spring up in all parts of Europe, and, as in the early
ages of mankind, the world was indebted to *cities* for
civilization and political institutions, so again modern
liberty was cradled in the bosom of the free cities of
Europe. "It was not the monarchies, it was not the
courts of the great princes,—it was the cities of northern Italy, which opened the way for the progress of
improvement, and lighted the torch of modern civilization."

Thus was Providence *politically* shaping the world for
the reception of Christianity, under the renovated form
of the Reformation.

And here we must not overlook the singular *distribution* of *political power*, at the *time* of the Reformation.
That the power might appear of God, and not of man,
Providence gave this to four of the mightiest monarchs
that ever wielded a sceptre. Henry VIII., was on the
throne of England; Francis I., on that of France;
Charles V., Emperor of the kingdoms of Germany and
Spain; and Pope Leo X., the most powerful, politic and
sagacious of the Popes, occupied the chair of St. Peter,
and reached his sceptre over all the monarchs of Europe.
But God employed none of them. And when they would
have pounced upon, and torn to pieces the Daniel of
Heaven's election, God shut the mouths of these lions,
that they should not harm a hair of his head.

But I pursue the subject no further at present. Let
us pause and reflect; and we shall review this great
transaction with increased admiration of the power and
wisdom of God. In carrying out his vast plans, *all the
inhabitants of the earth are reputed as nothing before him;*
he doeth according to his will in the army of heaven,
and among the inhabitants of the earth, and none can
stay his hand, or say unto him, what doest thou? Who,
then, would not fear thee, O God? Who would not
adore thee in the temple of thy power, and revere thee
in thy matchless wisdom, and praise thee in thy un-
speakable goodness? How much reason has the saint
to rejoice! Standing on the eternal rock, he is safe.

How much reason has the sinner to tremble! He stands, he trifles beneath the rock that shall grind him to powder.

"Be wise to-day, 'tis madness to defer."

CHAPTER IV.

THE REFORMATION. Europe clamors for reform. Causes. Abuses. Boniface VIII The Great Schism. Infallibility. Bad moral character of Popes—Alexander VI. Leo X. Elector of Saxony. Early Reformers. Waldenses—Nestorians. The Reformation a necessary effect—a child of Providence. Martin Luther; his origin, early education, history. Finds the Bible. His conversion. Luther the preacher—the Theological Professor—at Rome. "Pilate's staircase." Compelled to be a Reformer. His coadjutors. Opposition. Results.

"*All the inhabitants of the earth are reputed as nothing.*"

THE last chapter closed while yet speaking of the *causes* of the Reformation of the sixteenth century. These causes were numerous and multifarious. The crusades had broken up the stagnations of despotism—learning had revived—the art of printing was discovered—an adventurous spirit of discovery and conquest was abroad; the science of navigation, made abundantly practical by the invention of the mariner's compass, brought the nations of the earth into neighborhood and acquaintance. There was, too, a bold spirit of inquiry among philosophers, divines, and every class of the literati, which demanded reform. The inspiration of poetry breathed it. The spirit of the age boldly demanded immortal mind should be free. Mind is like the irrepressible spirit of liberty. You cannot chain it; you cannot imprison it. Though for a time it may be reserved in chains of darkness, the day of emancipation must come, hastened on by the very galling of its chains, and the gloominess of its prison.

The Reformation has been very justly denominated " a vast effort of the human mind to achieve its freedom."

Though its *religious* bearings were immense on the destinies of the world, it was more than a religious reform. It was an *intellectual* revolution.

The most shameful abuses in the church, the degeneracy of the clergy not excepting popes, and the abused common-sense of the people, clamored for reform. The long repressed spirit of liberty, smothered beneath the rubbish of ignorance and superstition, yet now beginning to labor in her dark caverns, and to make all Europe heave, fearfully demanded, by her oft-repeated irruptions, that the foot of Rome should no longer crush the world. *Causes* were at work which made the Reformation necessary as an *effect*. The world was prepared for it. Expectation was on the alert. The profoundest talents of the age were laboring to produce it. Suppressed, exiled, outraged piety began to emerge from her hiding places, to rise in the strength and beauty of her own dignity, and with a holy indignation to assert, and, in the name of Heaven, to demand, freedom for the sons of God. So clamorous, indeed, had Europe become for reform, that the pope, the clergy and a corrupt church were constrained to acknowledge its necessity. Accordingly, the Council of Constance, assembled by the emperor, (1414,) attempted to lop off some of the monstrous excrescences of the church. Yet this same council consigned to the flames John Huss, the pious and learned reformer, of Bohemia. Though frustrated in the attempt at ecclesiastical reformation, and deadly opposed to the popular reform of Wicklif, Huss and Jerome, and though reform was re-attempted with no better success seventeen years later, in the Council of Basle, yet much was gained to the general cause of liberty and religion. The necessity and feasibility of reform had been freely discussed in the high places of the church and of the empire, and though opposed and ostensibly arrested by the strong arm of Rome, facts were revealed, abuses exposed, principles established, which emboldened the potentates of Europe to proclaim against the usurpations of the Vatican. In France and Germany the famous Pragmatic Sanction of 1438 was made a law of the state, authorizing the *election of Bishops*, and the reform of the principal abuses of the church.

But, in further tracing out providential arrangements as at work, *ecclesiastically*, in bringing affairs to the desired crisis, we must go back a little.

The remarkable fourteenth century, signalized as the generator of new ideas, new schemes and activities, opened in the darkest days of the Papal church. The "mystery of iniquity" was now consummated—Popery had found its acme. Boniface VIII. now occupied the papal chair. In arrogance, in spiritual pride, oppression and blasphemy, he was surpassed by none who had preceded him. He claimed that, as "vicar of Jesus Christ, he had power to govern kings with a rod of iron, and to dash them in pieces as a potter's vessel." Though he exalted himself above all that is called God, and spoke great swelling words of vanity, yet his end was nigh, and his judgment did not tarry. Taken prisoner by an emmissary of France, and treated with indignity and rudeness, he dies in the extremity of his rage and mortification. Says the historian, (Sismondi,) "His eyes were haggard; his mouth white with foam; he gnashed his teeth in silence. He passed the day without nourishment, and the night without repose; and when he found that his strength was failing, and his end was nigh, he removed all his attendants, that there might be no witness to his final feebleness and parting struggle. After some interval, his domestics burst into the room, and beheld his body stretched on the bed, stiff and cold. The staff which he carried bore the marks of his teeth, and was covered with foam; his white locks were stained with blood; and his head was so closely wrapped in the counterpane, that he was believed to have anticipated his impending death by violence and suffocation."

Thus died the pretended vicegerent of God, the pattern of saints, the Head of the Church, and the almoner of Heaven's righteousness to dying men.

From this hour the strong arm of Popery was weakened. The power of the church was much diminished by the removal of the Popedom from Rome to Avignon in France, and still more by the "Great Schism of the West," which occurred in 1378, and continued half a century. There were now two rival popes, and at one time *three*, "assailing each other with excommunications, maledictions and all sorts of hostile measures"—not a little impairing their respective claims to *infallibility*, bringing into disrepute their ghostly characters, and effectually preparing the way for the abolition of their spiritual usurpation.

These things, together with *the bad moral character* of the clergy, from the Pope to the most beggarly mendicant—their affluence, avarice and luxury, had prepared the minds of the people to embrace the first opportunity to throw off the yoke of Rome. This consummation was rapidly hastened by the disgusting profligacy of Alexander VI. and the restless ambition and cruelty of Julius II. History rarely affords a specimen of so worthless a character as that of Pope Alexander. His youth was spent in profligacy and crime ; he obtained the pontifical chair by the most shameless bribery ; his palace, while Pope, was disgraced by family feuds and bloodshed ; by bachanalian entertainments and licentious revelry ; by farces and indecent songs ; and his death was compassed by the poison which he had prepared for one of his rich cardinals. Such was the Pope in 1492, on the very eve of the Reformation.

Stations of dignity and trust were filled by men raised from obscurity and ignorance ; or by sons of noblemen, and not unfrequently by mere children. A child of five years old was made Archbishop of Rheims, and the see of Narbonne was purchased for a boy of ten years. Nor was the papal chair itself exempt from the same disgraceful sacrilege. Rome was one vast scene of debauchery, in which the most powerful families in Italy contended for the pre-eminence. Benedict IX. was a boy brought up in profligacy—was made Pope at twelve years old, and remained in the practice of the scandalous sins of his youth.

Such abuses, crimes and usurpations, such despotism and corruption at the fountain head of the church, roused the indignation of princes and people not yet sunk below where the voice of a virtuous indignation reaches, and hastened on the Reformation. And mitred heads, and fulminating bulls, and all the array of the Scarlet Beast could not silence the clamor.   God was in it, confounding the wisdom of the wise, and giving understanding to babes.

It has not failed to arrest the attention of historians that Leo X., though a man of consummate skill and policy in the management of public affairs, prompt, energetic, provident ; yet, in reference to Luther and the rising Reformation, he seemed bereft of his wisdom and accustomed energy, while they who were undermining his throne, and plucking the ghostly crown from his head, were endued with uncommon sagacity.   In his attempts to crush Luther, and suppress the Reformation, nothing is so prominent as his hesitation. delays and mistakes.   In the mean time the good work was gaining ground ; the host of the Reformed receiving daily accessions ; the ball set in motion by an unseen Hand had gathered a power and velocity which kings and popes could not arrest.

Here I would just notice another providence : it is the raising up and rightly disposing the heart of the *Elector of Saxony*.   God fitted and used this noble prince for two great purposes : first, he gave him a controlling influence among the electors of the Emperor, which the Pope, deeply interested as he was in the election, could not afford to lose ; as he would, should he displease the Elector, by proclaiming his bull of excommunication against Luther : and, secondly, God gave his servant Luther a safe shelter beneath the wings of this excellent Prince.

But there were other causes of the Reformation.   We return, that we may again approach the great phenomenon of the sixteenth century through another series of providential arrangements.

Dark as the dark ages were, the lamp of truth and pure religion was never suffered to be extinguished.   Indeed, from the earliest corruptions of Christianity, God has not left himself without a succession of witnesses.   In the sixth century lived Vigilantius, the vehement remonstrant against relics, the invocation of saints, lighted candles in churches, vows of celibacy, pilgrimages, nocturnal watchings, fastings, prayers for the dead, and all the mummeries which had at that early period crept into the church.   In the ninth century, Claudius, the pious Bishop

of Turin, called the first Protestant Reformer, bore a noble
testimony to the truth. Peter of Bruges, Henry of Lau-
sanne, and Arnold of Brescia, raised their voices amidst
the general corruption, and in various ways and with various success pleaded for reform.* So did also the learned
and fearless Bishop of Lincoln, Greathead, in the thirteenth
century, and the excellent *Thomas Bradwardine*, Archbishop of Canterbury, and the noble Fitzralph, Archbishop
of Armagh, whose light from time to time made visible the
surrounding darkness. Nor may we pass unnoticed a
noble band of confessors and witnesses for the truth,
among whom we find the indefatigable Peter Pruys, Henry
the Italian, Marsilius of Padua, John of Garduno, who
was condemned by the Pope, 1330, and the learned,
dauntless and persecuted Barengarius, who, after having
withstood the storm of papal rage to a good old age, closed
his testimony in 1088. These were some of the lights
which shone amidst the darkness of the middle ages, and
by which an ever watchful Providence preserved his truth
from the general ruin.†

These, however, were but the casual outbreakings of
pent up fires that should soon burst out and burn with an
unquenchable flame. These were the lesser lights—the
precursors of the approaching morning. At length the
morning star arose. Wicklif appeared; the arm of
Providence, to pave the way for a glorious onward march
of the work of redemption; guilty of daring to think out
of the beaten track of the dark ages; guilty of question-
ing the arrogant claims of a haughty, avaricious, corrupt
priesthood, and guilty of publishing to the world the living
oracles of God, and teaching the people their right and
duty to read them. By his writings and lectures in the
University of Oxford; by his public instructions as
pastor at Lutterworth, and his translation of the Scriptures for the first time into English, he laid an immovable

---

* The fiery zeal of Arnold knew no bounds till he had carried the war of reform into
Rome itself, and kindled a fire in the very seat of St. Peter. but which in its turn kindled a fire about him, in which he perished, and his party (the Arnoldists,) was suppressed.

† The following are some of the sects, or Christian *communities* which stood up for
the truth, when the whole world had gone wandering after the Beast : The *Novitians*,
*Donatists, Paulicians, Cathari, Puritans, Waldenses, Petrobrusians, Henricians, Ar-
noldists, Paterines*, in Italy.

foundation for the reform of the church. The leaven so effectually wrought in the University, as to merit the charge of heresy from Archbishop Arundel : "Oxford," says he, "is a vine that bringeth forth wild and sour grapes, which being eaten by the fathers, the children's teeth are set on edge ; so that the whole province of Canterbury is tainted with a novel and damnable heresy :" an honorable testimony to the fidelity and influence of Wicklif. He had many zealous friends among the nobility, and even in the royal family ; which no doubt served as a shield to ward off the fiery darts of papal vengeance, and left our reformer to die a quiet death in the retirement of Lutterworth.

The impression produced by Wicklif's character and labors, was tremendous on all ranks and ages. It was as the letting out of many waters. Mountains could not hedge it in, seas could not limit it. No sooner was this new light extinguished by popish virulence in England than it begun to burn with redoubled splendor in Bohemia on the continent. Europe caught the light, and the cloud that had so long hung over Christendom began to scatter.

And here again mark the finger of Providence : Queen Anne, the wife of Richard II., of England, *a native of Bohemia*, having herself embraced the doctrines of Wicklif, became, through her attendants, the instrument of circulating the books of the reformer in Bohemia. Who can doubt "whether she did not come to the kingdom for such a time as this." God called her to the throne of England, that, having learned the truth there, she might introduce it, with a royal sanction, in her own native land. Huss and Jerome of Prague, by this means caught the fire of the English reformer, raised the banners of reformation, and ceased not, till a glorious martyrdom put out their lamp, to devote their great learning and their immense influence in defence of abused truth.

The execution of Huss as a heretic, furnishes a just though melancholy picture of the times of those early reformers. John Huss was Professor of Divinity in the University of Prague, and pastor of the church in that city ; a man as renowned for the purity and excellency

of his Christian character, as for his profound learning
and uncommon eloquence. But his light shone too bright
for the age. He was charged with heresy; arrested,
thrown into prison—condemned to the stake. At the
place of execution he was treated with the most barbarous
indignity. Seven Bishops strip him of his sacerdotal
dress—violently tear from him the insignia of his office—
put on his head a cap on which three devils were painted,
and the words *arch-heretic* written—burn his books before
his eyes. In the meantime the fires of death are kindled.
The undaunted martyr commends his spirit to Jesus, and,
serene and joyful in the prospect of a glorious immortality,
his happy spirit rises from the flames of wicked foes to
the bosom of flaming seraphim, who adore and burn in
the presence of the eternal throne.

But this was not enough: with savage fury his execu-
tioners beat down the stake, and demolished with clubs
and pokers all that remained of his half consumed body.
His heart, untouched by the fire, they roast on a spit,
and his cloak and other garments are also committed to
the flames, that not a memento might remain to his
friends. Yea, more, they not only remove the ashes, but
they scoop out the earth where he was burnt, to the depth
of four feet, and throw the whole into the Rhine. But
they could not extinguish the light of the Reformation.

From this new starting point the wheels of Providence
gathered strength, and rolled on the more rapidly as they
approached the goal. From the flames that consumed
these martyrs to the truth, there rose a light which shone
throughout all Germany. A spirit of inquiry was roused
in schools and universities, in the minds of the common
people and among the nobility, which could not be
repressed. Though often smothered in blood, it gathered
strength—the surface heaved, the internal fires burned
till the irruption came.

But I shall do palpable injustice not to notice some
whole communities which, during Zion's long and dreary
night, kept their fires burning and their lamps trimmed,
ready to meet the returning bridegroom. They were
found among the mountains of the Alps; in the valleys
of Peidmont and Languedock; in England, and over a

great part of Europe—known by the generic name of
Lollards, yet denominated Waldenses, Albigenses, Cathari,
Huguenots, from the valleys in which they resided, or
from some distinguished leader.   They had not bowed
the knee to Baal—had endured persecutions such as
make humanity blush—had trial of cruel mockings and
scourgings—of bonds and imprisonments—were stoned,
sawn asunder—tempted—slain—wandered about in sheep
skins and goat skins, afflicted and tormented.   They
wandered in deserts and mountains, in dens and caves
of the earth.   Since the scenes which transpired on
Calvary 1800 years ago, there has not been written so
black a page of man's history.   Yet their light shone, and
guided many an earth-worn pilgrim heavenward.   And
when the morning dawned—when the strong voice of
Wicklif, repeating but in louder notes the strains of
Claudius, Bradwardine, and Berenger, proclaimed the
approaching day—and the louder, and yet louder peals
of Huss and Jerome, Reuchlin and Hutten, broke in upon
the stillness of the night, these pious souls, (of whom the
world was not worthy,) these dwellers in the rocks and
caves of the earth were watching every prognostication
of the morning, and joyfully hailed the rising light.   And
no sooner were the banners of the Reformation unfurled,
than they, as tried and loyal subjects, came to the help of
the Lord.

And during the same period, and for centuries since,
the *Nestorians* have borne witness to the truth, and kept
alive the fire of true religion in the East, in circumstances
not very dissimilar from the Waldenses of the West.
When dark clouds settled down on the whole land, there
was light in *Goshen*—light amid the mountains of Kurdis-
tan.   And as now light returns upon the dark regions
of Asia, do we not find them as ready to welcome the
rising morning as were the dwellers among the Alps ?
The church has already been vastly indebted to the Nestorians in the work of propagating the gospel.   Never
has she had more valiant and successful Missionaries,
and that, too, under circumstances the most unpropitious.
Their missions form the connecting link between the
missions of primitive Christianity and modern missions

In the dark ages, (from the sixth to the fifteenth century,) we find their indefatigable missionaries among the rude, migratory tribes of Tartary, among the priest-ridden millions of India, and the supercilious natives of China. We find them, too, among the barbarous nations about the Caspian sea. In the tenth century, a Mogul Prince and 200,000 of his subjects, were converted to Christianity. Their Prince was the celebrated PRESTER JOHN. In 877, they had erected churches in all eastern Asia.

But without pursuing this line of providential development further, what presage have we here that Zion's King was about to introduce a new dispensation of his grace! He had fitted a thousand minds for the accomplishment of his purposes. Kings, emperors, councils, the literati, philosophers, poets, the church herself, all in their turn attempted a reform, and failed. Yet each did a work, and hastened a result. It was written in the records of Heaven that this should not be done by "might nor by power." The noble, the wise and mighty, should be set at nought—Goliath be overcome by the shepherd and his sling. The BIBLE should be the weapon by which to overcome the principalities and powers of sin, to demolish the strong-holds of the adversary, and to dislodge from their high places the unclean birds of the sanctuary : the Bible be the regenerator of the living temple, which should rebuild the sacred altar, and restore its fine gold. Hence the towering genius of Reuchlin, (the patron and teacher of the great Melancthon,) and the masterly mind of Erasmus, were now, by the hand of Providence, brought on the stage, the one to give Europe a translation of the Old Testament, and the other of the New ; and both to employ their profound learning in defence of the truth.

The sagacious eye of the world's wisdom could not but have seen that mighty events were struggling in the womb of Providence. The Reformation was a necessary *consequence* of what preceded. Internal fires were burning, the earth heaving, and soon they must find vent. Had not the irruption been in Germany, it must soon have been elsewhere. Had not Luther led, it must ere long have been conducted by another.

7*

Thus did the mighty hand of God order every circumstance—remove obstacles, provide instrumentalities for
the work, displaying in all the different series of events
which preceded the Reformation, and which, under God,
were the causes of it, the stately steppings of Providence
towards some magnificent result. Let us, therefore,
briefly survey,

2. *The great transaction itself*. The Reformation was
a great event—an event of great men, of great things and
great results; and the more closely it is scrutinized, the
more it will appear to be the work of God. It is not my
design to speak of the Reformation as a matter of *History*,
but as a child of Providence. Were we to trace it in its
progress, as we have in its preliminary steps, we should
everywhere discern the finger of God. I shall rather
speak of certain *characteristic acts* of the great drama,
than of the drama itself. The whole is too large a field.

From whatever point you view the Reformation, you
find it the child of Providence. Look at the *men* who
were called to be its conductors; or to the formidable
opposition it had to encounter; or to its *results*, and you
everywhere trace the footsteps of God.

When God is about to do a great work he first *prepares his instruments*. He selects and qualifies the men
by whom he will accomplish his purposes. So he did, as
we have seen, when he was about to enlarge the boundaries of his church by adding to its domains the American
continent. The bold spirit of adventure which characterized the latter part of the fifteenth century, was an electric shock to all Europe—as if an earthquake had shaken
the world, and raised from the midst of the ocean a great
continent. Hence such men as Columbus, the Cabots,
Gaspar Cortereal and Verrazzani. So, when He would
cut the cord that bound this infant nation to her mother,
and wean her from her mother's milk, and remove her
from the tuition of aristocrats and church dignitaries,
God raised up for the purpose such men as Franklin,
Hancock, Lee, Adams and Jefferson, and nerved the
arm of our immortal Washington. And so it has been
in all the great outbreakings that have convulsed the

world to make way for the church. He prepared his instruments.

It has been observed that great men appear in *constellations*. The truth is, they appear when, in providence, great occasions call for them. Great men are not only made *by* the times, but are endowed and moulded by the hand of God *for* the times. But nowhere do we find so marked a providence in the preparation of instruments as in the case of the Reformation. The leaders were all mighty men. Each was a host. Yet of all these mighties, Martin Luther was the mightiest.

But whence these giants, who, if they raise their voice, the earth trembleth—who shake the seven hills of Rome, and on their ruins rear a superstructure which reached to the heavens? Were they the scions of royalty—the sons of wisdom or of might? No. Martin Luther was taken from the cottage of a poor miner. Melancthon, the profound theologian and elegant scholar of the Reformation, was found in an armorer's workshop. Zuinglius was sought out by Him who knoweth the path which "the vulture's eye hath not seen," in a shepherd's hut among the Alps.

The history of Martin Luther is substantially the history of the Reformation. Would we come at once at the real genius of that great revolution, we must follow up the history of its controlling genius, from the time that little Martin was gathering sticks with his poor mother at the mines in Mansfeld, till he occupied the chair of Theology at Wittemburg, and was the most powerful and popular preacher of the day; or till he faced, single-handed and alone, the ravening beast of Rome at the Diet of Worms. Such as God made the instrument, such was the work.

Though pinchingly poor, John Luther, the woodcutter and the miner, resolved to educate young Martin. Thence forward mark his course. First, he was submitted to strict discipline and religious instruction under the roof of his parents. How much he was indebted to this, and how much the world, is not difficult to conceive. At an early age he is sent to school in the neighborhood of the mines. A new light had already broken in upon

the world, and the honest miner of Mansfeld determined
that his son should share in its benefits. At the age of
fourteen, we find him at the school of the Franciscans at
Magdeburg, yet so poor that he was obliged to occupy
his play-hours in begging his bread by singing. Here
he first heard Andrew Proles with great zeal, preaching
the necessity of reforming religion and the church.
Next he is at Eisenach, still poor, yet persevering, and
notwithstanding these, to common minds, insuperable
difficulties, our young reformer made rapid strides in his
studies, outstripping all his fellows.

We come now to the *second* link of the providential
chain : While begging his bread as a singing boy at Eisenach, he was often overwhelmed with grief, and ready to
despond. "One day in particular, after having been
repulsed from three houses, he was about to return fasting
to his lodging, when, having reached the Place St. George,
he stood before the house of an honest burgher, motion-
less, and lost in painful reflections. Must he for the want
of bread give up his studies, and return to the mines of
Mansfeld ?" Suddenly a door opens, a woman appears
on the threshhold—it is the wife of Conrad Cotta, called
"the pious Shunamite" of Eisenach. Touched with the
pitiless condition of the boy, she henceforth becomes his
patroness, his guardian angel, and from this time the
darkness from his horizon began to clear away. Soon we
find him a distinguished scholar in the University of
Erfurth, his genius universally admired, his progress in
knowledge wonderful. It now began to be predicted of
him that he would one day shake the world. The honors of the University thicken upon him. He applies
himself to the study of the law, where he aspires to the
highest honors of civic life. But God willed not so. He
is one day in the Library of the University, where he is
wont to spend his leisure moments. As he opens volume
after volume, a strange book at length attracts his attention. Though he had been two years in the University
and was now twenty years old, he had seen nothing like
it before. It is the *Bible*. He reads and reads again, and
would give a world for a Bible. Here is the *third* link.

Here lay hid the spark that should electrify the world—the golden egg of the Reformation.

But where next do we find our distinguished scholar—our doctor of philosophy—our humble reader of the Bible? Strange contrast! He is an Augustine monk, cloistered in gloomy walls; the companion of idle monks; doorkeeper, sweeper, common servant and beggar for the cloister. But what brought him here? He had read the Bible—was bowed to the ground as a sinner—and while in this state of mind he was literally smitten to the earth by a thunderbolt. This was the *fourth* link of the providential chain.

From this hour he resolved to be God's. But how could he serve God but in a cloister? The world was no place for him. He *must* be holy; he will therefore *work* out his salvation in the menial services and solitude of monastic life. But the hand of God was in this. It was the school of Providence to discipline him for his future work. Here, too, he must learn the great lesson (justification by faith) which should revolutionize the church and the world; here receive the sword that should demolish the mighty fabric of Romish superstition, and separate from the chaotic mass of a corrupt religion, the church reformed. And where, in accordance with the genius of the age, could this be learned but in a convent? From his youth up, Luther had believed in the power of monastic life *to change the heart*. He must, as he bitterly did, learn its entire inefficacy.

When he had learned this, when he was slain by the law, and lay, as supposed, literally dead upon the floor, a good "Annanias" appeared to raise him up and to conduct him to the peace-speaking blood of Jesus, and, in Christ's stead, to tell him *what he must do*. This messenger is Staupitz, the vicar-general, who from this time becomes Luther's teacher in holiness, and his guide and patron in his glorious career of reform. This is the next link in the chain. Staupitz conducted him to Christ; gave him a Bible; introduced him to a professor's chair in the University of Wittemburg, and to the friendship of the Elector of Saxony, and brought out the reluctant Monk as a public preacher; and, in a word, was the hand of Providence to conduct Luther forward to the great result of the Reformation.

Nor was it enough that Luther should serve a three years' apprenticeship in a convent. He must *go to Rome* —must trace up the corrupt stream to its fountain—must see what Romanism is at the seat of the Beast. His embassy to Rome was the next great providential movement which marked the early life of Luther. Here he beheld with his own eyes, the abominations of desolation standing in the place where they ought not. Though he had more than suspected the corruption of the *church*, he still retained a profound veneration for Rome. He thought of Rome as the seat of all holiness; the deep and broad well from which were drawn all the waters of salvation. Nothing but personal observation could cure him of this error. He found Rome the seat of abominations, the fountain of moral corruption. The profligacy, levity, idleness, and luxury of the priests, shocked him. He turned away from Rome in utter disgust and indignation. Nor was this all he learnt at Rome. It was here God instructed him more thoroughly in the perfect way. While performing some of the severe penances of the church, (as, for example, creeping on his knees up " Pilate's staircase,") he had a *practical* lesson of the inefficacy of *works ;* and the doctrine of *justification by faith,* seemed revealed to him as in a voice of thunder. And now was he prepared, on his return, to echo this voice from heaven till the very foundations of Rome should tremble.

Soon after this, Luther was made Theological Professor, or Doctor of the Scriptures. There was, in reference to the *oath* he was now required to take, another of those marked interpositions of Providence, to push him on in his work as a reformer. He was required to " *swear to defend the truth of the gospel with all his might.*" This though it had often been taken as a mere matter of *form,* was now received in good earnest. Luther now felt nimself commissioned by the University, by his Prince, and in the name of the Emperor, and by Rome herself, to be the fearless herald of the truth. He *must* now, in

House where Luther was Born.   Page 78

obedience to the highest authority on earth and of Heaven, be a *Reformer.**

Thus did the Hand of God resuscitate *a long and shamefully abused oath*, and snatch it from the hands of profanation, and arm it with a power that none could gainsay or resist.

Already has enough been said to develop the genius of the Reformation. I am not to give a history of it. It was the child of Providence—begotten, nourished, matured by the plastic hand of Heaven. Were we to follow Luther from his first putting forth his "Theses" for public discussion, till he laid down his armor at the dread summons of death, the head and leader of a great reformed church, we should see him in the act of accomplishing only what we have seen the hand of God preparing him for. He was raised up, fitted and protected for this self same work.† .

Or were we to trace the history of his great coadjutors in the work, such as Calvin, Melancthon, Reuchlin, Hutten, Erasmas, Spalatin, Staupitz, Martin Pollich, Zuingle, or the other giants of those days, we should discover, in proportion as God deigned to use them, respectively, in the execution of his great plan, the hand of God, fitting each to his respective place, assigning each his work, and nerving the muscles of his soul for the great combat.

Nor will it weaken our conviction that the Reformation was a stupendous act of Providence for the advancement of the true church and the spread of the true religion, if we notice the *opposition* it had to encounter, or on its final *results*.

Both as to character and amount, this opposition was such as no earthly power could resist. The advantage was all against the Reformers. The errors, vices, super-

---

* D'Aubigne's History of the Reformation.

† Not a few instances in his personal history illustrate the Divine care of him. Determined to cut him off by stratagem, at a period when his popularity precluded the use of force, the Cardinal Legate and Pope's Nuncio, invited the great Reformer and his chief Saxon friends to a dinner ; when, according to previous arrangement, the Pope's representative should propose the exchange of the usual glass of wine, and that a deadly poison should be infused into the portion designed for Luther. The pompous Cardinal requested "the honor of drinking the learned and illustrious Doctor's health." The Cardinal's attendant presented the two glasses. But Luther's glass, as he raised it to his mouth, fell into his plate, and discovered the murderous potion. Thus the Hand of an ever watchful Providence delivered his chosen one from the snare of the fowler.

stitions, impositions or crimes which they attacked, were nurtured in the very bosom of the church, and could challenge the authority of the highest powers in church or state ; while the Reformers were without power, either civil or ecclesiastical, the sons of obscurity, sought out, fitted, and distinguished in the work by a special Providence. Like the first disciples, they stood against the world.

3. And the *results* are too well known to need to be made a subject of extended remark. It was a revolution that has cast a new aspect over the whole world. It is under the shadow of the wings of the reformed church, that civilization has spread and prospered ; that the printing-press has flourished and shed forth its leaves for the healing of the nations—that learning has prospered ; the arts been cultivated and the sciences made to subserve the purposes of common life ; that enterprise has put forth its multifarious energies in the promotion of commerce, discovery, manufactures, and in the various forms of philanthropy and benevolence ; that the true science of government is better understood, and considerable advancement made in the principles of freedom ; a broad and immovable basis laid for free institutions ; and religion, pure and undefiled, has ventured to appear not only outside the cloister, or the sequestered valley, but on the wide arena of the world, in the face of Popes and inquisitors, in the face of nobles and kings, and boldly to assert its primeval claim to the earth. It was one of those vast movements of Providence, which, like angels' visits, are few and far between. It was one of those great deliverances, when Heaven deigns to interpose and give enlargement to Israel.

We cannot review this vast transaction without increased admiration of an ever-working, ever-watchful Providence, working all things after the counsel of his own will, with none to stay his hand, or say unto Him, what doest thou.

In concluding what I have to say on the Reformation, I may be indulged in one general remark : *How grand and magnificent, then, must that work be which can so intensely engage the mind of the eternal God !* Such is the

House where Luther Died.   Page 78.

work of Redemption. The unwearied hand of Providence has always been engaged, preparing for some *future* development of the glory of the body of Christ, which is the church. From Adam to Christ, the lines of Providence were all converging to the *Incarnation*. Every change and revolution was so shaped as to be preparatory to the advent of the Messiah. That first grand mark of consummation being reached, the next principal point of concentration is the *Millenium*, or the complete development of grace, and its victory over sin. Ever since Christ offered up the great sacrifice for sin, the whole energy of Providence has been engaged to mature the great plan and gather in its fruits.

Ride forth, then, victorious King, from conquering to conquer, till the kingdoms of this world become the kingdom of our Lord and of his Christ.

CHAPTER V.

Japheth in the tents of Shem: or, the Hand of God, as seen in the opening a way to India by the way of the Cape of Good Hope. The posterity of Japheth. The Portuguese empire in the East—its extent and extinction. Designs of Providence in opening India to Europe—not silks and satins, but to illustrate the evil of Idolatry, and the inefficacy of false religions and philosophy to reform men. The power of true religion.

" *God shall enlarge Japheth, and he shall dwell in the tents of Shem.*"—Gen. ix. 27.

A REMARKABLE prophecy, and remarkably fulfilled God has enlarged Japheth by giving his descendants, for a dwelling place, all Europe, Asia Minor, America, many of the islands of the sea, and the northern portions of Asia. Japheth has peopled half the globe. Besides his original possessions, and much gained by colonizing, he has greatly extended his dominions by *conquest.* The Greeks, the Romans, the English, have, successively, "dwelt in the tents of Shem."   At the present time, the offspring of Japheth, the English chiefly, wield the sceptre over scarcely less than two hundred millions of the seed of Shem.   This is worthy of remark, especially in connection with the fact, that Christianity has hitherto been confined, almost exclusively, to the posterity of Japheth. A line, encircling on the map of the world the nations descended from Japheth, incloses nearly all the Christianity at present in the world.   *Before* Christ, God committed the riches of his grace to the posterity of Shem; since, he has confined the same sacred trust to the children of Japheth.

The mind of the reader has already been directed to *one* of the enlargements of Japheth—the possession of the American continent.   I am now prepared to speak of another, an enlargement *eastward*, the discovery of the great East, by the Cape of Good Hope—another theatre on which should be acted the great drama of human salvation.

When, in the fifteenth century, God was about to purify and enlarge his church, when the King was preparing for a glorious onward march of the truth by providing resources, men, means, and all sorts of facilities, an enlargement of *territory* was by no means the least providential desideratum.   The church would soon need *room*; new provinces, new continents, whither to transplant the "vine" of Calvary.   But God never lacks expedients.   A spirit of bold adventure moves again over the face of the deep, and not only a *new continent* arises beyond the dark waves of the great Western sea, but, nearly at the same time, an *old continent*, scarcely more known, emerges from the thick darkness of paganism in the far East.

We have seen the church reformed and renovated, armed and strengthened for some grand onset upon the nations.   And we have seen the field already opened *westward*, wide enough, and promising enough to engage all her renerved energies.   But should the star of Bethlehem, now just emerging from the darkness of the past centuries, shine only westward?   Should the vast regions, peopled by so many myriads of immortals, and once cheered by the "star of the East," forever lie under the darkness of Paganism? The good pleasure of Heaven is here, as always, indicated by the stately steppings of Providence

While the Reformation is yet developing in Europe, and its energies are being matured for an onward movement, just the time when mind is beginning to assume its ndependence, and religion its vitality, all the wealth, and wickedness, and woe, of the East, with its teeming millions of deathless souls, are being laid open to the ameliorating process of reformed Christianity. It shall be our business to trace the *manner* in which this has been done; and to mark the hand of God as he has compassed such a result. It is not ours, however, to stop here to deplore, as we might, *man's delinquency*, as a reason why these vast and populous regions have not, since having been made accessible, been *sooner* Christianized and blessed, but rather to admire *God's efficiency* in introducing them to the West, and giving them into the hands of Christian nations at this particular time.

The adventurous spirit of the fifteenth century made known and accessible to the Christian world all the rich and populous countries of southern and eastern Asia, from the river Indus to the island of Japan. And it is not a little remarkable that the efforts which the Portuguese and Spaniards made to drive the Moors from their peninsula, were the beginning of these discoveries. As, from time to time, they pursued those native foes of the cross, back to Africa, and coasted about its shores, taking revenge for the long series of outrages they had suffered from the Moors, they so improved their maritime skill, and roused the enterprise of both monarch and people, that soon they are found pushing their adventurous barks southward, in attempts to find a south point to Africa. And, after many fruitless struggles, Dias finally doubled the Cape of Good Hope, in 1486, but made no important discoveries. This was reserved for Vasco de Gama, twelve years later. He visited India, formed commercial relations, and laid the foundation for an empire

Thus, while the territory of Mohammedanism was narrowing in Europe, and the progress of the Moors in

arts, sciences, and civilization, was forever arrested, vast
dominions were added to Christendom, at least prospectively, in the East, as had been in the West.   And though
for the present, uncultivated and unproductive, they are
capable, under proper culture, of yielding an abundant
harvest.

The Portuguese were soon in possession of a magnificent
empire.   Its extent, opulence, and the splendor with
which it was conducted, has scarcely a rival in the history of nations.   It stretched over one hundred degrees
of longitude, from the Red sea to Japan, embracing the
south of Persia, India, Birmah, China, and the numerous
islands of the Indian archipelago.   Not less than half the
entire population of the globe were thus thrown into the
arms of a nominally Christian nation.

But the sceptre of this vast empire soon passes away,
first to the Dutch, and then to the English.   The French
became competitors, playing no inconsiderable part in the
game for Oriental kingdoms.   But they were of Rome,
and Rome should not rule there.   Protestant England
has, at length, become almost the sole owner of the once
magnificent empire of the Portuguese.   From the Red
sea to Japan she has no rival.

Much has been written on the commercial and territorial importance of India.   The discoveries of De Gama
were very justly regarded as commencing a new era in
the world ; and history will never overlook the undoubted
benefits of the new relations which were, from this time,
formed between the West and the East.   Yet the sagacity of the world has lost sight of the chief design of
Providence in these discoveries.   Was it simply that Europe might be "replenished from the East," and "please
herself in the children of strangers," that the immense
territories of India were laid at her feet ?   Was it for
silks and satins, for luxuries and gewgaws—for no higher
objects than wealth and territorial aggrandizement, or
more extensive commercial relations, that the King of
nations made Europe master of Asia ?

These are the things the world has so much admired
in the nearer connection of Europe and Asia.   History,
eloquence, poetry, have wondered at these mere *incidents*

in the great scheme of Providence, overlooking the chief design, which we believe to be, first, and for a long series of years, *to furnish a theatre on which to make certain im portant developments*, and to teach the church and the world *certain important lessons;* and, secondly, to extend the triumphs of the Cross over all those countries.

India affords to such as intelligently and piously watch the hand of God in his magnificent movements in the work of redemption, a subject for intense and interesting study. While developments in the progress of the church of a different character were transpiring in America— God transferring his church thither, and planting her in a more congenial soil, and giving her room to take root and grow, India was, and has continued to be, the theatre of developments not less interesting. She has stood for centuries the teacher of nations. On that theatre, God has all this time been teaching.

1. *The evil of Idolatry.* In the great mental and religious revolution of the sixteenth century, God was preparing the sacramental host for a more formidable onset against the foes of Immanuel. On the one hand, he had allowed the enemy to intrench himself in the strongholds of the earth. The wealth, learning, philosophy, religion of the earliest civilized, and the most fertile and populous portions of the globe; their social habits, their every-day maxims, proverbs, and songs; their principles of action and habits of thinking were surrendered to the foes of the cross. Centuries had riveted the chains; and now sin stood as the strong man armed, frowning defiance on all who should question his right to the dominion of the earth. Idolatry was his strong-hold. On the other hand, the great King had come down to earth, and cleansed his temple, and enlarged the boundaries of the true Israel. The number of the faithful in Europe were vastly increased, and armed (by means of the Bible, education, the press, and the mariner's compass,) with a power before unknown. Colonies had been planted in this new Canaan, and here was maturing a rear guard, which may yet become the main army, and spread its wings eastward and westward, and become mighty to the pulling down of strong-holds. All seemed preparing

8*

for the conflict—the church to take possession of the earth.

But mark here the way of the Lord. Centuries are permitted to elapse before these wide wastes are inclosed in the garden of our God. Not only must the church be better prepared to take possession—her numbers and ability be so increased that she may supply her new allie. with the needed spiritual resources, and her active benevolence and spirituality be such that her image may, with honor to herself and to her God, be stamped on the heathen world; but, on the other hand, there must needs be an exhibition of the *malady* to be healed. It must be seen what a potent foe to truth Idolatry is—a great system of infidelity, ingeniously devised in the council-chamber of hell, and fatally suited to the desires of the human heart. The church, and the world too, must see what Idolatry is, in its power to enslave and crush immortal mind; in its devices to deceive; in its malignant influences to dry up the social and benevolent affections; in its withering blight on every starting germ of civilization and learning, and in the death-blow it strikes to every thing noble and virtuous.

Hence the providential subjection of those vast regions of Idolatry to Christian nations. By this means, the church has had a fair and protracted opportunity to contemplate Idolatry in all its odious features, and, at the same time, fairly to test her own professed principles and zeal for its abolition. Providentially, Christian men, of every condition in life, and for a long series of years, have resided among those pagan nations, and enjoyed every facility to estimate the curse of Paganism, both in its bearing on this life, and the life to come. But the mere *exposure of the evil* is not all.

2. India affords a striking example of *the inefficacy of philosophy to reform man* in this life, or to save him in the next. Brahmanism and Bhoodism are refined and skillfully formed systems of Idolatry—the combined wisdom of ages. Philosophy, metaphysics, worldly wisdom, were taxed to the utmost in their production. They present a fair specimen of what human reason can do. If these systems cannot ameliorate the condition of man

nere, and hold out hopes of a glorious immortality, no religion of human origin can.

But as the great experiment has been in progress some
thousand years, and during the last three hundred and
fifty under the eye of Christendom, what has been the
result? As a remedy for the moral maladies of man has
it been efficacious? Has the nation been reformed, or
individuals? Has it shed a ray of light on the dark
path-way to the tomb, or raised a single, cheering hope
beyond the veil of the flesh? Where has it wiped the
tear from sorrow's eye, or spoken peace to the troubled
spirit, or supplied the wants of the needy, or opened the
prison-doors to them that are bound? Where has it
spread its fostering wings over the rising genius of civilization, nurtured the institutions of learning, or been the
patron of virtue and morality? Three and a half centuries (since the eyes of Europe have been on India,)
have surely been a sufficient time—to say nothing of
the thirty or forty centuries which preceded—to test
the merits of a religion. And what has been the result?
It is stereotyped in the vices and superstitions, in the
crimes and ignorance, in the debasement and corruption
of those nations. In spite of the most scrupulous observ-
ance of rites, and the most costly austerities, they have
waxed worse and worse. In their religion, there is no
principle of veneration. The more religion they have,
the more corrupt they are.

Nor has Mohammedanism been scarcely more successful. Incorporating more of *truth*, its votaries are not
sunk so low as pagans, yet it has altogether failed of an-
swering the end for which man needs a religion.

India has, therefore, been made a theatre from which
the nations might learn the inefficacy of philosophy and
man's wisdom to produce a moral reformation. And
more than this: Providence has been there teaching,

3. *The inefficacy of a corrupt Christianity to renovate
and bless a nation.* As far back as history reaches, the
thick darkness of the East has been made visible by the
faint glimmerings of the light of truth. During all her
long and melancholy alienation from the true God, India
has, perhaps, never been without her witnesses for the

truth.   To say nothing of many relics of patriarchal religion, a large number of Jews, after the destruction of the first temple, and the conquest and captivity of the nation by Nebuchadnezzar, (588, B. C.,) yielding to the stern necessity of the conqueror's power, forsook their native land—the lovely hills and smiling valleys of Palestine and Mount Zion, whose very dust they loved, and their temple, the beauty of the whole earth, and sought an asylum amidst the idolatrous nations of India.   They carried with them the writings of the Old Testament, were accompanied with more or less of their religious teachers, established their synagogue worship, and became, in all things, Jewish communities, amidst a great pagan nation.   These are known by the name of *Black Jews*, in distinction from the Jerusalem or *White Jews*.

They are scattered throughout India, China, and Tartary.   To Dr. Buchanan, who visited them in 1806—8, and to whom we are indebted principally for the few interesting items we have of their history, they gave a list of *sixty-five* places, where societies of Black Jews then resided, and among which a constant communication is kept up.   Having been exposed to an Indian sun nearly twenty-four centuries, in complexion they are scarcely to be distinguished from the Hindoos.   These voluntary exiles have, during this long period, been remarkably preserved as a monument of the ancient economy.

The Jerusalem or White Jews, for very similar reasons, bade a reluctant farewell to their native Judea, after the destruction of the *second* temple, and the overthrow of the Jewish nation by the Romans under Titus.   Says a narrative preserved among them, "A numerous body of men, women, priests and Levites, departed from Jerusalem and came to this land.   There were among them men of repute for learning and wisdom; and God gave the people favor in the sight of the king, who, at that time, reigned here; and he granted them a place to dwell in, called Cranganore."   Others followed them from Judea, Spain, and other places.   Here they prospered a thousand years.   Since that period, they have been made to participate in the bitter cup of their dispersed brethren.   Dissensions within, and wars without, have diminished and scattered them; yet they are to be found, at this day, at Cochin, where they worship the God of their fathers, in their synagogues, every sabbath day. They have the Old Testament and many Hebrew manuscripts.

Thus has Providence, for nearly two thousand and four hundred years, preserved a succession of witnesses for the truth in the land of idols—not at the first, lights of great brilliancy, and growing more and more dim as the latter-day glory approached, and the great Light arose, but sufficient to keep alive, in the heart of a great nation of pagans, some idea of the true God.

Nor is this all: another succession of witnesses, of a still higher order, has existed there ever since the age of the apostles, in the *Syrian Christians.* Tradition reports that St. Thomas first introduced the gospel into those distant regions, and there established the Christian church. They are called, to this day, St. Thomas Christians. Like the Jewish church, just alluded to, their light shone brightest at the first, but grew dimmer as the light of the Reformation shed its healing rays on the East. So numerous and flourishing were they in the fourth century, that they were represented, in the council of Nice, (325,) by their patriarch, or archbishop.

On the arrival of Vasco de Gama, (1503,) he found more than *one hundred* flourishing Christian churches on the Malabar coast, and though sad havoc had been made by the emissaries of Rome, there were, at the time of Dr. Buchanan's visit, fifty-five churches, and about fifty thousand souls, who had not acknowledged the supremacy of the Pope. The churches, in the interior especially, would not yield to Rome, but continued to receive their bishops from Antioch, as they had done from the first. They are a branch of the *Nestorian Church*, which is, at present, exciting a laudable interest, and which, in the early ages of Christianity, was favorably known in the history of the church for the establishment of missions in India, China, and Tartary. They have the Sacred Scriptures, and other manuscripts, in the Syriac language, and use, in divine service on Lord's day, the Liturgy formerly used by the church at Antioch; and it is their honest pride that they date their origin back to that period, and to that land, where Christianity first rose, and to that particular spot where the disciples were first called Christians.

Their former glory has departed, and they are but the shadow of what they were; yet, their light still flickers amidst the wide extended darkness of that land of death. For centuries has this light shone on the surrounding darkness, which has but ill comprehended it. These Christian communities bore a decided testimony in favor of the religion of Jesus, and, through successive generations, exerted no inconsiderable influence in refining, liberalizing, and improving the moral condition of vast multitudes of pagans. In the ordering of an eventful Providence, Christianity has had witnesses there from its origin; and systems of Idolatry have been modified to meet the advancing state of the human mind, under the benign auspices of the gospel.*

From time to time, light has been breaking in from other quarters. The nations of Western Asia, have, from time immemorial, sustained commercial relations with India. An extensive trade was carried on through the Red Sea, and the Persian Gulph, and thence over land to the great emporiums of the West. Hence Christian travelers, merchants, civil functionaries, and various classes of adventurers, traversed these vast regions of the shadow of death. Many of these, at different periods, settled in the country; others were only sojourners. All added something to the general stock of a knowledge of Christianity—a further monument to the truth of God, in these wide fields of Idolatry. The Armenians, the Greeks, the Venetians and Genoese, each contributed a share to scatter light and truth in the East.

These were some of the agencies in operation before the discoveries of De Gama. And, what is worthy of special remark, they were effective just in proportion as they contained the *salt* of the pure religion. Their *illu-*

---

* The ideas which the Hindoos have of an Incarnation, as discovered, particularly in the history of their god, Krishna, and, perhaps, all they know of the Trinity, has been smuggled into Hindooism from Christianity.

mination was in proportion to the truth they embodied and illustrated.

But it is time to turn to what may be termed the *great effort* to convert India to the Christian faith. We have said the Portuguese established a magnificent empire in the East, embracing all the southern portions of Asia. A leading feature in their government every where, was to establish their religion, to erect churches, support priests, and convert the natives, whether by persuasion or force. Thus were the banners of the Romish religion fully, and for a long time, unfurled over more than three hundred millions of pagans. Every influence, (but light and love,) not excepting the horrors of the Inquisition, was used to swell the number of converts. Romanism has abounded in those countries. Tens of thousands of churches and priests, and millions of communicants, have represented,—rather *mis*-represented Christianity there, for three hundred years.

And what has been the result? Has not the leaven had time to work, and show what has been the efficacy of all that gorgeous array of the Romish faith and ritual, in ameliorating the temporal condition, and improving the moral state of myriads of converts to Rome? We can bear personal testimony that, in India, there has probably been nothing gained by the change. It has been little more nor less than passing from one set of rites, usages and superstitions, to another, as worthless and debasing, and from the worship of one set of images to that of another. In general, Romanism imposes less restraint on the immoral, than Hindooism.

It would, perhaps, be too much to say that India has received no good at the hands of Rome; yet we may safely say, the experiment, so long and so extensively tried, when viewed in the light of *renovating* India, has been a complete failure. Nor has its influence been but neutral. The little good it may have effected, is no compensation for the gross misrepresentation it has made of the Christian religion, and the consequent prejudice with which it has armed the Pagan mind against Christianity in any form.

Never, perhaps, has the Romish church had a more

faithful or successful missionary in the East, than the Abbe Dubois. Yet, after a residence of *thirty years*, and having made *ten thousand* converts, he leaves in despair of ever seeing any favorable *moral* change in the Hindoos, declaring that out of this immense multitude, he could recall but a single instance where he believed there was any moral renovation ; thus palpably conceding the complete impotency of Romanism, to raise, purify and bless a debased people.

Providence, on a large scale, has here furnished a practical illustration, that a spurious Christianity has not the power to renovate and raise to spiritual health and life a Pagan nation.

Another lesson designed to be taught on the broad arena of Paganism beyond the Cape, is, that nothing short of *spiritual Christianity*, can renovate the great East. What Romanism has so signally failed to do, the Bible, in the hands of the living preacher, is nobly doing. Habits and usages, inveterate and formidable, have been changed; prejudices removed, and character, individual, and in whole communities, completely transformed. Pure Christianity has shown itself omnipotent there. Already we number hundreds of thousands of Protestant Christians, in India alone, many of whom give pleasing evidence of a moral change. And nothing but increased means and men, and the smiles of Heaven, are needed to increase these successes to any extent.

We need no further guarantee that the gospel of Christ is potent enough to bring back to God, any and all those mighty nations of the East.

Such are the points which have already been illustrated through the discovery of India. But this is no more than the beginning. India, and all the countries of the East, are to be,—are already being, converted to God. What a field ! What teeming millions of immortal souls ! De Gama introduced to Europe half the population of the globe. Would we, therefore, scan the chief design of Providence, in the event of these Eastern discoveries, we must anticipate the day when all their nations, tongues and people, shall be gathered into the fold of the great Shepherd. Then shall the God of Japheth indeed dwell

in the tents of Shem, and they shall be one fold, and
the great purposes of Providence be consummated in
adding to the domains of the true church, all those populous territories which have so long a time lain in bondage to the prince of this world.

If we may infer the future designs of Providence,
from the past and the present, we shall entertain the most
stupendous expectations of what is yet to transpire on
that vast theatre.   At one time we saw the empire of all
the East, as by magic, laid prostrate at the foot of Rome.
Then, in a little time, a sudden and unexpected revolution transfers the vast possessions of the Portuguese into
Protestant hands.   From the time the Portuguese first
gained a foothold in India, till their magnificent empire
had passed away, and the English had supplanted them
and become master of their dominions, was scarcely
more than a single century.   The *transfer* has supplied a
marvelous chapter in the book of Providence.   The
ultimate design, we doubtless have not seen ; yet we
have seen enough to raise our admiration.   It is *through
Protestant England* that those great and populous nations
are opened for the entrance of the gospel.   British rule,
and admission and protection to the missionary, are
co-extensive.   A word and a blow, from the little Isle in
the West, and Despotism and Idolatry loose the chains
with which they had for so many centuries bound their
stupid victims, and more than half the population of the
globe are accessible to the embassador of the cross.   The
field is white for the harvest.

Obstacles have been removed.   Paganism is in its
dotage.   Unsupported by any state alliance, or any prop,
save that of abstract depravity, it can offer no formidable opposition to the introduction of Christianity.   The
haughty followers of the Arabian prophet, too, have been
humbled, and the power of their arm broken.   The
Romish Inquisition there has been silenced, and many a
strong-hold of the Papacy demolished.   The Bible has
been translated into every principal language ; the press
is established in almost every important position in the
great field, so many radiating points of light and truth ;
education is doing its work, preparing the minds of hun-

9

dreds of thousands to receive the healing influence of
the words of truth. An acquaintance has been formed
with the religions, the philosophy, the languages of these
Pagan nations ; with their manners, customs, history,
modes of thinking and reasoning. Dictionaries and
grammars have been prepared, and a great variety of
books. Schools have been established,—churches erected,
and, indeed, an extensive apparatus is ready for the
evangelical workman. Knowledge has been increased,
the blessings of civilization, and the results of modern
inventions and discoveries introduced, and, finally, the
benign influences of Christianity have already, to a no
inconsiderable extent, unfurled their banners over those
lands of darkness and spiritual death. Among the
130,000,000, of India, there is scarcely a village which is
not accessible to some, if not to all, the labors of the
missionary.

Or were we to contemplate the *success* which has
already attended the very partial endeavors which have
been made to convert India, we should still more admire
the Hand that doeth wonders, and look that, at no distant future, the great Gentile world shall pay their homage at the feet of their rightful Sovereign. Whole communities,—numerous, contiguous villages, as in the province of Krishnugar, South India and Ceylon, have cast
away their idols, and professed allegiance to Christ.

If we may take what *is*, as a presage of what shall be,
—if we may judge what the building shall be, by an
inspection of the foundation,—the superstructure from
the vast amount of materials we see in the course of
preparation, we must believe Providence has a stupendous plan yet to accomplish, in connection with the East.
The intelligent and pious reader of history will re-peruse
the record of God's dealings towards the Gentiles of
Asia,—especially will he ponder with new interest, that
single act of Providence, which, in the close of the fifteenth century, opened a high-way between Europe and
Asia, bringing the wants and woes of Asia to the very
doors of Anglo-Saxon Christianity, to prefer their own
claims for aid, and pouring the light and spiritual life of
Truth, as a fertilizing river, over the vast deserts of Asia.

The imperfect view which has here been taken of a subject which, of itself, cannot but interest the philosophical historian and the contemplative Christian, will, at least, leave on the mind of the reader the impression that God has some great design to accomplish, in respect to India : and it urges on every friend of humanity and of truth, the duty of following in the footsteps of Providence, and doing those things which, as a matter of means, shall carry out the magnificent plan of Him who worketh, and no man hindereth. The vast and protracted preparation indicates such a design. Three centuries and a half have elapsed in preparation. What shall the end be ?

Another obvious reflection is, that *God takes time* to carry on his work. Why has India so long been consigned to waste and spiritual desolation ? It has been a field for observation and experiment. Sin must have its *perfect work.* In its worst forms, it must have time and space to luxuriate,—to go to seed, and yield its noxious harvest. It must be permitted to show what it can do, and *all* it can do. It must show *itself.*

Finally, God here rebukes the impatience and distrust of his people. They murmur and faint, because wickedness and oppression abound, and God does not speedily avenge the cause of his elect, and bring wickedness to an end. God takes time. In the end, all shall be put in order.

And, with the same propriety, it might be asked—why has Central and South America, some of the richest and most beautiful portions of our globe, been consigned for so long a time, to waste and spiritual desolation been allowed to be trampled under foot, and devastated by the Papal Beast ? Rome has been trying *her* experiment there, and after a fair trial for centuries, we see *what Rome can do.* She has had the training of the aborigines of those countries all to herself, with every possible natural advantage ; and we do her no injustice, when we take their social, political, moral and religious condition, as a sample of the value of Romish missions, and of the transforming efficacy of Romish Christianity.

New developments are now being made on the Ameri

can continent, in respect to India and the great East
The present "California excitement," seems to be another
of the great pulsations of Providence, to open a passage
through the whole breadth of our continent, to form a
great commercial depot and thoroughfare on the Pacific,
and open a new line of communication with the whole
eastern world. It is an historical fact, often admired,
that what is called the "India trade," has never failed
to enrich and aggrandize every western nation which
has been able to secure it : and that every *route* through
which this commerce and intercourse has passed, has
been most signally benefited. Of the latter, the eye at
once fixes on Palmyra, Balbec, Alexandria, Venice ; all
owed their grandeur, wealth and importance, to the relations in which they stood to the India trade. We are
yet to see whether another "Tadmor of the Desert," is
not to spring up on the Pacific,—whether the stupendous
bay of San Francisco is not to be the great depot of
the Eastern trade,—whether a new route is not to be
opened to this trade, and its advantages now be transferred *another* step westward.

CHAPTER VI.

God in history. The Church safe. Expulsion of the Moors from Spain. Transfer of
India to Protestant hands. Philip II. and Holland. Spanish invincible Armada.
The bloody Mary of England. Dr. Cole and Elizabeth Edmonds. Cromwell and
Hampden to sail for America. Return of the Waldenses and Henry Arnaud. Gun-
powder plot. Cromwell's usurpation. Revolution of 1688. James II. and Louis
XIV. Peter the Great. Rare constellation of great men.

" *The Lord's portion is his people.   Jacob is the lot of his inheritance,*" &c.—Deut. xxxii. 9—14.

NOTHING can exceed the tender and unremitting care
of God for his people. They are termed "his portion,'
"his inheritance," "the apple of his eye."   "He found

him in a desert land and in a waste howling wilderness,
he led him about; he instructed him; he kept him as the
apple of his eye. As an eagle stirreth up her nest, fluttereth over her young, spreadeth abroad her wings,
taketh them, beareth them on her wings, so the Lord
alone did lead him, and there was no strange god with
him." And what can surpass the beauty and richness of
the idea that follows: "He made him ride on the high
places of the earth, that he might eat the increase of the
fields; and he made him to suck honey out of the rock,
and oil out of the flinty rock; butter of kine and milk of
sheep, with fat of lambs, and rams of the breed of Bashan,
and goats, with the fat of the kidneys of wheat; and
thou didst drink the pure blood of the grape;" expressions, though highly figurative, which indicate the *exu-
berance* of the Divine goodness, and afford convincing
proof of his never-failing care. God will honor them
that honor him. They that trust in him shall lack no
good thing.

That God has abundantly fulfilled such rich promises,
that he has uniformly acted towards his people as his
"portion," his "inheritance," the "apple of his eye," has
already been illustrated. We have seen the arm of the
Lord made bare to defend his inheritance in Jacob, and
his hands open to supply their wants. I shall now ask
you to follow me a little farther, and you shall see the
same mighty arm still engaged on Zion's behalf, and the
same exhaustless resources at her command. The Lord's
portion is his people.

I design, at present, to direct your minds to several
historical events which strikingly illustrate the agency of
Providence in the progress and establishment of the
Christian church. I can no more than select from a
great variety of Providential interpositions. Indeed, I
may remark at the outset, that the very *existence* of the
church supposes a ceaseless interposition of the Almighty
arm. It is a standing miracle, not that there should be
a nominal Christianity and a large and powerful Christian
church, for all this might be in perfect consistency with
worldly principles; the wonder is, that a *pure evangelical*
church should live in the world at all; that she has been

9*

allowed a permanent foothold amidst the perverse generations of men. The current of the world, the tide of human affairs, has always been opposed to her. Persecutions, wave after wave, have rolled over her; yet she has stood as an immovable rock amidst the angry floods. Civil power, philosophy, history, science, poetry, fashion, custom, wit, have all in their turn been made engines to assail the impregnable fortress of Christianity. Intrigue has spared no wicked device to undermine her foundations; cruelty and unrelenting hate have poured out the vials of their wrath in the horrors of the Inquisition, or let loose the bloodhounds of war to worry out and exterminate the saints of the Most High. Heresy, infidelity, superstitions, and fanaticism, misguided zeal, unhallowed invasions on her doctrines and ordinances, and all spurious forms of Christianity have, in their turn, done what they could to prostrate the fair fabric of religion, or so to undermine confidence in her, to arrest or neutralize her benevolent influences, as to make her appear to the world of little worth. The wisdom, policy, and spirit of the world—the maxims, principles, and acts of the worldly—have done any thing but foster the vine brought out of Egypt.

And what has been the result? The church has outrode every storm. She has passed unscathed by the lightnings of human violence. Like the oak that strikes its roots deeper, and clings to its rocky soil the more tenaciously, as the storm beats and the tempest rages, the church has been strengthened amidst the rigors of persecution, and nourished by the blood of her martyrs.

But if we descend to details, we shall be not the less gratified to discern the love of God engaged, and his omnipotent arm made bare to defend and favor his beloved Zion. I shall direct your minds to a few *historical events* which illustrate this interesting truth.

1. *The expulsion of the Moors from Spain.*

But a few years elapsed after Mohammed broached his impostures to the world, before Moslemism spread over nearly all Asia, the eastern part of Europe, and a great part of Africa. The portions of Africa adjacent to Spain early became its strong-holds. The countries now

called Morocco and Fez were then called Mauritania, and
its inhabitants Moors. They were of Arabian origin, and
seem to have been an enterprising, warlike, intelligent
people. They formed the channel through which the
knowledge of the arts and sciences, and an acquaintance
with civilization, traveled into Europe. Taking advantage of the distracted state of Spain, the Moors took possession of large portions of that country which they held
near eight centuries, from 713 to 1492. Here they
established a magnificent kingdom, cultivated learning,
while all the rest of Europe was sunk in barbarism, and
left behind them enduring monuments of their industry
and skill in the arts.

We may take, as some specimen of the magnificence
of the Saracen empire, the single city of Cordova; which,
in point of wealth and grandeur, was scarcely inferior to
its proud rival on the banks of the Tigris. A space of
twenty-four miles in length and six in breadth, along the
margin of the Guadalquiver, was occupied with streets,
gardens, palaces, and public edifices. For ten miles the
citizens might travel by the light of the lamps along an
uninterrupted extent of buildings. In the reign of Alma-
zor, Cordova could boast of 270,000 houses, 80,000 shops,
80 public schools, 50 hospitals, 911 baths, 3,877 mosques,
from the minarets of which 800,000 persons were daily
summoned to prayers. The seraglio of the caliph con-
sisted of the enormous number of 6,300 wives, concubines,
and black eunuchs. The caliph was attended to the field
by a guard of 12,000 horsemen, whose belts and scimi-
tars were studded with gold. Such was Cordova: and
the city of Grenada was, perhaps, equally celebrated for
its wealth, luxury, and learning.

At the period of which we now speak, nothing seemed
more probable than that the western world and all coming
generations, should receive their learning, civilization
and religion at the hands of the followers of the false
prophet. The tide of human affairs now indicated that
the crescent, instead of the cross, would monopolize the
vast resources of knowleage, of discoveries, inventions,
improvements in arts, advancement in the sciences, and
oi all the modern facilities for the propagation and estab-

lishment of religion which Christianity now enjoys. Had
not the tide of Mahommedan advancement been arrested
just at the time it was, (a year before the discovery of
America,) in all human probability the vast advantages
which now accrue to Christianity from the use of the
press, the mariner's compass, the application of steam to
the purposes of locomotion and the arts, and from the
various rich improvements of modern days, would have
been engines to propel onward the terrific car of Islam,
and crush in its course every rising germ of Christianity.

But He that watches the falling sparrow, and numbers
the hairs of your head, would not have it so. The mandate had gone out from the throne of the Majesty of
Heaven, saying to the rolling billows of Arabia's mad
fanaticism, "Thus far shalt thou come and no farther."
When the imperial city of Grenada yielded to the arms
of Ferdinand and Isabella, and the banners of the cross
waved triumphant over the red towers of the Alhambra,
the tide of Mahommedanism was turned back, and from
that good hour the religion of Calvary was fledged for
her immortal flight. She now began to rise from the
dust of her debasement, to be seated on the "white
horse," to be borne aloft and far away by the hand of
her God, and through the instrumentality of the facilities
which the world in its late progress has afforded, for the
spread and prosperity of religion. Henceforth these
facilities should be the friends and servants of Christ, and
not the slaves of Mohammed.

A few more historical references will set Providential
interposition in a still clearer light. God places the
Moslems for eight centuries in Spain, just in the position
where they might act most effectually as the handmaid
of Europe, in the restoration of learning and general advancement, uses them as long as he needed, then sends
them back to Africa just in time to give the empire of
letters and the power of knowledge to his church. *How*
their progress was arrested cannot be a matter void of
interest.

In the eighth century (732) it seemed that all Europe
must yield to the arms of the Moslems. From the rock

of Gibraltar to the Loire, nothing impeded their progress
Another such distance would have made England a province of the Grand Caliph : " the interpretation of the
Koran had been the scholastic divinity of Oxford and
Edinburgh ; our cathedrals supplanted by gorgeous
mosques, and our pulpits employed in demonstrating to a
circumcised people the truth of the apostleship and revelations of Mohammed. Such was the destiny that seemed
to impend over all Europe, from the Baltic to the Cy-
clades, when the standard of Islam floated over the walls
of Tours." But this cloud of devouring locusts should
be turned back. The hand of Providence was stretched
out to arrest the progress of the conqueror, and save the
church of Christ. CHARLES MARTEL was the "hammer"
in the hands of Omnipotence to break the power of the
foe, and save Europe, to be a field for the development of
God's truth. The finger of God is here remarkable.
France (Gaul) was attacked by an army of Saracens,
385,000 strong. They were met by the French, under
Charles, near Toulouse. The great Abdalrahman was
slain, and, "after a bloody battle, the Saracens, in the
close of the evening, returned to their camp. In the
disorder and despair of the night, the various tribes of
Yemen and Damascus, of Africa and Spain, were provoked to *turn their arms against each other ;* the remains
of their host were suddenly dissolved, and each emir consulted his safety by a hasty and separate flight." So fled
the Midianites, and fell on one another before Gideon and
his three hundred ; and the Philistines before Jonathan
and his armour-bearer ; and the Syrians when Israel
was afar off.

Mohammedanism should not have Europe. Again,
when in full tide of successful conquest, the Saracens
attack Italy, sail up the Tiber, ravage the country and
besiege Rome ; on attempting to land, they are furiously
driven back and cut to pieces. A *storm scatters one-
half of their ships*, and, unable to retreat, they are either
slaughtered or made prisoners. And again was Europe
near falling into the hands of the Turks in the 17th century, (1683,) when John Sobieski, king of Poland, defeated them.

No one can take his position on this summit of his
torical record, without feeling that he stands on a high
and narrow promontory between two broad seas, the one
receding and rolling back its turgid waves over the burning sands of Africa, with hollow murmurings of wounded
pride and dark chagrin ; the other, placid as when the
morning sun falls on the bosom of the peaceful ocean, its
deep blue waves gently, though irresistibly, rolling on,
and bearing the rich stores of grace and truth from land
to land,

> " Till, like a sea of glory,
>   It spread from pole to pole."

We, after the lapse of centuries, occupy a position to
appreciate the momentous and important interposition of
Providence at this juncture.   By turning back the tide
of Mohammedanism, the way was prepared for the Reformation ; that it might extend its peaceful, purifying
influences over the wide domains of Europe, and reach
the arms of its benevolence over the vast territories
about to be discovered, both in the East and in the West.
This singular interposition was by no means overlooked
at the time.   The downfall of Grenada sent a thrill of
joy throughout all Christendom, which echoed back in
"te deums" from every corner of Spain and Portugal,
from England, from Rome, and from the whole Christian
world. Infidelity was forced to exclaim—" Behold, what
hath God wrought ?"

2. Another event, which carried with it momentous
consequences in relation to Christianity, and challenges
our admiration, *is the transfer of the immense and populous territories of Asia from their Romish masters to the
hands of Protestants.*

I have alluded to a similar transfer in the early occu-
pation of North America.   The fact of the large possessions which the Portuguese gained in India, and so soon
and so completely lost, is still more remarkable.   From
the time the Portuguese first gained a foothold in India,
till their vast empire had fallen into the hands of the
English, scarcely more than a single century had elapsed.
The ultimate design of this transfer, doubtless, has not

yet transpired, yet we have seen enough already to excite our admiration of a wonder-working Providence. Through the influence of Protestant England, the great and populous nations of the East are open to the entrance of the gospel. The Romish Inquisition has been silenced; the powerful arm of idolatry has been broken; the haughty followers of the Arabian prophet have been humbled, and the strength of their power prostrated; knowledge has been increased, and the blessings of civilization and the results of modern inventions and discoveries have been introduced; and finally, Christianity, to no inconsiderable extent, unfurled her mild banners over those lands of darkness and spiritual death; and, prospectively, we can scarcely select an event pregnant with a richer harvest to the Christian church. In the singular, and, to all human sagacity, unexpected transfer of those idolatrous nations from Catholic to Protestant hands, we distinctly discern the finger of God. "Only a little more than a century ago it was as likely, to all appearance, that the Mogul empire, (or India,) would have passed into the hands of France, of Portugal, of Denmark, of Holland, or even of Russia, as of England. But under the jealous despotism of Russia, or the ascendency of a Romish power, India would have been closed against the missionary." We cannot, therefore, too much admire that special Providence which has given almost the entire heathen world, India, China, Birmah, Australasia, and many of the islands of the sea, into the hands of the only Protestant nation "capable of efficiently discharging the high mission of genuine Christianity throughout the East."

3. The long and bloody war which Spain about this time waged against Holland and the Low Countries, (1559) supplies another illustration. Philip II., Emperor of Spain, was a bigoted, cruel, intolerant Catholic. Husband of Mary, the bloody queen of England, and imbued with a like spirit, he worried out the saints of the Most High, by tortures the most barbarous, and deaths the most cruel. When he had "hung and burnt" as many as fell under the cognizance of inquisitorial vigilance in Spain, Piedmont, Milan, and Calabria, he directed his

parental regard towards his German possessions. Holland and the Low Countries became the prey of this ravening wolf. Here the seeds of the Reformation had been profusely sown and taken deep root. Philip determined to exterminate the rising heresy by a blow. But mark the end of his madness. See what God brought out of it: how he made the wrath of man to praise him, and restrained the remainder.

This religious despot resorted to the most violent measures to crush the rising germs of religion and liberty in that part of his empire. He set up the Inquisition, augmented the number of Bishops, and enacted the most severe and barbarous laws against all *innovators* in matters of religion. And when a persecuted people rose to repel these invasions on all right and conscience, the Duke of Alva, of bloody memory, was sent with a powerful army to quell the *rebellion*. A protracted and sanguinary war followed—on the one side for liberty, on the other for civil and religious despotism. But was liberty crushed—was the hated heresy of the Reformation exterminated? The issue was *the establishment of one of the most powerful Protestant States in Europe, the United Provinces of the Netherlands.*

Nor was this all that Providence brought out of it. Protestant England was drawn into the conflict. This led to those collisions in America, which broke the power of the Spanish yoke there, and, instead of the iron reign of Rome over all the western world, the way was prepared for the empire of liberty and Protestantism. And there was yet another issue: Philip, chagrined under his repulses in the Netherlands, determined on a grand onset upon England, which, while it should revenge on Queen Elizabeth for the aid she had lent the Hollanders in their late defence of the principles of the Reformation, should reduce England again to the domination of Rome.

This brings us to another of those grand interpositions of Providence in behalf of his adopted cause, viz:

4. *The destruction of the Invincible Armada of Spain.* Philip meditated signal vengeance on England. For this purpose he fitted out the most formidable naval armament that ever rode on the ocean. The project was no less

Invincible Armada. Page 108.

than the complete subjugation of England and the establishment of the religion of Rome throughout all Europe.
The crisis of Protestantism had come. Should England
—should the rising colonies of this New World—should
all Europe and Asia smile under the benign auspices of
the cross, or groan beneath the usurpations of Rome?
The vast empire of Philip was roused to strike a fatal
blow. The noise of preparation sounded in every part of
his dominions. " In all the ports of Sicily, Naples, Spain,
and Portugal, artizans were employed in building vessels
of uncommon size and force;" naval stores collected;
provisions amassed; armies levied; and plans laid for
fitting out such a fleet as had never before been seen in
Europe. Ministers, generals, admirals, men of every craft
and name were employed in forwarding the grand design.
Three years elapsed in the stupendous preparations. Who
could doubt that such preparations, conducted by officers
of such consummate skill, would finally be successful?
Confident of success, and ostentatious of their power, they
had already denominated this armament the *Invincible
Armada.*

The time for the actual invasion drew near. Troops
from all quarters were assembling; from Italy, Spain,
Flanders, Austria, the Netherlands, and the shores of the
Baltic. One general burst of enthusiasm pervaded every
nook and corner of the empire. Princes, dukes, nobles,
men of all ranks and conditions, equally embarked their
fortunes, lives, and honors, in an enterprise so promising
of wealth and glory, and so calculated to engage their
religious enthusiasm. And further to cherish the general
infatuation, the Pope had fulminated a fresh bull of excommunication against Elizabeth, declared her deposed,
dissolved her subjects from their oath of allegiance, and
granted a plenary indulgence to all who should engage in
the invasion. All were elated with the highest hopes of
success. And who could doubt that in a few short weeks
English power would be prostrate, and English Protestantism no more? But follow on a little, and behold the
Hand of Him who keepeth Israel as the apple of his eye.

This formidable armament had been consigned to the
command of the Marquis of Santa Croce, a sea officer of

10

great reputation and experience;—and who should dare whisper a doubt that such an armament, under such a commander, should not annihilate the Reformed Religion from the face of the earth. But mark its progress. The moment the Invincible Armada is ready for sea, the admiral *is seized with fever, and dies*. And by a singular concurrence the vice-admiral meets the same fate. The fleet is delayed. England gains time. An inexperienced admiral is appointed. The fleet sails (1588)—the next day meets a violent tempest which scatters the ships— some are sunk, and others compelled to put back into port. Again they are all at sea, and are descried approaching the shores of England, with fresh hopes in the prosecution of their enterprise. The English admiral sees the Armada, "coming full sail towards him, disposed in the form of a crecent, and stretching the distance of seven miles from the extremity of one division to that of the other." Never had so mighty a fleet rode the ocean before, and never, perhaps, the confidence of man so positive of success. Protestantism was, in anticipation, annihilated. These vessels brought the implements of torture by which the stern heretics of England were to pay the price of their defection from Rome. The writer has seen, in Queen Elizabeth's armory in the Tower of London, the thumb-screws, fetters, battle-axes, boarding-pikes, and the invincible banner, which were taken as spoils from the Armada.

But behold the hand of God here. Just as the lion, sure of his prey, was about to pounce on the lamb, Heaven interposes. The Lord of armies fought for his own cause. The firmness and courage of the English were less remarkable than the temerity and confusion of the enemy. The elements fought for the righteous cause. The fire, the wind and tempest were so many angels of death to the boasted *invincibility* of the Spaniards. The destruction of this vast and formidable armament was effected almost without human agency. *Deus flavit et dissipantur.*

The visionary scheme of Philip vanished like the summer's cloud. Never was a project more wisely planned, never preparations more ample, or hopes of success raised higher. Very slight obstacles were anticipated to the landing of the entire invading army on the coasts of England; and it was confidently expected that a single battle would decide the fate of England and of Protestantism forever. Yet Heaven does not permit a single Spaniard to step foot on English soil—the invaded sustain but slight damage or loss in any way, while in a very little time the ocean is strewed with the mangled corpses of their proud invaders, and with the wrecks of their noble vessels.

We have here another of those pivots on which the destiny of evangelical religion often turns. In all human probability, from this time forward, English greatness and English influence and power in her vast empire over the world, would be engaged to uphold Rome and the Inquisition—that her coal and iron, and her skill, would forge chains to bind immortal mind over one half of the globe —that her vast enterprise would be employed in the traffick of the souls of men. But Heaven had not so decreed. The eternal King had not yet yielded his right of empire on earth. A thrill of joy and thanksgiving now pervades every resting-place of Protestantism throughout the world. God had gotten the victory. They " sing unto the Lord a new song : for the Lord hath done marvelous things for them ; his right hand and his holy arm hath gotten him the victory." The well-concerted schemes of man are confounded, his, presumptuous expectations disappointed, and the impenetrable decrees of Divine Providence in the progress of his Church, established.

A Catholic coalition of the Irish and French against England in 1796 was a very similar instance of a remarkable interposition of Providence in behalf of the Reformed Religion. A vast conspiracy had been formed in Ireland against the British government. Two hundred thousand men were in readiness for the revolt. Overtures were made to the French republic for their assistance, and assurances given on the part of the Irish that five hundred thousand fighting men could be brought into the field on the arrival of the French. Hoche, the French General, at the head of one hundred thousand troops, burned with the desire to gratify his ambition in humbling the ancient foe of France. With twenty-five thousand of his troops he embarked for Ireland, flushed with the idea of a splendid victory. But not a Frenchman was permitted to step foot in Ireland. "A violent tempest arose immediately after the departure of the fleet; one ship of the line struck on a rock, and perished; several were damaged, and the fleet totally dispersed. Tempestuous weather continued the whole time the fleet was at sea." What escaped the violence of the elements and the attacks of the English, returned, broken and dispirited, to France. And the God of Hosts again made the winds and the waters his army by which to protect his cause from a Romish conspiracy, and to save from dismemberment a great protestant nation, which, as designed by Providence, has been used more effectually than any other nation to bring to all the tribes and kindreds of the earth a knowledge of the gospel.*

5. I shall pass lightly over several other events which illustrate not the less strikingly the same point.

Mary, the bloody Queen of England, was a violent persecutor of the Protestants. Having brought to the block and the stake multitudes in England, Scotland and Wales, she reached forth her hand to vex them of Ireland. She had signed a commission (1588,) authorizing the persecution and annihilation of all Irish heretics, which was committed for execution to Dr. Cole, a zealous son of Rome. The doctor immediately repairs to Ireland to execute the bloody mandate of the queen. At Chester, where he is to embark, he communicates to the mayor the nature of his errand to Ireland, at the same time pointing to a box, which, to use his language, contained "that which shall lash the heretics of Ireland." The good woman in the house where they were, (Elizabeth Edmonds,) a friend of the Protestants, who had a brother in Dublin, hearing these words, was not a little troubled. Therefore, watching her opportunity, she opens the box, takes out the commission, and places in its stead a sheet of paper in which she had carefully wrapped a pack of cards, with the knave of clubs uppermost. Suspecting nothing,

---

* See Alison's History of Europe.

Statue of Peter the Great.   Page 115.

the doctor, the wind and the weather favoring, next day set sail for Dublin. He immediately appears before the lord deputy and the privy council, makes his speech, declaring the nature of his commission, and presents his box to the lord deputy; which, on opening, nothing appears but a pack of cards, the knave of clubs staring his lordship in the face. The lord deputy and council were amazed, and the doctor was confounded; yet insisted that he started with a commission such as he had declared. The lord deputy answered: " Let us have another commission, and we will shuffle the cards in the mean time." The doctor, chagrined, returns to England, appears at court, obtains another commission, but is now detained by unfavorable winds, and while waiting, the queen is called to her dread account. And thus God preserved the Protestants of Ireland.* " Behold, he that keepeth Israel shall neither slumber nor sleep."

Again, Cromwell and Hampden are unexpectedly arrested when on the eve of joining the pilgrims in New England. This seemed a calamity, as they were just such men as the New World needed. But their detention, though involuntary, and seemingly calamitous, was, as developed in their future career, the very thing which secured the *liberties of England,* dissipated the cloud which hung over the Huguenots of France, and the Albigenses of Switzerland, and changed the face of all England.†

Other illustrations, no less apposite, we may find *in the detection of the famous gun-powder plot in* 1605—*in the usurpation of Oliver Cromwell in* 1649—in the English revolution, which brought to the throne of England William and Mary in 1688.

In the first instance a desperate confederacy had been formed by the adherents of Popery, to destroy, at one blow, James I., the Prince of Wales, and both houses of Parliament, by the explosion of an immense quantity of gun-powder, which had been concealed for the purpose under the House of Lords. A Protestant government

---

* MSS. of Sir James Ware, copied from papers of Richard, Earl of Cork—and found quoted by Mosheim. Vol. II, p. 42. Also, Universal History, Vol. IV., p. 278.
† Dr. Spring's Supremacy of God among the Nations.

once destroyed, they hoped to restore the power of Rome
But the hand of the Lord interposed—the nefarious plot
was providentially discovered,* and Protestantism still
safe.

Again the ark of God is in trouble in the reign of
Charles I.   The most strenuous efforts are made to bring
about a reconciliation between England and Rome.   But
a civil war breaks out between the King and the Parliament—Oliver Cromwell succeeds to the government, and
the tide of Roman domination is again rolled back.†

And again the restless emissaries of Popery combine
to vex the Church of God.   A confederacy is formed
between James II., of England, and Louis XIV., of
France, to crush, not only in England, but in all Europe,
the already wide-spread heresy of the German Reformer.
For a time they are elated with high hopes of success,
and nothing seemed more probable than that Protestantism would soon be prostrated in the dust, if not annihilated.   But was the ark in peril ?   By the most unfore-
seen incidents, James is driven from his throne,—a
wretched, forlorn exile, in a strange land.   The notable
revolution of 1688, occurs ; William and Mary, Protestant princes, are called to the throne of England ; and
never before was the cause of the Reformation so firmly
established in the British realm.   And more than this :
A Papist was, by the constitution, made for ever afterwards incapable of sitting on the throne of England !‡

The fixing of the succession to the English throne, in
the hands of Protestants, was itself an event of vast
magnitude, yet greatly magnified by other providential

* By a letter of caution sent to Lord Monteagle, that he should on a certain day absent himself from Parliament.

† The cannon of Cromwell's navies shook the Vatican, through the bravery of his
admiral, Blake—Gustavus, at another time, asserts the liberties of the Protestant North
on the field of Lutzen.   And, at a later period, Bonaparte lays his sacrilegious hands
on the Pope himself, and leads him away captive, and makes the seven hills of Rome
tremble.

‡ This dissolution continued in force, and England was divorced from Rome, and
consequently ceased to be a Papal state, till the passage of the late Catholic Emancipation Bill, (1833,) when the act of separation from idolatrous Rome was annulled, and
it became again admissible that Popish kings, and Popish subjects, should again wield
the political power of Great Britain.   And here, by the way, we may trace a remarkable providence in the *succession of the present royal family* to the throne of Britain.
The manner in which the Protestant branch of James VI. was preserved through the
amiable and pious Princess, Sophia Elizabeth, daughter of James I., and brought to
the throne while the male and Popish branch have come to nought, cannot but excite
the admiration of every believer in an overruling Providence.

events of the same period. Death removed not a few of the fiercest friends of Jacobinism and Popery, without which, a Protestant king could not have been seated on the throne of England. The French king, Louis XIV., died while he was yet contemplating an invasion of England; the Duke of Hamliton, just as he was going to France, where he was preparing to favor Rome; Queen Anne, "when the schemes of the party were becoming mature;" and the king of Sweden, when setting out for Norway, to use his influence against Britain.

Again, the hand of God is seen in moving the heart of Peter the Great, of Russia, to reform his people; to patronize schools of learning; to cause the Bible to be translated into the language of the country; commanding it to be kept in every household, and read by all. He was the hand of God to draw aside the veil of ignorance and superstition which had so long clouded the face of Russia, and to let in light, such as never shone there before, and has not ceased to shine, though feebly, ever since.

The kingdom of Prussia, too, furnishes an example how God so disposes of temporal power as to subserve the interests of His church. She has stood amidst the Catholic nations of Europe, as a rock in the midst of ocean's billows; far in advance of them all, in the improvements of life, in intellectual advancement, and in morality and religion; a city set on a hill, casting her light over the accumulated darkness of many generations. But whence her pre-eminence? Her history replies: Her infancy was cradled in the hand of Providence. Though rudely rocked by the vandal foot of a "seven years" war with the united powers of Europe, she, the youngest of the sisterhood of European states, soon attained a growth and vigor scarcely inferior to the oldest. Early in the fifteenth century, the emperor, Sigismond, gave the Marquisate of Bradenburg to the noble family of Hohenzollern. This family, in the sixteenth century, embraced the doctrines of the Reformation, became possessed of the Duchy of Prussia, and soon assumed the form, and, after many eventful struggles, in which the hand of God was abundantly manifested, the vigor and growth of an independent kingdom. And her present character, position and influence,—the religious character of her present sovereign and of her national institutions, afford a pleasing guarantee that God will not disappoint the high hopes raised by her protestant and providential origin, in making her the instrument of his power in the defence of his truth.

Or we may quote a single instance from the history of the *Waldenses*, so prolific in providential interpositions. I refer to their almost miraculous return to their native valleys, from which they had been driven by the persecutions of Rome. The miserable remnant that survived the assault, were scattered among the Swiss cantons, and in Holland, Prussia, and the Protestant states of Germany. Their homes had been peopled with Romanists, and their native valleys garrisoned by a foreign soldiery. Several attempts had been made to recover them, but in vain. In 1689, Henri Arnaud, one of their pastors, with incredible skill and courage, and at the head of but eight hundred brave mountaineers, forced his way back to the valleys, in spite of an opposing force of ten thousand well disciplined and armed French troops, and twelve thousand Peidmontese. The victories they gained, the sufferings they endured, the deliverances they experienced, are incredible on any mere human calculations, and to be accounted for only on the supposition of a special Divine interposition.

"Who but God inspired a destitute band of men with the *design* of entering their country, sword in hand, in opposition to their own prince, and to the king of France, then the terror of all Europe? Who but He, conducted and protected them in this enterprise, and finally crowned it with success, in spite of the vast efforts of those powers to disconcert it, and the vows of the Pope and his adherents to support the papal standard, and to destroy this little band of the elect?"

But why multiply examples; history is full of them. The Diet of Augsburg, (1530,) closes with full power and determination on the part of Rome, to put down by violence the Protestant cause. Rome had the power, and the Imperial arm was just raised to execute it. But mark the signal interposition of Providence. A war breaks out with *Turkey ;* Charles and Francis get at loggerheads ; the Duke of Mantua will not suffer a general council to be called in his city. All these events divert vengeance from the Protestants, and give them time for growth and strength. The wars of Charles V., and Francis I., are made to contribute to the cause of the Reformation, by having in their armies Protestant soldiers, who propagated the truth wherever they went. Not a few prominent reformers, especially in Italy, received their lessons of reform from this source. This same puissant Emperor Charles, allows a single, defenceless Monk, (Martin Luther,) to pass unharmed,—hated and doomed, yet so unmolested as not to be retarded in his great work. Henry VIII., of England, a cruel and superstitious king, a decided enemy of the Reformation, which he opposed by his arms and his pen, executes the plans of Providence, by shaking off the yoke of Rome. *He* did it to satiate his voluptuousness and ambition. God *allowed* him to do it, gloriously to subserve the cause of His truth. At the same time, Clement VII., to maintain some chimerical rights of the clergy, by hurling the thunders of the Vatican against Henry, lost all England, by the very means he adopted to retain her.* Rome again thought to increase the power of her church in Germany, by the scandalous traffick of Tetzel ; God made that traffick the occasion of the outbreaking of the pent-up fires of Reform, which were burning and heaving just beneath the surface. And Rome again thought to smother Protestantism in the blood of the Inquisition ; God made the Inquisition a principal cause of the Reformation in the United Provinces. During the persecution in England, under bloody Mary, the Puritans flee to *Geneva ;* are there brought in contact with the great Calvin, and

* On what a slender thread the Reformation in England, at one period, hung. Henry VIII., had effected a divorce of Queen Katherine,—had exasperated the Pope, who finally proposed, if Henry would by proxy acknowledge his authority, he would sanction the divorce. Henry consented. The Pope being informed of this, delayed to proceed against Henry, up to a certain day named. It was winter ; the traveling uncertain ; the messenger, (Henry's proxy,) was delayed. A respite was pleaded for, but denied by the Pope ; and the cardinals, hurrying through Henry's case, decided against the divorce, and thus throw down the gauntlet, which ended in severing England, and the English church, from Rome. The next day the messenger arrived ; but all was over. One day earlier, and England had remained a province of Rome.

become instructed more perfectly in the great principles of the Bible, by that eminent scholar and servant of God. These were the principles which these same Puritans brought to New England, and which lie at the foundation of all the distinguishing blessings of New England. But for the schooling of the Puritans for a time at Geneva, New England, and the religion and republicanism of New England, would have been another and an inferior thing.

I shall name but one other instance: it is the raising up, in the seventeenth century, *such a constellation of great and good men*, for the defence and establishment of the truth. In nothing, perhaps, are the footsteps of Providence more distinctly marked than in providing and fitting *men for the times*. Every great event, we see, has its master-spirit; every age, its controlling genius. And in the choice and preparation of these controlling spirits, the Hand of God is especially manifest. The Jewish economy could not be founded without an Abraham, nor the nation be delivered from bondage, and consolidated into a state, and brought under law, without a Moses; or conducted into Canaan, and settled there, without a Joshua; or restored, and the temple re-built after the discomfiture of the Babylonish captivity, without an Ezra and Nehemiah. There must be a Paul to give impulse, extension and permanency to Christianity; a Luther to act as the ruling spirit of the Reformation; a Cromwell, a Constantine, a Wilberforce, a Washington, to give impulse, unity and direction to the several great events in which, and *for* which they lived. In all such instances, there is indeed a "multitude of hearts beating, and a multitude of hands employed, for the accomplishment of the respective objects; and yet there was not a pulsation, nor a movement, but the ruling spirit animated and directed it."* Those great men were the primary agents, raised up for the very purpose; and we cannot doubt that He who made them such, made them in reference to the work he had for them to do.

Perhaps no century was more remarkable in this respect than the seventeenth. That was an age of great

---

* Dr. Sprague's sermon on Dr. Chalmers.

men,—especially of great authors, for the defence of the truth And the Hand of God here appears, especially in connection with the fact that this century stood in special need of such authors.

Protestantism was yet young, and knew not its strength, or the rich and varied stores on which it should feed. Truth was now to adorn her in a new and richer dress. The mine was to be opened deeper, and more of its invaluable treasures to be discovered and brought into use. And were there men adequate to such a work? There were giants in those days,—men mighty in word and in deed. Take from the long catalogue the following, as specimens: Lightfoot, Poole, Owen, Bunyan, Baxter, Flavel, Calamy, Howe, Bishop Burnet, Cudworth, Stillingfleet, Prideaux, Lock, Lloyd and Territin.

Or, as specimens of profane writers who essentially promoted the cause of Christianity by advancing science and learning, we may take such men as Archbishop Usher, Hervey, John Selden, Clarendon, Sir Matthew Hale, John Locke and Robert Boyle.*

Indeed, I may say, in a word, all veritable history is but an exponent of Providence; and it cannot but interest the mind of intelligent piety, to trace the mighty hand of God in all the changes and revolutions and incidents of our world's history. All are made, beautifully, to subserve the interests of the Church; all tend to the furtherance of *the one* great purpose of the Divine mind, the glory of God in the redemption of man.

The inference forced on us from the foregoing is, that *the preservation of the church*, amidst all the changes and revolutions of nations, and the stern and constant opposition of her enemies, is a standing providence, which the people of God can never cease more and more to admire. Often has the whole civil authority of the world been

---

* Robert Boyle was one of the most learned men of his age: but this is not what immortalizes his name in the annals of Christianity. He was the first Governor of the "Society for Propagating the Gospel in New England." He instituted public lectures for the defence of Christianity; manifested an unquenchable zeal for the diffusion of the gospel in India and in America, and among the native Welch and Irish; made munificent donations for the translation of the Scriptures into Malay, Arabic, Welch and Irish, and of Elliot's Bible into the language of the Massachusetts Indians, and for other religious books; and lastly, a legacy of £5,400 for the propagation of Christianity among the heathen. To his stern religious principles, he united the purest morals, a rare modesty and active benevolence.

confederated against her; often has she been brough.
to the brink of ruin; and often have great kings and
mighty kingdoms rejoiced over her supposed complete
overthrow; yet, she has stood; she has weathered
storms the most violent; withstood billows the most angry, for near six thousand years. When Moab, and Ammon, and Edom were mighty, she was weak; yet she
lived to see them all in ruins. When Babylon and Nineveh towered to heaven in their greatness and pride, she
was as nothing in their sight; yet Babylon and Nineveh
fell in undistinguished ruin, but she rose and triumphed
over their ashes. The monarchies of Persia, and Greece,
and Rome, rose and successively spread themselves over
the earth, and defied all human, if not all divine power,
to bring them down from their towering height. The
church was a thing despised, and nothing counted of;
yet she lived and prospered, and waved the banner of
her victory over their ruins; and this, too, in spite of all
their power, oftentimes employed for her destruction.
The Christian church, in her beginning, took root and
spread in despite of all the civil authority of the world.

Often did the Roman government set itself, in good
earnest, to extirpate her, root and branch, from the earth.
And under the tenth and last persecution, they boasted
that their design was accomplished; the church *was* extinct. Yet their boast is scarcely uttered, before the
Christian church rises triumphant over the Roman Empire, and that empire itself falls to ruin. Again, how
completely the voice of piety is suppressed, and her very
existence seems annihilated previous to the Reformation
in the sixteenth century; yet, soon we see her rising in
all her pristine strength and glory, and kings again bow
down to her, while the vaunting powers of Rome, under
imperial auspices, avail nothing. Philip II. of Spain,
Bloody Mary of England, and Louis XIV. of France, in
persecutions of exquisite cruelty and unwonted virulence,
each, in turn, raise their puissant arms to sweep Protestantism from the earth. Yet the church of God moves
on—through blood, through fire and faggots, purified, invigorated, enlarged, in proportion to the madness of their
folly and guilt. Again, Julian, the apostate, Voltaire,

MISSIONARY PREACHING TO THE SIRMANS. p. 122.

Paine, rise up in their wrath, to put down Christianity single handed. Yet she heeds their invectives as the moon did the barking of the petty cur. She moves on in her majesty, while they die in agony and shame, and their names become a stench in the whole earth.

Surely the hand of the Lord has held the ark. He has conducted it thus far, and will not forsake it now. He has reproved kings for her sake, saying: "Touch not mine anointed, and do my prophets no harm."

The Lord's portion is his people:—to lead them in a "waste, howling wilderness;" to instruct them; to keep them as the apple of his eye, is the sleepless care of the God of Jacob. And if, like the eagle that "stirreth up her nest, fluttereth over her young, spreadeth abroad her wings, taketh them, beareth them on her wings," the Lord, sometimes, by the sterner dispensations of his providence, rouses his people from their sloth, and teaches them to direct their reluctant souls heavenward, he is none the less mindful of their eternal well-being.

Let it, then, be our chief concern that we *be reconciled to God;* that our discordant spirits be hushed into harmony with the Spirit that controls all events in this wide universe according to his sovereign will. And then, though his chariot wheels roll on in their resistless course, we shall not be crushed, but, drawn by the sweet influences of everlasting love, our spirits shall find rest from every sorrow, and rest in God forever.

11

CHAPTER VII.

God in Modern Missions.—Their early history. Benevolent societies. The Moravians.—English Baptists' society. Birmah Missions. David Bogue and the London Missionary Society. Captain James Wilson and the South Sea Mission. The tradition of the *unseen God.*—Success. Destruction of Idols.—Gospel brought to Rurutu—Aitutaki—Rarotonga—Mangaia—Navigators' Islands.

"*And I saw another angel fly in the midst of heaven, having the everlasting gospel to preach unto them that dwell on the earth, and to every nation, and kindred, and tongue, and people.*" Rev. xiv. 6.

This angel is believed to prefigure the progress of the gospel, under the auspices of modern missions. The figure is sublime and apt. High in the air, where his course is unobstructed by mountain, lake, sea or desert, he moves majestically on, as if to extend his flight around the world. Nothing impedes his course. In trumpet tones he proclaims pardon to a rebel world. The dwellers on the mountains and in the vales, the inhabitants of the isles, hear the joyful sound, and respond in heart-felt melody as they receive the law of their God. The turbaned tribes of India, they that traverse the wide wastes of Africa, or inhabit the eternal snows of the poles, welcome the glad tidings, and praise Him who sitteth on the throne, and the adorable Lamb. As the angel speeds his flight, encompassed in a halo of celestial radiance, and scattering in his train the royal gifts of heaven, earth's remotest ends echo to the glad sounds of salvation by God's dear Son.

Such is the auspicious event symbolized by the flight of the angel. It would be a delightful anticipation to dwell on the glory and felicity of such a period; when sin shall no more invade the peaceful bosom of man; tears flow no more; men no longer hate and devour one another; fraud, oppression, wrong, be known no more :— righteousness shall reign; purity and peace triumph, and the earth be full of the glory of the Lord. But this would be to leap with mighty strides to that glorious goal

towards which the lines of Providence I am tracing are
all converging.   We must linger a little longer in the
outer court, and see how the stately structure of the temple is reared.

In preceding chapters, a variety of historical events
have been made to illustrate the hand of God as stretched
out to extend and protect his Zion.   An immense preparatory work was doing in three of the great quarters
of the globe.   In America, a nation of Protestants was
growing into manhood, and preparing, as a young man,
to run a race ; the church being founded on a more spiritual basis, was more free from political, social, and intellectual trammels than since the days of the apostles.   In
Asia, a great Christian and protestant empire was erecting in the very heart of idolatry ; while in Europe, a
brilliant succession of events were transpiring, all tending
to make room for the reformed church, and the doctrines
of the cross.   The Moors were driven out of Spain, and
thus the burning tide of Mohammedanism, which had so
long threatened to roll its fiery floods over all Europe,
was turned back on the deserts of Africa.   Queen Mary,
of bloody memory, is foiled in some of her most cruel
devices to exterminate from her dominions the religion of
Luther and of the cross.   The mad attempt of Philip II.
of Spain, to bind the chains of spiritual despotism on the
half protestant people of Holland and the low countries,
results in the establishment of one of the most powerful
protestant states in Europe.   The proud, presumptuous
attempt of the same bigoted prince to subjugate England
to the yoke of catholic Spain and the more galling yoke
of Rome, is signally frustrated in the destruction of the
Spanish "Invincible Armada."   Cromwell and Hampden
are providentially arrested when on the eve of joining the
pilgrims in New England, and thus the whole face of
things in England and in Europe is changed in reference
to the reformed church.   The *gun-powder plot* is discovered just in time to save a protestant government from
being buried in one common ruin.   The revolution of
1688 brings to the throne of England the protestant
princes, William and Mary, just in time to rescue the
periled cause of the reformed religion from the confede-

rated malice of James II. and Louis XIV., who now seemed about to crush it forever. Peter the Great unexpectedly becomes the defender of the faith in the Russias; and a rare constellation of great and good men, theologians, expositors, controversialists, historians, philosophers, logicians, orators and poets rise at this period, such as never appeared in the world before, men mighty in word and in deed, to develop the doctrines of the Reformation and to defend its truths. And to this list I may add the *American and French Revolutions* of the eighteenth century; the one of which secured to reformed Protestantism a free and a better soil on which to strike deep her roots and spread wide her branches; and the other struck a heavy blow on Papacy in Europe, and decreed that man should be free.

But to what point of convergency were the lines of Providence now tending? If I mistake not, all these events were but fledging the wings of the angel who was soon to commence his flight, preaching the everlasting gospel—preparatory steps to that system of efforts which has been devised, and is in progress for the conversion of the world to God.

I am now prepared to point out the hand of God in the progress of Christianity as seen in *the origin and success of Modern Missions.*

The early history of missions to the heathen everywhere bears marks of providential interposition. We have seen how the ever busy and wisely guiding Hand has prepared the way for the flight of the angel. We shall now see how he was, in the commencement of his flight, borne aloft on the wings of the same never-failing, sleepless Providence.

Special providences, in *the origin of modern benevolent societies,* and *corresponding providential movements in the different portions of the world* where these associations are destined to act, first challenge our admiration. And nothing here is more remarkable than the spontaneous and almost simultaneous up-shooting of a numerous constellation of benevolent associations at this particular period. Within the space of forty years (1792—1831,) there arose, from the kindly influences of a preceding

age, more than forty charitable institutions, halt ₙized so-
are missionary institutions, and the other half auxᵢₗₒded.
to the same great work. Whether or not we may ₋e
able to trace any striking interpositions of Providence in
the origin of particular associations, the hand of God is
abundantly manifested in bringing into existence, at
nearly the same time, such a beautiful and potent array
for the moral conquest of the world.

The whole early history of Moravian missions, the
earliest of modern missions, is a record of interesting
providences. Two young Greenlanders are providentially brought to Copenhagan—come to the notice of
the Moravian brethren—their history and condition is
searched out, (for true benevolence has many eyes, and
is fledged with angels' wings,) and a mission is immediately determined upon. Hence the origin of Moravian
missions.

That a congregation, not exceeding six hundred persons in all, and most of them exiles from their native land,
and poor, should originate the idea of missions to Green-
land, to the West Indies, to Labrador, to America, to Africa, and Asia, is, of itself, sufficiently providential to enlist our admiration. But that they should, from generation to generation, amidst incredible hardships and praise-
worthy self-denial, sustain these missions, is still more to
be admired. A volume would scarcely detail the all but
miraculous interpositions of Providence in behalf of those
missions. In the midst of extraordinary perils by sea and
by land, from the elements and from savage men, the
hand of God was, in a signal manner, with those devoted
and self-denying men, who, for Christ's and the gospel's
sake, braved the eternal snows of the north, or scorched
beneath the broiling sun of the equator. Oft did they
encounter famine, pestilence, shipwreck, and distressing
extremes of heat and cold; and the Lord delivered them
out of them all. When we take into the account the
fewness of their number, their circumscribed ability, and
the humbleness of their condition, the Moravians stood on
an enviable pre-eminence in the work of missions. Here,
emphatically, God ordained strength out of weakness,
making bare his own arm, and showing to the nations

11*

that He **can** conquer by the few or the many : David with his sling, single-handed, against Goliath.

A better day was dawning on the church. This little star which rose and shed its placid light over the dark waters of Paganism, was the precursor of a constellation that should soon rise and shine brighter and brighter till the whole earth should be radiant with their light.

Next in order rose the Baptist missionary society of England. It was not an orphan—it was the child of Providence. Its origin is worthy of note. An unwonted spirit of prayer prevails. A *new thought* enters the mind of one of the ministers met in association at Nottingham, in 1784. It is that one hour, on the first Monday evening of every month, should be devoted to prayer for the revival of religion, and the extension of the Redeemer's kingdom throughout the earth. Here commenced the monthly meeting for prayer ; and here a series of the most brilliant conquests over the empire of darkness. *Carey*, the pioneer of missions to India, was now brought to light, and the subject of the world's conversion began to be a topic of public discussion. The novel idea was now broached, to form a *society* to send out a mission ; and, after a little time, it was matured and realized, with a fund of £13 2s. 6d. Yet they had neither experience, nor a knowledge of any country where they might expect an open door for the gospel ; nor had they the men prepared to go forth on this untried enterprise.

But Providence had devised the great plan, and would now reveal it. While these things were transpiring in England, a corresponding part of the scheme was maturing in India. About the time that prayer began to be offered up for the conversion of the world, and the monthly meeting for this purpose was established, a surgeon, by the name of John Thomas, leaves England for Calcutta. The Lord stirs up his heart to attempt the spiritual benefit of the natives. Though unsuccessful in the attempt, his own heart becomes interested in the things of religion, and he was, on his return to England, baptized in 1785. He returns to India, gains more knowledge of the country and the condition of the heathen, and feels more than ever solicitous for their spiritual welfare.

In him Providence had provided the newly organized society with just such a helper and guide as they needed. Thomas being in London at the time referred to, is at once solicited to engage under the auspices of the society in the establishment of a mission in Bengal. And to what stately dimensions and vigor, and beneficent activity this child of Providence has since attained, all know who are acquainted with the history of the English Baptist Missionary Society.

And the American Baptist Mission in Birmah may claim paternity in the same Providence. Two missionaries while on their way to India, under the direction of the A. B.C. F. M., became Baptists; are naturally thrown, on their landing in Calcutta, among the English Baptist Mission; fall under their auspices, and as far as providential interposition and direction are concerned, may be regarded as a branch of the English Mission.

Nor can we but admire the wonder-workings of Providence as He wrought in the minds of Judson and Rice, and, by changing their views on a certain Christian *rite*, created, in some remote spot on the ocean, the germ of the American Baptist Missionary Society, roused that great and growing denomination to engage in the work of missions to the heathen, which they have since prosecuted with much energy and with signal success.

But look from another point; the formation of the London Missionary Society. The set time to enlarge Zion's boundaries had come. The angel had commenced his flight. Some ten years after the formation of the Baptist society, (1797,) the Rev. David Bogue, of Gosport, visits Bristol, to preach in one of Whitefield's tabernacles. But there was nothing remarkable in this. He had preached there many times before. But now, in the parlor of the tabernacle house, he first broaches the idea of uniting Christians of different denominations in an association for the spread of the gospel. The thought was contagious—as the leaven in the meal. Many a pious mind caught the idea. Circulars were sent out; addresses made; sermons preached; private conversations and correspondence maintained; the latent spirit of missions, which had for ages slept in the church, is now roused; a society is organized; funds promptly raised, and an auspicious commencement made on the islands of the Pacific.

But we shall be able to discern the finger of God more distinctly, if we allow the eye to pass cursorily over some of the particular missions of this Board. We may, at the very outset, record one of those interesting providential interpositions on which the eye of confiding piety delights to dwell. The first corps of missionaries were ready to embark; and a missionary ship, the Duff, was ready to convey them. But who should command it? They needed a skillful, wise, benevolent man, a controlling mind, who should come to the aid of the society at this crisis. Such was Capt. James Wilson. His eventful life in the East Indies had more, perhaps, than that of any man living, singled him out as an object of God's peculiar care; a chosen vessel, and a valued instrument in his work among the Gentiles.

The life of Wilson is a beautiful illustration of our subject: while engaged in an important and perilous service for the East India Company in their war with Hyder Ally, he was taken prisoner by the French; escaped from his prison by leaping from a wall forty feet high; swam the Coleroon river, an attempt accounted by the natives as certain death, on account of the multitude of alligators which infest it; was seized by some of Hyder Ally's peons; stripped; his hands tied behind his back, and he barbarously driven to head quarters. From thence, chained to a common soldier, he was driven, naked, barefoot and wounded, a distance of five hundred miles. Loaded with ponderous chains, he was now thrown into a prison, known as the Black Hole. Here he suffered incredible hardships from hunger, suffocation and excessive heat. Often a corpse was unchained from his arm in the morning, that a living sufferer might take its place. Amid such accumulated misery, he was preserved for twenty-two months. Emaciated, naked, famished and covered with ulcers, he was liberated. Yet in all this, he acknowledged not the hand that pre served him.

He was afterwards successful in business, accumulated a fortune, and returned to England in the same vessel in which Mr. Thomas of the Baptist Mission, (mark the hand of God here,) was passenger. Mr. Thomas often urged on his mind the great truths of religion, though apparently to little effect. Yet the eye of God was on him. He was a chosen vessel. Retired from foreign service to affluence and ease, he revelled in all the pleasures and gratifications which fortune and friends could bestow. Yet in the midst of nis enjoyments, a series of the most interesting incidents became the means of his conversion to a life of godliness. He became an eminent and devoted Christian. A magazine falls into his hands about this time, communicating an incipient plan of a mission to the South Sea Islands. The suggestion immediately arises in his mind that *here is work for him.* Willing to sacrifice the comfort and ease of an affluent and dignified retirement, he gratuitously tenders his services in this new and benevolent enterprise, to command the missionary ship. For gain, he had braved the stormy ocean; he will do it again for Christ. His services were accepted; and the early history of the South Sea Mission is ample voucher how much, under God, the success of that enterprise was indebted to the experience and skill, as well as to the piety and benevolence of the noble Wilson.

He was raised up, and by a rigid course of discipline, prepared for just such an untried and daring enterprise. While the friends of missions where maturing the plan for this bold expedition on the one hand, God was, by a singular process, on the other, preparing one who should take the command in an undertaking so novel and important.

The voyage was prosperous. Twenty-five laborers were taken out, and a mission established. For sixteen years they sow the precious seed upon a rock. No generous soil receives it; no friendly sun or fertilizing shower, causes it to vegetate. They seemed to labor in vain. The heavens over them are brass, and the earth iron. Desolating wars, and abominable, cruel idolatries, are the all-absorbing themes of the natives. But the dav

of deliverance is at hand—and in a manner to show tha'
the hand which wrought it was the Lord's.

The missionaries are unexpectedly driven from the
islands by the fury of war, and their fond hopes of seeing
their labors successful, and the cross planted in those
regions of death, seemed completely blasted. But *this*
was *God's time to work.* When the field had been
abandoned to the ravages of war, and amidst the very
desolations of all their expectations of success, the work
of conversion began. The good seed of the word had,
unknown to the missionaries, taken deep root in the
minds of two domestics who had been employed in their
family. Though "buried long in dust," the eye of Providence watched it, and would not suffer the precious
seed to be lost. Others gathered around these first fruits,
earnests of a glorious harvest. The wars ceased; the
missionaries returned; and what must have been their
joy and astonishment, to be welcomed back by a large
company of praying people!* They had now only to
cast the seed as profusely as they could, into a soil prepared to their hands.

There is, too, a beautiful counterpart to this signal
Providence. While these things are transpiring at the
islands, a dark cloud of discouragement gathers over the
society at home. Years of fruitless toil had elapsed, and
the Directors entertained serious thoughts of abandoning
the mission altogether. This disheartening resolution
was overruled by the determinate friendship and munificence of Dr. Haweis, and the irretractable attachment
to the enterprise of the Rev. Matthew Wilks. The mission was sustained. Letters of encouragement were
written to the Islands; and what is worthy of remark,
while these letters were on their way, they were passed by
a ship conveying to England not only the news of the
overthrow of Idolatry, but the rejected idols themselves.

Nor should we here overlook another Providence in
the auspicious commencement of this mission. The
shock of an earthquake is felt in Tahiti, a thing, till then,
unknown to the Tahitians. This creates no little alarm,

* Williams' Missionary Enterprises in the South Sea Islands.

and gives rise to many conflicting opinions as to the meaning of such a phenomenon. At length, an old chief rehearses to the people a tradition which existed on the island, viz. : that there is an UNSEEN GOD, and that strangers would, at some period, visit the island to tell them about this Being. In his opinion, he said, the earthquake was caused by this unseen God, and that the men who should tell them about him, must be near at hand. In a few days a strange sail is seen standing into the bay. It was the Duff, Capt. James Wilson, with the first missionaries for Tahiti.

The destruction of their idols was the beginning of a series of successes which, for more than forty years, have blessed those numerous groups of islands, so that, within two thousand miles of Tahiti, the radiating point of light in those dark seas, there is not a single island which has not been illumined by the Sun of Righteousness. Where will you find a parallel to this in all the annals of Christianity ?

Instances like the following might be recounted to almost any extent. An epidemic prevails on the island of Rurutu, an island some three hundred miles south of Tahiti. The superstitious inhabitants, believing it to be the infliction of some angry god, two of their chiefs determine to build each a large boat, and, with as many of their people as could be conveyed, to commit themselves to the winds and the waves, in search of some happier isle. They feared, if they stayed, "being devoured by the gods." A violent storm overtakes them ; one canoe yields to its fury, and nearly the whole crew perish ; the other is driven about for three weeks, over the trackless deep, they know not whither, in the most pitiable condition for the want of food and water. But an unerring hand guided them. They were driven to the Society Islands. Totally unacquainted with Christianity, or the comforts of civilization, these untutored savages were not a little astonished at the improved condition of the Society Islanders. Their books, schools, temporal comforts, mode of worship, and especially the account they now heard of the true God, were novel and astounding. They were at once convinced of the superiority and the divinity of

the Christian religion, and believed they had been con
ducted here that they might become acquainted with a
more excellent way.   They became immediately interested in the gospel; made astonishing proficiency in
learning, and after a few months returned to their native
isle, accompanied, at their earnest request, by two native missionaries, who brought light into the land of
darkness.

This remarkable providence not only brought to the
notice of the mission a new island, full of benighted, immortal souls, and was the first of a series of events which
soon added this lovely isle to the domains of Immanuel's
empire, but in connection with this, appeared the first
germ of the missionary spirit among the native converts
of the South Sea Islands.   Freely they had received, and
from this time forward, freely did they give, till island
after island, group after group, were encircled in the
extended arms of Christian benevolence.

The history of the South Sea Islands is a history of
providential interpositions.   Pomare, King of Tahiti,
proposed to his assembled chiefs the adoption of Christianity and the destruction of their idol gods.   Many
chiefs strenuously oppose.   A powerful chief comes forward, accompanied by his wife.   They cordially second
the king's proposition, declaring that they had, for some
time past, been contemplating the destruction of their
own idols.   This state of mind had been induced by the
death of a beloved and only daughter.   Having in vain
sought help from priests and gods, by all that rich sacrifices and profuse presents could avail, they were bitterly
enraged at their gods, and ready to cast them away as
useless.   The scale now seemed turning in favor of
Christianity; when another occurrence threatened more
than to balance it.   *Tapua*, another mighty chief and a
formidable warrior, who had conquered many islands,
was present at this consultation, and threatened by every
means in his power to oppose the king's proposition to
destroy the idols.   But his puissant arm was soon palsied,
and his haughty spirit yielded to the all-conquering scythe
of death.   His timely removal left behind no formidable
obstacle to the destruction of idolatry and the introduc-

tion of Christianity.* But for the death of this chief,
Christianity, it is believed, could not have been introduced.

Who can read the record of such events, and not discern the hand of God? What miracles once effected,
may now be achieved by the special interpositions of
Providence.

The introduction of the gospel at Aitutaki, was similar
to that of Tahiti. The death of a chief's daughter so
incensed the parents against the gods, and impaired the
confidence of the people in their aid, that they immediately abandoned them. There is, perhaps, not a more
marked interposition of Providence in the whole history
of Christianity, than in the extensive and almost simultaneous movements among the Pagan nations of the
Pacific to cast away their idols and to embrace a new
religion.

The people of another Island—Mangaia—brutally
abuse the first teachers sent them, and drive them from
their shores. A disease breaks out among them, which
spares neither age nor youth, high nor low. They believe it to be the vengeance of the "God of the strangers;"
and from this time they received the missionaries gladly,
and cordially embraced the religion of the cross.

In another instance a native Christian woman of Tahiti
is providentially cast on the beautiful but idolatrous Island
of Rarotonga. She speaks freely of the change which
Christianity had produced on her native island. These
things came to the ears of the king, and as a consequence
the king and royal household, the chiefs and people, were
prepared to receive the new religion, as it was shortly
after introduced. In another instance, a foul wind ar-
rests the "Messenger of Peace," (the name of the missionary vessel,) which was bearing Mr. Williams from
one island to another in his errands of mercy, and he is,
much to his disappointment, and after contending in vain
for several days with the elements, compelled to put in at

* While the king was meditating and proposing to destroy the idol gods, the young
man who kept them formed the bold resolution of doing the deed. A day is fixed;
a pile of combustibles prepared; the people are gathered around, and the idols are
brought out and thrown on the pile.

the Island of Mangaia.   Here had been gained from the
moral wastes of Paganism a beautiful vineyard.   The
vine brought out of Egypt had been planted here, and had
taken some root, and began to put forth its tender branches,
but the vandal foot of war was raised over it, and but one
day later and the hedge would have been broken down,
and that vine trodden under foot.   The heathen chiefs
had determined, by one decisive blow, to rid themselves
of the whole Christian party.   Mr. W., with two or three
Christian chiefs, hastened on shore, repaired to the hostile
chiefs, and, before the deadly attack of the morrow came,
the raging tempest was assuaged—the war prevented.
And the happy result was the dissolution of the league
against the Christians, and the removal of most of the
heathen to the Christian settlement.

It is, indeed, a fact worthy of remark, that no considerable Island in the South Seas embraced Christianity without a *war*, though always defensive on the part of the
Christians.   Providence here singularly interposed, discomfited the heathen, gave the victory to his people, and
established the religion of the cross.

I shall adduce but one illustration more :   It was long in
the heart of the indefatigable Williams, (since murdered
and eaten by the savages,) to carry the news of salvation
to the Navigators' or Samoa Islands.   The reluctance of
his wife dissuaded him from the enterprise.   But the
thousands of that interesting group shall not perish without the light of the Gospel.   Two or three years pass,
and the design in the mind of Williams seems to be abandoned.   His wife is brought by the heavy hand of God
to suffer a protracted and severe illness.   She revolves in
her mind why the hand of God is thus laid on her, and
what is *the* lesson he would have her learn.   She says to
her husband, "I freely consent to your absence in your
contemplated visit to the Navigators' Islands."   Nor was
the hand of God less manifest in the progress than in the
commencement of this important, and, in many respects,
hazardous undertaking.

They touch on their way at the Island of Tongatabu—
an active respectable looking native presents himself, says
he is a chief of the Navigators' Islands, and related to the

most influential families. His assertions are corroborated; and he desires and obtains a passage to his native islands in the mission ship, promising to do all in his power to favor the introduction of the gospel there. During the voyage he informs Mr. Williams that he need anticipate but one formidable obstacle to the realization of his wishes in relation to the Navigators' Islands: it was the violent opposition which might be met from *Tamafainga*, a kind of high-priest, in whom it was said "the spirit of the gods dwelt." If *he* opposed, all further attempts would be vain. But they are wafted on by the favorable breeze, and seem soon about to land on the desired spot. But adverse winds blow, and a furious storm drives them from their course. Their sails are rent, the vessel crippled, and several of the men sick with influenza. All these things seemed against them—why could they not have been conveyed by that favoring breeze to the destined landing? for they came on an errand of mercy, and Heaven is not wont to frown on such enterprises.

After several days painful delay they arrive, and what must have been their admiration of the dealings of Providence, when they were told that *Tamafainga was dead!* He was killed but ten days before. The storm had detained them, that they might arrive precisely at *the right time*, to introduce the new religion. Ten days earlier, their efforts would have been abortive on account of the opposition of the high-priest. A few days later his successor would have been appointed, and all their attempts equally fruitless.

Thus the gospel was introduced into those islands under the most favorable auspices, and followed by the most unprecedented success.

But I pause for the present. To write a history of missionary providences would be to write a history of missions.

Our subject affords *a delightful assurance of ultimate success in all our well-directed efforts to convert the world.* We need only to recur to the illustrations already adduced, to convey to our minds infinite satisfaction that He who has begun the good work will carry it on. He that can make the winds, the waves, the pestilence, the fury of war, his ministers, can work and none can hinder. The Lord hath sworn and he cannot go back, that he will give to his Son the heathen for his inheritance, and the uttermost parts of the earth for a possession. The angel having the everlasting gospel to preach to them that dwell on the face of the whole earth, has begun his glorious flight. Move on, thou blessed messenger of peace, till earth's remotest bounds shall join in the grand jubilee of the world's redemption.

CHAPTER VIII.

MODERN MISSIONS continued.—Henry Obookiah and the Sandwich Islands. Vancouver and the Council. Dr. Vanderkemp and South Africa. Africaner. Hand of God in the Origin of Benevolent Societies. Remarkable preservation of Missionaries.

"*And I saw another angel fly in the midst of Heaven, having the everlasting gospel to preach to them that dwell on the face of the earth.*" Rev. xiv. 6.

IN the last chapter, attention was directed to an interesting period in the history of Christianity. We saw the angel, having the everlasting gospel to preach, directing his adventurous flight over the broad Pacific, scattering blessings from his wings on the beautiful isles that sit on its bosom. "Truly, the isles *waited* for the law of their God." In not a few instances, the people, in expectation of the missionary ship, cast away their idols, erected places for public worship, and *waited* for the coming of the "Messenger of Peace." It is related that in several instances, before the gospel was introduced, though expected, "they were known to assemble at six o'clock on Sabbath morning, sit in silence an hour or more, and repeat this a second, and even a third time, during the day.'

Before leaving this new and wide theatre on which

God has of late, and in a most extraordinary manner, been pleased to display the riches of his grace, I shall recount yet another instance of remarkable providential interposition. The illustration is familiar—you will discern the finger of God in the tale.

An orphan boy on one of the Sandwich Islands, of twelve years old, is seen escaping from a scene of the most disgusting carnage. He bears on his back an infant brother of only two months old. They are pursued; the infant is transfixed with a spear, while the lad is spared and led away the captive of war. He is the only survivor of his family. The father and mother, with these two boys, had, on the approach of the enemy to their village, fled to the mountains; but were soon sought out and cut to pieces before the face of their children. Henry, the surviving boy, remained for some time with the man whom he had seen kill his father and his mother—is at length found by an uncle, who takes him to his house, and keeps him one or two years. Again is he, with his aunt, a prisoner of war—makes his escape—secretes himself at a little distance, whence he soon saw his aunt conducted from the prison to a precipice, from which she was thrown headlong, and dashed to pieces. Now alone in the world and disconsolate, he determines to end a miserable existence in the same way he had seen his relative meet her tragic death. As soon as the enemy disappeared from the precipice, he approached to execute his horrid purpose. But being discovered by one of the hostile party, he is rescued just in time to save a life which should be the hand of Providence to bring life and immortality to light among his benighted countrymen.

Again we find him, by some means once more restored to his uncle; yet weary of life, and the last of his race, he never ceases to bemoan his parents. In this state of despondency and wretchedness, he conceives the strange idea of seeking an asylum in some foreign country.

While in this state of mind an American ship arrives. Young *Obookiah* was immediately on board to seek a passage to America. His uncle refused to let him go, and shut him up in his house. But the young adventurer

12*

finds means to escape, and is again on board, and is
allowed to sail.

But mark the next link in the chain.   There is on
board this vessel a pious young man, (Russel Hubbard,)
a student of Yale College, who becomes a friend of young
Henry, and takes much pains to instruct him in the rudiments of learning, of which he was totally ignorant.

After a few months we find Henry in New Haven.
Wandering about the college yard, he attracts the attention of E. W. Dwight, who, from this time, becomes his
friend and teacher—is introduced into the family of Dr.
Dwight, and finally comes to the knowledge of Samuel
J. Mills, who takes him to his father's, in Torringford.
Thence, after some time, he is transferred to Andover—
becomes a Christian—lives in different places in Massachusetts, Connecticut and New Hampshire—every where
adorns a good profession—manifests a burning zeal for
the salvation of his countrymen, and much solicitude for
the salvation of all men.   At length we find him in the
mission school at Cornwall—the same decided, consistent
Christian ; the industrious scholar; the amiable companion, ever loved and highly respected.

He has by this time produced a strong interest in favor
of the Sandwich Islands.   A mission thither was always
his fond hope and the object of his unremitting toil.   It
was a much cherished idea that he might return, a messenger of peace, to his deluded countrymen ; and for this
purpose he used all diligence to be prepared.   But, strange
dispensation of Providence! he is cut down by the relentless hand of death, before he sees one of his benevolent
schemes for his native island executed.

But let us pause here and mark the hand of God.   The
time of blessed visitation had come for the isles of the sea.
The English churches had already taken of the spoil of
their idols, and were rejoicing and being enriched by
their conquests.   The American Zion must participate
in the honor and profit of the war.   Hence Henry Obookiah, an obscure boy, without father or mother, kindred
or tie, to bind him to his native land, must be brought to
our shores ; be removed from place to place, from institution to institution, everywhere fanning into a flame the

smoking flax of a missionary spirit, and giving it some definite direction; be made the occasion of rousing the slumbering energies of the church on behalf of the heathen, and of kindling a spirit of prayer and benevolence in the hearts of God's people; and finally, and principally, his short and interesting career, and, perhaps, more than all, his widely lamented *death*, should originate and mature a scheme of missions to those islands, the present aspect of which presents scenes of interest scarcely inferior to those of the apostolic age. Behold, what a great matter a little fire kindleth!

But there is another aspect in which we must view the pleasing interposition. While Henry Obookiah was being used as the hand of Providence in preparing (through Mills and Hall, Griffin and Dwight, and others on whom his influence bore,) the American church to engage in a plan of benevolent action, definitely directed towards the islands of the Pacific, there was a process transpiring *at* the islands still more interesting, if possible, and more strongly marked as the handi-work of God. Already had the decree passed for the destruction of idolatry, and those islands, too, were *waiting* for the law of their God.

An incident here will illustrate. I give it as taken from the lips of the Rev. Mr. Richards on his late visit to this country. On the arrival of our first company of missionaries, a consultation of the king and chiefs was held, whether they should be allowed to remain. Different opinions were advanced, supported by as different reasons. The second day of these deliberations had nearly closed without any decisive result. Now there came into the council the aged secretary of the late king, who had just returned from a neighboring island. He had long been a sort of chronicler of the nation. His mind, in the absence of written documents, was a kind of historical depot. His opinion was asked, and his decision determined the momentous question, whether the "glad tidings of great joy," which had then, for the first time, reached the islands, should be proclaimed, or the darkness of death which then brooded over them become darker than before.

Addressing the young king, he said: "what did the late king, your father, enjoin on you as touching these men who now ask your protection and a residence among us ?"   "He left in charge nothing concerning these men," said the young king.   "Did he not repeat to you what *Vancouver* said to him, as he looked upon our gods, and pitied our folly ?—how he said that not many years would elapse before Englishmen would come and teach a better religion, and that you must protect such teachers, and listen to them, and embrace their religion?   Now they have come, and what would your father have you do with them ?"

He resumed his seat ; the young king recalled the charge of his royal sire, and this "little matter" fixed the decision that opened the flood-gates of mercy to thousands of the most abject of our race, and formed the commencement of a successful career of benevolent action which shall not cease with time.   Discern ye not the finger of God here ?

But the history of the introduction of the gospel at the Sandwich Islands, is too strikingly illustrative of a superintending Providence, to be passed without further detail. Yet the history of other missions may furnish illustrations no less interesting.   We shall here, at every step, trace the foot-prints of providential interposition.

For some time previous to the introduction of the gospel at those Islands, Providence was actively preparing the way for such an event.   The Islands were now brought to the notice of civilized and Christian nations ; a few such men as Vancouver had visited them and done much to prepare the native mind favorably to receive the means of civil and religious renovation, when they should be offered ; the conflicting interests of different chiefs had been very much annihilated in the conquests of Kamehameha, who had consolidated the whole group under one government, and thus prepared the way for a *national* reformation.   As in the days of Augustus Cesar and the advent of Christ, the clangor of war was hushed, and facilities, as at no former period, afforded for the spread of the truth.   And, more than all, a *prediction* existed that the time drew nigh when a "*communication should be made to them from heaven entirely different from any thing they had known, and that the tabus of the coun-*

try should be destroyed." This singular prediction, the result, no doubt, of that presentiment or general expectation which is wont to pervade the public mind on the eve of some great national change, did much to prepossess the minds of the popular mass to let go their idols, and accept the gospel when offered. It was the dim shadow of events yet hid in the dark future ; it was the still, small voice of God, announcing his purposes of mercy to these long-benighted islands.

A few specific instances will indicate how God provided himself with some of the chief instruments in the late extraordinary work at the islands, and how he removed obstacles.

A female child is born in an obscure corner of the Island of Maui. Her parents, who had once basked in the sunshine of the royal favor, are now languishing in the shades of neglect, destitute and depressed. Twice, when an infant, was she providentially saved from drowning. Wrapped in a roll of *kapa,* she was laid by her parents on the top of a double canoe, from which, as tossed by the waves, she fell into the sea. The floating *kapa* being discovered in time, she was drawn as from a watery grave. Again, when in her childhood, being near the sea with her mother, she was caught by a huge wave, rolling suddenly in, and in its recoil carried her beyond her depth, and was for the moment given up for lost. She was now a third time rescued from the jaws of death; yet none but the Great Deliverer knew for what a noble purpose.

It was a stormy period of Hawaiian history. Her childhood was spent amidst scenes of violence and blood. A revolution is in progress ; a ferocious, warlike king of Hawaii, (Kamehameha,) gains the dominion of the islands ; the destinies of the family of *Kaahumanu,* (the heroine of my tale,) begin to rise. Her father being one of the conqueror's chief supporters, she, like the renowned Noor Mahal, of oriental memory, is brought to the notice of this western Mogul,—is numbered among his wives, —becomes his favorite queen, and at his death, as regent, holds the kingdom in trust for his son.

While a bigoted idolater, proud, haughty, independent,

she gave indications of possessing the elements of the noble character which was afterwards exhibited in the humble, zealous Christian, the pious Regent and the enlightened philanthropist.

To her, principally, was owing the abolition of the *tabu* system and of image worship, and to her, more than to any other person, was the American mission indebted for permission to remain on the islands after the expiration of their year's probation, and for their success. While yet unreclaimed from the bondage of idolatry, her proud, independent spirit, led her to seize the first opportunity, (offered by the death of her late royal husband,) to disenthrall herself and the chief women of the nation from the chains and degradation of the tabu. Placed providentially next the throne, where she could speak with authority, and supported by several chief women of royal blood, she boldly asserted the "rights of woman, unrestrained by a lordly husband," and protested against the unreasonable disabilities under which they had been placed. She demanded equal privileges with *men*, in respect to eating and drinking, and the termination of those distinctions and restraints which were felt to be degrading and oppressive.

This important step gained, she had unwittingly opened the way for the introduction of the gospel. She favored the plans and wishes of the mission from the first, and was an efficient instrument in its establishment and in its progress, though not herself brought under its vital power. A withering sickness is at length sent upon her, and she seems nigh unto death. The missionaries are now afforded the opportunity to show what kindness, sympathy and hope, the gospel holds out to them who languish and draw near to death. She appreciates their sympathies and instructions ; seems deeply impressed ; becomes a firmer friend of the mission, yet is not converted. A few years more roll away, and we find her in a mission school ; the truth is gradually gaining ascendency in her mind ; she yields to its power, and becomes a humble, lovely, decided, energetic Christian.

In the mean time, by the death of the young king, she again becomes Regent of the kingdom, and loses no opportunity to use her great influence, whether in the formation of laws, the restraint of sin, or the encouragement of virtue ; in the promotion of education ; in tours over the islands to foster the new work of reform, or in her personal teachings ; and more than all, in the example of a pure, unostentatious, effective piety, to hasten the complete subjugation of her islands to the rule of Immanuel.

I hazard nothing in saying, if posterity shall do justice to her memory, history will accord to Kaahumanu a high rank as a ruler, a statesman and a Christian. She lived and reigned in troublous times. The nation was just emerging from barbarism. A complete revolution was to be effected, from the throne to the meanest subject. The fountains of the great deep were broken up, and a new order of things was to be established in government, in morals and in religion ; and it is believed the annals of history present few persons, under the circumstances in which she lived and reigned, who have acquitted themselves better towards man and towards God,—more essentially aiding the progress of Divine truth and of civil liberty.

Having mentioned the death of the young king, (Lihoiho,) we are reminded of another remarkable providential interposition, without which all the awakened elements of reform might have been crushed in the bud. The young king was a wayward, unstable, dissipated youth, easily led astray by wicked foreigners. He promised little as a Reformer of the nation,—was likely to prove a formidable obstacle. But what a singular interposition of the hand of God now! The king suddenly conceives the idea of going to England, uninvited, unannounced, and seemingly for no adequate or definite purpose. The excellent Kaahumanu now becomes Regent. A few months elapse, and the king dies in England ; and a few months more and his remains are brought back to the island in the frigate Blonde, commanded by the excellent Lord Byron, (cousin of the poet,) who, perhaps, fulfilled the most important mission of Providence in the whole matter. The counsels he gave to the chiefs and people, his noble bearing towards the mission and its ob-

jects, the notoriety and character he gave to the mission,
the rebuke which his enlightened and enlarged philanthropy, administered to the narrow, selfish and wicked
policy of many foreigners at the islands, all conspired to
make the visit of the Blonde most opportune and influential for good. It was worth, to the cause of moral reformation, the sending into the Pacific of the whole British
navy.

The king being removed, and certain ill-affected chiefs
absent as a part of the king's suite, the good work went
on apace.   Now Kaahumanu, (whose regency continued
nine years,) aided by the excellent chief Kalanimoku,
who, from a very early period in the mission, was a
staunch supporter, and Kaumualii, late king of Kauai,
who had been as early and as heartily enlisted on behalf
of Reform, on account of the safe return of his son from
America, and the kind attentions and expense bestowed
on him there to educate him, (another important link in
the providential chain,) set herself in good earnest to the
work of radical Reform at her islands.   And so deeply
had its foundations been laid before any very formidable
adverse influences were permitted to return upon them,
that they could not now be removed from their place.

That a restless, roving, dissipated youth, clad in the
robes of savage royalty, should conceive the freak of
going to England, made but a small ripple on the waters
of the great world; yet it was again a first link in a most
interesting series of events: a little fire that kindled a
great matter.

Among the hostile chiefs, the mission had not a more
formidable foe than Boki, the governor of Oahu. He
had accompanied the king to England, and returned, having learned to admire only the worse features of civilized
life. His vacillating course, wishing to seem to be carrying out the policy of the Regency, while at heart opposed
to it, his hostility to the Reforms of Kaahumanu, and
his connivance at the wicked devices of certain wicked
foreigners, and his readiness to aid them in their schemes
to evade or break down the laws of the government,
made him truly a formidable foe. So mature did his hostility at length become, that he headed an insurrection

against the government, with the intent to assume the reins himself.

But mark the hand of God here, and you will see how he and many of his insurrectionary and most to be feared adherents, are put out of the way. Nothing is easier with Him who turns the hearts of men as the rivers of water are turned.

Boki suddenly conceives the notion of an expedition to a distant island, to cut sandal wood, hoping thereby to repair his dilapidated fortunes. Pursuing his preparations on the Sabbath, he embarks in two vessels, with more than four hundred of his adherents, natives and foreigners, most of whom *hate the light* which now for the first time is dawning on the islands. Never, perhaps, were two vessels ever freighted with more rancorous hostility to the bands and cords of a pure religion.

And did they return in all safety? No: the Lord had separated them from his people, that he might destroy them. When far out at sea, a storm arose. The vessel in which Boki embarked, is heard of no more. The other returns with only twenty survivors, twelve natives and eight foreigners. Like Pharaoh and his host, the sea opened its mouth and swallowed them up alive. Such was probably the fate of the vessel in which Boki sailed. The other was overtaken by a mortal sickness; one hundred and eighty died, and twenty were left sick on a distant island.

Thus did God disarm the strong man, and bring to nought the devices of the wicked. His little church on those late favored islands, is as the apple of his eye. As of old, He "suffered no man to do them wrong; yea, He reproved kings for their sake, saying, touch not mine anointed, and do my prophets no harm."

Were it needful, a great variety of similar instances might be adduced; such as the very timely visit of the Rev. William Ellis, London missionary from the Society islands, and Messrs. Tyerman and Bennet, deputation from the London society, with several South Sea converts. Nothing could be more opportune than their arrival at this time, to counsel, encourage and assist our mission in its incipient stages, and when few in number,

13

and of small resources and experience ; and especially
opportune and providential was the visit of the South
Sea converts.   They were not only living illustrations
of what the gospel can do, but they brought a report of
the success of the gospel on their islands, and the readiness of the chiefs and people to abandon their idols, and
embrace Christianity, which was more influential in per-
suading the kings, chiefs and people of the Sandwich
Islands, than the eloquence of scores of foreign missionaries.

Or such as the visits to the islands of the United States
sloops-of-war, Peacock and Vincennes, whose command-
ers and officers, by their gentlemanly conduct and enlightened Christian philanthropy, imposed a timely check,
and, by the uprightness of their intercourse with chiefs
and people, administered a timely and salutary rebuke
on the waywardness of a class of loose and vicious foreign residents.   And in nothing, perhaps, was the hand
of God more conspicuous than in the manner in which
the shameless outrages, from time to time committed by
this same class of foreigners, such as ship-masters, sailors,
naval officers, were overruled for the furtherance of the
gospel.   Not an attack was made on the mission which
did not add character to the missionaries, give notoriety
and reputation to the mission and its work, and deepen,
in the minds of its patrons, the conviction that a great
and a good work was in successful progress.

But we have, perhaps, lingered too long on those specks
on the ocean.   Our apology is, that the arm of the Lord
is there wonderfully revealed.

We turn now in another direction, where the footsteps
of Providence are quite as visible in the establishment of
another mission.   I refer to South Africa ; and at a time
when her moral atmosphere was darker than the ebon
hue of her people.   Scarcely has any portion of the human family been so debased and abused as the South
Africans.   And as the day of deliverance drew near, the
bondage of sin grew more and more cruel.   The corrupt
mass became, of itself, yearly more corrupt, till it seemed
that a few years more must have exterminated a wretched
race from the face of the earth.   They approached the

climax of their misery. They had learned that sin is an evil thing, and bitter, yet its *dregs* they had not drunken till they were subjected to the relentless despotism and the shameless outrages of the Dutch boers. They were treated as brute beasts—were shot down in their hunting excursions as the jackal or the hyena. A daughter of a Dutch governor was heard to boast how many natives she had shot with her own hands.

Yet there was deliverance for the poor Hottentot. The star of hope rose out of the darkest cloud that ever brooded over a wretched land. Providence was all this time preparing for them the full horn of salvation. An iniquitous government was filling up its measure, and hastening to its doom; while another nation, which Heaven has appointed to open the door of the nations to the gospel, was ready to take possession, and the almoners of Heaven's mercy were laying in rich stores for distribution among the needy sons of Ham. How events so unexpected and extraordinary were brought to pass, may be seen better from another point of observation.

A little pleasure boat is seen sailing on the river Maese, near Dort, in Holland. It contains a fine looking, gentlemanly man, in middle age, with his wife and daughter. They glide along in all the gay luxuriance of a life of ease, and, perhaps, never feel more secure of life and pleasure. A cloud has risen—the sky is overcast—a squall disturbs the waters of the placid stream. The boat is upset, and the wife and daughter are drowned. The husband, after a long struggle and hair breadth escape of death, having been carried down the stream nearly a mile, is picked up by the crew of a vessel, which, providentially, had at *this very moment* been loosed from her moorings.

As the bereaved father and disconsolate husband returned to his solitary dwelling, his citizens recognized in him Dr. Vanderkemp, the gentleman of affluence and pleasure, who had come to spend at Dort the remainder of his days in literary pursuits and rural amusements. They had known him only as the man of the world, the traveler, the scholar, the infidel. Though a son of an excellent Dutch clergyman, and a scholar of the first

rank in the university of Leyden, he chose the army as
the road to honor and affluence. Here he served sixteen
years; when, unfortunately, he made a wreck of moral
character by imbibing principles of the grossest infidelity.
Next, we find him in the University of Edinburgh, pursuing studies preparatory to the practice of medicine.
Next honorably and successfully exercising his profession on the island of Zealand; and, finally, the retired
gentleman at Dort.

But from the hour that God sent his tempest and sunk
his little bark, and buried his hopes beneath the waves,
and made the earth around look dark, a change comes
over the scene. The infidel is reclaimed. The retired
soldier, the man of leisure, the scholar, that was laying
down his armor, and yielding ingloriously to the fascina-
tions of pleasure, enlists anew. When the Great Captain had need of another Paul, to bear his name to the
Gentiles—to raise the standard of the cross in Africa, he
arrested the proud and unbelieving VANDERKEMP—cut off
his family with a stroke—covered his pleasant home with
desolation—loosed his strong hold on earth, and then
opened the way to him—to his vast learning, his long accumulating experience and wisdom—his enterprise and
wealth, an ample field in South Africa.

On the ensuing Sabbath he is found in the long-neglected sanctuary, commemorating the death of our blessed
Lord—and as Christ is evidently set before him, *crucified and slain for the remission of sins,* his heart is subdued
by the power of divine grace, and he receives the Lamb
of God as the great sacrifice and atonement, and henceforward he seeks to do the will of his new master.

About this time the London Missionary Society began
to direct attention to the long-neglected and abused continent of Africa. An address of that society reached
Vanderkemp. Men, money, influence, learning, experience were wanted for the noble enterprise. He had them
all—his warm heart took fire: "Lord, what wilt thou
have me to do?" Though the meridian of his life was
passed, its remaining suns shall shine on the benighted
land of Ham. His purpose is fixed—and soon the winds
are wafting him to the land of the Hottentots and the

Caffres; where he labors, the indefatigable and successful missionary, thirteen years.

But this is not all: while an instrumentality is preparing in Europe, the field for its operation is opening in
Africa: while young Vanderkemp is cultivating his gigantic mind at the university, and storing it with knowledge,
he knew not why—while for sixteen years he was sub-
jecting himself to the hardships of war, that he might
"endure hardship as a good soldier"—or pursuing his professional studies at Edinburgh—or gaining wisdom and
experience in professional life, a corresponding line of
Providence is discovered at the Cape of Good Hope.
The power of the Dutch, who have long abused and
humbled the natives, and done much to *scourge* them into
a compliance with almost any change, is on the wane;
and while the attention of the London Missionary Society
is directed thither, and only three years previous to the
embarking of Dr. Vanderkemp, South Africa is thrown
into the hands of the British, and a wide and effectual
door opened for the admission of the gospel of peace.
And now, over those once sterile regions, where not a
plant of virtue could grow, the Rose of Sharon blooms.
Thousands of once wretched Hottentots sing for joy, and
the dreary habitations of the Caffres are vocal with the
praises of our God.

Before quitting this interesting portion of benevolence
and providential development, I must allude at least to a
single individual instance. I refer to the conversion of
AFRICANER, the most formidable and blood-thirsty chief
that ever prowled over the plains or hid in the mountains
of Africa. He was the terror of every tribe; the traveler feared him more than all other dangers that might
befall him; and he most emphatically breathed out threatenings and slaughter against the disciples of Christ. He
had attacked and burnt out the mission which had settled
on his territory, and dispersed the missionaries under circumstances the most distressing. But, thanks to the
power of sovereign grace, this lion could be tamed. The
Lion of the tribe of Judah was stronger than he. His
heart at length relented. Saul was among the prophets.
He received the missionary into his kraal—listened to the

13*

message of redeeming love, and found it the power of
God to salvation.   Henceforth he was gentle as a lamb—
docile as a child.   And he became as famous as a peace-
maker as he had been as a rioter in blood and carnage.
God arrested him—and through him gave the gospel free
access to many tribes, and made him a nursing father to
all who chose the new and more excellent way.

Copious extracts might be taken from the history of
modern missions illustrative of the same thing.   But we
need not multiply examples.   I have undertaken to give
only specimens of the manner in which God has guided
the flight of the angel—removing out of his way every
obstacle, giving success under the most untoward circumstances—making the wrath of man praise Him—and
using the winds, the floods, pestilence, fire and sword, to
subserve the great purposes of his mercy in the spread of
the gospel.

While watching the ways of an all-controlling Providence in the progress of Christianity the last fifty years,
other items in this connection deserve attention: As *the
almost simultaneous origin of modern benevolent societies—
their providential history—*and *the remarkable preservation
of their missionaries from the hand of violence.*

It is always interesting to watch the processes of Divine
Wisdom.   His purposes never fail through omissions,
oversights, or mistakes.   One thing is always made to
answer to another.   When he has opened a field and
prepared it for the seed, he never fails for the want of laborers.   Or when he has raised up and prepared his laborers, his plans never fail from a lack of pecuniary means.
Not only has he all hearts in his hands, but the silver
and the gold are his.   In accordance with the universal
wisdom by which he sees from the beginning to the end,
and his universal supremacy over all, by which, with infinite ease, he accomplishes all his purposes, we find there
has sprung into existence a beautiful sisterhood of benevolent societies.

Is there an increasing demand for the Bible, which shall
soon grow into a universal demand from the four quarters
of the earth?   There is a mysterious moving on the
minds of a few pious persons in London—they meet to

provide means to give the Bible to the poor in Wales—
whence came the first feeble cry.   Hence a Bible Society.
But how little did those pious few expect so soon to become a mighty host—how little expect their deliberations
would issue in the formation of a Bible society, destined,
with its collateral streams, to supply the whole world with
the waters of life—in less than a quarter of a century to
issue ten millions of Bibles ; or since its formation twenty-
six millions—and in whole nations supplying every family
with the word of life.

Or have vicissitudes in nations, and changes in empires opened new and large territories for occupancy by
the gospel, a spirit of benevolence begins to pervade the
church.   The holy fire, kindled by some invisible agency,
begins to burn, and spread from heart to heart.   And as
genuine piety is social, and holy and benevolent desires
seek the company of their kindred, a holy confederacy
springs into existence to meet the new demand.   Hence
a missionary society.   Providence created the demand—
and the same unerring councillor and unfailing executor,
furnishes the corresponding supply.   And hence, too,
tract, education, and home missionary societies, and all
those combinations of holy and benevolent energies, the
objects of which are to carry forward, in their respective
departments at home and abroad, the evangelization of
the world.   They are the legitimate offspring of Providence, begotten in the council chamber of eternity, and
brought into existence nearly at the same time, and at
the identical moment when the wheels of Providence, in
their sure and irresistible revolution among the nations,
had arrived at a point where such instrumentalities could
be used.

I have already alluded to the providential origin of benevolent societies.—It is enough that they rose into being
at *precisely the right time,* and at the bidding of *Him who
spake and it was done.*   "It is remarkable, says a late
British writer," (Rev. Mr. Thorp,) "that these noble institutions of Christian benevolence originated at the momentous crisis when the pagan kingdoms begun to shake
under the visitations of Divine wrath.   It was amidst the
rage and madness of atheism—amidst the horrors and

chaos of anarchy and revolution, that these societies rose with placid dignity; combining, as they rose, the wealth, the talent, the influence, and the energies of myriads of Christians, in various nations, and all denominations, in one general effort to rescue the heathen world from the bondage of corruption. Verily, the finger of God is here. It is the Lord's doing, and it is marvelous in our sight."

And there is much in the progressive, providential history of these societies, which merits a passing notice here. Take the Church Missionary Society of England, and in reference to a single particular, viz: an increase of *funds* to suit every exigency, and we shall see it. Items like the following are recorded in her history: In the fourteenth year of the society's existence, her funds rose from sixteen thousand dollars to fifty-two thousand. That was the year the East India Bill passed, which laid open to the benevolent efforts of British Christians the one hundred millions of Hindoostan. In her twenty-seventh year, her funds rose from two hundred and four thousand dollars to two hundred and thirty-five thousand. This was the year of jubilee in the West Indies, when a new and effectual door was opened to the society by the act of emancipation. Again, in 1838, her funds rose from three hundred and forty-seven thousand dollars to four hundred and four thousand. It was in this year that the spirit was poured out from on high, upon the province of *Krishnughar*, and an unwonted demand made for laborers in this newly opened vineyard. Thirty or forty villages almost immediately embraced Christianity; which number has since been doubled, and some four thousand natives numbered as converts.

God provides for every exigency. We should not soon find an end of quoting providential interpositions in the history of benevolent societies.

There is one point more: *the remarkable preservation of missionaries.* It must have arrested the attention of even the casual observer, that this class of men have been peculiarly under the protecting hand of Heaven. How various have been the vicissitudes of their lives, yet how few their casualties. By sea and by land, they have been subjected to all sorts of perils. Their dwelling-place has often been among robbers, and generally among savage men, and in barbarous climes. In the missionary enterprise it is no unfrequent occurrence that expeditions are undertaken by a few defenceless men, in the face of hostile and despotic governments, and in despite of dangers from climate, wild beasts, deserts, rivers, or human foes, which, to the eye that sees not the protecting Hand, seems incredible and presumptuous. Yet how very few have fallen by violence. Of the thousands that have rode on the angry billows, or dwelt in the midst of thick perils, few have made their grave in the deep, or come to an untimely end.

Remarkable preservations stand on the records of the flight of the "angel having the everlasting gospel to preach." God has kept his embassadors to the Gentiles, as the apple of his eye. It is enough that I adduce a few instances as specimens:

To pass over the many exceedingly interesting inci dents in the lives of the early missionaries to the North American Indians, in which the most barbarous plots for their lives were frustrated, and the most inveterate hostility of priests and chiefs, disarmed the moment it seemed just about to burst on the heads of the missionaries ; and, also, instances not a few in the early history of Moravian missions, in which they escaped death so narrowly ; or, as they seemed inclined to believe, so *miraculously*, as to induce the belief among them, that they did experience the literal fulfillment of the promise : " They shall take up serpents, and if they drink any deadly thing, it shall not hurt them :" I will quote from the records of providential preservation, the following : "Irritated by the unwelcome restraints of Christianity, several dissolute young men, on one of the South Sea islands, determined on the assassination of Mr. Williams and his colleagues. The time fixed to strike the first horrid blow was when Mr. W. should be on his way to a neighboring island, in the regular discharge of his official duties. To make sure their opportunity, four of the conspirators volunteered their services to convey him thither. His fate seemed inevitable. The hour for starting had arrived, when Mr. W. discovered that his boat was wholly unfit for the sea,

and the voyage, much to his regret, was abandoned
But the assassins did not abandon their murderous design
so.   On the following day he was again saved, by the
providential interposition of a friend, from the execution
of a plot which had been laid to murder him in his own
house.   Again and again did he escape death, the fatally
aimed dart being warded off by an unseen hand."

The South Africa mission abounds in such incidents :
a ruffian raises a dagger to plunge it in the heart of Mr.
Kramar.   Providentially a little girl is standing by, who
wards off the blow.   Again, an abandoned wretch forms
the murderous design of cutting off the whole mission—
missionaries, teachers, church and people, by throwing
poison into their well.   But the Keeper of Israel, who
never slumbers nor sleeps, had again set a *child* to watch,
and warn his chosen ones of harm.   Her timely notice
saved the mission, and brought the culprit to condign
punishment.

Again, a party of Bushmen lay in ambush near the
house of Mr. Kicherer, and were preparing to discharge
a volley of poisoned arrows at him, as he sat near an open
window ; but the same little girl that saved the life of Mr.
Kramar was near to act as the mouth of God, to give the
timely warning, and, as the hand of Providence, to rescue
his servant from a premature death.   And in another
case, a criminal, having escaped from prison at the Cape,
and insinuated himself into the family of Mr. K., formed
the murderous design of assassinating his host, and moving
off with his cattle and goods to some remote horde.   But
as the villain enters the room to strike the deadly blow,
Mr. K. is roused as by an unseen hand, and, in his terror,
put to flight the murderer.

Read the whole history of missions, and you will find
on almost every page, a record of some kindly interposi
tion of the Divine Hand in the preservation of nis chosen
vessels, to bear his name among the Gentiles.   We might
call up such examples as Judson, Hough and Wade,
amidst the mad Birmese, waiting but a signal to execute
the bloody mandate of the king.   The signal is given—
which was the roar of British cannon ; yet the execu-
tioners, petrified with fear, cannot perform their bloody

mission, and the missionaries live ; or such examples as those of Bingham, Richards, and others at the Sandwich Islands, when ferociously attacked by infuriated gangs of seamen.

The idea of a special interposition here, is strikingly illustrated by a statement recently made by one of the Secretaries of the American Board.

" From the organization of the American Board of Commissioners for Foreign Missions, in September, 1810, to the death of Dr. Armstrong, the number of outward and home voyages, between the United States and foreign lands, made by persons in the employment of the Board, excluding twenty-seven, of whose completion intelligence has not yet been received, is seven hundred and four. These voyages have been made by four hundred and ninety-six persons, male and female, not including twelve now on their way to foreign lands for the first time. Of these voyages actually completed, four hundred and sixty-seven have each been from fifteen to eighteen thousand miles in length. If those voyages along the coast of the United States, on the great lakes, and on the western rivers, and those from one port to another in foreign countries, varying from five hundred to three thousand miles each, are included, and to them are added the voyages made by the children of missionaries, the whole number of voyages will exceed one thousand ; besides many shorter trips on seas, rivers and lakes. In all these, no individual connected with the Board has been shipwrecked, or has lost his life by drowning.

The number of ordained missionaries sent out by the Board, is two hundred and fifty-three ; physicians, twenty ; other male assistants, one hundred and twenty-two ; and females, four hundred and fifty-seven ; in all, eight hundred and fifty-two ; none of whom, so far as information has been received, have lost their lives, or been seriously injured, in their journeyings to or from their fields of labor, by land or water. Three—Messrs. Munson and Lyman, in Sumatra, and Doct. Satterlee, west of the Pawnee country—lost their lives by savage violence while on exploring tours ; and Rev. Mr. Benham, of the Siam mission, was drowned while crossing a river near nis own house. With these exceptions, all the explorations and other journeyings of these eight hundred and fifty-two missionary laborers have been, so far as can now be called to mind, without loss of life or serious accident.

Going back to the commencement of the operations of the Board, none of its treasurers, secretaries or agents, amounting to about fifty persons in all, have, in their various and extended journeyings by land and water, and in the almost pathless wilderness on the western frontiers and the contiguous Indian countries, met with any serious accident or calamity, till Dr. Armstrong perished in the wreck of the steamer Atlantic."

In conclusion, a single inference urges itself on our attention. It is this: God's tender regard and watchful care over his own cause. This cause is as the apple of his eye. No weapon raised against it has ever prospered. Not one jot or tittle of all he has said can fail; not one purpose be left unfulfilled. Has He said he will give the kingdom to his Son, and shall he not bring it to pass? Nothing can oppose his will; nothing hinder his arm once made bare to carry out his purposes. With what unwavering confidence, then, we may trust in God.

CHAPTER IX.

THE WESLEYAN REFORMATION; its origin and leaders; its rapid growth and wide extension; its great moral results.

METHODISM is one of the most extraórdinary facts of modern history. Its origin, the rapidity of its growth, its extension over so great a portion of Christendom, and the influence it has exerted, in so short a period of time, on the destinies of man in time and for eternity, give it a place in history, and especially designate it as a great providential arrangement, which may not be passed in this connection without some special notice. The Wesleyan Reformation is the third great religious movement in the onward march of the Christian church since her deliverance from the thraldom of the dark ages. The Reformation of the 16th century, developed and conducted by Martin Luther and the extraordinary men of his time, was a wonderful event, which, at every step of its progress, bears upon it the impress of the Divine Hand. The great religious movement of the 17th century, which we may call the Puritan Reformation, will ever stand as one of the great landmarks of history, far reaching in its influence, and permanent as the truth and the church of God. The great movement of the 18th century, which we have denominated the Wesleyan Reformation, was another of the few leading events of a kindred character, which ever and anon, at great intervals, revolutionize society and bless the world.

The first of the three named, was an intellectual, a civil, an ecclesiastical, and, incidental though not slightly, a moral and religious Reformation. It was a deliverance from the darkness of the middle ages, and from the religious and civil despotism of the Romish hierarchy. Yet the restoration of the Bible, and of sound doctrine to the church and to the mass of the people, was followed by a reformation of manners and a restoration of the spirit of piety. The second was the struggle of civil and religious liberty to emancipate itself from the persecuting hierarchy and the half reformed religion of England in the 18th century. This was a remarkable advance both in respect to the progress of civil government and of the Christian church; and the result of the movement has left its mark on the history of the world, never to be effaced so long as the virtues and institutions of the Puritans and their descendants shall bless the world. The third great religious movement named, was, in some respects, more extraordinary than either of the preceding. It assumed neither a civil, intellectual, nor ecclesiastical position. It begun purely as a *religious* movement—as the revival of a pure, evangelical religion. It sprung up in the bosom of the Established church, at a time when

spiritual religion in that church was at an exceedingly
low ebb. "In the days of Wesley many of her clergy
were openly and sadly scandulous." Many even but
miserably educated ; and "even the better educated were
often too busy in hunting, drinking, and card-playing, to
afford the time, or too lazy, to make the exertion, to write
their own sermons. "Livings" were too often bestowed
on unworthy persons through family considerations, and
the flock was but slightly cared for except for the fleece.
The consequence was that the living soul of religion had
departed, and "the church," in the words of Bishop
Leighton, "had become a fair carcass without a spirit.

Grieved at the low condition in which he found vital
godliness, when once roused himself to feel the importance of it in his own soul, Wesley, with the extraordinary
men who had been raised up to be his coadjutors, set
earnestly to work, not to oppose the church to which he
belonged and to which he was truly attached, not to form
a new organization either within or outside of it, but to
raise the standard of vital godliness, and to quicken into
life the dormant energies of that church.

The Wesleyan Reformation was truly a child of Providence. Its history is rich in illustrations of our general
theme, and we may be excused for making some special
reference to it. We shall here discern, in a most striking manner, the mighty Hand at work, carrying out the
purposes of his mercy through this great and eminently
useful branch of the family of the faithful. If contemplated simply as a great providential system, it presents a
striking phenomenon in the history of the Christian church
and of the world. Its origin and extent, and the wide-
spread moral influence it has exerted on the world, give
it an interest in the eye of the sacred and philosophic
historian, which he scarcely meets in any other branch
of the Christian church.

Methodism, as a distinct religious sect, is not yet three
quarters of a century old. Nor is it scarcely more than
a hundred years since "Methodist Societies," out of
which the present Wesleyan and Methodist churches
grew, were first known as bodies of religious worshipers.
The *name* had been applied to a little club of young men

in Christ Church College, Oxford, organized, at first, by Charles Wesley as early as 1729, principally for the purposes of religious improvement and the furtherance of plans of usefulness. In this little band, of which John and Charles Wesley and George Whitefield were leading members, lay hid the germ of that wonderful system, which God has since made so potent an engine to advance a living and active piety both on the old and new continent. The next ten years was the period of germination. The good seed was nourished by the kindly influences of the prayers and tears of a burning, unostentatious piety, and quickened into life by the silent breathing of the Holy Spirit. The year 1739, was a memorable epoch in the annals of Methodism. The swelling germ now burst. The evening of January 1st, 1739, was the Pentecostal epoch of the Methodist church. Here was the baptism of the Holy Ghost, and the beginning of a spiritual work such as had not been witnessed since the days of the apostles. "When the day of Pentecost was fully come, they were all with one accord in one place. And suddenly there came a sound from heaven as of a rushing mighty wind, and filled all the house where they were sitting."

"The evening of the first of January," says the record, "was a memorable occasion. John Wesley, Charles Wesley, and George Whitefield, who had just returned from America, met, with about sixty others, at a love-feast, held at the Fetter Lane Society. This meeting held all night. About 3 o'clock in the morning, as they were continuing instant in prayer, the power of God came mightily, as in the days of Pentecost, upon them. Some cried out for exceeding joy, and others fell to the ground. As soon as they recovered a little from the awe and amazement with which the presence of the Divine Majesty had inspired them, the assembled company broke out in one voice, "We praise thee, O God, we acknowledge thee to be the Lord." From this love-feast, the Wesleys and Whitefield went forth to labor with a new unction from on high. Whitefield went to Bristol, and the Wesleys remained in London. The most extraordinary results followed. Their words were the power of God unto salvation.

On visiting Bristol three months after, Wesley found Whitefield preaching daily, *out of doors*, to thousands, the churches being closed against him by the clergy. Here Wesley commenced his field-preaching. He preached every day, generally on the open commons of the city and in the adjoining fields, to audiences varying in number from one thousand to six thousand people. The most surprising effects followed. "Persons would cry out aloud, with the utmost vehemence, as in the agonies of death. Fervent prayer being made for them, they would soon sing a new song, even thanksgiving to God. Some would be seized with violent trembling, and fall down to the ground. They would drop as if struck by lightning, one after another on every side. Prayer being earnestly made for them, they would soon arise full of peace and joy in the Holy Ghost. It often happened that the persons who had gone to the meetings to oppose the proceedings, who stood biting their lips in wrath and knitting their brows in scorn, would drop suddenly on the ground, cry out in agony and remain in the greatest distress, till, after supplication and prayer, they would be restored to liberty, their hearts filled with joy, and their mouths with praise. These persons, so strikingly converted, become, many of them, ornaments to Christianity, and among them arose some of the most efficient and successful of Wesley's lay coadjutors."

The effects of the preaching of these men were perfectly astonishing. Nothing had appeared like it since the days of the apostles. At a time of the most melancholy spiritual lethargy, both in the Established church and among the Dissenters; when "learned prelates, preaching to almost empty seats, were producing but little impression on the fashionable audiences of the metropolis, with difficulty keeping their communicants within the bounds of descent morality," Wesley and Whitefield were preaching with the most astonishing effect among the abandoned crowds in Moorfields, to the lawless, brutal, and irreligious colliers of Kingswood, and the scarcely less abandoned multitudes that gathered about them on

Kensington Common and Blackheath.   Five, ten, twenty, and, Whitefield thinks on one occasion, *sixty* thousand people were assembled, to hear from their lips the words of eternal life.   Tears flowed from eyes unused to weep; the most hardened were overcome; the most profligate arrested and reclaimed ; the lion was changed to the lamb; thousands, and soon "tens of thousands," were rescued from a state of ignorance, degradation, sin, and misery, and blessed in this world, and given a hope for the world to come.   Lady Huntington says she went one day to hear one of these preachers (Thomas Maxfield) *expound*, expecting little from him, but before he had proceeded far she became so interested and impressed that she quite forget herself and seemed as one immovably fixed to her seat.

The remarkable religious movement which occurred in this country near the middle of the last century, known as " the Great Awakening," was but another part of the Wesleyan movement in Great Britain.   Edwards, Dickinson, and the Tennants, were but coadjutors with Whitefield and the Wesleys.   In New England, the work, under Edwards, though of a kindred character, had, in its earlier stages, a separate development.   In the southern and middle States, it was, for the most part, but an extension of the English movement.   The preaching of the same men who moved the countless multitudes of Moorfields and Kingswood, were producing the same wonderful effects from Philadelphia to Charleston, and finally in New England.   A new revolutionary element had been cast into the great stagnations of churchism, both in the old world and in the new ; a coal from the upper altar had fallen among the hay, wood, and stubble of formalism, and had kindled a fire which no human power could extinguish.   Every wind that blew against it, did but increase its strength and give its extension. Under the influence of this new principle, men pressed home the necessity of immediate repentance—of a change of heart—of a new inward life conformed to the word of God and the divine image.   This great idea—the idea of the new birth—so vital to Christianity and the very life of the gospel, had been sadly lost sight of in Great

14 *

Britain, and to a great extent in the American church. Even among the descendants of the Puritans, there was a deplorable declension of spiritual religion. The years 1739 and '40, were years of the right hand of the Lord. A power went out from the little band which met in the "Fetter Lane Society," which shook the British Isles, and seemed to gather new strength through the length and breadth of the American colonies.

The preaching of the men whom Providence called and fitted to be the leaders in this movement, was attended with a *moral power*, especially on the thoughtless and corrupt *masses*, which had been unknown for ages; and which took every class of religionists quite by surprise. Yet this power often operated in a manner which but ill-harmonized with the preconcieved orthodoxy of the times; and it still more confounded the long entertained ideas of ecclesiastical order. It was like the "living creatures" of Ezekiel: "they turned not when they went; they went, every one, straight forward," quite regardless of all human prescriptions or restrictive rules for the operation of spiritual influences.

But we are concerned rather with the providential history of Methodism. Whence this mighty river, so broad, so deep, so fertilizing as it rolls on, not always in a gentle stream; sometimes in the rushing tumbling violence of the cataract; never stagnant; sometimes overflowing its banks, tearing away landmarks, and producing apparent, if not real, devastation. Whence this river? John Wesley, we are told, was the founder of Methodism. And so he was, in the sense in which the commencement of a great river is the point where its several contributary streams unite and roll on in one great body to the ocean. We must go to the head-waters; we must traverse many a weary mile among the mountains, to where the pushing waters gush from beneath the rocks, and send their silvery streams down upon the plain beneath.

John Wesley was an extraordinary man, and was indeed the father of Methodism, as we find it developed and reduced to a system. He was of the "three mighties." He was of the few who have gone forth, heaven-commissioned, sometimes to produce a civil, sometimes a relig-

ious revolution, and whose names represent the great
providential changes by which the Divine purposes are
accomplished. Warriors, statesmen, philosophers, scholars, divines, have fulfilled their mission, and left their mark
upon their age. Yet where is the man since Martin Luther,
that has left his mind so deeply impressed on so large a
part of the Christian church; and more especially who
has left so indelible an impress of his heart? Wesley was
a child of Providence, made what he was by a special
training. He was no more the originator of Methodism,
than Luther was of the Reformation. John Wesley was
the product of several preceding generations. We trace
the character, the spirit, the principles of Wesleyanism
to the father, the mother, the grandfather, and the great
grandfather of John. John Wesley, the elder, was as
true a Methodist as his illustrious grandson. Ejected
from his parish, and persecuted even unto death, he could,
in his time and place, do little but to bequeath his spirit
and example to his worthy descendant and namesake.
Once he resolved to seek an asylum from persecution in
the wilds of America. But this might not be. "Had he
left England for either Surinam or Maryland, the circumstances which resulted in the originating and establishing
Methodism, under the great John Wesley, could never
have existed."

Wesley was, in his person, as signally preserved by
Providence, as he was, by the same agency, fitted for his
work. When six years old, he was remarkably rescued
from a burning house. A moment later he would have
been buried in the falling timbers and perished in the
flames. This providential escape made a deep impression on the mind of the child. He grew up with the impression that God had preserved him for some great and
good work. The same circumstance led his mother to
devote extraordinary attention to his moral and religious
training. She was "particularly careful of his soul."
At eight years of age, he was admitted to communion
with the church; at eleven, sent to Charter House School,
London, and at sixteen, he entered the University at Oxford. On his voyage to America, he did but narrowly
escape a grave in the deep; and often, in his after-life,

was he brought into the most imminent perils by sea and by land; and more than all, by the infuriated mob. But God delivered him out of them all.

Once on his passage from Savannah to Frederica in a flat-boat, he wrapped himself in his cloak and lay down to sleep on the quarter-deck. In the middle of the night, when sound asleep, he rolled off into the sea, and did not awake till his mouth was full of water. Instantly recovering his presence of mind, he swam to the boat and was saved.

Wesley was fitted to be the genius and moving spirit of Methodism. His training at Oxford, first as a pupil and then as a Fellow; his visit to America, which was quite a failure except as a matter of valuable discipline to himself; his acquaintance and intercourse with the Moravians; the unreasonable persecutions to which he was subjected, and the trials he experienced in the separation from him of some of his best friends and fellow-laborers, all contributed essentially to give him that vigor of mind, and firmness and energy of character, which he so eminently possessed. Most manifestly does the hand of the Lord appear in fitting Wesley for his mission. His capabilities for labor, both mental and physical, were prodigious. Perhaps there never lived a man that performed so much work, and for so long a period of time, as this great itinerating Bishop. He traveled near 5,000 miles, annually, on horseback; preached a thousand sermons a year—forty thousand in all; read much; wrote much; carried on an extensive correspondence; extensively cared for the wants of the poor; administered medicine to the sick; and had the care of all the churches. And he continued to perform these prodigious labors, and bear his burdens during a period of more than fifty years; till he arrived at the age of fourscore years and eight.

Wesley had no design of originating a new sect, or organizing a separate church. He aimed only at a general revival of piety in the Established church. To accomplish this, was the most ardent desire of his heart; and to this, all his labors were at first directed. He aimed " to spread scriptural holiness over the earth." Yet such were the orderings of Providence as to make him the

founder of a new sect, and the originator of a new church.
And not only was a separate *existence* forced upon this
new and numerous class of Christians, but nearly all the
peculiarities of their separate economy were the offspring
of the same Providence. The class-meeting and its
leader, the love-feast and its tickets, the quarterly meeting and itineracy, were no part of Wesley's theory.
They were purely providential; expedients to meet necessities created by the unexpected progress of the work.

The class-meeting arose out of the early practice of
appointing one person to call on eleven others, to collect
the penny a week for the poor. To this duty was soon
superadded the office of a spiritual oversight, the company
was called a "class and its leader;" and instead of calling at the home of each member, they met together; and
hence the effective institution called a class-meeting. Again
Wesley was wont, personally, to visit the members of his
flock once in three months, to inquire into their spiritual
condition, and to give suitable advice. To the worthy,
he gave *tickets* as testimonials of fitness for the communion. Hence, quarterly meetings, and the functions of the
presiding elder, and love-feast tickets. And "circuits"
and "itineracy" grew as naturally out of the necessities
created by the missionary character of the scheme.

The history of the Methodist church in America is full
of illustrations to our purpose. It was truly a "little one"
in its beginning; it soon filled the whole land. It is, perhaps, in this country that Methodism finds the most congenial soil, and has its happiest development. Eighty-
seven years ago, (in 1766,) the first Methodist meeting
was held in the city of New York. It was not a "class-
meeting," though it was a class with a leader. It was
not a religious meeting, though it was a meeting of persons with their leader, who had once professed themselves to be religious men. Philip Embury was a Methodist from Ireland, and once a local preacher. He, with
other Methodists, had come to America; lost their relish
for divine things, become engrossed in the spirit of the
world, and yielded sadly to its temptations. Others arrived the next year from Ireland, among whom was a
pious woman, a true "mother in Israel," who, hearing of

the defection of Embury and his associates, and ascertaining the place of their evening resort, suddenly entered the room, snatched from their hands the pack of cards with which they were playing, cast them into the fire, and boldly rebuked the delinquents. Turning to Embury, she said : "You must preach to us, or we shall all go to hell together, and God will require our blood at your hands." "But where shall I preach, and to whom?" "Preach in your own house, and to our present company." Stung to the heart and prostrated in penitence, he did preach to the five persons present. And from that good hour Methodism had a name and a place in America. Soon we find a congregation worshiping in an upper room in 120 William street, (the building is still standing,) whence their sound went out into all the land.

During the public ministry of a single man, (Asbury the first Bishop,) the American Methodist church increased from 600 members to 200,000, and her preachers from six, or seven, to 700. The little societies collected by Mr. Embury and Capt. Webb, the well-known "priest in the red coat," have multiplied till a million and a half of Methodists, 12,467 churches accommodating 4,000,000 of hearers, cover our land from the Atlantic to the Pacific, with schools, colleges, benevolent institutions, a colossal Book Concern, and an effective corps of 7,000 preachers. And during the eighty-seven years since the first Methodist sermon was preached in New York, not only has the membership of that church increased from five to a million and a half, but there have been erected 4,220 church edifices, (one for every week of her existence,) at a cost of more than $14,000,000, besides an expenditure, during the last twenty-five years, of not less than $1,000,- 000 annually in rebuilding and remodeling churches and for educational purposes. Indeed, Methodism has spread with an unexampled rapidity till it has extended, not only over England, Scotland, Ireland, and the United States, but over Canada, New Brunswick, Nova Scotia, and the West India Islands. In truth, wherever the Christian name is known, wherever the banners of the Cross are unfurled, the zealous, indefatigable followers of Wesley are to be met.

We have spoken of Methodism as, in its genius and organization, a great Home Missionary scheme. It has, too, its Foreign Missions, the providential history of which is full of interest. The Wesleyan Society of England, is one of the most efficient societies in the world. It has the largest fund, and its missions bless every continent, and a "multitude of Isles are glad thereof." From what small beginnings, and how unexpectedly, some of these missions sprung into being, and attained their present magnitude and efficiency! We may refer to the missions on the West India Islands, through which the gospel has been so successfully and extensively preached to the slave population.

In the year 1758, Nathaniel Gilbert, Speaker of the House of Assembly in Antigua, was in London, with some negroes in his service. They hear the Methodists preach; are converted; Wesley baptizes them, with the presentiment that it is the beginning of a great work. Gilbert returns to the Island; and himself deeply effected with the condition of the negroes, he begins to preach to them, and soon forms among them a society, after Wesley's rules, of 200 persons. After the death of Gilbert, two women kept the society together till the arrival, in 1778, of John Baxter, a class-leader from England, whose business had brought him thither. Under his guidance and teachings the work goes forward, numbers increase, and the slaves build a house of worship.

They now apply to Wesley for a preacher, but he has no one to send. At length the indefatigable Dr. Coke, is accidentally thrown upon the Island. He was on his way to Nova Scotia, when a succession of violent gales, a leak in the vessel and a lack of water, compel the captain to steer for the Island of Antigua. Dr. Coke is received with joy, and from that auspicious hour a mission is established. It *was* the "beginning of a great work." The little one became a thousand; and was soon multiplied to tens of thousands. It was the beginning of that great and successful scheme of missions which, till this day, has so richly blessed the whole cluster of the West India Islands. It is the glory of Methodism that it preaches the "gospel to the poor." And far distant be the day

when it shall lose this distinctive and honorable witness
that it is of God and the gospel of his dear Son.

A very pleasant and promising feature of Methodist
missions, is the "German Mission." Its object is the
German population of our country; and it has already
grown to a magnitude of great interest, though it be yet
in its incipiency. It has already 116 missions; 138 missionaries; 75 local preachers; 10,000 church members
and probationers; and 6,000 children in Sabbath schools.
The field of its operations extends from Boston to St. Louis,
occupying all the principally places where this population
is to be found. Yet it had a very small beginning, and
in this beginning we meet, most beautifully displayed, the
hand of sovereign Mercy.

There was known in Cincinnati, a few years ago, a
German, of a well cultivated mind, but of a badly cultivated heart; skeptical; infidel; God-despising and heav-
en-daring. One evening, as a matter of amusement and
perhaps ridicule, he turned into a Methodist meeting.
He was deeply impressed; overcome; sorely convicted
of sin; and finally converted. And soon his soul is stirred
in him, to preach the gospel to his countrymen. He applies for license as a local preacher, and becomes a missionary to the Germans of Cincinnati. His labors the
first year are, apparently, without success. He is appointed the second year, and is successful. Hence the
origin of the present, prosperous mission among the Germans of this country, and also the mission to Germany.

William Nast, now the Rev. Dr. Nast of Cincinnati,
has, since the all-controlling Hand conducted him to that
Methodist meeting, been extensively used as an efficient
and honored instrument, to carry forward this work. By
his preaching and missionary labors, by his public discussions with Romanists and infidels, and by his editorial
labors and other writings, he has abundantly vindicated
the ways of God in so remarkably bringing him into the
work.

But it is not my design to multiply examples, but rather
to present the great Wesleyan Reformation as one of
those stupendous schemes of Providence by which he is
advancing his cause on the earth; remarkable in its

origin as an unpretending attempt to revive the languishing spirit of piety in the Established church; remarkable for the character of its early leaders, who were men of great power and of unparalleled success; remarkable for its rapid growth, its wide extension, and its extraordinary moral results; and more remarkable in its adaptation to reach the *masses* of the people. It is the religion of the "poor;" which is but to say, it is the religion of the New Testament. It is the religion, too, of the outcasts of Ham, as we find them dispersed among us either north or south. Not less than 170,000 slaves in America, are this day members of the Methodist church.

When, therefore, we look upon Methodism in the magnitude of its members and its broad extension over the earth; when we contemplate it as the most stupendous missionary system which graces the Christian church and blesses the world; when we view it in its original design, as well as in its peculiar adaptedness to preach a simple, unadorned gospel to the masses of our lapsed race; and when we learn from its history that it has so eminently realized the design of its great founder and its early friends, we can only respond that *the Hand of the Lord has done it.* The sublime realization is before us. It has spread itself into every nook and corner of our broad land. As a colossal missionary scheme, it has gone pioneer to the uttermost bounds of our settlements, and furnished thousands of hamlets with a simple, burning gospel, which otherwise must have waited a generation at least for the good seed of the word of life. While a portion of its preachers, men of taste, learning, and refinement; preachers, writers, and scholars of a high order, have been preaching to enlightened and cultivated audiences in our towns and villages, thousands have been doing the most laborious and self-denying work on the very frontiers of civilized life, and in places where but for them the gospel would not be preached.

Methodism, at the present time, represents a body of believers, in America, England, Europe, Asia, and Africa, and on the numerous Isles of the sea, bound together by essentially the same creed, spirit, and practice, which, in number, scarcely falls short of two millions of church

15

members with 12,000 preachers, and a much larger number of local preachers and assistants; 850 foreign missionaries, and near 9,000 assistant missionaries. Nearly one million of dollars are raised in England and America for foreign missionary purposes, besides large amounts for other benevolent and educational purposes. Four hundred of the above named missionaries, and half a million of the money, are to be accredited to the Wesleyan Missionary Society of England, while in America, Methodism may claim as the offspring of her beneficence and energy, nine colleges, fifty-four seminaries, 9,000 Sabbath schools, 94,000 teachers, and 500,000 scholars; and above all, a Home Missionary work, surpassing any thing of the kind in existence.

Such is the extraordinary realization, in less than three quarters of a century, of this great providential scheme of church order. No separate organization existed in this country till 1784, and not so early in England. It was the great religious movement of the 18th century. Its history will more and more interest the pious and reflecting mind. We admire it because it is approved of God as a great providential agency for the advancement of his truth; and though we may not, in all its details and doctrines, be able perfectly to harmonize with it, yet we honor it because we see God so clearly revealed in in its history.

CHAPTER X.

HAND OF GOD in facilities and resources by which to spread Christianity. The supremacy of England and America: prevalence of the English language, and European manners, habits and dress. Modern improvements; facilities for locomotion. Isthmus of Suez and Darien. Commercial relations. Post-Office.

"Behold, I will do a new thing; I will even make a way in the wilderness, and rivers in the desert."—Isaiah, xliii. 19.

NOTHING more interests the pious mind than to trace the footsteps of Providence in the progress of evangelical truth. It invigorates our faith; fires our zeal; gives strength and reality to our hopes, and infuses new vigor into our efforts. We are looking for the day as not distant, when the kingdoms of this world shall become the kingdoms of our Lord and of his Christ. The Proprietor and Governor of this world is soon to take possession of his own; to wrest it from the hands of the usurper, and give it to the saints of the Most High. Already we discern tokens of such an event; providential dispensations, preparing the way, removing obstacles, gathering resources, providing men and materials; multiplying facilities, till we already begin to speak with confidence that the day of Christianity's triumph is near.

Beautifully have all things, from the beginning, been brought into subserviency to this end. "Political changes and state revolutions; war and peace; victory and defeat; plenty and famine; the wisdom of the wise and the imbecility of the weak; the virtues and the vices of mankind, and all the minute or mighty movements of man, are under the control of an invisible and Almighty hand, which, without breaking in upon the established laws of nature, or intrenching on the freedom of human actions, makes them all subservient to the purposes of his infinite wisdom and perfection," in the progress of the great work of human redemption. Here all opposition, however skillfully concerted, is unavailing. No weapon ever formed against truth has prospered. Its victories have been as certain as they have been triumphant and glorious. Apparent defeats are final, and oftentimes illustrious victories. The rage of persecution is either restrained, or overruled for good. However furiously the troubled waters have beat against the ark of the true Israel; however madly dashed on the Rock of our salvation, that ark—that rock, has remained immovable as the everlasting hills. He that walketh on the waves of the sea, hath said to their proud billows, "peace, be still." He fulfilleth all his purposes; he executeth all his will. He maketh a way in the wilderness, and rivers in the desert.

In preceding chapters I have shown how God has done this, in carrying forward the cause of Christianity in different periods of its progress. In the last two, I gave a practical view, at least, of the hand of God in the enterprise of modern missions. In continuation of the main subject, three topics remain to be discussed :

I. The hand of God as seen in the FACILITIES which the present state of the world, and the present condition of man, afford to the speedy and universal spread of the gospel.

II. The present aspect of the world *as a field open* for the reception of the gospel.

III. The duty of Christians in regard to the world's conversion.

My purpose, in the discussion of these points, is to delineate, as accurately as possible, the present aspect of the great field, which, as disciples of Christ, we are commanded immediately to evangelize. I may, from the fluctuating character of the records, make the picture more or less accurate, but, I trust, sufficiently accurate to supply motives of much encouragement to our "labors of love" to a dying world, and which shall exalt the God of our salvation.

I. The hand of God as seen in the FACILITIES which the present state of the world, and the present condition of man, afford to the speedy and universal spread of the gospel.

I should occupy too much space were I to attempt, on so fruitful a topic, to draw a complete picture ; yet I should do injustice to the general subject, were I to be too brief. The following particulars will furnish ample illustration :

1. *The unwonted acquisition of power and territory, by Christian nations, furnishes extraordinary facilities for the universal diffusion of the gospel.* The disposition of nations is purely providential. God alone setteth up one, and putteth down another. As king of nations He has, at the present time, and for purposes we can scarcely mistake, given an almost unlimited supremacy to the two most enlightened and Christian nations. England and America give laws to the world ; rather, I will say, the Anglo-Saxon race are extending an all-controlling influence over nearly the entire earth. Where will you fix

the limits of English power, or where bound the influence of them who speak the English language? Will you circumscribe it within the vast boundaries of the ancient Roman empire? Will you fix on the Indus or the Ganges as its eastern boundary, or on the Mississippi as its western? You will have circumnavigated the globe before you will have found the goal beyond which *Anglo-Saxon* power and influence do not reach. Traverse the earth from pole to pole, and you can scarcely point out the spot where you may not trace the footsteps of Anglo-Saxon skill, improvement, civilization and religion. The sun, in his diurnal journey, never ceases to look down on some portion of the British empire. And, though the territorial possessions of the United States are much less than those of Great Britain, her moral influence on the world may not be less; at least the inference is fair that it is destined not to be less.

Nor has the empire of the Anglo Saxons yet found a *limit.* Her sons in America are stretching themselves over a vast continent. They are planting the institutions of freedom, and displaying the improvements of civilization, and diffusing the benign influences of religion from the Atlantic to the Pacific. While England, on the other hand, is pushing her conquests, either directly by war, or more laudably by negotiation and treaty, by colonies, by commerce, or otherwise, into almost every part of the habitable globe. She is enlarging her borders in western and central Asia. She dictates terms of peace and war in Syria, Cabool, or Afghanistan. She sits an arbiter among the nations. If she turn her victorious arm against the "Celestial Empire," a way is prepared before her. Every valley is exalted, every hill made low. Nothing can withstand the power of her arm, for Heaven has nerved it, till the purposes of His wisdom and His grace be accomplished. She reaches out her sceptre, too, over numerous and distant islands of the sea, and gives laws to more of the human race than were known to exist on the whole face of the earth in the proudest days of the Roman empire. Africa, too, on almost every side, is beginning to feel the benign sway of English power. In the south, on the east and west, that ill-fated continent,

15*

so long the abode of ignorance, cruelty and superstition
—so long the subject of outrages which disgrace the page
of man's history, is begirt with those same Anglo-Saxon
influences, which ere long shall be to her as the cloud
that interposed between Israel and her pursuers,—a cloud
of *darkness* and confusion to them who would, with hands
of robbery and blood, invade the peaceful dwellings of
the sons of Ham, and bring them to a bondage more
cruel than death, but a *luminous* cloud to them who will
receive from the hands of the white man the light of religion and science, of the arts and civilization.

Whatever may be said of English ambition, or of her
pride, avarice or oppression,—or whatever opinion the
political moralist may form of the *justness* of many of
her negotiations (which are little else than terms dictated
by a stronger to a weaker power,) one thing is undeniable;
wherever English power is felt, there the arm of protection and assistance is extended to the missionary. No
sooner is the roar of British cannon heard off the coast
of Birmah, or at the Cape of Good Hope, than the captured missionaries are set free, and allowed to return to
their work.*

This is all our present subject demands. Wherever
the British flag waves, the messenger of peace and pardon may pursue his work unmolested; traverse the whole
land, in its length and breadth, and fear no danger; employ the means of education, erect school-houses, build
churches, translate the Bible, prepare books, and apply
the various instrumentalities for the regeneration of a
benighted nation, without the chilling apprehension that
the jealousy or fickleness of the government, or some
freak of human depravity may at any time frustrate all
his plans and banish him from the country. Sheltered
under the wings of the Almighty, which are spread over
him in the shape of British dominion, he commences his
work, confidently expecting to be able to finish it.

I do not mean to intimate that the English nation, as
such, has any such noble and benevolent design in her
conquests and dominion; "howbeit she meaneth not so

* As in the case of Mr. Judson, Dr. Vanderkemp, Read, &c.

neither doth her heart think so," but that the Almighty
Ruler of the nations has chosen her as his arm, by which
to break to pieces the gates of brass, and cut asunder the
bars of iron, which have for so many centuries shut up
the heathen world in gross darkness, and bound them fast
in the bondage of Satan.   The time of their emancipation has come, and an all-controlling Providence, who
has at command all the resources of earth, has chosen
this nation as his instrument by which to accomplish so
noble and grand a purpose.

I need not ask who it is that has taken the reins of
government from so many hands, and given them to a
Christian nation.   This, and on a magnificent scale, too,
is one of those divine arrangements which we cannot too
much admire. ⋅ What unbounded facilities are thus afforded for the diffusion of the gospel throughout the length
and breadth of the earth.   Do the embassadors of the Cross
need protection in Birmah or China?   These nations
are delivered into the hands of England, and the needed
protection secured.   Is the existence and prosperity of a
mission in Abyssinia suspended on the will of the king
who may soon be succeeded by a prince hostile to Christianity?   Mark the divine interposition here.   A British
fleet appears in the Red Sea.   Aden, the Gibralter of that
sea, and the key to Abyssinia is captured, just in time
to afford an asylum to the mission.*

We cannot but discern the hand of God in the wisdom
and benevolence of the arrangement which has given
such a decided supremacy to the nations of Christendom.
The word of their power is felt to the ends of the earth.
England is the Rome of the day.   In respect to the spread
of the gospel, she holds a position not dissimilar from the
Roman empire in apostolic days.   This will be further
illustrated as we proceed.

2. Another facility for the universal spread of the gospel, in which the hand of Providence is clearly discernible, *is the very great prevalence of the English language,*

---

* Aden was taken by the British, in 1841. But for this timely interposition of Providence, the present interesting mission must have been broken up on the death of the
present king.

and a corresponding desire to become acquainted with that language.

The English language is a store-house. It contains treasures of knowledge, of history, of wisdom, theoretical and practical. It embodies a record of the arts and sciences, of civilization and religion. It abounds, too, in political wisdom, opens the surest road to social and civil honors; is rich in biblical learning and criticism; and, indeed, affords to all who can read and speak it, an immense advantage in their progress from barbarism to civilization and Christianity. We can scarcely conceive a man to have free access to the treasures of English literature, science and religion, and to use his privileges, and yet remain a Pagan or Mohammedan. He may be professedly so, yet he will be a Christian or an infidel.

Language is a mighty thing. The Romans understood this when they spared no pains to diffuse the Latin language throughout their distant provinces. By this means they diffused the feelings and sentiments of Rome. Thus Italy not only gave *laws* to the many nations which composed her mighty empire, but, by sending, through the sure channel of her language, her fashions, customs and thoughts, she effectually made them *Roman*. The influence of the introduction into a Pagan nation, of a *Christian language*, containing a Christian literature, science, history and theology, and forming a constant channel of communication for the every-day sentiments of a Christian people, can only be estimated by those who know the power of language over the national character, and the social and religious habits. When a pagan nation gives up its language, it essentially gives up those rites, superstitions and fooleries which almost entirely make up its religion.

The English language is fast being diffused over the whole earth. Not only is it co-extensive with the vast domains of the Anglo-Saxons, but you can scarcely visit a people, tribe or nation, where you will not hear the fa miliar accents of your mother tongue. And, as extensive as the British empire, too, is the desire to become acquainted with this language. The Hindoo and the Tahitian, the proud Chinese and the poor Esquimaux,

St. Petersburg. Page 177.

makes it the height of his ambition to be able to read and
speak the language of so noble a race.

The time is not distant when half the population of our
globe shall speak the English language. Such, at least,
are the present intimations of Providence. And it is not
difficult to see what must be the bearing of such a fact
on the destiny of the whole world. If language be a
mighty thing, and if the English language be laden with
such stores as has been said, we may hail the singular
prevalence of our language as a delightful presage that
Truth is soon to prevail.

But there is, in connection with this thought about
languages, a kindred fact of a more general character,
which still more distinctly indicates a providential agency
engaged to remove obstacles to the spread of the truth.
I refer to the remarkable *decrease of the number* of languages. Not a few of the languages, which have so long
made our world a *Babel*,—producing confusion and dispersion, *alienating* the different branches of the same
great family, have within the last century ceased to be
spoken ; and as many Pagan languages are scarcely more
than spoken languages, having nothing that deserves the
name of literature ; they have virtually ceased to be
languages. And the number is yearly becoming less.
The spread of the English language, easy international
communication, and the supremacy of the nations speaking the English language, are fast bringing the long separated portions of the human race again into one great
family. Through the medium of six or seven of the
principal languages now used, by far the greater portion
of the world's population may now be addressed. Let
the missionary address, verbally and through the press,
as many of earth's inhabitants as he can through the
medium of the English, French, German, Arabic, Hin-
doostanee, Chinese, and one language of Africa,* and he
will probably have reached more than four fifths of the
whole. And causes are in progress to diminish the number of languages still more. Truth only is permanent.
And those languages only, can live, under the reign of

---

* See remarks in Chapter XVI, on the affinity of African languages.

Truth, whose literature, science and theology, are the utterances of Truth.

Hence we look that the language of the little Isle—yet ιot so much the language of England, as the language of Puritanism ; the Puritanism of Oliver Cromwell and New England, the language of English liberty, of Republicanism, of true science, of Protestantism, of religious freedom and of piety, shall become well nigh universal. Other languages, as they shall become inoculated with the vitality of Truth, shall have a longer or shorter, a feebler or a more vigorous life. Nevertheless, we look for the time to come when the *cause* of the melancholy catastrophe at Babel shall be removed, and "the whole earth" shall again be of one language and one speech."

The influence which this wide extension of the English language must have in the evangelization of the world, it is not difficult to conceive. It affords an immense facility for the propagation of the gospel to the ends of the earth. And who has furnished it to our hands ? Who has done this *new thing, and made a way in the wilderness,* by which access is open to half the inhabitants of the globe ? The Lord is his name, and we will praise him. He is hereby breaking down the partition wall that has separated us from the Gentile world.

3. Akin to this, there is a disposition equally extensive *to conform to European habits, manners and dress ; to adopt the improvements of civilized and Christian nations ; to be governed by their laws, and profited by their superior wisdom.*

These things, though not religion or morality, are nearly connected with both. They are often the channels through which religion and morality are introduced and established. When a people consent to give up a false philosophy for the true ; Pagan literature for Christian ; when they concede the superiority of civilized government to the despotism and cruelty of Paganism, and freely avail themselves of the improvements of civilized life, and no longer despise its costume and social habits, we predict, with much certainty, that they are not far from the kingdom of heaven. They have emancipated themselves from the bondage of *prejudice,* and condescended to yield to the sober dictates of reason. Serious obstacles to their conversion are removed, and we may expect to find their minds open to receive the truth.

If, on looking abroad over the face of the earth, we find such, in the orderings of divine Providence, to be the actual condition of large portions of the heathen world, we may, without fear of disappointment, await some favorable result.

4. *Facilities for the spread of the truth arising from modern improvements in modes of conveyance.* Before knowledge shall be so increased as to cover the whole earth, many must go to and fro. Distances must be contracted ; nations be brought into neighborhood, and close international relations formed.

Such is precisely what we see at the present day. For all purposes of business or social intercourse, Liverpool is now as near New York, as, forty years ago, Boston was to Albany. Nor is China so far from us now, as London was at that period. For this extraordinary change, we are principally indebted to the application of the power of *steam* to the purposes of locomotion. The introduction of the railroad car and the steam-ship, forms altogether a new era in the business and reformation of the world. And especially is the influence of this new order of things felt in the work of evangelization. The Roman empire was vastly indebted for its greatness and glory, to the facilities of communication which connected its capital with its remotest frontier. By means of its great national roads, constructed at an enormous expense, and connecting Rome with the capital of every province of the empire, (vestiges of which, after fifteen centuries, still remain,) that vast empire was consolidated and strengthened. The imperial arm could thus reach to the remotest corner of the empire. Posts were, by this means, established ; intelligence communicated ; a knowledge of science, literature and improvements diffused ; and the great purposes of government easily answered. Indeed, as already intimated, this was the feature of the Roman empire which made it so effectual an instrument in the early extension of the gospel.

When a superintending Providence would convey his messengers throughout the Roman world, he provided. as never before, *facilities of conveyance.*

But not the provinces of the Roman empire, but now the nations and kingdoms of the *whole earth* are brought into juxta-position by means of improved modes of conveyance. Nations are no longer alienated by formidable distances, or unknown seas. There is scarcely a tribe on the surface of the globe, which is not easily accessible to those who hold in their hands the everlasting gospel. A voyage around the world—a visit to the remotest islands of the Pacific, is but an enterprise of a few months. Do philanthropists of different nations wish to meet for mutual consultation—do Christians of every clime desire to mingle their councils, such a meeting is practicable. A world's convention may be convened.

Already has *steam navigation* wrought a mighty change. It has changed the whole moral, social, and political world. It has brought nations into neighborhood; made them acquainted with one-another's advantages and disadvantages, virtues and vices, and thus struck a death-blow to a thousand prejudices and superstitions, and made many tribes of rude barbarians ashamed of their ignorance and barbarism, and resolved to imitate their improved neighbors.

It has wrought a mighty change on the *habits* of the sluggish nations of the East. The paddle-wheels of improvement, and the terrific puffs of the fire and smoke of reform, have broken up the stagnant waters of every nation from Constantinople to Japan. It has infused a spirit of enterprise; a promptness in business habits; an idea of the power of true science, and shown the practicability and vast advantages to a nation of progressive improvement, which nothing before has ever done. It becomes a ready medium for the interchange of ideas. The Chinese and American may now meet on common ground, and talk of government, of science and religion. They may weigh the merits of their respective systems, compare practical results as exhibited in the character of their respective nations, and deduce a motive for improvement. It affords, too, every needed facility for the conveyance of the agents of philanthropy and benevolence to every nation on earth. It is a presage of vast good that all the tribes of the earth are, at length, brought into so close neighborhood as to afford a ready interchange of thoughts, and a comparison of habits. While the missionary from America is teaching a pure gospel in Bombay or Batavia, and exemplifying the graces of our holy religion, the Imaum of Muscat, a bishop from the mountains of Persia, a Chinese mandarine, or some Henry Obookiah, from an unknown island, is gazing and wondering at what he beholds in a land of free institutions, and of a pure religion. They return to their respective countries to relate and recommend what they have seen, and heard, and felt.

Discern we not the hand of God here? Has blind chance produced such a state of things? Do we not rather here read the gracious interposition of Heaven in behalf of a world lying in wickedness? Something here seems to say, *the winter is past, the rain is over and gone, the flowers appear on the earth, the time of the singing of birds is come.* The day of earth's redemption is at hand.

But the progress of improvement in modes of conveyance has yet found no limit. We have yet no engine for locomotion which is, of its kind, perfect. Its machinery, both as to material and workmanship, is constantly undergoing improvement. The sciences on which it depends are but in their infancy, and, of consequence, their practical results are imperfect. We may, therefore, expect vast improvements in our means of international communication, which shall make them safer and more expeditious. And not only this, but are we not to look for further *inventions*, which shall as far excel our present modes of conveyance, as these surpass those in the days of our grandfathers?

The supposition is a fair one, and not without some plausible grounds. Several years elapsed, after the discovery that *steam* might be made a locomotive power, before it was applied to purposes of any essential importance. Franklin, sometime after the discovery had been announced, ventured the prediction that the time would come when a vessel should be propelled by steam at the

16

rate of seven or eight miles an hour; that the day *might* come when the Atlantic should be crossed in a steamship; and the distance from New York to Philadelphia be traversed in a single day and night.

Few had the mind of Franklin, or penetrated so far into futurity, or anticipated more accurately the expansive intellect and inventive genius of man, or the advances of science. Yet how far he fell short of the present reality.

The supposition is more than probable that the coming half century shall be as fertile, in useful inventions, as the last half has been. Already modes of conveyance have been invented, which, if they can be made practical, and be brought to perfection, will as far surpass steam-ships and railroad cars, as these surpass, in celerity of motion and convenience, the Dutch schooner which navigated the North river forty years ago, or the Jersey cart which plied between New York and Philadelphia. The expectation that *air balloons* shall, within that period, become practical and safe means of crossing mountains, rivers, seas, and deserts, as, with a bird-like celerity, the inhabitants of one nation shall, on errands of mercy, or tours of business or pleasure, wish to visit the inhabitants of another, is no more absurd, does at this day no more transcend our conceptions of what may be, than the idea of the present facilities for traveling and freight would have surpassed the conceptions of men fifty years ago. And should the close of the next fifty years witness our *atmosphere* a high way to the nations, by means of *airships*, there will be as little reason for surprise.* Indeed, should this be the "*new thing*" which inventive Heaven shall do; this the "way," which, in these latter days, He will open for the more speedy acceleration of his work on earth, it would but beautifully accord with the description of its progress given in Rev. xiv. 6: "And I saw an angel *fly in the midst of heaven*, having the everlasting

* Indeed, little is wanting now to realize all I have supposed, but the invention of some mode of *guiding* the balloon in a horizontal direction. This attained, and the point is gained. Tribes and nations, now quite inaccessible, would be thrown open to us. The following notice recently appeared in a New York paper: "AN AERIAL CAR for navigating the air at will, in all directions, was exhibited in the Tabernacle, Feb 23d, 1849, to be propelled by a steam-propeller of ten-horse power.

gospel to preach." Again, the wonderful mode of communication through the Magnetic Telegraph, by which means intercourse may be held, business transacted, and knowledge communicated instantly between places thousands of miles asunder, can, by no means, be passed unnoticed here. The bearing of this new and extraordinary mode of communication, for good or for evil on the world, will be tremendous. If overruled for good, as we may expect, it will doubtless prove one of the most efficient arrangements which Providence has ever devised for the enlarging and Christianizing the world. Long hath God made the winds his ministers; now shall he make the fiery flames his messengers.

There can be no doubt that all these human improvements are under the special direction of a superintending Providence. He has not so vastly increased the means of going "to and fro," without a design that knowledge shall increase and speedily cover the earth. The present *accessibleness* of the world for all the appliances by which it is to be converted, is exceedingly interesting. What surer indication can we have that God is about to do a great work among the nations of the earth! Infinite Wisdom prepares not his instrumentalities in vain. "The earth helps the woman," by doing the most expensive part of missionary labor in providing the facilities of conveyance and intercourse. But I pass to our next particular, which is of a kindred character.

5. I should be overlooking what will doubtless, in a few years, be regarded as an exceedingly interesting item in the annals of international improvement, if I did not allude, at least, to two contemplated works which are destined to produce tremendous transformations in the political and moral world. I mean *the joining of the Atlantic and Pacific Oceans, and the Mediterranean and Red Seas by means of ship canals.*

The practicability of the latter of these enterprises, as to any physical obstructions, has not, as I am aware, been called in question. And misgivings, as to the former, have been quite removed by the late surveys of Mr. Bailey, a half-pay British officer. The proximity of the two oceans between North and South America, the interposi-

tion of lake Nicaragua, and the river San Juan, occupying a greater portion of this route, and the singular depression, at this place, of the Andes, are obvious indications
of Providence pointing out this to be a future highway
for the nations.* The navigation of the globe is, at present, impeded by formidable obstacles. Not a vessel from
either of the great maritime nations can now visit Asia
or the Pacific ocean, without first doubling the tempestuous Cape of Good Hope, or the more tempestuous Horn,
and by a circuitous route of several thousand miles.
One half the time and expense of navigation, and more
than one half the danger, will be removed the day the
above named passages be opened.

Columbus saw this, and sought a passage to the Pacific
between the two continents. The Spaniards, sensible of
its advantages, have, from time to time, projected plans
for its accomplishment. The governments of Central
America have proposed schemes for which they have
asked the co-operation of the United States, and the
Netherlands. The American Senate, and the courts of
Europe, have accorded to it, in some degree at least, the
importance it may claim. Readily has it been acknowledged to be "the mightiest event in favor of the peaceful
intercouse of nations, which the physical circumstances
of the globe present to the enterprise of man."

The influence of this enterprise, if once completed, (the
cost of which is estimated at not above twenty-five millions of dollars,) would be vast beyond conception. It
would soon bring the moral and political wastes of Central America into the pale of civilization and a pure
Christianity. It would bring the present semi-barbarous
and unproductive provinces of the whole western coast
of America, from Patagonia to Bhering Straits, into the
family of nations, develop the vast resources which these
immense territories are capable of contributing to national wealth and influence, and thus vastly enhance the
resources of the world for the accomplishment of any
great moral enterprise.

---

* Similar remarks might be made respecting a passage for a rail-way through the
Rocky mountains.

That garden of the world, though now overrun, physically, morally, and politically, with a useless, if not noxious growth of most unlovely luxuriance, where once flourished the magnificent cities of Copan, Palenque, and Aztalan, would again smile with its marts of trade ; and its beautiful plains be covered with the sure tokens of improvement and prosperity. There would, as it were, be added to the world a vast accession of territory and population. Numerous nations and tribes ; immense bodies of the human race, would, by this means, be inducted into the rank of nations, improved, assimilated, and prepared to act in concert for the general advancement of the world.*

Similar remarks might be offered in reference to the other great enterprise—the connecting the Mediterranean and Red seas at the Isthmus of Suez. But I pass on.

Is that, I ask, a visionary expectation, which anticipates the time as near, when the steam-ship shall send up its dark volumes of smoke among the Andes, or over the desert of Egypt ; or disturb, with its impertinent wheels, the calm waters of the Pacific ? It is no more visionary than (forty years ago) that the Atlantic and the great lakes should be connected, or a voyage to India should be made by steam. Already is this indicated to be one of the great schemes of Providence for the elevation and moral improvement of our race. And we may rest assured that when *He* shall wish to bring the nations into still nearer proximity—when, to accelerate still faster the work of the world's amelioration, he will so quicken and mature the wisdom and enterprise of man, and so remove present political inabilities and obstructions, that this "*new thing*" may be done, and this "WAY in the wilderness" be prepared for the redemption of the world.

---

* The following is from a report of M. Le Humboldt to the Academy of Science: " The examination of localities, by commission (of the French government,) has terminated—the result as favorable as expected. The chain of the Cordilleras does not extend, as supposed, across the Isthmus, but a valley, very favorable for the operation, has been discovered. The natural position of the waters is also favorable. Three rivers, over which an easy control may be established, and which may be made partially navigable, would be connected with the canal. The excavations necessary would not exceed twelve and a half miles. The fall, regulated by four locks, one hundred and thirty-eight feet. Total length of the canal, forty-nine miles—width at surface, one hundred and thirty-five feet—width at base, fifty-five feet—depth, forty feet—navigable for vessels of one thousand to one thousand four hundred tons—cost, one hundred and twenty-four millions franks "

6. The same grand scheme of preparation for the universal spread of the gospel, as conducted by the hand of an all-controling Providence, is further indicated *by the extensive commercial relations* which England and America, at present, hold over the whole face of the earth.

No people can, to any great extent, meet and barter their commodities without, at the same time, an interchange of thoughts. Continued commerce will introduce into a pagan nation much besides merchandize. The improvements, the literature and science, the manners and religion of the more civilized, follow in the wake of their commerce. Here, principally, the people of different nations have the opportunity of free and friendly intercourse. Masters of vessels, supercargoes, indeed, men of almost every class are, at this day, dispersed through almost every nation, province or island—adventurers, agents, men, as in the navy, for the protection of commerce, functionaries of government—and all these enjoy rare opportunities of preparing the way for the glorious gospel.

And it is a remarkable fact that these rare privileges of exerting an influence far and wide on the barbarous nations of the earth, are, providentially, confided to the hands of the two principal Christian nations. Where will you find a people or tribe that sustains no commercial relation with England or America? To the same extent God has confided to these nations the solemn trust of acting as the almoners of Heaven's riches to the world. If they betray this trust, if they act unworthy this high prerogative, God will take it from them and give it to whom he shall choose. Yet we cannot contemplate such an arrangement without discovering in it a presage of speedy and universal good to all people and kindreds of the earth.

7. The extensive establishment over the world of *the post-office system,* is another kindred providential arrangement of immense moment in the civilization and the Christianizing of the world. The mere announcement of this may not develop its true importance; yet a moment's reflection will assign, among the facilities for the spread of the gospel, a high place to an establishment which enables men, dwelling at the two extremities of the

earth, to transact business, and interchange thoughts and feelings. But for the *post-office*, the facilities afforded for the amelioration of the world by means of our extended navigation; our commercial relations; the wide prevalence of the English language; and a tendency among unevangelized nations to imitate the manners and imbibe the sentiments of the more civilized nations, would, to a great extent, be neutralized.

8. Finally, we must not leave out of the account the immense accessions of *wealth* which have recently been, and which are still being, brought to light. To pass over the exhaustless treasures which have within a few years been discovered in *coal deposits* and *beds* of *iron*, some extending hundreds of miles, (as in Illinois and Missouri,) remarkable discoveries have of late been made of the more precious metals and minerals, which have of a sudden added immensely to the pecuniary resources of the world. In the interior of Africa, near Cossan, on the eastern side of the Sommat, and also on the banks of the Gamamil, gold has recently been discovered by Russian engineers in the service of the Egyptian government, which exceeds in abundance and richness the far famed mines of Siberia, and threaten to rival the wonderful discoveries of California. Gold has also been recently found in the island of Borneo, in different parts of Europe, in Rhode Island, New Jersey, North Carolina, Virginia, Georgia, and in other places of the United States, and in Canada; new discoveries in Mexico and Central America, to say nothing of the exhaustless treasures of the world-famed California and Oregon. Yet it is, perhaps, more to our purpose to notice the late discoveries of minerals and metals which are usually esteemed less precious. An exceedingly rich *silver* mine has just been opened in *Spain*, and another in California. *Coal* has been found abundantly on Vancouver's island, just in the right spot to provide for the steam navigation of the Pacific, when the new route to the " Indies" shall be opened over the American continent—Missouri and Illinois supplying in their place. *Cobalt* has just been found in Cornwall, England, —a dying material which produces the splendid Tyrian purple, and is, ounce for ounce, of equal value with gold.

And a valuable spring of *mineral oil*, or naptha, has been discovered in a coal pit near Alfreton, Derbyshire. Besides gold and silver, the mineral wealth of New Mexico and California is immense; mineral springs, salt in the greatest abundance, platina, till of late worth its weight in gold, mercury, copper in vast quantities, iron ore and coal. All these vast resources of nature, so long hid from the research of man, are brought to light now for some *purpose*. They have been kept safely treasured up in the capacious store-house of the great Proprietor till he has need of them.

But I will pursue the subject no farther at present. A few brief reflections urge themselves upon us.

1. The tremendous responsibility of England and America. The destiny of the world is, under God, suspended on the course of conduct which they pursue. If they act decidedly in favor of a sound morality and pure religion; if they hesitate not to use, in all proper ways, their immense advantages to fill the world with blessings, they may wield a moral power for its renovation, such as no nation could at any former period. The resources of these two nations, in wealth and territory; in power; in learning and truth; in useful arts and inventions; in industry and enterprise; in almost every thing needed to secure influence abroad, are enormous. But why has God committed to their hands such prodigious resources? Doubtless that they may fulfill his designs in the renovation of the world. If they are faithless here, God will not hold them guiltless. The nation or kingdom that will not serve Him shall perish.

2. The responsibility of travelers, visitors, and sojourners in foreign lands. They appear abroad as the representatives of Christianity. Nations less civilized, and debased by a false religion, estimate the value of Christianity very much as they see it exemplified in the everyday life of those calling themselves Christians. How important, then, that Christian travelers and sojourners among such nations, should not *mis*-represent our religion and its thousand concomitant blessings. And on the other hand, no class of persons may be so extensively and permanently useful as they who have it in their power

to be examples of Christian faith and practice among unevangelized nations, and who may introduce among them the better manners and customs, and the comforts and improvements in common life which obtain among Christian nations.

3. We have here forcibly urged on us the duty we owe to *sailors*. No class of men may on the one hand do more mischief abroad, or on the other, more effectually carry out the purposes of divine mercy towards our world, than they " who go down to the sea in ships, who do business in great waters." Their field is peculiarly the world. Let them go forth sanctified men, everywhere zealous for the honor of their God, and their influence will be immense beyond calculation.

4. With what pleasing interest and profound solemnity ought we to regard the present condition of the world! Never before has God provided such resources for its recovery. Never before has he brought it into a position so favorable to receive the truth, and never imposed on his people so solemn obligations. What thrilling motives have we here to *action!* Are we *servants* of Christ? Never were we more encouraged, or so loudly called on to live for our Divine Master. Are we permitted to co-operate with God? Never before were we urged on by such irresistible arguments. If God is making a short work on the earth,—if He is consummating his plans with unprecedented and glorious rapidity, how ought we to double our diligence, that we may keep pace with his stately steppings.

CHAPTER XI.

"Behold I will do a new thing—I will even make a way in the wilderness, and rivers in the desert." Isa. xliii. 19.

PROVIDENCE makes no vain preparations. The end is never less sublime than is indicated by the beginning. Immense facilities now exist for the general diffusion of the gospel. I have named the unwonted acquisition of territory by the two great Protestant nations, and their extraordinary supremacy among the nations of the earth —the prevalence of the English language—a disposition to adopt European manners, habits and dress, to be benefited by the improvements of Christian nations, and to be governed by their laws—modern improvements in modes of conveyance—the extensive commercial relations of the two great Christian nations, and the present extensive arrangements for social and international communication by means of *posts*. I shall now adduce two or three particulars more.

8. *The general peace*, which at present pervades the earth, furnishes another facility for the universal extension of our religion. This is purely providential, and is a narbinger of prosperity to Zion. The temple of Janus has been shut more than a quarter of a century; during which there has been no general war, and the partial warfares which have been carried on, have been peculiarly overruled to the spread of the gospel.

When God was about to bring his Son into the world, he hushed the world into peace—committed the government of the earth principally to *one nation*, whose head, unlike his predecessors, loved peace more than conquest. Here, under God, lay hid the mystery of the rapidity with which the gospel spread in the days of the apostles. The wings of the Roman eagle were spread to protect her citizens at the farthest verge of the known world. When

Paul said, *I am a Roman citizen*, he found protection amidst the *mob*. Under the benign auspices of the Augustan age, the gospel had free course and was glorified.

Again has the clangor of battle ceased—except it be as the distant murmur of waters in some dark cavern. No more do we hear the thunder of the battle-field, or "see garments rolled in blood." But who hath stationed his angels at "the four corners of the earth to hold the four winds of the earth, that the wind should not blow on the earth, nor on the sea, nor on any green tree"—giving the world another respite from the turmoil and confusion of war? And for what purpose, if not that the everlasting gospel may be preached to all nations and kindreds, and God's elect be sealed? The moment the torch of war be lighted, and hostile armies invade a nation, the banners of the Cross are furled. Thus is the mighty arm of God made bare, to restrain the wrath of man, and to give protection and success to his servants.

The demon of war is only *restrained*, not annihilated In the far distant, and scarcely below the horizon, the dark cloud of war is still lying. Ever and anon, as if resting on the bosom of troubled waters, its black folds loom above the line of vision, and threaten a storm. Yet it soon disappears beneath its own native billows, and the sun of peace again shines. Then again it sends up its lurid fires, and its distant thunders roar. Yet we have, at least for a little space longer, security, in the dispensations of Providence, that the days of the Divine forbearance are not yet past. The principal nations of the earth are strangely bound together by mutual ties of friendship, philanthropy and interest. If there was at this time no other security for a general peace, we have a strong one in the *commercial relations*, which exist between the principal nations. The capital embarked by these nations in *commerce*, to say nothing of *benevolence*, is as *bonds* given by them to keep the peace of the world. War would not only peril a vast amount of their property, but would destroy a good trade. England might almost as well sack and burn Liverpool as New-York—Russia as well make St. Petersburg the spoil of war as London.

9. Again is the hand of God strikingly visible *in the*

*present advanced and the yet advancing condition of knowl-
edge, civilization and freedom.* In these respects, too,
God has brought the world into a posture favorable to
the progress of Christianity.

Christianity is by no means a religion of ignorance and
barbarism. It luxuriates in the light; walks hand in hand
with learning, and only brings forth its fruit in all its native richness, when nurtured in the genial soil of civilization and freedom.

Now, if, on looking abroad in the world, you discover
an advanced and a yet advancing state of these three
great auxiliaries and accompaniments of a manly, well
developed, all-commanding piety, are you not to regard
them as *tokens* of providential schemes about to be carried
out, and as monitions to duty, and facilities for executing
the plans of Heaven in setting up Messiah's kingdom on
earth?

The present progress in knowledge finds no parallel in
any preceding age of the world. Learning, heretofore,
had been confined not only to a few nations, but to a few
individuals of these nations. Now, there is something
approximating a universal diffusion of knowledge. There
are few people or tribes in whose bosom there has not,
within the last twenty years, been kindled an unwonted
ambition to be able to read, and become acquainted, at
least, with the rudiments of useful knowledge. The progress of truth, whether as to facts or principles, whether
in the sciences or in the practical affairs of life, has
within a few years past been astonishingly onward. Fiction, romance, legendary tales, gross superstitions, Pagan
mythology, which but a short time since held such bane-
ful supremacy over the mind of the vast majority of mankind, have, to no inconsiderable extent, given place to the
desire and pursuit of rational knowledge.

It is but a few years since the literary trumpery of Paganism—the Koran and Sonnah of the Mahomedans, the
Targums and Talmuds of the Jews, and the nonsensical
traditions, legends, and ghostly tales of Romanism, en
grossed nearly all the learning in the world. Truth stood
alone, and was desolate. She sighed in vain for any to
do her reverence, while the world was gone after fiction

and falsehood. History, philosophy, geography, physics, metaphysics and theology, were unknown, except as dimly seen, befogged and mystified in the sacred books of paganism. Socrates fell a martyr to true science. The Copernican system of the heavenly bodies, at a much later date, was condemned as a heresy, by the sapient Inquisition of the seventeenth century : and Galileo, for certain astronomical discoveries made by his newly constructed telescope, and which went to confirm the Copernican heresy, was condemned, by the same ghostly court, to all the horrors of perpetual banishment, and forced to purchase his liberty by retracting his opinions. Virgilius, archbishop of Saultzburgh, was excommunicated by the Church of Rome, and Spigelius, archbishop of Upsal in Sweden, suffered martyrdom at the stake for entertaining the theory of the spherical form of the earth. The discoveries and signal advances made in science by the immortal Bacon, were believed by his ignorant cotemporaries to be the works of magic. They were denounced to the court of Rome as "his dangerous opinions and astonishing operations," attributing them to the agency of the devil. The great adversary of human knowledge and of the immortal soul had almost completely monopolized the *mind* of the entire family of man. He had either buried it in sordid ignorance, or, if he could not repress its deathless activity, he had prostituted its energies to purposes the most vile and worthless.

But the infernal chain is now, measurably, broken; man is intellectually emancipated; there is freedom of thought, freedom of research, and full scope given to all the inventive and acquisitive powers of mind.

Late advancements in science have vastly facilitated all the operations of life, and thrown open to the unrestricted range of the mind, fields of immeasurable knowledge. *Astronomy* has brought within the scope of our intellectual vision boundless fields, all radiant with starry gems, which, when plied with telescopic aid, become a resplendent galaxy of worlds, all fitted up for the habitation and happiness of immortal beings like ourselves. Nothing, perhaps, like these discoveries, enlarges the boundaries of human thought, elevates man above him-

17

self—makes him feel the original nobility of his nature—
the divine lineage of his race, and at the same time, that
he is but a speck of wide creation, a polluted speck of
insignificance :—nothing so effectually magnifies in his
estimation the great and eternal God, or gives him such
sublime, extatic ideas of the magnificent empire over
which God sways the sceptre, and of the importance of
His law, and the necessity that he sustain its awful
sanctions—nothing so makes guilty man feel how unpar-
donable his guilt, how fearful his condition—how infinite
are God's resources by which to make his enemies
wretched or his friends happy.

Had science done no more than to spread out before
us the fields developed by modern astronomy, it would
deserve a mention in this connection. It presents man,
in his relations to the universe, as a nobler being. It
furnishes his devotion with new motives. It creates increased incentives to Christian activity. It enhances in
our esteem the value of the immortal soul. If to be allied
to a king be an honor—if to be the son of an earthly potentate furnish motives strong enough to move the whole
soul, what is it to be allied to, to be Son of the great
King? *heir* of the *only* Potentate, the King of kings and
the Lord of lords? A science which throws open to us
so much of the material magnificence of Jehovah, cannot, when sanctified, but make the Christian a more noble, devoted, active being, and cherish a caste of piety
more efficient for the conversion of the world.

But there are sciences of less pretension, whose late
progress yet more directly contributes to the advancement and permanent establishment of Christianity. We
cannot contemplate recent advancements in philosophy,
natural history, geography, chemistry, mineralogy, geology, or the many useful *discoveries* and *inventions* of a
few past years, or the present condition of religious
knowledge or biblical study, without the delightful conviction that Christianity is fast gathering strength, and
rallying her forces for the conquest of the world.

The inventions of human skill, the applications of
science and knowledge to the useful purposes of life, con
tribute to the comfort, convenience and improvement of

man ; facilitate his labor, multiply his resources, and make him a nobler and more influential being ; better fitted to serve his God, and to do good to man. By these means the use of minerals and metals are brought to his aid ; new substances are discovered, and new uses ascertained of those already known ; his wealth is increased, and of consequence his means of doing good. In his improved condition man is another kind of being ; belongs to another order of things—which, under the reign of the Messiah, God is about to introduce.

The earth is a vast magazine. Treasured in its bowels are minerals, metals and precious stones, which, when drawn out and wrought and applied to use, become the means of almost every improvement which distinguishes a barbarous from a civilized, intelligent and free people. Instruments, machinery, weapons of war and peace, materials and apparatus for book-making, publishing and circulation ; the means of navigation, and of locomotion on land and through the air, and all the manifold machinery which augments the energies, increases the comforts and promotes the general improvement of mankind, are drawn out of the earth. Geography ascertains their location, natural history, in her departments of geology and mineralogy, penetrates the earth and points them out to the research and skill of man. Chemistry there erects her laboratory, and by a great variety of patient and interesting experiments, ascertains their properties and capabilities, and takes cognizance of their changes ; while natural philosophy steps in to point out the phenomena, which, in different aspects and changes they exhibit, the laws by which they are governed, and the uses to which they may be applied. But for the aid of these sciences, in searching out and applying the properties of the *magnet*, the mariner would have still been feeling his way along his native shore. The few books we should have would be executed by the tedious and expensive process of the pen ; and for the want of an acquaintance with the uses of *iron*, we should be thrown back into the darkness of barbarism. The inventions and discoveries which now so much bless the world and favor the improvement

of man, would never have been made.*   America and
many islands of the sea, and other large territories, had
not been discovered.   Most of the world had remained a
bleak waste, a roaming ground for a few savages ; and
the few nations which, from natural proximity, would
form some neighborhood relations, had been raised but
little above a state of barbarism.   Commercial relations
had not existed ; and nearly all the advantages derived
from international communication had been wanting.
The interchange of thoughts by means of books, traveling and commerce would be almost unknown.   Isolated
man would never rise above the in statu quo position of
his insignificance and ignorance.

If, under God, the plastic hand of science has done so
much already, to re-mould and improve the world ; so
much to *prepare* the nations to receive the gospel and to
facilitate its diffusion, while, as yet, science itself has been
but half fledged for its more adventurous flight, what
may we not expect through her instrumentality, when
she shall arrive at the state of perfection towards which
she is so rapidly tending?   Nature has but begun to yield
up her resources to facilitate the progress of human culture and moral improvement.   Science but begun to appropriate these resources to the universal amelioration of
our race.   Yet already we see enough to confirm the
hopes of expectant piety and our confidence in God's unerring word, that Providence is gathering up his resources,
and preparing his machinery for a mighty onward movement in the work of redemption.

That the condition of the world is rapidly advancing,
is not only the hope of many, and the general expectation
of all, but there are yet more tangible grounds for our
anticipations.   There has recently grown up in the heart
of man almost everywhere a strange and unprecedented
sensibility to all that pertains to the best interests of *man*.

* Few are aware of the immense and multifarious facilities and resources which
have been furnished through science, to counteract *physical evil*, to improve the condition of society ; to promote social and domestic enjoyment, and to facilitate the progress of the race in every useful and ornamental art.   Among these we may name the
steam for locomotion ; gas for lights and balloons ; Davy's safety lamp ; the cotton
gin ; magnetic telegraphs, mariner's compass, &c.
The Millenium may be less a result of supernatural agency than is generally supposed

Is there a vice that afflicts humanity, that vice is assailed
as an enemy of the race.   Is there oppression, persecution, ignorance, superstition; *any* foe to the progress and
well-being of man, the genius of modern philanthropy is
instantly roused in remonstrance, and fired with indignation, and demands redress, the expulsion and decapitation
of the foe.   So prevalent and all-controlling is such a
sentiment now, that Mammon and Infidelity itself are
obliged to render homage to it.   Infidelity no longer sits
growling in the cavern of his dark misanthropy.   He
sees he must come out and mingle with his race, and put
on the garments of charity.   He appears in the stolen
robes of Christianity, the philanthropist, the reformer,
the Christian.   His virulence has taken the *form* of compassion for man.   The advancement and highest interests of his race are his ostensible aim.   Though he strike
with the same weapon, his sword is unsheathed for truth;
though he kill with the same poison, it is poison disguised
in the sweets of paradise.

But the thought presents itself in a more pleasing
aspect.   The human intellect and human research are,
at the present day, remarkably employed in promoting a
common brotherhood of our race, and in advancing its
highest interests.   Late advances, not only in the sciences
of history, geography and philosophy, but yet more in
archeology, *comparative* philology, and, especially, in eth-
nology, are most effectually contributing to bring all the
kindreds and tribes of the great family of man unto one
great brotherhood, and to protect and advance the interests of every member.   The new science of ethnol-
ogy, for the cultivation of which there is already a respectable organization in this country, is peculiarly producing such a result.   For the object of this science, as
the name imports, is the study of man as a social being;
as the member of a family, tribe, or nation.   Whatever
relates to man in his physical being; his races, habits,
locations, sustenance or language; and all that connects
the present and past generations as component parts of
the one great human family; their intellectual efforts,
their sciences, their struggles, their progress of development, are comprised in the objects of this science.   "It

17*

is the science and history of the human race itself, and
of the relations in which it stands towards itself, and
towards the external world."

Never before was science contributing so generously
to prepare the world for its universal emancipation.
Railways, steamships, magnetic telegraphs, are penetrating into and astounding the most benighted regions.
" Franklin drew the lightning from the clouds, but Morse
gave it voice, and bade it go forth and speak to every
nation, and kindred, and tongue. It is the voice which
is to enter the darkest recesses of the heathen world and
teach them how degradingly they contrast with the
genius which gave it utterance."

The advanced state of knowledge here supposed, is
necessary to the *full development and revelation of truth.*
Even the written revelation is to us, and has been in all
passed ages, a *progressive* revelation.   As God had regard
to the *then* condition of society, the existing condition of
knowledge, civilization and improvement, in originally
making known his will, imparting the light as the world
was able to receive it ; in like manner the book containing this revelation, emits more or less light, according to
the existing condition of the human mind and the human
heart, and according to the advanced condition of the
world.   The sun always shines the same, though the
quantity of sunshine *we* may enjoy, will vary as clouds
intercept our rays.   Truth is the same, however different
may be the quantity apprehended by us.

Biblical knowledge, the science of theology, has also
wonderfully advanced within the few past years.   Biblical researches have been casting new light on the sacred
page, or rather educing new light from it.   The most
laudable progress is now making in those collateral
studies which bring us to the study of the Bible with new
interest and zest, and make the sacred volume the repository to us of *more* available truth than it has ever been
before.   The true principles of interpretation are being
better understood ; the most pleasing advances have recently been made in sacred geography, history and archeology ; and thus the Bible is made to shed a clearer and
a more profuse light ; duty becomes plainer and more im-

perative ; the promises richer and more comprehensive ;
the threatenings more terrific ; God more lovely to the
obedient, more dreadful to the wicked. The motives
for extending the gospel are increased, and the guilt of
neglect aggravated. Again, the Bible has been translated into more than one hundred and sixty different languages, enabling as many tribes and nations to read the
word of God in the tongue in which they were born.
Already is the Bible unsealed to every principal nation
on earth.

Or if we turn to the *execution* of our benevolent purposes *in spreading the gospel*, we shall not the less feel
our indebtedness, under God, to the facilities in question.
It is only among a *free, intelligent,* and *civilized* people.
that are found the *qualifications* and *resources* for appre-
ciating and prosecuting the work of Foreign Missions.
In no other work is there brought in requisition such a
combination of moral, mental and physical power.

Learning of all sorts is now, to an unprecedented extent, made to subserve the cause of truth. Eloquence,
poetry, history, literature, science, the arts and philosophy, are all made to contribute their respective quotas to
defend, enrich, adorn and advance the truth.

We are also indebted to modern improvements for the
cheapness and *rapidity* with which books are made and
circulated in every nook and corner of the earth. A
single Bible Society manufactures a thousand Bibles a
day. Yet we have by no means arrived at perfection
here. All these improvements are progressive, and are
yearly progressing. And we should indeed be blind to
the movements of an ever-busy Providence, if we did
not discern in them mighty preparations for the onward
progress of His cause.

And so I may say in respect to the present advanced
and advancing state of *civilization*. Never before was
the world so nearly civilized ; and never so many and
such powerful means at work to make civilization universal. The political, literary and commercial supremacy of the two or three most civilized nations. cannot
but exert a powerful influence on the whole barbarian

world, to which they either give law or hold in some sort of dependence.

The bearing of this on the spread of the gospel, is too obvious to need comment. It prepares the way of the Lord before him. It provides a soil made ready for the good seed. It furnishes the resources by which to sustain the institutions of Christianity when once established, and to make it permanent, and to extend its blessings over fields which lie still beyond. Both the agency and the design of Providence are here abundantly obvious.

There remains one other particular not to be overlooked : It is the *advanced and the still advancing progress of freedom*. Christianity has as little affinity to despotism and tyranny, as to ignorance and barbarism ; and we cannot but hail, as especially auspicious to the diffusion of the gospel, every advancement in the cause of freedom. But as we turn our eyes again towards the revolving wheels of Providence, what do we find God hath wrought here ? How is he already bringing the nations of the earth into a state that shall give to the Prince of Peace, and to the religion of meekness and mercy, an unmolested dwelling on earth.

Political liberty has, within a few years, made rapid advances. Government has become a science. The will of an individual has ceased to be law. It is now very generally conceded that the design of government is to secure the welfare of the governed. Not a potentate in Europe can sit on his throne without conceding in some form this principle. Absolute despotism is almost antiquated. "A monster of so frightful mein," has slunk away before the light of liberty, into the dark regions of ignorance and barbarism. The public sentiment of mankind has undergone an astonishing revolution during the last century. The progress of free principles has been by no means confined to America. The seed which took such deep root in the bosoms of the Puritans of the seventeenth century, had, if not so rapid and ostensible, as sure and sturdy, a growth in Europe as in America. Here, committed to an unoccupied soil, they took readier root, and sprung up more luxuriantly ; there they struck their roots not the less deep, or ascended

with not the less perseverance, though obstructed in
their ascent by a previous growth.

Since the upheaving of Europe, by the wars of Napoleon Bonaparte, there is not a nation in Europe which
has not made progress in liberal principles. All things
have been verging towards constitutional and representative government. Revolutions in France, Prussia,
Saxony, Spain and Portugal, cannot be mistaken, as out-
bursts of the pent up spirit of liberty. And so we may
say of the late revolutionary movements in Ireland,
Scotland, Germany, Switzerland, and even in *Italy*.
They are the upheavings of the suppressed fires of liberty, giving no doubtful premonitions of the no distant
downfall of the grim throne of despotism.

The policy pursued by the present Pope pays a homage to liberty which we scarcely expected. Driven by
the force of public sentiment, and the conviction of an
advanced condition of the world in point of liberty, the
Pope of *unchanging* Rome so far changes the policy of
Rome as to make a sort of concession to constitutional
government, and to grant his subjects a sort of constitution ; and in some other respects to relax the rigid muscles of despotism which have always characterized Rome.
We will not accept this as an index, that Rome has at
heart changed, but that the *world has changed*, and that
Rome feels if she would live in the world, she must, in
some degree, conform herself to the advanced condition
in which she finds the world. Had we been ignorant
before of the present progress of liberty and the increase
of light in the world, the line of policy pursued by the
present Pope would keep us informed on these matters.
As a concession to these degenerate times of liberal principles, Pius IX. has instituted a system of national repre-
sentation in the shape of a council of delegates from the
different provinces, who are to assemble at Rome for the
purpose of discussing with the government the affairs of
the administration, and aiding it in its efforts for the good
of the people. This measure has been hailed by the Pope's
subjects with the liveliest demonstrations of joy and
thanksgiving. And well it might be ; for this was a new
thing from the pontifical throne. In the palmier days o

Rome, despotism and darkness were the order of Papal rule.   Then the Scriptures and the Fathers of the Church were quoted as proof that Columbus was a heretic and an infidel for suggesting there was another continent ; and a clergyman actually published a sermon to show that Jenner, for endeavoring to check the ravages of the small-pox, was the beast of the Apocalypse.

The present popular movement of Italy is a matter of intense interest to the whole Christian world.   It looks like the precursor of an explosion which shall blow to atoms the throne of despotism throughout Europe.   The times are ominous of eventful changes in Europe.   Austria, and all Catholic Germany is rocked on a volcano. The stagnations of Spain and Portugal are moving, and France seems every year approaching nearer the verge of revolution.   "Indeed," says Dr. Baird, "I think that all continental Europe is going to be shaken to its very centre before many years pass away."*

Late acts of toleration in Turkey, India and China, herald the approach of universal freedom.   The Emperor of China has recently issued an edict, in reply to the petition of Keying, High Imperial Commissioner, granting toleration to Christianity.   The law of inheritance in India has recently been so modified as to remove the former disabilities which Hindoos suffered on becoming Christians.   Caste is no longer a legal disability.   Young Hindoos from mission schools are alike eligible to office with those from government schools.   And the Sultan of the Turkish empire has favored a system of respresentative government and of common-school education ; and more recently the Sublime Porte has issued an order for the protection, as Protestants, of the evangelical Armenians. A hatti sherif (order of the cabinet) was issued by the Sublime Porte in 1841, placing all the inhabitants of the Turkish empire upon a footing of equal rights.   And though insurmountable difficulties to its execution have as yet stood in the way, it is a presage of the rising spirit of liberty, even in that most despotic nation.   And more recently still—at the late annual feast called "Courban

* These pages were penned before the eventful Revolution of 1848.

Beiram"—an imperial order was issued, constituting the Protestant subjects of the empire into a separate and independent community, like that of the Armenians, Greeks or Latins.

"Reform," says Mr. Dwight, "is the order of the day in every department of the Government. The Sultan and his ministers are laboring to do away with old abuses, and to secure to every man his rights. The power of inflicting capital punishment for apostasy from Mohammedanism, has been taken away from the Turk; and the Sultan has given a solemn pledge to the English embassador, that *there shall be no more religious persecution in his Empire.* Sir Stratford Canning is disposed to stand firmly on this ground, and insist on it as a conceded right, that men shall not persecute for religious opinion."

In *Hungary*, the law against entering the Protestant communion is abrogated. Every inhabitant may adopt which church he please, Romish or Protestant, without annoyance. Under the former law of intolerance, eight hundred to one thousand Protestants embraced Popery yearly; under the law of tolerance, nine hundred Romanists in one year have come over to the Reformed faith, and only thirty-five have gone to Romanism. And what is much in point here, and truly surprising, the cabinet of Vienna abrogated the oppressive law.

There has, too, during the same period, been a corresponding movement to loose the chains of *personal* bondage. The time was when one half of the world might kidnap and enslave, under circumstances which makes the blood run cold in its currents, the other half, reduce them to "durance vile," and continue them in cruel bondage at pleasure, and yet scarcely a whisper of remonstrance be raised in defence of rights so egregiously violated. But another spirit is now moving on the face of the deep. It is the spirit of universal freedom. Slavery is fast passing away, to be numbered among the works of darkness that *were*—a relic of barbarism. The jubilee-trumpet sounded, in 1834, throughout the realms of the British empire. The West Indies were made free; and since that time the same glad sound has been heard in India; at Malacca, Penang and Singapore; among the forty-five millions of the serfs of Russia ; in Wallachia at Algiers, and among the Moors at the strong piratical naunt at Tunis; in the republic of Uruguay and Montevideo, South America, and on the island of Trinidad. The slave trade has been abolished by the Imaum of Muscat, the Shah of Persia, and throughout the Turkish empire.

It was announced some time ago that the slave trade had been abolished by the Bey of Tunis. It now appears that slavery is fast coming to an end there. A letter from Malta, 1842, says, "I went, while in Tunis, to see the demolished slave market. Hundreds of years, human beings had been exposed for sale in that place, like cattle. How strange, that a Mussulman state should tear down that den of traffick for the bodies and souls of men, while in Christian America this foul system still flourishes in such vigor! I made many inquiries as to the feeling of the Moors on this subject. I am most happy to say that the greater part are in favor of the Bey, while all obey. If slaves are now sold in Tunis, it is contraband, and with the greatest secresy. The prohibition is complete and absolute. And many of the courtiers of the Bey, following his noble example, are liberating their slaves."

The General Assembly of Wallachia having passed an act of emancipation, March, 1847, Prince Bibesco, (the head of the government,) with whom this truly magnanimous act of philanthropy originated, thanked the head of the Church and the Assembly for having passed a law which, as he said, the spirit of the age and the progress of civilization had so long demanded.

The French Chambers have begun the work of emancipation in their colonies. Indeed, the whole world is coming to a sense of justice on this subject—not only Christendom, but Moslems and barbarians. The slave trade, with almost united voice, is branded as piracy by all nations. Indeed, such has become the public sentiment of all Christendom and of the whole civilized world on this subject, that no nation may be the supporters and abettors of slavery, except at the peril of its good reputation. Philanthropy will weep, and humanity will point the finger of scorn.

Other indications that international relations are as-

suming an auspicious aspect in respect to the universal
extension of the gospel, may be read in the records of a
Congress of nations which from time to time meet to ad-
just affairs, otherwise adjusted by balls and bayonets —of
world's Conventions, which do much to cement national
ties; and of arbitrations instead of arms, by which to
compromise disputes. Not long since, commissioners from
England, Russia, Turkey and Persia met at Erzeroom,
"to settle disputed boundaries, and to arrange other difficulties."

Nations, that by a proud isolation had strongly barricaded themselves within the walls of a hateful and repul-
sive despotism, have been invaded by the light of liberty
and the love of Christianity. Austria, with all her argus-
eyed vigilance, cannot shut out the all-pervading genius
of liberty. Already has it cheered with the hope of better
things, the cottages of the poor, and, with fearful omen,
looked in at the windows of palaces. And China, though
ensconced within a yet higher wall, has been compelled
to surrender, and to condescend to the mutual courtesies
of national intercourse. Her strong-holds are broken
down; her walls of brass are razed; her gulph of separation from European intercourse is bridged. The great
family of nations, so long estranged, is being drawn together, becoming acquainted, and learning their mutual
duties. The world is becoming free.

The Press, too, has been emancipated from its former
shackles; religion is breaking loose from the domination
of priestcraft; opinion is becoming free; discussion untrammeled; and the feeling is fast taking possession of
the human mind, *that man must everywhere be free.*

Thus, again, has God prepared his way before him.
He has made ready the field; and may we not now expect that the Lord of the harvest shall send forth his laborers profusely to scatter the seed, and in due time to
gather an abundant harvest? All things are now ready;
the hand of the Lord is stretched out, and who shall turn
it back? He is preparing the world for the kingdom of
his Son, and shall not the Prince and the Saviour speedily
come and take possession? Ride forth, victorious King,
conquering and to conquer, till the kingdoms of this world

18

become the kingdom of our Lord.   Hushed be the voice
of war; palsied be the arm of Despotism, that Religion,
pure and undefiled, the first-born of Heaven, the immortal daughter of the skies, may find a peaceful dwelling on
earth.

10. I shall advert to but one other particular: Within
the last generation, God, in the vast revolutions of his providence, has *removed*, to a great extent, *the most formidable
obstacles to the universal spread of the gospel*.   The mightiest bulwarks behind which Satan has ever intrenched
himself are Paganism, the religion of Mohammed, and the
Papacy.   The great desideratum in the council-chamber
of the infernal king has always been how man's innate
religious feeling should be satisfied, and yet God not be
served.   How could the heart be kept from God, the
clamors of conscience be silenced, and yet the demands
of an instinctive religious feeling be answered?   The arch
enemy of man's immortal hopes solved the problem.   The
solution appears in the cunning devices he has sought
out by which to beguile unwary souls.   He has varied
his plans to suit times and circumstances, the condition of
man, the progress of society, the character of human governments, and the condition of the human mind.

Idolatry, multiform in its systems, yet one in essence
and spirit, concedes to reason and conscience the *existence of one supreme God*, yet disrobes this divine Being
of the attributes which make him God, by multiplying
subordinate deities, attributing to them the most unworthy characters, and making them the chief objects of
worship.   Knowing God, they glorify him not as God.

Such a religion was suited to a gross age of the world,
—an age of subtilty and ambition on the part of a few,
and superstition, debasement and ignorance on the part
of the many.   But when Christ had come, and new light
had risen on the world, and the general condition and
character of man had advanced, the same object was
gained through two great modifications of idolatry, better adapted to the intellectual and moral condition of the
world.   Western Asia, and a part of Africa, became
too much illumined by the Sun of Righteousness longer
to submit to idolatry in its grosser form.   Hence for

those regions there was got up a *reformed* Paganism,
yclept Mohammedanism, taking the place, and subserving
the purposes of idolatry in its original form.

While among the more contemplative nations of Europe, where the public mind had become still more enlightened and advanced, and could not be satisfied even
with Paganism *reformed and partly Christianized*, Christianity had to be *paganized.* Europe would be *Christian.*
So mote it be, said Satan ; and old pagan Rome rose
again to life by his enchantments,—and he clothed this
monstrous image in a garb stolen from Heaven's ward-
robe, and commanded all men to worship it. The religion of Rome is the last new edition of the same old
idolatry, with a new title, amended, enlarged, on finer
paper, with gilt edging and better bound, suited to the
spirit and taste of the age.

These are the three strong-holds of human depravity
and Satanic power, by which man's arch foe has from
generation to generation held the human mind in the
most abject thraldom.

Now what I affirm, is, that these three enormous systems of iniquity are on the wane. Such, in the irresistible movements of Providence, have been the overturn-
ings among the nations, that their great power to bind
and to trample under foot the immortal mind, is broken.
Paganism is in its dotage. It evidently belongs to a condition of the world which is rapidly passing away. Mohammedanism, embodying in itself the seeds of its own
dissolution, already bears marks of decrepitude, and only
lives and stands as it is propped up by a little doubtful
political power. And Romanism, though in its dying
spasms it ever and anon exhibits an unnatural return of
former life, presents no doubtful marks of its approaching
doom. We are not ignorant of the strange phenomena
at Oxford, or of Rome's unnatural appearance of youth
and vigor in America. While she is gaining individuals
in England, and making a desperate struggle to gain a
foothold in the new world, she is losing whole provinces
in Europe. Look at the general condition of Romanism.
How many of its limbs have already perished,—how
many more are, to all human appearance, doomed to a

speedy decay.   What mean the ruins of the Papacy over a great part of Asia, and in Central and South America? The Inquisition once flourished in India, in all the bloody pre-eminence of torture and death ; and China,* and Japan, were the arena of numerous and flourishing churches. But where now are the walls of its dismal dungeons; its courts of inquest ; the gorgeous palaces of its inquisitors, and its horrific implements of torture ?   They are crumbled to the dust.   The hand of Heaven's vengeance has passed over them and left them but the ruined monument of deadly intolerance.   And what mean those ruined heaps of colleges, schools, churches and other public edifices, met on the islands of Bombay and Salsette, in Goozaret, and on the whole western coast of India ? Or the vast dilapidations of Central and South America? A late traveler in Central America speaks of passing seven ruined churches in a single day, and of finding as many more under a single curate.   Edifices, two or three hundred feet in length, and of proportionate dimensions, of solid structure, and costly materials, and elegant architecture, once the receptacles of vast multitudes of Rome's faithful and most bigoted sons, are either a ruinous heap, or the decaying sanctuaries of a miserable remnant of a once flourishing church.

Surely the wheels of Providence are rolling on.   Obstacles which have so long hindered the progress of the everlasting gospel, are fast being removed.   The arm of Omnipotence is made bare.   God is doing a " new thing" on the earth ; He is "making a way in the wilderness, and rivers in the desert."

In concluding what I designed to say on the *facilities,* which, as results of providential movements, the present age affords for the speedy and universal spread of the gospel, and the complete establishment of Messiah's kingdom, many useful and interesting reflections might be appended.   The present aspects of Providence towards

---

* Such was the success of Popery in China, that many mandarins embraced its doctrines ; one province alone contained ninety churches, and forty-five oratories.   A splendid church was built within the palace.   The mother, wife and son of the Emperor, Yung Ceith, professed Christianity, and China seemed on the eve of being united to the papal see.

our world are most solemn and delightful. What overpowering arguments here, urging us on to duty. Does
God carry out his plans through human instrumentality?
How loudly, then, do the movements of his Providence
call us to be willing instruments. Never before were we
so imperatively urged to more fervency of spirit, to more
diligence in duty. The wheels of Providence now run
high and fast, leaving behind them more events in ten
years than was wont a little while ago to transpire in a
hundred years.

To give point and pungency to such reflections, allow
the eye to take a retrograde glance over the extraordinary providential developments which I have named.
How singularly has God confided to the two most civilized and Christian nations,—the Anglo-Saxon race,—
vast heathen territories, and, by extensive commercial
relations, connected them with every nation on the
face of the earth; how diffused is the English language;
how popular European habits, manners and dress, and
the improvements, experience and laws of civilized nations; what unwonted improvements in modes of conveyance, and the facilities of an enlarged post-office system; how is the clangor of war hushed, and the world
left in almost universal peace; what recent advances in
knowledge, civilization and freedom; and how has the
vigor departed from those mighty systems of false religions which have heretofore beguiled Christianity of the
fairest portions of the earth.

Let us ponder these things, and be wise; wait and
work; pray and watch, till the end be, that we may rest,
and stand in our lot at the end of the days!

18*

CHAPTER XII.

THE FIELD PREPARED. General Remarks;—First, PAPAL COUNTRIES, or Europe; their condition now, and fifty years ago. France—the Revolution—Napoleon. 1845, an epoch;—present condition of Europe Character of her monarchs. Catholic countries;—Spain and Rome—Austria—France, an open field. France and Rome. Geneva. Benevolent and reforming societies. Religion in high places. Mind awake. Liberty. Condition of Romanism and Protestantism.

" Lift up your eyes, and look on the fields; for they are white already to harvest.—John iv. 35.

WE have, in the two preceding chapters, spoken of the hand of God as visible in the *facilities* which the present state of the world, and condition of man, affords to the universal spread of the gospel. We now proceed to a survey of our next topic.

II. The present aspect of the world as a field open for the admission of the gospel.

More than a general survey of so vast and complicated a field, would transcend our prescribed limits. Before attempting any geographical delineation of the great missionary field, I shall direct attention to some of its general features. A brief survey will carry conviction to the mind that the ever busy hand of Providence has brought the world into a position peculiarly favorable to receive the gospel. I have spoken of the rank assigned by Providence to the two great Protestant nations. By territorial importance, commercial relations, and intellectual and moral superiority, England and America hold in their hands the destinies of the world. Why did North America so soon pass into Protestant hands, if not to give the religion of the Reformation a wider field and a fertile soil, that it might bear fruit for the enriching of the nations? Why did not the magnificent empire of the Moguls in Hindoostan either remain in the hands of the Portuguese,—and there seemed no earthly reason why it should not,—or pass into the possession of Russia, France, Holland or Turkey? France fixed an eager eye on the

East, and lost no advantage to gain it. Russia has long
been watching for it, and Holland called much of it her
own. Yet England has unfurled her banner over the
strong-holds of more than one hundred millions of Hindoos, and virtually rules over more than thrice that number in Farther India and China. Why are these populous
nations of idolatry laid at the feet of Protestantism, if
not that they may learn the living oracles of God ? Why
is Paganism grown old and ready to die, and Mohammedanism only propped up by interested civil power, and
Romanism struggling to prolong a morbid existence, by a
spasmodic activity which betokens corruption at the
heart, and mortification in the extremities, if it be not
that those things which are "ready to die," have nearly
come to an end ? What means the recent unparalleled
progress in civilization, government, freedom and knowledge, if it be not that the great controlling mind has purposes of vast moment to answer by such resources ?

The press has been made the handmaid of Christianity,
and the improvements in the arts, advancements in science, inventions and discoveries, have been made to subserve the cause of evangelical religion, and to propagate
it over the earth. Such, too, is the political condition of
the world as to invite our benevolent efforts to send the
gospel to almost every nation.

Could we for a moment entertain the idea of abandoning the work of missions, we should meet a severe rebuke
from the finger of Providence, pointing to the *success*
which has already crowned the but partial efforts of the
church to convert the world, and the munitions of war
already accumulated to complete the conquest. More
than fifteen hundred efficient missionaries are this moment in the field, some scorching beneath a meridian sun,
some shivering amid the eternal snows of Lapland,—occupying more than twelve hundred principal stations, and
many subordinate ones, traversing vast regions of heathen
territory, and preaching the unsearchable riches of the
cross to some millions of the votaries of idolatry. This
sacramental host is assisted by above five thousand native and other helpers, and by not less than fifty printing establishments. They number in their ranks some

two hundred thousand communicants in their differen
churches, and a yet larger number of children and
adults in their schools.*

But such statistics do not, perhaps, introduce us to the
most accurate estimate of missionary labor and success.
Take another series :—the Bible has been translated into
more than one hundred and sixty languages, or principal
dialects, spoken by seven hundred and fifty millions of
the earth's population. Thousands of associations are
in operation for publishing and circulating the sacred
volume, and more than thirty million copies or portions
of the Bible have been put in circulation since 1804.
Half this number has been issued during this period by
the British and Foreign Bible Society alone.

Corresponding to this, too, is the progress of education
among the unevangelized, the demand for schools, and
Christian books, and 'advancement in the useful arts and
in general knowledge. It is a fact of much interest, that,
in the order of things, induced by missionary labors and
influences, the Bible is the first and the principal book
brought to the notice of the heathen. This is usually
the first book translated into the vernacular tongue, and
sometimes the only one to which their more aspiring
youth may resort for assistance in their great eagerness
to learn the English language.

We cannot pursue this general survey without everywhere discerning the busy Hand of preparation compass-
ing ends of vast magnitude to the kingdom of Christ.
The way of the Lord is preparing before him ; and not
to discern the special interposition of Providence here,
would be to close our eyes against the noonday sun.
But a general view does not suffice here. Allow the eye
once more to pass over the world. Geographical or political boundaries will not subserve our purpose at present, so well as religious or moral divisions. Spread before you, then, a map adjusted to the fourfold religious
listinctions of *Papal, Pagan, Jewish* and *Mohammedan,*
including the lapsed Christian churches of the East.

We begin with Papal countries. In our survey of

---

* See Dr. John Harris' Great Commission.

the field over which Romanism breathes its withering breath, our remarks may be chiefly confined to the south of Europe. The religion of Rome is by no means confined within these limits; yet her territories beyond, are but colonies from the parent stock. As the trunk is full of vigor and life, or as it withers and dies, so are the branches. Popery, in South America, in the East or West Indies, in Central America or Canada, cannot retain the strength of its manhood, if there be weakness or decay at the seat of life in Italy, or in France, Spain and Austria.

What is the present state of Europe, compared with its condition fifty years ago,—and what the present condition of Romanism, and of Protestantism? An answer to these queries will present Europe before us as a field open to evangelical labor, and, by consequence, indicate the measure of our duty.

We are struck with admiration at the *change* which Europe has passed through during the last half century. It is but fifty-three years, (Oct. 10th, 1793,) since France "voted Christianity out of existence," and with impious hands assailed the Temple of Truth, and decreed that one stone should not be left on another, till the whole should be thrown down; and in the temple which she built, she set up her image, the goddess of reason. And the reign of terror which followed, was terrific and bloody beyond any thing recorded in the annals of the apostasy. Revelation was trodden under foot, and evangelical piety scouted from the nation. Her voice was nowhere heard, except as echoed in blood and groans, or from the remote valley or solitary glen.

Indeed, the religious history of France is exceedingly bold and instructive, greatly abounding in materials suited to my present purpose. France early received the doctrines of the Cross—early corrupted them—and, though bigoted and superstitious, she readily admitted the Reformed religion of Germany. Two thousand Protestant churches were established in France during the first twenty years of the Reformation. Protestantism took deep root and flourished; and was at length protected by the famous Edict of Nantes, which was extended over

them by Henry IV., himself a Catholic. Under this benign shield, Protestantism prospered for nearly a century.
At length times grew dark, clouds gathered. The perfidy
and artifice of Richelieu first sought to beguile the Protestants into the Romish communion. Priestly rage and
cruel bigotry then assailed them. The Jesuits had decreed their ruin ; and the weak and credulous Louis XIV.,
trampling on the most solemn obligations, and regardless
of all laws, human or divine, revoked the Edict of Nantes,
and let loose the blood-hounds of persecution on the defenceless Protestants. Thousands, hundreds of thousands,
now became voluntary exiles from their country. A
dark century followed. Its history is written in blood—
disgraced with outrage, superstition and crime. The
church was corrupt, the nation a hot-bed of iniquity.
An explosion was inevitable. It came in 1789. It was
as if a volcano had discharged its fiery contents on all
Europe. It was "fire and blood, and vapor of smoke." Yet
this was the signal of better things—the lowering cloud,
the fearful thunder, and the vivid lightning which often
precede a smiling sunshine. It was the explosion of
French infidelity, licentiousness and despotism. For a
time the sun was darkened, and the moon was turned to
blood; the sea and the waves roaring, and men's hearts
failing them. But the atmosphere was purified. The
terrific reign of Napoleon did much to advance the cause
of liberty. The return of the Bourbons could not suppress the spirit of reform and of freedom, which had now
taken deep root in France. The revolution of 1830 was
a report of progress. And the yet more decisive revolution of 1848 brings us a further report of the doings of
that ever watchful Providence, in whose hands are held
the destinies of France.

In Spain and Portugal the flickering light of Protestantism was almost immediately quenched in the blood of
the Inquisition. The voice of piety was stifled. No
one dared read the word of God, much less to give the
sacred volume to his neighbor, or to favor the cause of
education. Italy, under the very thunders of the Vatican, was completely barricaded from the Reformed religion. Belgium, the South of Germany, Austria, and

every foot of Papal territory in Europe, were almost entirely inaccessible to the introduction of Protestantism in any form.   An iron-handed religious despotism would tolerate nothing but the religion of Rome.   Neither the press might propagate, nor education foster, nor the pulpit enforce the doctrines of the Reformation.

Such was the condition of the Catholic states of Europe.   Nor was there much more than a nominal Protestantism in the Northern states of Europe.   The heart of the Germans had stagnated in rationalism, while the Hollander, the Dane, and the Swede, lay dormant in a frigid orthodoxy.   Protestantism was hushed in the slumbers of spiritual death, Rome imposed her yoke, and immortal mind, long debased and humbled, scarcely felt the galling bondage.

But this general stagnation was soon to be broken up. The "reign of terror" came, and in its bloody footsteps followed the terrific reign of Napoleon.   Heretofore the atmosphere had been murky and mortiferous.   The earth yet exhaled the bloody vapor of the revolution, and a lurid sky still bespoke the angry frown of indignant Heaven.   The heavens are again overcast—the thunders roar ; the lightnings blaze—Europe is convulsed—the earth is terribly shaken.   The hero of Corsica comes—a burning comet rolling over all Europe.   Every green tree is burnt up—thrones are crushed—kingdoms crumble—the foundations of the great deep are broken up. As the wars of the crusades, by the eruptions they produced in the civil, social and religious state of Europe, were active causes introducing the notable revolution of the sixteenth century, so we may regard the terrific career of Napoleon Bonaparte as the fearful ushering in of a new and glorious dispensation in the Christian church.   Out of the dark and tempestuous sea which then brooded over Europe, the Sun of Righteousness rose with renewed radiance.   From that period the scarlet beast has staggered from weakness, and Protestantism has been gathering up her strength, and buckling on her armor.   The date of 1815 is destined to be as illustrious in the annals of the Christian church as it is in the great world of politics.

The wars of Napoleon were singularly the scourge of European infidelity, and the means of its correction. Europe felt that a mighty hand was stretched over her, and she trembled. The French revolution had spread the pall of death over Christianity. Revelation was de-throned, and to rationalism and infidelity was given the empire of Europe. This was the portentous calm that followed the strange commotions of 1793. Nor was it strange that another concussion should *undo* what the revolution had done. The devastating wars of Napoleon produced a shock which taught all Europe that Jehovah is the God of nations; that an appeal in this hour of wide-spread catastrophe must be made only to Him, and that the time had come when Eternal Justice would vin-dicate the rights of nations. Says the Emperor Alexan-der, of Russia, who from about this time to his death is believed to have been a humble follower of the Lamb, "the burning of Moscow lighted the flame of religion in my soul;" and he did but speak the thoughts of many hearts, as the car of the conqueror rolled on. "I was a youth," says Professor Tholock, from whose authority I derive these facts, "when Germany was called to contend for her freedom. But I well remember that this memora-ble event awakened religious desires in hearts that had remained, till then, strangers to every Christian sentiment. Every one was penetrated with this thought, that if aid came not from on high, none was to be expected on earth; and that the moment was come for the display of the Eternal Justice which governs the world." The inhab-itants of Prussia, in particular, felt this; and from this time the heart of their king was open to the truths of Christianity. Germany began to feel that she could not, in so grave a period, forsake the God of her fathers.

From this time evangelical religion was revived—the writings of the Reformers, which had been neglected and despised, were now read and revered—the anniversary of the Reformation was celebrated in 1817—sermons, books, lectures, science, literature, theology, from this time, bore the impress of the reformed religion. Schools, religious and philosophical associations, and the press, bear a living and delightful testimony in favor of a pure

Christianity. There undoubtedly arose out of the troubled waters of Napoleon's reign a spirit of advancement in religion, in general intelligence, in free institutions, in the science of government, and in the better understanding of human rights. That such results should come out of scenes so terrific and unpropitious, is but another illustration of the workings of that inscrutable Providence which bringeth order out of confusion, and good out of evil.*

Europe and the world once more hushed in peace, the angel having the everlasting gospel to preach recommenced his flight.

From the battle of Waterloo, June 18th, 1815, commenced a new era in *education* throughout Europe. Read the records of Prussia, Sweden, Denmark, Norway. The loud demand for education by the common people of Europe dates no farther back than 1815; and the late improvements in modes of education are equally modern. It is since that date that Prussia has, in some respects, outstripped even republican America in the education of her people—that Sweden has surpassed any other country in great scholars and literary enterprise—that national school systems and parish district schools have been introduced into monarchical Europe.†

It was from that eventful period, too, that the American church had given her eagle's wings that she might fly to the ends of the earth, bearing to the famishing nations the bread of life. And it was upon the clearing away of the dark chaos which disappeared with the sulphurous smoke of Waterloo, that there arose a beautiful constellation of *benevolent societies*, whose light has already shone to the ends of the earth. And, finally, from that same period, civil and religious liberty has been advancing by sure and rapid strides, and the physical and political, the moral and religious character of Europe has undergone astonishing ameliorations. The press has, in a great degree, been manumitted from a thraldom of many centuries; and Europe, in spite of Rome and the Vatican, is

---

* Mr. Headly, in his book, entitled "Napoleon and his Marshals," confirms the views advanced above, which were penned more than five years since.
† Dr. Robert Baird's Northern Europe.

in the rapid progress of receiving a Christian literature.
Europe, as a field for the circulation of the Bible and
religious books, was never open as it now is; and never
the Bible so extensively read. For several years past,
two hundred thousand copies of the Bible have been put
in circulation in France alone: or more than three millions since the battle of Waterloo—and as many copies
of the New Testament. In Belgium, till recently one
of the most bigoted and superstitious of the Papal states,
there have been circulated, within the same period, three
hundred thousand copies of the sacred volume; and there
has been a large distribution, through every nation in
Europe, not excepting Spain, Portugal and Italy.*

The late religious excitement in France, the movement
under Ronge and Czerski in Germany, the late evangelical
movement in Scotland, and the tendencies to the same
result in England—the late manly and self-denying resistance to oppression of the evangelical pastors of Switzerland, the numerous conversions of Jews, and the increased interest felt in their behalf, indicate the sure
designs of Providence in the spread of the gospel over
all those Papal countries. They are the pillar of cloud
and of fire going before the people of God, to lead them
to victory and to glory.

In France, says one who has resided several years in
the country, " the most encouraging accounts of the progress of truth are coming to us from all parts of the
kingdom. The masses of the people are demanding the
Bible; and in some places, the dignitaries of the church
are coming down from their lofty positions, and, in self-
defence, are giving the famishing multitudes the Bread of
Life, which they have so long withheld. Thousands of
Romanists desire the word of God. The feeling con-
tinues and extends. The people are tired of the yoke of
the priests. If we had ten times as much money, and
ten times as many men, they could all be immediately

---

* In Belgium the demand for the Bible is unprecedented: and the decree of the
Bishop of Rome against the reading of it, only excites the curiosity of the people, and
makes them more anxious to procure a book the Pope is afraid of. In Holland great
numbers of the sacred Scriptures have been distributed, as also among the Carpathian
mountains. In Ireland, too, more than forty Romish priests, and forty thousand lay
men have, within a few years, come over to the Protestant church.

employed. It would be easy to open a new church every month, every week, and to cover with churches al¹ France." In the department of "Saintonge, foity communes are open to the Evangelical Society—in Yonne, twenty important posts are accessible." "What is now passing under our eyes is somewhat like what occurred in France in the age of the Reformation," when two thousand Reformed churches were established in France during the first twenty years.

Nor is this movement by any means confined to France. In Germany, while there is scarcely less of development, there is perhaps more of an undercurrent in favor of evangelical principles. The phlegmatic mind of Germany was, perhaps, never more awake. The intellectual movement is a strong one, pervading Romanists and Protestants, Rationalists and the evangelical; and we may expect the utterance shall not be less distinct than the cogitation, when the day for action shall fully come. Such a day has begun to dawn. The Reformation of Ronge and Czerski, though not so evangelical and orthodox as we could wish, is a great movement, when regarded in its anti-Romish character. It has fearlessly raised the standard of revolt from Rome; and we may take the readiness with which tens of thousands rally about this standard, as a signal of the ripeness of Germany to disenthral herself from spiritual bondage. The Ronge movement was commenced in 1844, by eighteen persons, who were in the habit of meeting in a small town in Germany, to study the Scriptures. Two years from that time, it was stated by Doctor Guistiniana, that there "is not a kingdom, duchy or town in Germany, where there is not a Reformed church." The whole number of dissenting Catholics who have attached themselves to the new communion under Ronge and Czerski, is estimated to be one hundred and fifty thousand, who assemble in more than three hundred places for public worship.

This anti-Romish movement is finding its way among the immigrant German population of America, where it is making progress under auspices more favorable to truth than in Germany. The late meeting of Germans in the Tabernacle, New-York, 1846, "to declare publicly theii

secession from Rome, and to form themselves into a
Christian church, recognizing the Bible as their only
rule of faith and practice," was a delightful token for
good to our country, to the German people among us,
and to the triumph of the truth.*

Nor may we overlook in this survey, the condition of
Romanism in South America, in Central America and in
Mexico. "Things throughout South America are now
exceedingly favorable to the introduction of the gospel.
The severance of South America from the European
world, has tended greatly to weaken the hold of Popery:
and every day the field is becoming wider and riper for
the harvest."

And Central America and Mexico are essentially in the
same condition. Romanism, like thousands of its temples, is there in a state of dilapidation. Every revolution is at the expense of the despotism of the priesthood.
Mexico, just at this time, is, providentially, brought into
a condition of great interest in a religious point of view.
Precisely what God will bring out of the unrighteous war
we are waging against Mexico, we cannot predict. We
cannot but indulge the sanguine expectation that this
war, however unjust and unnecessary on the part of the
United States, is, in the permissive purposes of God, a
providential occurrence, that shall overthrow another of
the strong-holds of popery, and open a vast field for the
diffusion of the principles of the Reformation and the
Bible. A reverend gentleman writing from Mexico,
says a political party exists there whose avowed object
is to limit the power of the priests; to confine them to
their proper duties; to break down the overgrown religious establishments of the country, and to devote their
great wealth to the cause of popular education. They
are not protestants, yet they desire to have the Scriptures circulated as a means of opening the eyes of the
people to the abuses of the church.

---

* Another meeting, a sign of the times, too, has taken place in the Broadway Tabernacle. It was a meeting of *Protestants* to congratulate Pope Pius IX., on account of
his *liberal principles!* And another meeting still, the New England Society, the genuine descendants of the Puritans, to be sure—all good Protestants—not a *Jesuit* among
them—met, forsooth, to commemorate the spiritual emancipation of their fathers—with
Bishop Hughes for their invited guest, and a toast and congratulations for Bishop
Hughes' master at Rome!!

Another general feature of the present condition of Europe, betokening the hand of God at work for her amelioration, is the *character of her present monarchs.*

How different the noble-minded and republican king, Bernadotte, who has just vacated the throne of Sweden, from the super-aristocratic Gustavus, III., and his weak, unstable son, who jointly occupied the throne from 1792 to 1809. And the present incumbent of the Swedish throne is spoken of by Dr. Baird, as one of the most interesting men in Europe. The son of Bernadotte,* is a man near 45 years, he was Chancellor of the University of Upsula ; a man of extensive knowledge and fine literary attainments, and deeply interested in modern improvements and benevolent enterprises. The Queen, too, is spoken of as a most lovely character, the mother of five interesting children, a daughter and four sons, who are said to be admirably brought up.

Or compare the present intelligent King of Denmark with the imbecile Christian VII.; or the pious, noble-hearted King of Prussia, and his saintly Queen, with any of the line of excellent Princes who preceded him, and you cannot overlook the interesting fact that Providence has so disposed of the political power of Northern Europe, as beautifully to throw open those nations to receive a pure gospel.

Or if we extend the comparison to the present comparatively liberal and enlightened policy of the cabinets of the Catholic powers of Europe, we shall discern the hand of God quite as industriously at work to prepare the soil of Europe for the good seed of the word.

Spanish despotism has appeared so modified in some recent movements of the Cortes, as to foster the hope of some important amelioration. Convents are abolished and their vast revenues taken away ; all recourse to mass dispensations forbidden, and all confirmations of ecclesiastical appointments rejected. Henceforth no money shall be sent to Rome, nor any nuncio from thence be

---

* Bernadotte was a Frenchman : a Marshal in the army of Napoleon ; elected by the Diet Crown Prince of Sweden, 1810 ; made king, 1818 ; a man of noble mein, of a liberal mind, sound judgment, engaging manners, and an amiable heart ; a patriarchal king, and an honest man.

19*

allowed to reside in Spain.   This virtual separation from
Italy cannot but work a mighty change in Europe, and
set in motion an influence which shall not stop till it
reach the Andes of South America.   Austria, too, has
become more liberal ; and Italy has been obliged to relax
her iron sinews in her wholesale dealing of despotism
among the nations.   Indeed, there has been a very
marked progress of civil liberty in Europe during the last
half century.

But would we get a true picture of Europe as a field
inviting the evangelical laborer, we must direct the eye
to *France*.   What Great Britain and the United States
are to the world, France is to the Papal world.   Indeed,
France, once evangelized, would take her place among
the "three mighties."   Should she not be " the most
honorable of three," yet she should have a "name among
three."   The Anglo-Saxon race excepted, no nation has
so great an influence over mankind as France.   Her
language is the court language of nearly all Europe.
The nations of the continent are wont to receive their
philosophy at her hands, and to sit at the feet of her
Gamaliels.   And not only Europe, but the ends of the
earth would feel the evangelization, not to say of France,
but merely of the French capital.

We may, therefore, judge of the prospects of Europe
by the encouragement and reception which evangelical
labors meet in France.

I have alluded to the fact that 200,000 copies of the
Bible have recently been put in circulation in France, in
a single year, 33,000 *sold* by colporteurs in three months;
and more than 3,000,000 since 1815.   When the London
Missionary Society sent a deputation to France, 1802, to
inquire into the state of religion, and publish the New
Testament in the French language, it required a search
of four days among the booksellers of Paris, before a copy
of the Bible could be found.   And it is but thirty years
since you would have scarcely found an orthodox, evangelical minister in France, or a pious Frenchman, who was
willing to be employed as a colporteur or an evangelist.
Great as has been the change in Protestantism since the
purchase of peace by the blood of Waterloo, it has been

\ stly greater since the revolution of 1830.   A pure gospel is preached in hundreds of places, more than it was at that period.   Now hundreds of Frenchmen glory in the cross, in being willing to submit to toil, trial and obloquy for the good work's sake.   Bibles are now published and offered for sale in the city and the country, in the chief marts, and at the door of the private cabin, while a quarter of a century ago, it was almost impossible to find a single copy in any store, either in Paris or any city in the kingdom.   Roused from the fatal lethargy of Infidelity, France is at length convinced that she must have religion, and Christianity, in some form, is receiving an unwonted patronage from all classes of her people.*

As a further evidence of this, we may refer to the *spirit of benevolent enterprise*, which has, within a few years past, like the sun after a dark and tempestuous night, risen on France, scattering the darkness and mists of the past, and sending its light and its vivifying influences over the whole land.   Bible, Tract and Missionary Societies, are educing, gathering and combining the benevolent energies of a people who are peculiarly fitted for benevolent action.   Paris, already modestly treading in the footsteps of London and New York, annually gathers together the different bands of the sacramental host, that they may collectively rejoice in their triumphs, and recruit their strength for new encounters.   As an example of their pious zeal and benevolent activity, the Evangelical Society of France employs twenty-five ordained ministers, seven evangelists, twenty-nine school teachers, eight colporteurs, and supports six students, preparing for evangelists.   The Paris Society employs one hundred and forty-six laborers, of whom thirty-four are preachers.   And, if we admit into the account the amount of labor performed *in* France, whether by the French clergy or by different Evangelical Societies, as

---

* "I am surprised," says Rev. Dr. Bushnell, "by what I see of the condition and character of the French people.   They are fast becoming a new people.   The revolution was a terrible, yet I am convinced, a great good to France.   It has broken up the old system, and blown it as chaff to the winds.   Priestcraft has come to a full end; the lordly manners of the hierarchy are utterly swept away.   Industry is called into action; wealth is increasing; education is becoming a topic of greater interest.   No country in Europe is advancing so rapidly as France."

the Geneva and the American Evangelical Societies, and
Bible, Tract and Book Societies, we meet no less than
four hundred preachers, of whom one hundred are
evangelists. There are, also, three hundred colporteurs,
and a large number of pious school-masters ; in all, a
goodly host, who, in honesty and godly sincerity, and
in the midst of great sacrifice and reproach, are raising
their voice in testimony of the truth.*   And Romish
virulence dare not harm a hair of their heads.   Is this
the France of 1793 ?

Such men as Dr. Malan and Professor Monod, Roussel
and Audabez, bright and shining lights, and worthy to
tread in the footsteps of the immortal Calvin, are traversing the nation from East to West, and North to South,
preaching publicly and privately, by day and by night, to
multitudes of the dispersed children of God, who are
hungering for the bread of life ; and to greater multitudes
of Romanists, who are allowed to occupy the places of
preaching to the voluntary exclusion of the Protestants.
These deluded children of Rome hear the strange things
that are thus brought to their ears, and admire the simplicity of an unadulterated gospel, and many embrace it.
It is a fact worthy of the most joyful reiteration, that most
of the above list of evangelical laborers are converts from
Romanism, now engaged to demolish, by the mighty arm
of truth, what once, by ignorance and superstition, they
contributed to build up.   An hundred Romish priests
have been converted in France.

"Never," says Rev. N. Roussel, "have the Roman
Catholic people been more disgusted with the superstition
of their church and the avarice of their priests, than at
present ; and never has there been a more favorable opportunity of declaring the gospel to them."   We need
here to descend to particulars : the following we may
take as illustrations of the hand of God in France at the
present moment :

The departments in which the work of God has been

---

* A single fact connected with the agents of this distribution is worthy a passing notice : of the two hundred French distributors or colporteurs, employed by the British
and Foreign Bible Society, during the same period, one hundred and seventy-five were
formerly Romanists, and the superintendent was not only a Romanist, but a pupil of
the Jesuits.

the most marked, are Yonne, Haute Vienne, Saintonge, Charente.

In the department of Yonne, is the ancient and celebrated city of Sens, whose Archbishop takes the title of *Primate of the Gauls,* and where priestly influence has been from time immemorial overpowering. Could protestantism find room in Sens? Heaven had decided it; but how? A physician of Sens is brought to Lyons,* where, with his wife, he spends some time. His wife becomes acquainted with a pious, respectable widow, whose exemplary deportment and well-ordered family quite excite her curiosity to know by what means this family differ so widely from Romish families of her acquaintance. It was the fruit, she found, of a pure and holy religion. She visited the widow; admired her deportment and conversation, and received from her hands some religious books. The physician and his wife return to Sens, but with minds troubled and uneasy. They sought rest in such instructions as Sens afforded, but found none. They then said, "let us read the tracts the good widow of Lyons gave us." They read them; acquire new views of Christianity; become seriously concerned for their souls, and begin to pray. And so it was with other persons, all Romanists, who were present and read the tracts with them.

While this was doing in Sens, the hand of Providence is working a counterpart in Paris. A poor laboring man, a weaver, feels his heart stirred in him to serve his Divine Master, and begs at the door of the British and Foreign Bible Society to be sent as a colporteur to *Sens.* He goes; falls upon the house of the physician. He and his wife receive him gladly. They are instructed; converted; their house becomes a rallying point of protestantism and piety. A congregation is formed; a pastor is sent for; Mr. Audebez goes and soon finds hundreds, yea thousands, flock to hear him. The whole city is moved. Men of every age and rank show an eager de-

---

* Did space permit, we might go a step further back and trace the *providential history* of the evangelical church in Lyons, and we should find matter for profound ad miration. She is peculiarly a child of Providence. A clerical visitor, after spending several weeks at Lyons, declares that no church answered so nearly to his ideal of what a Christian church should be, as the church in Lyons.

sire to know the gospel. Old soldiers, veterans in prof-ligacy, yield to the sacred word, and weep like children.

The work extends to the whole adjacent country; Mr. A. cannot meet the growing demand for labor; another pastor is called, and shortly the whole department seem about to renounce Rome. Mr. Audebez goes to Paris and asks for more laborers; says he can place forty in the department of Yonne, and doubts not that shortly he shall have place for an hundred.*

A similar movement is going forward in Haute Vienne and Lower Charente. It is the opinion of an eye wit-ness that the "entire Roman Catholic population of Lower Charente would be brought over to the protestant faith, or at least to the protestant communion, if we only had laborers ready to send into the field, which is so un-expectedly open for us."

In the department of Haute Vienne, the work has been, if possible, yet more extraordinary. After laboring six months at Villefavard, Mr. Roussel has the happiness of seeing the *entire Romish population* join the protestant faith, and attend their worship. At Baledent, one half follow Mr. Roussel; at Limoges, Mr. R. established pro-testant worship, which was attended by hundreds of Ro-manists. At Rancon, whither he was called by a letter signed by *eighty* heads of families, eleven of whom were members of the Municipal Council, the Mayor of the city acquiescing, he preached to six hundred persons in a barn. Other communes were waiting to receive his visit and to hear from him the words of life.

We may take the following as an illustration of the eagerness of large portions of the French people for evangelical preaching:

Says Mr. Roussel, "I was in Rancon last week, it was a market day, and the peasants of the neighboring com-munes came from all parts. A man came to my room, who was sent by his village, to ask me what they must do to get a pastor. We were conversing on the subject

---

* At a later date, (May, 1847,) Mr. Audebez says before the General Assembly of the Free Church of Scotland: "If men and money could be secured, it would be easy to es-tablish five hundred places of public worship in France, now that the greater part of France is disposed to Protestantism." And the speech of the Rev Mr. Cordes, of Ge-neva, was equally cheering, says the Report.

when four other persons entered my chamber, and asked
me if I would not come soon and establish worship in
their commune. I had not finished a reply when a third
delegation came to ask what steps they must take to get
a pastor. Before these had gone, there came still four
peasants, from four different villages, to say that all the
inhabitants wished to become Protestants. Lastly, a
fifth delegation came to request the establishment of
evangelical worship." "A stranger might suppose these
persons had concerted together, all to come on the same
day; but for myself, knowing the state of the country, I
was not at all surprised."

Again, Mr. Roussel comes into the department of Charente, distributes ten thousand tracts—the bishop issues
a mandate forbidding—more are sold than before. The
priests preach against reform—the sale increases. A
colporteur is imprisoned; he preaches to the prisoners,
and when he comes out, sells more Bibles than ever. A
barn is open to Mr. R., who there preaches to two thousand attentive hearers, one half of whom could only get
so near as to *try* to hear. And "this," says he, "is but
a specimen of the readiness of the people to hear a pure
gospel."

"Everywhere," says another, "Popery seems shaken.
The priests can only hold back their flocks with an arm
of iron, by intrigues of all kinds; and even then the men
frequently escape from them. To these the Romish religion appears superannuated, they can see nothing but the
frauds of the ambitious clergy, who grow rich on the labor of the poor people." "There are few villages in
France in which the word of God has not been offered,
and some copies been left. And though the priests may
burn the book of life, and utter a thousand lies against it,
the people begin to perceive that the Romish religion and
the Bible cannot exist together."

The *missionary spirit* of the evangelical church of
France and her two theological schools are further tokens
for good. The one augurs good for France, in supplying
her waste places with those who shall water them from
the wells of salvation; and the other is a sure pledge of
the spirit and power of religion in a church. As they

water they shall also be watered again. As they mete, so it shall be measured to them. The divinity schools at Montauban and Geneva, under the auspices of their excellent professors, are verdant spots—wells of salvation, whose waters shall fertilize nations not a few.

Before quitting France I would call attention to a single fact: It is *the singular connection between the French nation and the Papacy.* This is a matter of deep historical interest. And if this providential relation is still to continue, we cannot contemplate the extraordinary religious movement now going forward in France, without anticipating some movement as extraordinary in the church of Rome. France has not only been the right arm of the Papacy in the support she has lent Rome, but she has been the mighty angel with the chain in his hand, to chain the Scarlet Beast, when he has essayed to go beyond his prescribed limits. When Rome was to be exalted, France has done it; when to be humbled, France has been the instrument. France was the first to confer temporal and political power on the Bishop of Rome, and the first to lay hands on a Pope, making him prisoner, humble him, and kill him with mortification and rage. Yet no power has done so much since the days of Pepin, to uphold the Papacy. In 756, Pepin, King of the French, moved by the touching letter of St. Peter himself, direct from heaven, (with the trifling exception of having passed through the hands of Pope Stephen III., and received his *approval and emendation,*) crossed the Alps, took up arms for the Pope, overcame the King of Lombardy, and left the Pope in possession of the exarchate of Revenna and its dependencies. Thus the universal bishop became a temporal prince; added "the sceptre to the keys," and France did it. Pepin conferred this splendid donation on the Pope in supreme and absolute dominion, as a recompense "for the remission of his sins and the salvation of his soul." Charlemagne received from the hands of the Pope the crown of imperial Rome, and thus recognized and became pledged to support the unwarrantable usurpation of Anti-christ.

This famous letter—and we are happy to be able to quote from a veritable correspondence of St. Peter himself—was addressed to the most excellent Prince, Pepin, and to Charles and Charloman, his sons, and to all bish-ops, abbots, priests, and monks ; as, also, to dukes, courts and people. It begins thus: "The Apostle Peter, to-gether with the Virgin Mary, and the thrones, dominions, &c., gives notice, commands, &c.;" the letter ending with the very *apostolic* injunction : "If you will not *fight for me*, I declare to you by the Holy Trinity and by my apostleship, that *you shall have no share in heaven.*"

Pope Boniface VIII. was most signally humbled by Philip the Fair, of France. Philip demanded a general council to depose the Pope ; and the Pope as readily thun-dered his bull of excommunication against Philip. The King, roused to madness, levied an army, seized his Ho-liness, and treated him with the greatest indignity. He soon after died of an illness engendered by his mortifica-tion and rage. Again we trace the hand of France raised against Rome in the Great Western Schism—the elevation of a *French* Pope—the removal of the Papal seat to Avignon, and the subsequent wars of rival popes. Here we may date the first great shaking of the mighty fabric of Rome. Here the Beast received his incura-ble wound. Again, France, under *Napoleon*, humbles the Pope, and breaks the strong arm of his temporal power.

The political power and influence of France, her treas-ures, her diplomacy, her armies and navies, have been laid an offering on the altar of Rome. And France, too, has done more than all other papal countries to *extend the Romish faith.* She furnishes near one half of the missionaries of Rome, (total, three thousand in number,) and about one half of the receipts of all her missionary societies, (total amount, nine hundred thousand dol-lars.) The government is foremost, too, in opening the way, by its power and diplomacy, for Papal missionaries ; and freely lends its ships of war to transport Romish priests to distant continents and islands, and its cannon, to compel the people to receive them.

What France will do next, doth not yet appear. The present auspicious movement in that nation certainly cherishes the hope that this right arm of the Papacy may

20

ere long, prove a right arm to conduct Rome to Christ This we may at least hope *evangelical* France will do—though papal France may once more lend her power to uphold Rome.

The recent revival of evangelical religion in Geneva, the city of Calvin, and where Beza made bare his giant arm in defence of the Reformation, may not be overlooked in our estimate of providential movements in Europe. Geneva has been called the Jerusalem of the continent. Once purified and filled with the sweet waters of life, it would be a fountain, whose streams should flow to Europe and the world. Already France receives her healing waters, and her deserts rejoice.

Late movements in behalf of *reform* indicate moral advancement in Europe. The temperance reformation has crept into the palaces of kings, and numbers in its ranks nobles and princes, while associations for carrying out various plans of benevolent action are springing into existence in almost every quarter of the continent. The travels, labor, and reception, of the Rev. Dr. Baird afford a forcible and edifying illustration of what Europe now is as a field prepared for the good seed of the word. Fifteen years ago, how would the monarchical people and aristocratic princes of Europe have received a protestant, an American, a republican, a man whose principal and sole object was to search out the moral destitutions of the land, and to overflow its moral wastes with the pure waters of life? How he has been everywhere hailed as the precursor of better days to the lapsed churches of Europe, we know. How he would have been received at any former period since the expulsion of Protestantism from France, Spain, Belgium, and Italy, is matter of no doubtful conjecture.

Europe does not, perhaps, present a more pleasing feature, or one of more delightful promise, than in the *increase of evangelical religion in high places.* I have already alluded to instances of this in king's palaces, of crowned heads guided by pious hearts. What a charming example of the power of religion is the Duchess of Orleans, whom the Protestants of France had fondly hoped to hail as their Queen—Count Gasparin, a young

French nobleman of great promise and decided piety, a
man of fine talents, and the most fearless champion for
the truth the Protestants of France have had for half a
century. To which may be added, the late Duchess de
Brogli and her excellent brother, the Baron de Stael, and
not a few of kindred spirits, who now adorn the higher
ranks of life in France and on the continent of Europe.

Or, in another sphere, we meet such men as Dr Merle
d' Aubigne, Prof. Monad, G. de Felice, Dr. Malan, and
the indefatigable, spirit-stirring Roussel, and Mr. Cordes
of Lyons. Indeed, the evangelical church in the ancient
city of Lyons is a beacon of great promise. In the very
heart of Catholic France is a church of near four hundred
members, and the truths of the gospel preached to immense numbers every Lord's day. Or, I might speak of
the late wonderful movement in favor of religious liberty
in Germany, Switzerland, and Belgium.

In reference to the latter we must note in passing, another interesting providential interposition in the destiny
of nations. Rome and her priests espoused the cause of
the Belgic revolution, hoping to be rid of the Protestant
influence which a union with Holland had imposed upon
them. Never did men more grossly mistake the inten-
tions of Providence. The result was a *constitution* for
Belgium, securing perfect religious liberty. No country
in Europe enjoys so complete religious liberty.

The finger of God is most distinctly seen at the present
time in Europe in the *progress of free principles*. The
science of government has undergone an almost entire
revolution within the last half century. The idea of the
absolute divine right of kings is exploded as one of the
last relics of a feudal age, and the republican notion that
a government is for the people, is not only being conceded, but is fast becoming universal. Europe is engaged in a war of opinion. On the one side, for constitutional government; on the other, for arbitrary power
and hereditary succession. Every revolution produces a
result in favor of popular sovereignty, and detracts in the
same proportion from the divine right of legitimacy. In
France, Germany, Spain, Portugal, and Italy, civil liberty

is in the ascendant.*   All continental Europe seem about
to be shaken to its very centre.

The revolutionary tendencies of Europe are especially
interesting on account of the connection between free institutions and Protestant Christianity.   Both are the fruit
of free inquiry.   Church reform is very likely to follow
political reform.   As the government of reason and law
takes the place of arbitrary power, obstacles are removed
to the free access of the gospel.   While, on the other
hand, every Bible, or sound religious book that is distributed in Europe; every protestant school that is established; every evangelical sermon that is preached; every
Bible doctrine or moral sentiment that is enforced, is a
stone loosed from the foundation of the twofold dominion
of Popery and civil despotism.

Another feature not to be overlooked, is, *the general
waking up of the mind of Europe*, at the present time, on
the great subject of religion.   The Romanists may call it
a woful tendency to infidelity.   It has in it, to say the
least, a strong suspicion and disgust of Romanism.   The
public mind is unusually awake to the absurdity of papal
rites and superstitions.   The spirit of inquiry is abroad,
and, dispossessed of its predilections for Popery, the mind
of thousands is open to receive the truth in its unadorned
simplicity.

Little need now be said on our second inquiry.   *The
present condition of Romanism and of Protestantism.*   The
inference from the above is irresistible.   In a worldly
point of view, Rome possesses immense advantages for
propagating her faith; and she is making desperate efforts to regain her lost dominions.   The finger of prophecy and the strong arm of Providence are marking her as
the object of Heaven's maledictions.   "The souls of the
martyrs beneath the altar are uttering their solemn petitions against her.   Thousands are becoming weary of her
vain superstitions and her ghostly tyranny.   Her very opposition is becoming more feeble.   Fire and faggots have
failed.   Her military and her diplomatic power is gone.

* We wait in hope till the opening of the next scene.   The darkness of despotism has
for a little while settled down on Europe; but the curtain shall again be drawn, and the
glorious drama of 1848 be finished.

She no longer stands up in the presence of kings, thirst-
ing for the blood of the saints."* Her power is diminishing with the advance of knowledge, piety, and civil
liberty. Before the advancing light of the Bible, Rome
is stripped of her meretricious charms. Where she once
threatened, she now implores, or condescends to reason.
"She, who once roared, and the nations trembled; she
who frowned, and kings grew pale," is now as tame, and
where public sentiment compels, as obsequious, as an en
feebled, famishing old lioness.

Protestantism, on the other hand, though for a long
time enveloped in a dark cloud, is now as a bridegroom
coming out of his chamber, and rejoiceth as a strong man
to run a race. Worried out by the proud usurpations of
Rome, and crushed beneath the heavy foot of popish oppression, Protestantism has been chased off the soil on
which, for some time after the Reformation, she seemed indigenous. On the very ground where Luther taught,
and Calvin and Melancthon defended the truth of revelation, Protestantism had almost ceased to be. But a remnant, according to the election of grace, remained. All
had not bowed the knee to Baal—all had not received
the mark of the beast. The day of their redemption
seems to draw near. Again do they rise in all the vigor
of youth, and put on the helmet of salvation. In their recent efforts to resuscitate the languishing churches on the
continent, and to strengthen the things that remain, they
have found richly verified the promise, "They that wait
upon the Lord shall renew their strength; they shall
mount up with wings as eagles, they shall run and not be
weary, they shall walk and not faint."

The present condition of Protestantism in Europe,
speaks volumes in favor of her speedy evangelization.
Or if viewed as a providential movement, it indicates the
prepared state of Europe to receive a pure gospel.

If the picture before us is a fair one—if Europe, in her
general features, and in respect to the present condition
of Popery and Protestantism be such as has been described, the question of *duty* in respect to this portion of

the world, is irresistibly forced upon us. In the vision of
our faith, and in the arms of our benevolence, we are to
encompass the whole earth. Not a nook or corner may
be overlooked. No rank or condition of men, no climate
or color, may form a barrier to the universal benevolence of the Christian. Yet the Christian philanthropist
and philosopher must, above all other men, watch the
finger of Providence. Where God is at work there he
must work. Where he finds an open door, there he must
enter, looking to God that he will make it a wide and
effectual door. In carrying out his great plans in human
redemption, it suits the purposes of God sometimes to
advance his work simultaneously in nearly every portion
of the great field, and sometimes to confine his agency to
particular portions of it. We must watch the Divine
mind and work where He works.

At the present time the mighty hand of God is stretched
out over nearly the whole of the vast field. At no former
period has He given so distinct indications that he was
about to give all the kingdoms of the earth to his Son.
Yet the agency of his Providence is more distinctive in
some portions of the world than in others. There is in
the order of time and place a preference in the Divine
mind. Some nations shall come in before others. We
must study this preference. The finger of Providence
will point it out, and then we must direct our efforts, our
prayers and benefactions, to the point or points where the
lines of Providence the most prominently converge.

At present Europe is one of these *special* points of
convergency.

This will enable each one of us to determine our personal duty towards that interesting portion of the world.
Looking to the present condition of Europe—her opening and inviting field, her wants, and the indications of
Divine Providence towards her, what, in benefactions, in
prayer and personal effort, is the measure of our duty?
This determined, in the fear of God, and with the approval
of an enlightened conscience, it only remains to be said,
the "Am. and For. Christian Union" is a channel by
which to convey our benefactions to the aid of a feeble.

yet determined Protestantism, in her struggles to rear
her head amidst the opposing principalities and powers
of Papal Europe.

> "The liberal deviseth liberal things ;
> And by liberal things shall he stand."

CHAPTER XIII.

Continued. Second, PAGAN COUNTRIES. Paganism in its dotage. Fifty years ago
scarcely a tribe of Pagans accessible. 1793, another epoch. Pagan nations, how accessible. Facilities. War. The effective force in the field. Resources of Providence in laborers, education, and the press. Tolleration. Success. Krishnugar. South
India.

"*Lift up your eyes, and look on the fields, for they are white
already to harvest.*" John iv. 35.

THE subject of the last chapter was the GREAT FIELD,
open and prepared to receive the good seed. Attention
was then directed to the countries over which the Papacy
holds its iron sway. We were able to trace very distinctly the hand of God in the present condition of those
countries. Morally, politically, ecclesiastically, and in
reference to the state of education, they are brought into
an unprecedented state of readiness to receive the gospel. He that runneth, may there read the agency of the
Omnipotent arm.

I come now to invite you to a like survey of the
territories of Paganism.

Asia, with her teeming millions, at once starts up before us as the principal theatre of Pagan abominations.
Though Paganism is by no means confined to Asia, nor
is Asia all Pagan, yet we look there for the capital, and
the chief resources of Satan's empire. *There* are the
great *systems* of Idolatry, which have so signally perverted
human reason, extinguished human sympathies, and dried
up the fountain of man's noblest affections. On many

islands of the sea, and in large portions of Africa, and in parts of Northern Europe, there is idolatry, gross abominable, debasing, yet not so systematized; not so interwoven with the science and literature of the people—with the very warp and woof of their existence. In Asia, the great battle is to be fought—the attack must be made at the capital, while the outposts must not be overlooked.

Our present inquiry relates to the *present condition* of Pagan countries, and the *preparedness* of the countries over which this cloud of death has cast its shadow, *for the promulgation of the gospel.*

Paganism is fast sinking beneath its western horizon. Its mighty temples are crumbling to the dust, with no hope that they shall ever again be rebuilt. Its altars are prostrate; the glory of its priesthood has departed; the potency of its spell is broken. It is but the stupendous ruin of a gorgeous edifice. The kings of the earth brought their glory and honor into it. All nations bowed before its gilded altar, and revered its thousand gods. But its foundations are undermined; its sanctuary is assailed; its outposts are taken. The stone cut out of the mountain without hands is fast jostling from their places their strong-holds, and nation after nation is yielding allegiance to King Emanuel.

Precisely to what extent Idolatry is on the wane, and Christianity coming in to possess its vacated territory, we may not be able to determine. The following facts afford indubitable evidence that *something* is doing, which ought to expand the pious heart in grateful aspirations of praise to Him that worketh and no man hindereth, that openeth and no man shutteth. It is the hand of an ever-busy Almighty Providence.

Paganism is on the decline. It is but a few years since its great systems were in the vigor of manhood. Fifty years ago Brahmunism and Bhudism, the two systems which prevailed over all Eastern Asia, holding in mental and spiritual bondage more than half the population of the globe, held their empire undisputed. With difficulty could an evangelical missionary find foothold anywhere in their wide domains. India, China, Birmah, Japan, Tartary, and the numberless and populous islands of the

sea, were almost entirely inaccessible. When, in 1792,
the English Baptists first turned their faces towards the
heathen world, they knew not whither to direct their
steps. Nor was it scarcely less an experiment with the
London Missionary Society in 1796, or with the American
Board in 1812. The world seemed closed against them.
Heathen nations were barricaded against Christian influences by a double wall. Both *ecclesiastical* and *political*
power shut the door against them. Pride and prejudice,
superstition and ignorance, and love of license from the
restraints of religion, united with the ambition and avarice
of the priest and the will of the despot, to keep out the
light of the gospel. Consequently, darkness and despotism reigned, and unbroken generations went down to the
shades of death unpitied and unwarned.

But what a change has come over the world since the
disgorging of the volcano in Europe in 1793.*   That was
not merely an explosion of French Infidelity. Mysterious
though it may seem, yet the convulsion, called the French
revolution, was shortly felt to the remotest boundaries of
Paganism. From that mighty furnace, heaving and boiling with liquid fire, and consuming the hay, wood and
stubble of its own impurity, there seemed to arise a re-
generative spirit, which passed over the face of the whole
earth. " The church, started out of the sleep of the last
century by the shock that engulphed the monarchy of
France, began to grope her way in the early twilight, and
with weak faith and dim vision, to gird herself for her

---

* This date has several times been referred to in the foregoing pages as an important
epoch. If we subtract from it 1260, (a well known prophetic period,) we shall have
533; which latter we find to be the date of the celebrated edict of Justinian, which
established Popery by acknowledging the Pope the head of all the churches. May we
not, therefore, take 1793 as the beginning of the "time of the end," or the fall of Anti-
christ? Another epoch in the rise of Anti-christ was 583-4, when the Pope first set up
the claim of *Infallibility*. Add 1260, and we have 1843-4 as another step in "the time
of the end." Another yet more important epoch in the establishment of the great
Papal apostasy, was 606, when the emperor Phocas acknowledged Boniface universal
Bishop or Pope; and we may look, therefore, that 1866 shall be a yet more illustrious
period in its downfall. But the end may not be yet. For the Pope was not established
as a *temporal* prince till the year 756; to which add the years of his gigantic age, (1260,)
and we have 2016 as the date of the *final* end of Popery. Whether the dying struggles
of the Beast shall be protracted to that date, is yet to be seen.
  It should have been added that 1843-4 is the epoch from which dates the commencement of the modern Reformation in Germany. The bold and energetic manifesto of
John Ronge, against Papal Infallibility, was dated October 1, 1844. We have yet to see
whether a stone was not then set rolling which will crush more than the "toes" of this
huge colossus. This German movement was announced by a leading journalist in
this country as a " NEW PAGE TO THE HISTORY OF THE REFORMATION IN GERMANY.'

work, as the light of the world and the pillar and ground
of the truth."

From that hour idolatry the more rapidly declined, and
an extensive system of means began to come into being
to introduce Christianity. And, what is more, from that
time, political power in the East, which had for some
time previous been shifting, alternately, from the hands
of Pagans and Papists, became confirmed in the hands of
Protestants, and thus the way was opened, and protection
secured for the introduction of the gospel into the populous regions of the East. In India, and over the islands
of the Eastern Archipelago, Protestant rule is paramount.
In Birmah and China, the same power is, at least, indirectly dominant, so as virtually to secure access and
protection to the missionary. Thus political obstacles to
the evangelization of those nations, are in a great measure
removed.

And the hand of God is no less signally manifest in
providing *facilities* for the same work. What, under the
smiles of Heaven, has been *done* towards evangelizing
those countries we may regard as the *fulcrum* of Providence for the doing of vastly greater things. The Bible
has been translated into all their principal languages, the
press is established in almost every important position in
the vast field, and already the light of truth radiates from
these points over those dark fields of death. And education is doing its appropriate work, to prepare the minds
of hundreds of thousands of Pagans to receive the healing waters of life. Much, too, has been done to open the
way by the extensive knowledge which has been acquired
of the *religions*, the philosophy, and the language of
Pagan nations, of their manners, customs, history and
modes of reasoning. Dictionaries and grammars have
been prepared for the study of languages, and a great
variety of elementary and common reading books for the
instruction of the people. Schools have been established,
and churches gathered over large portions of the heathen
world. Thus has Providence put into the hands of the laborer who shall now enter the field, vast resources—an extensive apparatus, which he may bring to his aid—tools with
which to work. Among the one hundred and thirty millions

of Hindoostan, there is scarcely a village which is not accessible to some, if not all the labors of the missionary. And few are the islands of the sea which will not welcome to their shores the messenger of peace.   The vast empire of China, as an issue of the late war, is now added to the great field, and invites Christian enterprise.   Africa—the Pagan portion we mean, has, by one movement of Providence after another, become, to an extent hitherto unknown, accessible to the messages of mercy.   An entrance has already been partially effected on the East and on the West, and an effectual door been opened on the South.

Every missionary station, every press, or school, is an entering-wedge to indefinite enlargement.   Every degree of success opens the door to what lies beyond, and increases the probability of greater success.

We have already spoken of the present increased facilities of *intercourse* with Pagan nations—extensive commercial relations—the unprecedented prevalence of the English language, and the residence among heathen nations of so many Europeans, many of them highly intelligent, and some of them eminently pious.   By these and other means, the unevangelized are becoming acquainted with us, and we with them.   We meet and compare notes—learn their character and condition, their wants and their woes; and they are made acquainted with the advantages which a people derive from the improvements of civilization, from true science, and a divine religion. It is almost impossible for a nation at the present day to close their doors against the diffusive light of liberty, knowledge, civilization and Christianity.   The remotest nations, by the rapidity of recent modes of communication, have become neighbors.   These are so many telegraphic lines, to convey knowledge, and to diffuse light over the darkest nook and corner of the earth.   They are providential arrangements, giving facilities to the church to send abroad the everlasting gospel.   The field is prepared either for the good seed or for tares.   We do well not to sleep.

Nor should we pass unnoticed the instrumentality of *war* in preparing the world to receive the gospel.   War is the *sledge-hammer* of Providence to break in pieces the

great things which he will destroy.   The wrath of man
is made to praise Him.   Wicked passions as roused in
the war spirit, are made to subvert and remove some of
the most formidable obstacles to the progress of the truth.
When God would batter down the despotism of Europe,
and smite the head of Rome, he let loose upon them the
blood-hound of Corsica.   Napoleon Bonaparte was his
hammer.   When he would demolish the time-honored
and seemingly insurmountable obstacles which India presented, to ever becoming a Christian nation, he commis
sioned a people of fierce countenance, and skillful in
carnage, and mighty in power, first to punish them for
their abominable idolatries, and next to remove difficulties to their evangelization—to give protection to the
missionary, and to supply facilities for his work.   When
he would cut the bars of iron, and break the gates of
brass which shut out China from the family of nations
and the benign influences of Christianity, he again commissioned the scourge of war and British cannon.   Or
when he would break up the feudal institutions of Mount
Lebanon, and prepare the way for the peaceful reign of
the gospel, he broke those flinty rocks by the hammer of
war.   "Light, knowledge, and the gospel itself, have followed on the bloody heels of war; and the flowers of
learning and liberty have blossomed on the field of the
crushed skeleton."   We regard with interest the *providential issue* of the late war with Mexico.

But we shall take a different view of the field as providentially prepared.   Fix the eye for a moment on the
effective force in the field—the *resources* and facilities at
command, and the *success*, which has already crowned
the past, and the conviction will deepen that the hand of
the Lord is in the work.   In *success* Providence furnishes
an illustration of the power and purity of Christianity;
and the *effective force*, in the form of laborers, with the
facilities and resources put into their hands, is a providential instrumentality made ready for the work.

Since the commencement of the present century, God
has brought into the field a corps of laborers, and accumulated an instrumentality far surpassing the conception of
the common observer.   At that period, they were but a

South Sea Islanders.   P. ge 230.

very little band,—a few skirmishing parties. Now they
have become a thousand,—an army organized, consolidated and furnished. We are safe in stating in round numbers the whole number of efficient laborers employed in
the different departments, as sappers and miners of the
colossal fabric of idolatry, in round numbers as follows :

1,500 Ordained ministers, European and American.
2,000 Assistants, male and female, from the same
       countries.
5,000 Native preachers and catechists.
200,000 Native members of churches.
250,000 Pupils in mission schools.

In this short list we have an army of, we may say,
9,000 salaried agents of benevolence, engaged in preaching the gospel, or in some of the varied offices of education or religious instruction ; and we might add a yet
greater number of unpaid agents, as native helpers, assistants, and sabbath school teachers, who are furthering
the same good cause. And to this we may add the influence, by example and precept, of two hundred thousand church members. In a greater or less degree they
are illustrating the power of the gospel, and putting shame
on the vanities of idolatry. And to this, again, we must
add a less numerous, but an effective corps of foreign
helpers, in different military, civil, mercantile and diplomatic services. The influence abroad of such men as
Sir Stratford Canning and Sir Edmond Lyons in the Levant, and W. C. Money and Lord Wm. Bentinck in India,
is immense beyond computation. Scores of such men
have been, and are still using the influence of their stations, and employing their great talents to further the
cause of Christianity among the heathen. And the wealth,
the talent, the Christian example and influence of hundreds, yea, of thousands, of devoted men and women, in
the more ordinary ranks and employments, go to make up
an immense machinery, furnished by Providence to carry
forward his work.

From more than fifty printing establishments, issue
forth the Bible and religious books by thousands, daily

which are scattered, by an agency made ready, over those vast fields of spiritual death.

The pecuniary resources of the foreign missionary en-terprise have likewise become considerable. About $2,500,000 are annually raised and expended for this purpose—half a million by the churches in the United States, and two millions in Europe. The above aggre-gate includes only what is given directly for this purpose through Foreign Missionary Societies—exclusive, of course, of considerable sums contributed to the same cause, directly or indirectly, by foreign residents in heathen lands, and of still larger sums which go, indirectly at least, to favor the same enterprise, through other benevo-lent societies, as the Bible, Tract and Education, Sea-men's Friend, Jews, and Colonization. Three millions would probably fall quite within the limit of the revenues of this branch of benevolence.

In like manner the same inventive Providence has brought into being, for the same purpose, an immense *system of education* abroad. Including the learners at colleges, seminaries, high schools, boarding schools, and common free schools, we count not less than two hundred and fifty thousand heathen youth and adults, who are re-ceiving a Christian education. Through these pupils the light of truth is sent—faintly it may be—into nearly as many heathen families, and each of these school-rooms is made a preaching place for the missionary, I speak now of the system of education only as a machinery made ready for future operations. An amount of mind is hereby rescued from the ruins of Idolatry, and capacitated to exert a tremendous influence in demolishing the whole fabric. Of this we have a happy illustration in the edu-cated Hindoo youth at Calcutta. Hundreds of native young men are there educated at the Hindoo college—first, they become sceptics—thoroughly despise and aban-don the fooleries of Hindooism, and as soon as they fairly come in contact with the truth, some of them are con-verted; and there is, perhaps, not so influential a class of defenders of the truth, and propagators of the gospel, as these same educated, converted natives. Thus Providence has secured in *mind* a rich resource for the further progress of the work.

The moral conquest of India will probably be achieved as her physical conquest by the British has been—by *her own sons.* Our dependence, under God, lies in a *native agency.* We may never hope to send men in sufficient numbers from abroad, to supply her hundred millions: nor is this desirable. An agency must be created on the field. We look for this in those nurseries of learning and religion, which Providence has raised up in those schools.

But where, as in most cases, actual conversion is not the result, yet the number of *readers* is increased by tens of thousands, and thus the field on which the good seed may be sown is proportionably enlarged.

But we must not overlook a new feature in education in India, for we shall here again trace the footsteps of Providence. A late act of the governor-general has given a new impulse to native education. Moral and intellectual qualifications only, are henceforth to be regarded in conferring governmental offices on natives. The candidates are to be selected from the best qualified in the schools; governmental schools, public or private schools, missionary or non-missionary, are all to be put on an equal footing. This forms a new epoch in Indian education. Heretofore everything has been ruled by *caste,* favoritism or patronage. In a country like ours, the people are, to a great extent, self-governed. In India, all offices, from the highest to the lowest, are held by official agents appointed directly by Government. Consequently, the patronage of Government is immense, monopolizing, all-absorbing. Hence we can scarcely conceive the impulse given to education the moment this vast source of patronage is open, as a stimulant to the most deserving in the schools. "It makes the seminaries the nursery of the service, and the service the stimulant of the seminaries."

It introduces the enlightened principles of European governments, diffuses European knowledge and science, (which have heretofore been confined very much to the capital,) into the districts, and places men of enlightened minds in situations of the highest trust and responsibility.

And Indian education presents another new feature worthy of a passing remark. But a few years since nearly the whole of the immense educational patronage of the East India Company's government went to pro-mote *oriental* learning, and of consequence to nurture Hindoo superstition and Idolatry. Now, thanks to Heaven for the wise and philanthropic policy of Lord William Bentinck, truth, in the form of European litera-erature and science, has taken the place of falsehood and error, as formerly taught amidst the dreary lore of ori-entalism. And if nothing were at work to undermine and demolish the whole fabric of Brahminical supersti-tion, this would do it ; so interwoven is Hindoo learning and Hindoo religion, that one must fall with the other. Thus mightily is the hand of God at work to demolish falsehood, and build up truth in that vast country.

Akin to this is another providential feature. The Hindoo law of inheritance heretofore presented a most formidable obstacle to the conversion of that people. The moment a man forsook the religion of his fathers, he made a complete forfeiture of property and rights. He beggared himself and his family. But He in whose hands are the hearts of all men, has moved on the minds of the ruling powers, to remove this obstacle too. The Govern-ment, by assuming the ground in a late act, that "all the religions professed by any of its subjects shall be equally tolerated and protected," has, at a blow, annihilated one of the most formidable obstacles to the conversion of the Hindoos. The Hindoo or the Mohammedan may now become a Christian, and abandon his caste, and yet suffer no disability or oppression.

Another important item in this connection, is the late divorce of the English Government from all patronage of Idolatry. Formerly large appropriations, as a result of treaty stipulations, were made to the support of certain temples and Brahminical establishments, and a ruinous patronage was lent to certain pilgrimages and festivals, especially those of Juganauth ; and a very unchristian-like indulgence was granted to certain cruel and abom-inable rites and practices. The prohibition of infanticide was the first decisive act of the Government—the suppression of the suttee followed ; and after a few years more the Government completely divorced itself from the vile and abominable thing which God hates; and we may now expect that the influence of that Government, in the final suppression of Idolatry, and the establishment of Christianity, shall be vastly increased.

But progress in Toleration, so distinctly marking a providential movement in the advancement of truth in the world, is not confined to India. Similar edicts have recently gone out from the Emperor of China, and from the Sublime Porte of the Turkish empire. In reply to a petition of the High Commissioner, Keying, the Emperor of China has decreed toleration to Christianity ; and the Sultan of Turkey "engages to take effectual measures to prevent, henceforward," the persecution and putting to death of the man who shall change his religion. The bold, fearless and energetic remonstrance of Lord Aberdeen, organ of the British Government, in a letter addressed (1844) to Sir Statford Canning, Embassador at Constantinople, speaks the mandates of Providence at the present day. Opinion shall be free.

So much for facilities and resources. Let us now see what preparation for future progress there is in the *success* which has already attended our missionary enterprises. We shall again see that the fields are white already for the harvest—the reapers stand with sickle in hand—an immense power is accumulated for future progress. Past *success* not only supplies materials for future progress, but it indicates the removal of obstacles, and holds out the most cheering encouragement to a still more rapid success, and carries conviction to the mind of the heathen of the *power* of Christianity.

What, then, has been *done?* It will subserve our present purpose to confine our inquiries chiefly to India, Birmah, and the islands of the Pacific.

The provinces of Krishnugar, Tinnevelly, Madura, Ceylon, and Western India, afford not only a wide and effectual *door* for the entrance of the missionary, but an unprecedented vantage ground has been gained at these points for the prosecution of all future labors ; and they

21*

may therefore very justly be introduced here as illustrations of the present providential condition of the world.

Krishnugar, a province in Bengal, was a strong-hold of Brahmanism. No efforts seem to have been made for its conversion till 1832, when a few schools were established. Preaching commenced in 1835. The next year thirty-five were admitted to the church—the word was preached, and five hundred inquirers were found seeking the way of life. From that time the work made a gradual yet irresistible progress, till it has at length extended to no less than seventy-two villages, and numbers as the subjects of its power, more than five thousand converts. Churches have been erected, and filled with attentive and devout hearers; and schools established in which some thousands are receiving a Christian education. Christian ordinances are instituted; the gospel preached, and the press is sending out the leaves of the tree of life. A territory of eighty miles in extent is thus brought under religious culture. A fire is here kindled, whose light may shine far and wide over the vast regions of darkness which still cover India—an altar erected there from which may be taken coals to light up more fires throughout those dismal regions of death.

The Bishop of Calcutta, after visiting this province, thus describes the progress of improvement since the work commenced: "A few months since all was jungle—now every thing is teeming with Christian civilization. What building is this? I asked. "It is the girls' school." And this? "The house for the mistress." And that large building? "The mission house." And those small ones? "They are out-offices." And that wall? "It incloses the garden." And where is the new church, of which you talk, to stand? "Here," was the answer, "and I will show you the ground plan." It was like magic. And not a brick of all this had been laid when I passed through the same place in 1839. What a blessing is Christianity! How it raises, civilizes, dignifies man! How it turns, literally as well as figuratively, the wilderness and solitary place into the garden of the Lord!"

In the progress the gospel has made in the southern

portion of the peninsula, we meet the same pledge of future success—a promising starting point for future operations. "In Tinnevelly," says the same authority, Bishop Wilson, "the word of the Lord runs and is glorified more rapidly, and to a far wider extent. The inquirers and converts of the Gospel Propagation, and the Church Missionary Societies, amount to thirty-five thousand. Such awakenings have not been surpassed since the days of the apostles, and there seems every prospect of all the South of India, containing millions of souls, becoming, ere long, the Lord's."

Some idea may be got of the progress of Christianity in Southern India, from the following statistics of the Church Missionary Society. There are connected with this single institution, aside from the missionaries themselves, the following native agency: 267 native catechists—192 school-masters—6,842 baptized persons, 1,245 of whom were added the last year—19,706 candidates for baptism—1,468 communicants—30,000 persons under Christian instruction—and 461 villages under the care of the Mission. "The power of divine grace," says one, "seems to me to have been so sudden and mighty as to strike with wonder every mind susceptible of religious impressions." "I have but very little doubt," writes another, "the whole population of Tinnevelly will soon renounce Heathenism and come over to Christianity,"

If regarded in no other light, what resources has Providence here gathered, in the operations and success of this single society, for the future prosecution of the work. And were we to add here similar items furnished by the Reports of the American Board, the London and other Missionary societies, we should discover a cumulative power by which to act in time to come, truly encouraging; especially when taken in connection with the open door of access, and the readiness of the native mind to receive the gospel. Hundreds of villages have cast away their idols, and not a few are the temples which have been unceremoniously cleared of the emblems of idolatry, and elevated to the worship of the true God. These are verdant spots on which the good seed has taken root, and

fruit is now abundantly ripening with which to feed the famishing tribes around

The American Mission at Madura has seven churches, fifteen stated congregations, one seminary, five boarding-schools, ninety free schools, and four thousand pupils in the various stages of learning. Forty villages have put themselves under the care of the Mission, and one hundred would do the same if the number of missionaries would allow of assuming such a responsibility.

A specimen of the preparedness of this field to receive the good seed, may be gathered from a late appeal of the American Mission at Madura: "We are not aware," say they, "that there is, on the whole district of Madura, a town, village or hamlet, in which we could not, as far as the feelings of the people are concerned, establish schools and Christian instruction to any extent your pecuniary means will allow. The whole district, in the most accurate and strictest sense, is open to the reception of divine truth and the Christian teacher. Yea, more—there is scarcely a town or village from which we have not received a formal request, an earnest entreaty to send them a teacher. A population surrounds us, who speak one language, equalling more than half that of the United States. From one end of the land to the other, in city, town or country, the living minister will find the way prepared before him, to preach the tidings of a Saviour's love, and to distribute all the Bibles and Tracts the American church will furnish." Again the same missionaries say, "Never do we pass through the streets of these villages without being assailed by the question, Why do you not send a missionary here?—we will receive him gladly; we will send our children to your schools; you must not pass us by."

Such language is true, too, of other parts of India. Every missionary station is a door of entrance to a wide field beyond. And more than this is true: the Bible and the religious book is going before the living preacher, and preparing fields for his future labors, and creating demands which nothing but evangelical truth can satisfy. On a tour in the Northern Concan, beyond the reach of any direct missionary labors, Dr. Wilson finds a Brahmin reading a portion of the New Testament to a company of natives who are eagerly listening. In Goozarat he meets some natives, about one hundred in number, residing in seven different places, at considerable distances apart, who professed to be converts to Christianity. He found, on inquiry, they had not had intercourse with any missionary, but had received the knowledge they possessed of Christianity principally from books, aided by a native Christian from Bengal. They had openly professed Christianity, one of their number acting as their head and teacher. "I believe," says the same missionary, "that instances of this nature are not unfrequent."

Another missionary has recently reported a very similar case. "Recently two men came from another village, to inform us that a thousand persons—in consequence of reading some of our books—were desirous of putting themselves under our protection. The same messengers mentioned half a dozen villages where a similar change has been produced by the reading of Christian books."

Says Mr. Mather, of the London Missionary Society, "I had an interview with Mr. Hill, at Berhampore, and he told me that he and Mr. Lacroix were in conference with about five hundred natives, who were promising to come over to Christianity." And "about a year ago a proposal was made by a sect of about two hundred persons, that I should be their Gooroo, (spiritual guide,) that they would attend my instructions, and that together we would fully investigate Christianity."

Such cases as the following are now occurring : While a missionary was waiting at a rest-house, he "saw the villagers assemble, and heard them addressed on the folly and wickedness of Idolatry, by a native, who was also a resident of the village. This man was not acquainted with any missionary, but had learned what he knew of the truth from books and tracts."

Such instances afford delightful testimony, not only that the field is ripe for the harvest, but that there are agencies at work, which facilitate the progress of evangelization in a ratio hitherto unknown, and give pleasing promise of speedy and complete success.

And here I would not withhold again the high authority of Bishop Wilson; who, after a residence of some fifteen years in India, discourses thus : " The fields in India
are white already for the harvest.   Nothing has, I believe, been seen like it.   An outburst of the native mind
seems at hand.   The diffusion of education ; the striking
benefits of medical science ; the opening of an exhaustless commerce on all hands ; the recently ascertained
riches of the soil ; the extent and magnificence of the rivers and mines ; its superb harbors, including its almost
interminable coasts ; the rapid increase of settlers from
Great Britain and America ; the security of person and
property under British rule ; the number of offices thrown
open to native merit ; the railroad contemplated and almost begun ; and the incredible rapidity of communication by steam, uniting the whole world, as it were, into
one vast family, are bringing on a crisis in the native
mind most favorable to the introduction of Christianity."
Again the Bishop speaks of his " firm belief that Hindooism will soon altogether hide its head—the crescent of
Mohammed already turns pale—worn out and effete superstition sinking before the mere progress of science and
civilization, before the startling knowledge of history, the
lights of chronological learning and the laws of evidence,
of the incredible progress of religious principle ; of the
more favorable disposition of Indian rulers towards Christianity ; and of the decidedly improved moral and religious character of the servants of the Honorable Company."   All of which help to make up the sum total of
what God is doing to prepare that vast and populous land
to receive the gospel of his Son.

Similar testimony flows in upon us, unsolicited, from
other quarters.   The excellent Rhenius, German missionary in Southern India, says, " The Lord Jesus Christ is
certainly magnifying his name in these parts ; Idolatry is
rapidly diminishing ; this wilderness begins everywhere
to blossom ; many souls are delivered, not only from the
bondage of Idolatry, but from sin in general ; villages are
coming in constantly, casting away their idols, and giving
up their temples to be used as Christian churches.   I
could furnish you with cooley loads of their neglected

idols." Say the corresponding committee of the Church Missionary Society, "The barriers of caste are rapidly breaking down; there is an increasing spirit of inquiry about religion, and for moral and religious instruction; deep-rooted prejudice against religious instruction no longer general; the promotion of secular education a leading topic." "A great desire has arisen among the youth of Calcutta to obtain and read the New Testament. We have not to go as formerly, and beg them to accept it. They come of their own accord, and solicit this blessed book. This desire is now prevalent among the pupils and students of schools of all grades."

A feather indicates the course of the wind—so little facts are sure pledges of great and wide-spread changes: "Young Hindoos, who have received an English education, are establishing English schools in their own villages, and thus render themselves useful to their country, and effectually advance the truth. Rich zemindars pay them a small salary, and the parents of the children contribute their share for their support."

Brahmins see the impending danger, and use every effort to turn it away; yet they say, "When Christianity obtains a permanent influence, we shall join your ranks." They are not ignorant of the influence of Christian schools over the minds of their youth. One recently said, "As soon as the boys learn to read, they become Christians; hence I take my boy from school." A wealthy Brahmin, near Benares, recently gave up his son into the hands of a missionary with these remarkable words: "I feel convinced, after reading your sacred Shasters, that they contain the true religion. I have not the power to come up to the purity of its precepts, but here is my son, take him as your child; feed him at your table, and bring him up a Christian; at the same time making over to him ten thousand rupees, (five thousand dollars,) to defray the expenses of his son's education." This is a new thing in India. The effect on the mind of the Hindoos will be incalculable; a heavier blow has perhaps never been struck on the strong-holds of Idolatry.

In no part of the great field has God provided a more powerful moral momentum for the future progress of the

work than in Ceylon, Birmah, and China.   But we may
here forego details.   Were we to take a survey of those
countries, as providentially opened, and of the work as
already in progress there, we should meet the same open
field, the same preparation of mind, the same accumulation of power by which to urge onward the evangelica!
car, which we have seen in the instances already contemplated : missions established and a fund of experience gained ; obstacles removed ; translations of the
Scriptures, the press at work, and a store of religious
books made ready ; a strong native agency, and efficient,
extended educational systems in readiness for the work,
and extended mental preparation in many thousands of
native minds, all so many resources and facilities in the
hands of God for the future progress of the work.

A voice from the four winds proclaims the no distant
fall of Paganism.   It speaks of the "crumbling of idol
temples," "colleges of Hindoo learning deserted," "general abatement of prejudice against Christianity," "the
gradual increasing influence of missions and respect for
missionaries," "six thousand eight hundred natives converted through the Church Missionary Society the last
year," "every prospect that India will, perhaps, in a single generation, renounce Idolatry."   Indeed, writes one,
"the feeling is becoming general among the people of the
East, that some extraordinary change is at hand, which
is to be effected through the diffusion of Christianity."
And well may they look for such an event when they see
so much that is ominous in the signs of the times ; in the
neglect of rites and ceremonies essential to their idolatrous systems ; in the divisions and schisms among their
priests, as in the fierce conflicts recently carried on in
Bombay and Calcutta ; in the conversion to Christianity
of not a few of their priests ; in the public discussions, as
in Calcutta, where mighty champions for the truth and
for the demolition of Brahminism have been raised up
from the people themselves ; in the many newspapers and
periodicals, both for and against Christianity, published in
Calcutta, Bombay, and Madrass, and in the already wide
diffusion of Christian and European learning.

In the sacred city of Benares, among the gorgeous

Arabian Scene.

monuments of Idolatry, stands a remarkable shaft, which is reputed once to have towered to the very clouds, but has been gradually sinking for many years. This the Hindoos regard as an index to their waning and sinking religion. When the shaft shall have sunk to the surface, and mother earth shall close in upon it, Hindooism shall be no more.

CHAPTER XIV.

THE FIELD PREPARED. Islands of the Pacific. Native agency. Liberality of native Churches. Outpouring of the Spirit and answers to Prayer. The first Monday of January. *Timing* of things. England in India—her influence. Success, a cumulative force for progress. The world at the feet of the Church.

" Look on the fields, for they are white already to harvest."

BEFORE closing our review of Pagan territories, we must cast a glance over the isle-dotted waters of the Pacific. Here God is doing a new thing under the sun; is constructing a new world, perhaps another continent, through the instrumentality of an infinite number of insignificant animalcules. Numerous islands, smiling in all the luxuriance of a new creation, have arisen from the bottom of the ocean, fabricated by the incessant toils of these minute workmen. They rise to the surface of the water, the waves contribute to convey materials to form a soil; the birds of the air are commissioned to bring and plant seeds on them; a luxuriant vegetation springs up; man at length comes, and a new field is open for the ravages of sin, and a new field over which victorious grace shall yet raise her victorious banners.

We have already traced the hand of God in bringing these several groups of islands to the notice of the civilized world and of the church; how it was done just at the right time; when religion and knowledge had become matured for a vigorous onset upon the powers of darkness; when an unwonted spirit of benevolence had been roused in the church, and the angel of evangelism was prepared for his immortal flight. We are now concerned only with the present condition of those islands. They have already, for the most part, been brought within the dominions of nominal Christianity. Ninety islands are said to have received the law of their God, and a population of some four hundred thousand have nominally embraced Christianity. Eight of these islands have been converted solely through a native agency, and forty or fifty are, at the present time, under the instruction of none but native laborers. In schools, in the power of the press, in a religious literature, in the experience and ability of laborers, in governmental protection and aid, and in a consistent exemplification of the power of Christianity in a multitude of converts, perhaps God has nowhere accumulated a more efficient power for the future prosecution of his work.*

In four groups of these islands, where, thirty years ago, the people were gross idolaters and cannibals, are now forty thousand church members. In a district of the island of New Zealand, the average attendance on divine worship is seven thousand five hundred, and one thousand four hundred candidates for baptism. From the Sandwich Islands we now receive such reports as these: Printed by the mission, in a single year, ten and a half millions of pages, nearly half of which were the Scriptures; seven boarding-schools with three hundred and sixty-one scholars; four select schools; a boarding-school for the children of the chiefs; a mission seminary with one hundred pupils, to which is attached a theological class; a female seminary with sixty pupils, and three

---

* We may take the following as a specimen of the influence of the *school system* on the future destinies of the people: The seminary at Lahainaluna (Sandwich Islands,) has sent out two hundred and ninety-six pupils, of whom forty-two have died, two hundred and fifty-four in the field. Of these, one hundred and eight are engaged in the work of teaching; forty-three in the service of government; thirty-one, though not engaged in teaching, are usefully employed in letting their light shine. Of the remaining seventy-eight, some are engaged in honorable employments, while others are idle, or worse than idle. One hundred and fifteen are in good standing in the church. The institution is thus scattering blessings throughout the islands; its graduates are everywhere the leading members of society, in matters, civil, religious, and literary. "In manual labor they are several times more valuable than other natives, having acquired habits of industry, and learned how to work while at school."

huudred and fifty-seven common schools, taught by five hundred and five teachers, and containing twenty thousand scholars. And to this prospective, though already in a degree effective, force, we add the daily preaching and the faithful instructions of eighty missionaries and assistant missionaries, with six hundred native teachers and catechists, with the goodly profession and the ordinary activities of twenty-four thousand church members, and several thousands of inquirers and candidates, who, in the judgment of charity, are the children of God, and we have before us an instrumentality by which we may expect soon to see all those beautiful islands laid at the feet of the Redeemer; and vast resources secured for the prosecution of the work elsewhere. Or who can contemplate the vast amount of knowledge and civilization that has been secured in other islands of the Pacific; the Christian instruction that has been imparted; the educational systems that are in operation; the missionary experience that has been gained; the native agency that is prepared; and the divine power that has been exemplified by tens of thousands of living examples, and not read in these things a sure pledge for the speedy consummation of the work?

Or who can look for a moment at the Feegee Islands, and not be impressed that now is the accepted year of the Lord? Where, but a few years ago, was a population of gross, greedy cannibals, now are happy, peaceful communities.

There is, perhaps, at present, not a more marked or encouraging feature of the missionary work than the prevalent conviction of the value of a *native agency*, and the fact that every principal mission is directing its efforts especially to create such an agency. Mission colleges, in full growth or in embryo, with a theological class attached, are fast gathering in the choicest material from the lower schools, and preparing it for future service. A new agency is thus coming into existence, whose progress is in geometrical ratio, and which shall, ere long, supply a native ministry, native preachers, literati, professional men of all classes; book-makers and publishers; civilians, statesmen, and rulers. No feature, perhaps, more distinctly indicates the designs of Providence in reference to the conversion of the world. Hopeless, indeed, is the task of ever supplying the heathen world with preachers from abroad; but the work assumes another aspect the moment the eye turns to the *native agency*, which, in germ at least, is met in every mission school and seminary from Oregon to Japan, east or west. Such agency is already acting far more extensively and efficiently, perhaps, than is generally known. The late German missionary, Rhenius, was wont to preach in one hundred villages on every Sabbath day. That number of native preachers and catechists, on Saturday, received the word at his mouth, and thence went and preached in as many different places. Some entire printing establishments, as the extensive one in Bombay, are conducted wholly by native skill and labor.* Extensive school establishments are, in their details, carried on by the same agency. We wonder how a single missionary can act as pastor to a church of eight thousand members, scattered over an almost inaccessible country of thirty miles in extent. The wonder ceases when told that this church embraces thirty congregations, which assemble in as many different places, under the immediate care and instruction of as many catechists or sub-pastors. The heads of departments and the funds, in the missionary work, must, for some time to come, be furnished principally from abroad, but the details of the work are fast passing into native hands. Some fifty islands in the Pacific are said already to be under the instruction of natives alone. "Mount Lebanon," says a high authority, "will furnish missionaries for the sixty millions speaking the Arabic language, and noble missionaries too."

Another promising feature is the *liberality* and *self-denial* of the native churches. In their deep poverty they are contributing liberally to send the gospel to the dark regions beyond them. The American Board

---

* Thomas Graham, the superintendent of the American press at Bombay, was one of those young lads who accompanied the Rev. Gordon Hall on his late tour, and alone witnessed the dying moments of that excellent man, and gave him his humble sepulture, far from friends, and among idolatrous strangers. Thomas was a poor boy, who early came under the care of the mission; was nurtured and elevated by them—converted by the grace of God—and, after rendering various useful services, was at length raised to this responsible and important trust.

recently reported one hundred dollars received from a church at the Sandwich Islands for the education of a girl in the female seminary in Ceylon, collected during one year at the monthly concert for prayer. Mr. Williams tells a beautiful story in, point here. When on a visit to the native Christians at Aitutaki, he was explaining the manner in which the British Christians raised money to send the gospel to the heathen. They expressed their regret that they had no money to give. He replied: "If you have no money, you have something to buy money with." What? "The pigs I brought you; they have increased abundantly, and if every family would set apart one, and when the ships come, sell them for money, a valuable contribution might be raised." The idea delighted them; and the next morning the squealing of pigs, which were receiving a mark in the ear for the purpose, was heard from one end of the settlement to the other. A ship came; the pledges were sold, and the avails realized; and soon the native treasurer paid over for missionary purposes £103. It was their *first* money.

We are permitted to chronicle such instances as the following: The people of Tahiti and of the neighboring islands, contributed £527 in one year to the British and Foreign Bible Society. The London Missionary Society acknowledged in one year, £17,748 from their mission churches; £5,000 of which was from Southern India, as a contribution to the Jubilee Fund; half of the latter sum was contributed by the native church at Nagercoil; £160 at one station in Jamaica. The English Baptist Missionary Society report £1,200 contributed in a single year by their mission churches towards the support of their pastors. The Rev. Mr. Davis, pastor of a mission church of Africans, at New Amsterdam, South America, says, "During the five years of my pastorate there, that congregation contributed £7,000 to various objects of charity." As early as 1821, we find a native missionary society organized at Tahiti, and a "great number of missionaries sent thence to other islands." The church at Hilo, Sandwich Islands, contributed to different benevolent purposes, from four hundred to six hundred

dollars annually. The Sandwich Island churches contributed last year, thirteen thousand seven hundred and
eighty-two dollars, to different benevolent purposes, five
thousand of which came from the Hawaiian Bible Society, which is one of the best auxiliary Bible Societies in
the world.

Much importance may, very justly, be attached to the
self-denying and benevolent spirit of these churches, as
indicative of God's purpose soon to convert the world.
While enjoying, themselves, scarcely more than the bare
necessity of subsistence, they have begun their Christian
existence in a noble recognition of the first principles of
the gospel. From such a generation of Christians, the
church and the world may expect much.

Laudable efforts, too, drawing heavily on the slender
resources of native converts, are at the same time making,
especially in the Pacific Ocean, to build church edifices
for themselves, and in part, or in whole, to support their
pastors. In the records of those missions we are frequently meeting items like the following: "Erecting a
stone church, one hundred and twenty-five feet by sixty,
and three temporary buildings at the same time at out-
stations." "The walls of another church rising at one
point, and materials collecting at another." In the year
1840, there were built, or in progress of building, at the
Sandwich Islands, *eight* large churches, one of which was
one hundred and forty-four feet by seventy-eight. For the
building of one, the King gave three thousand dollars, the
chiefs and people having already given two thousand five
hundred dollars.

And while these noble efforts are making to provide
suitable and durable edifices for the worship of God. efforts equally laudable are making to provide needed ac-
commodations for schools. At four stations, at the Sandwich Islands, eighty school-houses were built in a single
year—forty-two in connection with one station—"large,
pleasantly situated, with verandas and play-grounds
around them." And not a few of these same churches
are contributing from one hundred, to four hundred and
five hundred dollars a year for the support of their pastors. The church in Honolulu, in 1845, raised five hun

dred and seventy dollars for the support of their pastor. The church of Wailuku paid for the same purpose, in 1844, seven hundred and twenty-five dollars, besides supporting a native preacher at an out-station, and contributing fifty-four dollars at the monthly concert for prayer, and building a church at an out-station. The church at Lahaina contributed, in the same year, as follows : Three hundred and twenty-one dollars for the support of their pastor; two thousand and four hundred dollars for rebuilding a church; one hundred and eighty dollars for the support of school teachers. The church of Molokai, besides the entire support of their pastor, contributed, in the same year, six hundred and seventy-eight dollars to different objects of benevolence.

The following paragraph recently appeared in one of our religious papers. It will further illustrate the point in hand. "We have learned with surprise, and yet delight, that a Foreign Missionary Society in the Sandwich Islands has sent to the American Home Missionary Society a donation for planting the gospel in our own west! Think of it! The converted heathen of yesterday rallying to bless our own land. Awake! ye sleepy and careless ones in our churches, who have never felt or done any thing in the cause of domestic missions. Make haste! or these converts from heathenism will be the means of saving your own kindred.

"Nor have the liberality and public spirit of the Hawaiian people been manifested merely in supporting their pastors and erecting houses of worship. It is estimated that, during the seven years ending December, 1844, they had contributed nineteen thousand nine hundred and eighty-seven dollars : and during the last year, they had raised not less than three thousand one hundred and five dollars."*

Other encouraging features, indicating the hand of God as stretched out to bless our missionary enterprises, appear in the *extraordinary outpouring of the Spirit* on mission churches, and *signal answers to prayer.* The recent extraordinary outpourings of the Spirit and revivals of

* Report of American Board for 1845.

religion on the Island of Ceylon, at the Sandwich Islands, and among the Choctaws, Armenians and Nestorians, are indications full of hope.   Perhaps in the whole history of religious revivals, the power of the Spirit has not been more signally manifested, revealing the mighty hand of God.   Should similar displays of Divine power be expe-- rienced by every Christian mission now in operation, (a thing not more improbable,) we might hail such an event as the long expected conversion of the world.

Akin to this, are *the signal answers to prayer*, which Heaven has, within a few years past, vouchsafed.   I will illustrate only by answers to prayer on a single occasion : The friends of missions have been wont, for some years past, to observe the first Monday of January as a day of prayer for the outpouring of the Spirit on the world, and especially for the success of foreign missions.   Results like the following have come to my knowledge.   Others, more observing of God's movements among the heathen, may add to the list.   A few instances will be given where prayer seems to have been answered, on a remote part of the globe, *on the very day*, and perhaps the same hour, it was offered :

On the first Monday of January, 1833, there was an extraordinay and unaccountable religious movement on the minds of a class of natives who had been for a few months under Christian instruction at Ahmednuggur. The writer, then the only missionary at the station, in- vited all who wished to be Christians, to meet him for re- ligious conversation and inquiry ; when, to his surprise, *thirteen* responded to the call ; all, apparently, deeply con- victed of sin, and wishing to be pointed to the Saviour. The number was in a few days increased to *sixteen*, most of whom subsequently became members of the church.   And this self same day was distinguished in other places by the power of the same blessed Spirit.   In Richmond, Va., the pastors and churches were assembled for prayer.   The lamented Armstrong, late Secretary of the American Board, was there.   He had been a trusty friend of missions before ; "but the time when his whole soul seemed to be peculiarly moved for the heathen, and he was, as it were, newly baptized with the missionary spirit, was at the meeting for prayer for the conversion of the world, held on the first Monday of January, 1833 Standing among the ministers, and before the assembled churches of Richmond, with a countenance glowing with love, he said, " My brethren, I am ashamed that there are so many of us here in this Christian land. We must go to the heathen." " That day of prayer," says one who was present, "made an impression on many hearts, which was deep and lasting." This was doubtless the way in which God was preparing him to perform the labors to which he was soon to be called, in connection with the foreign missionary work.

At a subsequent period, Rev. Mr. Spaulding, of Ceylon, says, " I was called up at midnight, on the first Monday in January, by one of the girls of the Oodooville school, and informed that the whole school was assembled in the large lecture room for prayer. On going thither, and seeing all present to hear what the Lord would command them, I found them in a most interesting state of mind ; and this was the beginning of the great revival of religion in Ceylon. Inquiring how this thing originated, Mr. S. found the larger girls, (the younger ones having retired,) had assembled for their evening prayer meeting, and not being willing to separate at the usual hour, the interest became so intense that one after another called up a friend to share in the good feeling, till, at length, the whole school were assembled.

The first Monday of January, 1838, presented a scene of thrilling interest at the Sandwich Islands. "At the rising of the sun, the church and congregation at Honolulu, filling one of the largest houses of worship on the islands, united in solemn prayer for the outpouring of the spirit of God." And thence followed a series of protracted meetings throughout the islands, and a general revival of religion blessed the nation. This was the beginning of what is known as the "great revival." By midsummer, more than five thousand had been received into the church, and two thousand four hundred stood propounded for membership. Though there had been some favorable indications of a spiritual movement some time previous, and the preceding Sabbath had been a day of unusual interest at Honolulu, yet we may date the be ginning of the great revival on that day. Now the windows of heaven were opened, and the refreshing rain came; and, as the fruits of the remarkable work, there were gathered into the churches, (1838—40,) twenty thousand persons; and more than three thousand remained as candidates for admission.

On the first Monday of January, 1846, two of the older girls in Miss Fisk's school at Ooroomiah, linger after morning prayers. She inquires the reason; finds they feel themselves to be lost sinners, and ask that they may spend the day in retirement. In a few days they are rejoicing in the hope of sins forgiven. Five others come to Miss F. the same day, and ask what they shall do to be saved? and, with no knowledge of what had taken place in Miss Fisk's school, a considerable number of Mr. Stoddard's scholars came to him with the same inquiry. From this hour we date the commencement of the present powerful, extensive revival of religion, which has already pervaded, not only the two seminaries, but the city of Ooroomiah and the adjacent villages, and has spread even among the mountains, and already numbers more than one hundred and fifty converts; to say nothing of the deep and far-reaching moral influence which this religious movement has produced on the Nestorian mind in general, and the conviction of the power of evangelical truth. Nor was this all: just two years before, (Monday, January, 1844,) there were decisive indications of the mighty workings of the spirit at the same station, producing a happy effect on the hearts of the native Christians and missionaries, but resulting in the conversion of only one individual, and he a young man the most unlikely to be thus effected. But he afterwards became a most efficient helper in the mission, and, perhaps, did more than any other one, to *prepare the way* for the great work now in progress. God first prepares his instruments, then does his work.

On the same day, (1846,) the spirit was poured out from on high, upon the Choctaws. "A pleasant state of things existed a few days previous, but on Monday, (January 5th,) the spirit came down in power, and a mighty work began," and did not end till more than two hundred were gathered into the church, which did not number before above seven hundred. "Before they call I will answer, and while they are yet speaking, I will hear."

But I must avoid so much detail. I shall group, in the briefest possible space, a variety of providential interpositions, which should by no means be passed in silence. We shall discover in them many interesting *coincidences* and *junctures*, which cannot but convey to the mind of the Christian a pleasing conviction that *God is in the work*, and, therefore, it cannot fail. They are such as these :

The *timing* of things so as to make one answer to another ; as the discovery of the South Sea Islands just before that wonderful period, when, amidst the "throes of kingdoms and the convulsions of the civilized world," a missionary spirit was wonderfully diffused among British Christians. The idol gods at the Sandwich Islands are cast away while missionaries are yet on their way thither. A wise Providence had raised up and fitted such characters as Kaahumanu, Kalanimaki, and Kaumualii ; characters so peculiarly suited to the crisis as obviously to indicate that they were the agents of Heaven, raised up for this very purpose. These islands became consolidated under one government, and the conflicting interests of different chiefs annihilated just in time to prepare the whole group for a *national* reform. The young and dissolute king, from whom the mission had much to fear and nothing to hope, is cut off by death in a foreign land, and his remains are sent back in charge of the noble Byron, whose influence is nobly employed on behalf of the mission. The most despicable and decidedly hostile chief, Boki, (Governor of Oahu,) is sacrificed to a mad project of his own devising. From small beginnings, and in a manner peculiarly providential, an extraordinary instrument for reform is prepared in the person of Kaahumanu, and raised to the highest pinnacle of power. The rebellion in Kanai results in the final prostration of the Anti-christian party. And the *timely* visit of Van Couver, of the Blonde, the Peacock, the Vincennes, and the noble bearing of their chief officers towards the incipient mission, and the salutary influence exerted by them on

the minds of the chiefs and people, are providential intei
positions worthy of record.

Nor was this all.   The mission schools were taken
under the patronage of the government, just at the time
when it had become impossible to sustain them by the
mission.

And who has not traced, with grateful admiration, the
origin and growth of the missionary spirit; how it has
expanded and warmed the heart of the church in proportion as the field opened to receive the gospel; the increasing philanthropy of Christendom, a sensibility to
every thing that effects the well-being of man, and the
general *expectation* of the world's speedy conversion?
Whence this, but a divine premonition, a dark foreboding
of idolatry's doom?   Says an intelligent missionary,
"the feeling is becoming general that some extraordinary
change is near at hand, which is to be effected by the
diffusion of Christianity."   A singular presentiment prevails among the Mohammedans; and a strange, irrepressible restlessness in Italy and other papal countries, predicts some mighty change in great Babylon.   Even in
the Vatican, "Prelates and Cardinals, and the late dying
Pope, have visions of threatening tempests, of disaster
and trouble, from whence there is no escape."

Again, we have the footsteps of Providence in the
machinery prepared; in organized action, societies—the
army marshalled and ready for the field; in the improved
character of nominal Christians residing in pagan lands;
in the late divorce of the connection which has hitherto
existed between the English Government and Hindoo
idolatry; in the suppression of the Suttee and Infanticide; in the extreme sensitiveness of Anti-christian powers
to the prevalence of pure Christianity, rousing the spirit
of persecution, indicative of the progress of Christianity;
in the oppression and extortion of the priesthood, which
is *driving* many from their long-cherished superstition to
take refuge under the mild banners of the gospel; in the
decrease of the Papal priesthood;* in the increased at-

---

* Statistics which have recently been presented, on the decrease of the clerica:
order, show a diminution of the Romish clergy, amounting to near 900,000 within the
last fifty years.

tention of Pagan nations to the study of the English language ; and in the present advanced condition of knowledge, civilization and freedom. Advancement in the arts and sciences, in civilization and civil liberty, is a no doubtful presage that the kingdom of the Messiah is at hand. It is the hand of the Lord preparing for the universal spread of the gospel. Religion is found eventually to come down to the social and intellectual condition of a people. Nothing in the past history of Christianity warrants us to expect that a pure, healthful Christianity will long remain among a people ignorant and unacquainted with the arts of civilized life.

The moral change, too, which, during the last forty years, has taken place among European and American residents in heathen countries, is an indication of, and a preparation for, coming good. In India, it is a presage of much good. Then, scarcely a righteous man could be found there. There was no church, no Sabbath, no chaplaincies, no mercantile house closed on the Sabbath. "English residents were as much strangers to the gospel as the Hindoos or the Mohammedans." But now how changed. Not a mercantile house is now open on the Sabbath.* Instead of an "universal, unblushing disregard of religion," there are scattered over India, in its length and breadth, delightful specimens of piety. More lovely, active, and benevolent Christians are not to be met, than they whose light shines in that land of darkness. How different a starting point has the gospel now, how increased the resources of piety for its onward progress!

We cannot too profoundly admire the wonder-working hand that has given, as before noticed, such preponderance in Pagan countries, to the present two great *maritime* nations; that such a country as India, which has once given religion, science, and civilization to all the East, should now be thrown into Anglo-Saxon hands; into the hands of a nation of such extent and power and maritime skill, and such resources and intelligence and

* A late number of the Bombay Times states that the Governor-general has directed that henceforth there shall be no labor on the public works throughout Hindoostan, on the Sabbath. The same paper adds, "A similar measure introduced three years since by Sir George Arthur into Bombay, has been eminently successful."

piety, and every advantage for propagating the gospe..
There has, perhaps, never been an arrangement of Providence, in all the revolutions of nations, which, when
rightly viewed, excites a profounder wonder. The religious and intellectual influence of India has always been,
and is likely to be, great over the whole East.   Once
converted to Christianity, she may again send her missionaries, not as formerly, to propagate error, but to carry
the full horn of salvation to the remotest extremities of
Asia.

Time would fail to trace out the many ways in which
the wealth, power, and learning of England are contributing to prepare the way of the Lord in India. The
power of her arms and the skill of her statesmen have
done it by securing protection for the missionary ; while
the researches of her scholars have been accumulating a
power in the hands of the same missionary for the prosecution of his work.   Colebrook and Sir Wm. Jones, and
the many philosophers, linguists, historians, and literati,
who have gained immortality in Indian lore, have been
unconsciously forging the weapons of the missionary
warfare.   Every acquisition in true science, every advanced step in literature, history, geography, is a blow
struck at the heart of Hindooism, so interwoven is error
into the very warp and woof of Hindoo learning.

And the British Christian will here pardon us for saying that we think the providence worthy of much admiration, that so strong and encouraging a missionary spirit
should pervade the *American* Church, that the gospel
should be so extensively sent from this country, the land
of revivals, of general intelligence, and freedom ; that
religion of *such a type* should be so prominently stamped
on pagan nations.

The hand of God is abundantly visible, too, in the
increased demand for the Sacred Scriptures. I speak
now more especially of anti-christian nations. The *people*
in almost every portion of the world show an unwonted
desire to become acquainted with the Christian's Bible,
though generally opposed by the priesthood.   Whence
this desire, if not wrought into the world's mind by the
Spirit from on high ?   The Bible and the Paganism of

India, or of Rome, cannot long live together. We may, therefore, regard this desire to possess and read the pure word of God, both as a providential preparation and a premonition of the speedy coming of the Messiah's kingdom.

Finally, the present condition of the Pagan world, as providentially prepared to receive the gospel, is full of encouragement. The field is open, explored; a knowledge of different countries has been gained, of manners, customs, languages, and religions; a rich fund of experience has been acquired. Providence has accumulated vast resources for the work, and provided immense facilities. The missionary work is almost necessarily *progressive.* Not only does each missionary station create resources and facilities for its own extension, but the success of one station prepares the way for the establishment of another, and the work thus becomes self-propagating in an accelerating ratio. Take the missions of the American Board for an example. The success of these missions, if estimated only by the number of conversions, (by no means a fair estimate of real results,) "has been twelve times as great during the last ten years, as it was in the whole previous twenty-six years of the Board's history." Ten years ago there were 2,000 members of the Board's mission churches, now there are more than 24,000. All that has been done is a cumulative force for onward progress.

Our *success,* again, urges on the Pagan mind our most convincing, tangible argument for the divinity of our religion. Christianity now has its *monuments* in every Pagan country. It has *transformed character,* morally, socially, politically. We can now point to these monuments, and challenge investigation for the divine original of our religion. It has refined, elevated, purified character. It has done in a few short years what the wisest and most refined systems of idolatry and oriental philosophy have not begun to do in as many centuries. We can point to living illustrations of the power of the gospel; how it has gone up to the springs of moral corruption, and cast in the salt there. We can point to individuals, to families, communities, *nations,* that

have been transformed, civilized, elevated, and radi
cally improved by the simple power of the gospel. This
is the lever of Providence, by which to overthrow the
whole Pagan world, and on its mouldering ruins to rear
the beautiful superstructure of his everlasting truth. The
blind votaries of idolatry are not so blind as not to see
this, and not so disingenuous as not sometimes to acknowledge it. "We look," says a Sandwich Islander, "at the
power with which the gospel has been attended in effecting the entire overthrow of idolatry among us, and which
we believe no human means could have induced us to
abandon." In like manner, a Hindoo Brahmin is made
to pay the same unwilling homage to the truth, when, on
hearing the gospel preached, he said, "Nothing can stand
before the atonement of the Lord Jesus Christ."

Thus are we furnished, from the success of missions,
not only with the means of still greater success, but with
an overwhelming argument on the heathen mind, in favor
of the truth of Christianity.

With a few exceptions, found in Central Africa, or in
the ill-defined regions of Tartary and Kamschatka, the
God that worketh wonders, has, in the mysterious workings of his providence, opened the entire world to the
gospel. The Macedonian cry comes to us from every
nation, and tongue, and people, and kindred on the face
of the earth. In past ages of the church, the prayers of
God's people went up, that the Great Master would grant
access to the unevangelized nations, and raise up and
qualify men for the work. Those prayers have been
heard. The world lies in a ready, in a beseeching posture, at the feet of the children of the Highest.

CHAPTER XV.

MOHAMMEDAN COUNTRIES AND MOHAMMEDANISM. The design, origin, character, success, extent of Islamism. Mohammed a Reformer—not an Impostor. Whence the power and permanency of Mohammedanism? Promise to Ishmael—hope for him. The power of Islam on the wane. Turks the watch-dogs of Providence, to hold in check the Beast and the Dragon. Turkish reforms—Toleration—Innovations—A pleasing reflection.

" And Abraham said unto God, O that Ishmael might live before thee !"—Gen. xvii. 18.

WE shall now turn to Mohammedan countries, and attempt to trace the hand of God as there at work, to prepare the lands which have so long languished under the pale light of the crescent, to receive the gospel of the Messiah. Our inquiry now relates to the present condition of Mohammedanism and Mohammedan countries, as providentially prepared to receive Christianity.

It will not be irrelevant, first, to take a brief survey of this extraordinary form of faith—its design, origin, character, success, and extent. We shall all along keep the eye steadily fixed on the providential agency engaged in this stupendous system. The whole enormous fabric of Mohammedanism is one vast monument, or arrangement of Providence, in conducting the affairs, especially the moral affairs, of this world.

We may then, first, inquire *why* Mohammedanism was ever permitted to be—what was the providential *design* to be accomplished by that extraordinary man, who rose in Arabia in the seventh century? We do not see great systems of religion, and mighty empires rise and flourish, and for centuries exert a controlling influence over large portions of the world, without a correspondingly important divine purpose. What is this purpose in reference to Mohammedanism? We may not pretend fully to answer this question, yet we may doubtless point out some of the purposes, which lay in the divine mind, when he permitted the Man of Mecca to embark in the arduous enterprise of giving to the world a new religion.

23*

Three points here claim our attention: The design of God in this system; the design of Mohammed, and the design of Satan.

The design of God seems to have been, first, to fulfill his promise to a great branch of the Abrahamic family, the posterity of Ishmael; and secondly, to check effectually the power and progress of idolatry, and to scourge a corrupt Christianity; to rebuke and humble an apostate church by making her enemy a fairer example of God's truth than she was herself. The design of Mohammed—bating the aspirations of ambition—seems to have been to destroy idolatry, and to give the world a new religion, and a better one, than he had met elsewhere. And the design of the devil was to make the new system a great delusion, by which he might hope to retain in bondage that large portion of the human race, which had become too much enlightened, longer to be held by a system of gross idolatry.

A moment's glance at the origin, progress, and character of Islamism, will confirm what I have said. In the 9th chapter of the Revelations, a corrupt Christianity, personified in the first Pope, perhaps, is represented as a "star fallen from heaven unto the earth," to whom was given the key of the bottomless pit. The propagation of false doctrines, especially on the nature of the Trinity, and the worship of images, saints, and angels, afforded to the prophet a plausible pretext, and prepared the way for Mohammed and his religion. He opened the pit, "and there arose a smoke out of the pit as the smoke of a great furnace, and the sun and the air were darkened by reason of the smoke of the pit:" a striking description of Mohammedanism as a *religious* power. It is a grand *delusion*, which blinds the eyes of men, or so bedims and perverts their vision that they can only see as through a glass darkly. But it was more than a religious power. It was a great civil and military power. "And there came out of the smoke *locusts* on the earth, and unto them was given *power*, as the scorpions of the earth have power. And the shapes of the locusts were like unto horses prepared unto battle; and on their heads were, as it were, crowns like gold, and their faces were as the faces of men. And they had hair as the hair of women, and their teeth were as the teeth of lions. And they had breast-plates, as it were breast-plates of iron, and the sound of their wings was as the sound of chariots of many horses running to battle. And they had a king over them, which is the angel of the bottomless pit."

No one can more accurately describe an Arabian army. Numerous as the swarms of "locusts" from the southern shore ; vindictive and deadly as the "scorpion;" consisting chiefly of cavalry, with turbans on their heads resembling "crowns ;" with long hair as the "hair of women," thus bearing some marks of gentleness and timidity, yet they have teeth "like the teeth of lions." They have faces as the "faces of men," appear like men, yet they are unchained tigers. They ravage and destroy without mercy. They are a well organized army, have a king over them, as one commissioned by the destroying angel ; are actuated by one spirit ; harmonize in their object, to scourge a corrupt church, and to destroy idolatry. They have "breast-plates of iron ;" are protected by a strong civil power. They produce a great tumult in the world ; fly from one country to another, like an army with chariots and many horsemen.

They had power to hurt *five months*—one hundred and fifty years. Mohammed began publicly to announce his divine commission in the year 612—and the violence of his aggressions was stayed on the building of Bagdad, and the transfer of the Caliphate thither, A. D. 762. The *smoke*, however, the religious delusion, continued. The fierce military character—the flying, furious, stinging, scorpion-like locusts, abated in their ravages ; yet the civil and religious dominion over the fairest portions of the world continued, and is to continue, till it shall have accomplished its twelve hundred and sixty years.

At the close of the one hundred and fifty years, the banners of the crescent waved victorious over the whole Roman empire. Arabia had yielded to the Prophet before his death. Syria, Persia and Egypt were soon made the vassals of his proud successors. Within twelve years after the Hegira, thirty-six thousand cities, towns and castles, are said to have been subjugated to the new conquerors; four thousand Christian temples destroyed, and one thousand four hundred mosques dedicated to the Prophet. Africa was soon subdued—the Moors converted to the new religion; who, in their turn, descend into Spain, and there establish a magnificent empire. "The victorious standard of the crescent was raised on the cold mountains of Tartary, and on the burning sands of Ethiopia." The Moslem empire extended from the Atlantic to Japan—across the entire continents of Africa and Asia—into Spain, and France as far North as the Loire, and over the Indian islands, embracing Sumatra, Java, Borneo, Celebes, and the Manillas. The island of Goram, one of the spice islands, may be taken as the eastern boundary of Islamism.

The Moslems appeared even under the walls of Vienna, whence they were turned back, and Europe saved from the scourge of the East, by the noble Poles, as they had been driven out of France by the intrepid Charles Martel. At the close of its first century, the Saracenic empire embraced the fairest and the largest portion of the civilized world.

But let us return to the *design:* First, I said God designed now to fulfill his promise to the posterity of *Ishmael.* Ishmael was a child of Abraham, and though *the* blessing should descend through Isaac, the child of promise, yet *a* blessing was reserved for Ishmael. As God was pronouncing the blessing on the seed of promise, Abraham, with a father's tenderness, "said unto God, O that Ishmael might live before thee." Is there no blessing for Ishmael? "And God said—as for Ishmael I have heard thee: Behold, I have blessed him, and will make him fruitful, and will multiply him exceedingly: twelve princes shall he beget, and I will make him a great nation." We are, I think, to look for a parallel—though often by way of contrast—in the histories of the posterity of Isaac and Ishmael. Both should inherit a blessing—both have a numerous natural seed—twelve patriarchs should proceed from each—they should live side by side, though in perpetual rivalry. They were both sons, the one the legitimate heir, the other a spurious offspring. The one should have the true Revelation, the true Religion, and the true Messiah; the other a spurious Revelation, a spurious Religion and a spurious Messiah. The blessing on Ishmael was principally of a temporal nature. His posterity should be exceedingly numerous. And, as a matter of history, it was more numerous than that of Isaac. And it should live in perpetual hostility with the other great branch of the Abrahamic family. But are we not to look for a spiritual blessing on Ishmael, that shall correspond with his constituted relationship to Isaac? Was not the religion of the Arabs or Ishmaelites *before* Mohammed, a reflection, a base imitation of Judaism—the bastard religion of the promise? yet containing many valuable truths of patriarchal theism. When Israel's Messiah appeared, they might have looked that Ishmael's Messiah should soon follow. Islamism is then the Christianity of Ishmael, and the Popery of Judaism. It is a faithful image and reflection, as some one says, of the *defects* of Judaism. In Judaism, Isaac new-modelled and improved the faith and morals of men through his literal descendants, the Jews; Ishmael did the same through his literal descendants, the Arabs. Mohammedanism, like Christianity, on the other line, was an advance, "a considerable reformation," on the then existing system of religion among the spurious seed. One is the light of the sun, the other the light of the moon as reflected from the sun.

Again, in permitting this system, God designed effectually to check the power and progress of Idolatry, and to scourge a corrupt Christianity. The spirit of Mohammed was singularly transfused through all the ranks of his followers: it was an implacable hatred of Idolatry. Wherever the Moslem was found, he was the hammer of God to break in pieces the idols of the heathen. Nor was he a less signal scourge to a corrupt Christianity, or a formal Judaism. Islamism has been, in its turn, both the censor and the corrector, the scourge and the reformer of eastern Christianity. The illegitimate offspring has stolen from the armory of the true seed many valuable weapons of truth, which he has turned with signal vengeance against his brother. Mohammed was a Reformer. He introduced into Western Asia a better religion than at the

time existed there. There was more truth—more of
divine revelation—less of Idolatry in his religion, than in
any of the existing forms of faith there prevalent, not
excepting the Christianity of his time. God rebuked and
humbled an apostate church, "a fallen star," by giving
an enemy rule over her. And another thing he did: by
the iron arm of Mohammed he has restrained the bloody
hand of persecution. The blood-hounds of Islam have
been set to watch the lions of Anti-christ. And well
have they watched them. And they are not yet forgetful
of their commission, as late acts of the Turkish government in behalf of the persecuted Armenians doth show.

The character of Mohammedanism has, perhaps, been
as imperfectly understood as its design. I do not think
Mohammed an impostor. He was probably an honest
man—though ambitious and enthusiastic. His religion,
(not the abuses and corruptions of it by others,) was to
him a truth, and an improvement on any system he was
acquainted with. The Christianity of his time was a
vile alloy; Judaism no better, and Paganism worse. He
set himself to devise and establish a better. He seized
on the great truths of religion by that "inspiration which
giveth man understanding"—appropriating what he knew
of truth in Judaism or Christianity, his great aim being
to counteract and destroy the Idolatry of his own countrymen. On this it was a notable advance. It was an
acknowledgment of one God, of self-denying duty, and
of future rewards and punishments. To him the whole
world seemed given up to Idolatry. The absurd and
false notions on the subject of the Trinity, had laid the
Christians under the charge of worshiping a plurality
of Gods, to say nothing of the prevalent worship of
images, saints and angels. His spirit was stirred within
him. Hence he became the bold champion of the great
truth, *God is one.*

Mohammed commenced his career under a favorable
combination of circumstances. The world was providentially brought into a condition especially favorable to
his success. Mohammed looked on the world, with the
eye of intuitive philosophy. "He compares the nations
and religions of the earth," says Gibbon, "discovers the

weakness of the Persian and Roman monarchies, beholds, with pity and indignation, the degeneracy of the times, and resolves to unite, under one God and one King, the invincible spirit and the primitive virtues of the Arabs." The political condition of the world was favorable. The leaven of liberty, generated in the religion of calvary, had prepared the world for a great revolution. And the moral and religious aspect of the world was still more favorable. The idolatries of Western Asia were in a tottering state. The advent of the Messiah had cast light over the whole world. Many dark places had been enlightened, and the darkness of other places had been made visible. Christianity had reached Arabia, and had loosed the bonds of Idolatry, and "produced a fermentation there." Both Christianity and Judaism were in a condition which afforded a plausible pretext and encouragement to the career of the Prophet. And no doubt, in the then extreme military inactivity of Asia, he was not a little indebted for his success to the power of arms. But are any, or all of these causes sufficient to account for such success?—especially for the *permanency* of it? Was there not rather a considerable mixture of *truth* in the confused medley of the religion of Mecca, to which we are rather to refer certain well known results. It was military prowess, for example, that conquered the barbarous, ignorant, besotted Tartars—an exceedingly rude people, roaming herds of shepherds and warriors, who neither lived in houses nor cultivated the ground. Yet their subjugation to Bagdad, wrought in them an extraordinary transformation. They soon formed for themselves a regular government, cultivated their large and fertile plains, cherished the arts of peace, and congregated in large cities. A new and independent kingdom here arose, which soon proved a powerful rival to Bagdad itself. What wrought this extraordinary transformation? Must we not look for something beyond mere military force and a happy juncture, to account for the power which this religion held over *mind*, and the civil, social and moral changes which it wrought?

By the mere force of arms the barbarous Moors invaded Spain, and made themselves possessors of that rich

276 HAND OF GOD IN HISTORY.

and beautiful portion of Europe. But what enlightened and civilized them—what reared for them a regular government, and a magnificent empire—made them rule in the world of letters, and become the teachers of Europe? What made them to excel all the nations of their time, in the arts, in science, and in agriculture? "While the greatest portion of the western world was buried in the darkest ignorance, the Moors in Spain lived in the enjoyment of all those arts which beautify and polish society." "Agriculture, too, was better understood by the Arabs of Spain than by any other people." When an ambitious priesthood were urging their expulsion, the Spanish barons plead, "with great power of argument and eloquence, that this detested people were the most valuable part of the Spanish population." They were characterized by "frugality, temperance and industry." The manufactures of the country were very much in their hands—the arts, sciences and navigation.*

Or we may ask what gave rise to the college at Bagdad, with its six thousand pupils and professors—or made Grand Cairo a chief seat of letters, with its twenty colleges, and its royal library of one hundred thousand manuscripts—or what placed a library of two hundred and eighty thousand volumes in Cordova, and more than seventy libraries in the kingdom of Andalusia—and adorned the towns on the north coast of Africa with literary institutions; and made the sun of science rise in Africa, and soften the manners of the savage Moors by philosophy and song? The Moors formed the connecting link between ancient and modern literature—introduced literature and science into Europe, and were the depositories of knowledge for the West. The mathematics, astronomy, anatomy, surgery, chemistry, and botany, were pursued by the Moors far in advance of their age. Or whence came it to pass that Cordova became the "centre of politeness, taste and genius?" A religion which pro-

* The introduction of cotton, and sugar cane—articles of oriental growth—into Europe by the Saracens, first gave that impulse to European art and luxury, and to the spirit, consequently, of commercial enterprise, which issued eventually in the opening of a maritime communication to India and the remote East, and in the discovery and settlement of the New World.

duces such fruits must have something in it besides error, superstition, enthusiasm, and military prowess.

Mungo Park found, quite in the interior of Africa, a degree of elevation and improvement which quite aston·ished him; it was so unlike what he had seen among other African tribes—"a people of very different descrip·tion from other black Pagan nations," who had adopted many of the arts of civilized life—subjected themselves to government and political institutions—practiced agri·culture, and learned the necessary and even some of the ornamental arts—dwelt in towns, some of which con·tained ten thousand and even thirty thousand inhabitants, surrounded by well cultivated fields, and the improve·ments and comforts of civilized life. All these improve·ments had been introduced into Africa by the *Mohamme-dans.* Previous to this introduction, the same tribes were as wild, fierce savages as the natives towards the South, where the missionaries of Islam had never penetrated.

A glance at the religion which Mohammed set himself to propound, will discover the secret. He started out with the great leading truth of the DIVINE UNITY. "He proclaimed himself a Prophet sent from heaven to preach the unity of the Godhead, and to restore to its purity the religion of Abraham and Ishmael." And a principal means by which he was to accomplish his mission, was the destruction of Idolatry and superstition. The Oriental Christian Church at once fell under the ban of his male·diction, because found shamefully allied to the great sys·tem of Idolatry.

If we descend to practical results, we shall meet—not the religion of the New Testament—but a religion con·siderably in advance of any thing which came within the Prophet's acquaintance. He essentially mitigated the horrors of war. "In avenging my injuries," said he, "molest not the harmless votaries of domestic seclusion; spare the weakness of the softer sex, the infant at the breast, and those who, in the course of nature, are hasten·ing from this scene of mortality. Abstain from demol·ishing the dwellings of the unresisting inhabitants; destroy not their means of subsistence; respect their fruit trees; and touch not the palm, so useful to the Syrians for its

24

shade, and delightful for its verdure. Take care to do
that which is right and just, for those who do otherwise,
shall not prosper. When you make any covenant or article, stand to it, and be as good as your word. As you
go on, you will find some religious persons that live retired
in monasteries, who propose to themselves to serve God
that way. Let them alone, and neither kill them nor destroy their monasteries." This was quite in advance of
his age in reference to war. We must not be too ready
to charge on Mohammed the abuses of his system, by
many of his followers, or to forget that, as with other
men, his impetuous nature sometimes hurried him into
excesses in practice, which his theory condemned. It is
not to be denied, that fraud and perfidy, injustice and
cruelty, were too often made subservient to the propagation of his faith; and that in his last days ambition was
his ruling passion.

Again, we find Mohammed inculcating charity, forbearance, patience, resignation to the Divine will; prayer
five times a day; a regard for the sabbath as appointed
by him; future rewards and punishment; mercy to captives taken in war; the prohibition of wine; that reli
gion is not in the rite or form, but in the power of an
internal principle: we find him enacting laws against
gaming and infanticide; on inheritance and the rights of
property; correcting many grievous abuses, and inculcating many valuable moral precepts.

He did not enjoin *universal charity*, but implacable
hatred of all infidels. This is but of a piece with the
great design of the system.

Thus we see what God designed by this religion, and
what he has brought out of it; what Mohammed designed by it; and what the devil has used it for, viz. as
a grand *delusion* by which to blind men's minds, and to
betray a countless multitude to perdition. Mohammedanism, if contemplated simply as a device of the enemy,
stands before the world in the character of one of his
great *counterfeits*. "It has always been the policy of
Satan to forestall the purposes of God, and to set up a
counterfeit of that which the Lord hath declared he will
do." We may, therefore, regard the religion of the Caaba

before Mohammed, as Satan's counterfeit of Judaism; and Mohammedanism, or the religion of Mecca, *after* Mohammed, as the counterfeit of Christianity. Satan is a shrewd observer of providence and of revelation, and he advances in his systems of deception with the *times*, with the advance of man, and the condition of the world Every new dispensation of grace is, on his part, accompanied by a new dispensation of falsehood, not absolute falsehood, but *perverted truth* and practical falsehood. Satan is no *inventor* but a vile imitator. His systems of error are as much like God's systems of truth, as a counterfeit coin is like a genuine one. The shape, the size the lettering, the whole external, are much the same; yet one is a base alloy, the other is pure gold. Mohammedanism is not a simple counterfeit of Christianity alone That bad pre-eminence must be accorded to Popery. It is a successful counterfeit both of Christianity and Judaism, with accommodation in some of its features to the mind and the heart of the Pagan. While it incorporates in itself much of truth, it incorporates more of worldly wisdom and satanic craft.

But I have already transcended my prescribed limits in a review of the past; we will now turn to the present.

We have found Mohammedanism to be, on a large scale, a minister of Providence to carry forward the great plans of human redemption. It has been God's hammer, to break in pieces the idols of a large portion of the heathen world; his scourge, to inflict summary and severe judgments on an apostate church, and to check the vast power she has accumulated by which to persecute the saints; and his channel in which, during the dark ages, to preserve, and by which to communicate to his chosen inheritance, (the spiritual seed of Abraham,) a knowledge of the arts and sciences, of literature, and of the various means of refinement and civilization. Poor Ishmael, though often with an ill grace, and sometimes with vengeance in his heart, has all his days been made to serve the posterity of Isaac, the seed of promise.

"O that Ishmael might live before thee." Is there a blessing for Ishmael? As we turn to Mohammedan countries we seem to see hope smiling over the black

tents of Kedar. Writers well versed in the affairs of
Islam, who look on Mohammedanism as a corruption of
Judaism, "an anti-christian heresy," "a confused form of
Christianity," a "bastard Christianity" as Carlyle calls it,
think they see a tendency of convergence in Mohammedanism and Christianity; the "imperfect becoming absorbed in the perfect; the moon of Mohammedanism
resigning its borrowed rays to meet in the undivided
light of the everlasting gospel," the Sun of Righteousness.*
Is there any thing in the present condition of Mohammedanism to indicate such a convergence? A brief survey
of Islamism, physically, politically, and morally, as now
to be seen, may throw some light on this question.

We have seen the Mohammedan empire stretching
over the fairest portions of the globe, from the Chinese
sea to the walls of Vienna and the gates of Rome, and its
proud waves stayed only by the broad Atlantic. The
earth once trembled before the throne of the haughty
Moslems, "till princes were ambitious of its alliance."
Such Moslems as Ghengis Khan, Tamerlane, and the
great Moguls in the East, and Abbasides of Western
Asia, and the Ommiades of Spain, have ruled the world
with a rod of iron. Even as late as the close of the last
century the authority of the divan of Constantinople was
generally respected. But where is the political power
of Islam now? It is numbered among the things that
were. Except in Turkey, we search for it almost in
vain. And we shall soon see how little of power the
Moslems possess even in Turkey.

Though the religion of Mohammed embraces in it
some truth, to which we are to attribute much of the
power and permanency which it has enjoyed; yet we
must bear in mind it is characteristically a religion of the
sword. As a distinctive system it exists by *force*. Yet
when once forced on a community, or a nation, and allowed to develop itself, it has, with much error, brought
forth some good fruit. But "all they that take the sword,
shall perish with the sword," shall perish *with the laying
down* of the sword. We need not apprehend that the

---

* Foster's Mohammedanism Unveiled

religion of the Koran shall outlive the civil and military power of the Moslems. But what is the condition of this power at the present time? For an answer to this question, we must look to Constantinople and the Turkish empire.

Writing from the East, one says: "A deplorable anarchy prevails in Turkey. The European powers thought to strengthen the Ottoman empire by an armed interference in her internal quarrels, but they have only added fuel to the flame. Turkey is in the agonies of dissolution, and will soon be a corpse. There is no law, no safety, no security for property in this unhappy country. Is not this a sign that the last hour is coming for the followers of Mohammed?" Before Napoleon Bonaparte had inflicted the incurable wound on Rome, or exerted his dread commission in heaven's retributive justice on Austria, Russia and Prussia, for their wrongs on poor Poland, he had already aimed as deadly a thrust at the Sublime Porte; and but for the interference, in either case, of Protestant England, he would, in all human probability, have totally demolished the monstrous fabrics both of Popery and Islamism. By his expedition and success in Egypt, he not only himself struck a heavy blow on Turkish power, but he revealed to the whole political world the weakness of the Turkish empire. Hordes of Turks, Arabs, and Mamelukes, were seen to be no match for an European soldiery. Turkey has since lain a prey at the feet of Christian nations, to be seized the moment the victors can agree on the division of the spoil. Her people are demoralized; her institutions and opinions antiquated; her army without discipline or bravery; her government superannuated and without authority; a nation with no homogeneity, or moral and political cohesion; without manufactures or commerce, with little money, and less justice in her rulers, or security for her people; that is to say, all the vital parts of society are struck with death.*

And so she remains, with no inherent power of her own by which to restore herself, or to preserve herself **as**

---

* Correspondence of the New York Observer.

she is, but only propped up by the jealousy of European
nations. Strenuous attempts have been made of late
years to reinstate the decayed energies of the Moslems.
She remains but the shadow of what she was, "a sad
spectacle of inevitable dissolution." We need only take
the most cursory survey of Mohammedan countries as
they now are, and the conclusion will be forced upon us
that the power of Islam is on the wane. Many of its
empires, celebrated in the history of past times, have
already become Christian, or are subjected to Christian
powers. The empire of the great Moguls is no more.
Persia has little either of power or independence. Like
Turkey, she only exists by sufferance. Afghanistan has
been terrified and humbled. Algiers is subjected to a
Christian nation. "Greece, awaking from her long stu-
por, uttered the cry of liberty, in the name of glorious
ancestors, and a heroic struggle achieved her independence." The right arm of Turkey was palsied at the
battle of Navarino. Already there is not a Moslem power
that can stand of itself.

But political power to Mohammedanism is essential to
its existence; empire and territorial extension, essential
parts of the promise to Ishmael; and as we see these
passing away, we may receive it as an undoubted omen
that the religion of the Moslems is drawing near its end.
"The great obstacle," says an intelligent missionary, "to
the conversion of the Mohammedans, is their *power*, and
their pride of power, but the fact that their power is passing away, has produced a great change among them."
Infidelity cannot compare the present condition of Mohammedanism with the past, without recognizing the
hand of God in the change.

Nor will the same providential feature appear less distinct in a *religious* survey of the system. The *moral*
power of Islam is as effectually weakened or annihilated
as its political power. "Immorality," says one, "has
awfully increased among the Mohammedans of Asiatic
Turkey;" and others speak of the "decline of Mohammedanism in spirit and zeal;" "enthusiasm gone;" "fasts
unobserved, and the prescribed prayers and the ritua
neglected." The power and spirit have well nigh de-

parted, and nothing remains but the death-stricken body,
ready to crumble to decay. And in correspondence with
all this, we meet a physical wasting away of the once
gigantic power of the Moslems. "*Depopulation*," says a
correspondent from that quarter, "has been going on
rapidly during the year 1838, the plague, small-pox, and
other diseases, carried off in one province most of the
children under two years old." In another district
"where three hundred yoke of oxen used to be employed,
the ground is now tilled with twelve. The country is
drained of its inhabitants, too, by the frequent draughts
of young men to serve in the army. There is every indication that the strength of the empire is gone. The
waters of the great Euphrates are drying up."

"*And power was given unto him to continue forty and
two months,*" 1260 years; which period has almost ex-
pired. The Rev. Dr. Grant, whose authority in this
matter we may quote with much confidence, speaks thus
of the approaching end of the great Eastern Anti-christ:
"In Persia it is commonly believed that the existing
Mohammedan power is near its end. Calculations have
been made by one of their seers, which lead them to believe that its days are numbered, and limited to a very
few remaining years. In Turkey, in Mesopotamia, and
even among the wild mountains of central Koordistan,
where the subject was gravely canvassed, I found a prevailing impression that the arm of the Mohammedan
power is soon to be broken; and such, too, is the general
belief among the Moslems of Egypt and Syria. Moreover, such is the posture of things in the East, and such
the increasing developments of Providence, that a general
expectation of the speedy downfall of the empire of Mohammed prevails throughout Christendom; while those
of us who have resided within the borders of that empire,
have been sensibly impressed with the fact that we were
the tenants of a falling edifice.

"A missionary, long resident in the metropolis of
Turkey, remarked, that 'it requires no prophecies to
satisfy us that the Mohammedan power is falling to ruins,
and must soon be at an end.' The astonishing changes
now taking place portend its overthrow. The Moslem

feels that 'fate' has so decreed it; and the Christian may here learn that the Almighty has set bounds to its duration, and that its days are fast hastening to a close."

But Mohammedan countries present another aspect. Certain encouraging features pleasantly contrast with the foregoing. While the waters of the great Euphrates are gradually drying up, while the gigantic structure of Islam is falling to decay, there is springing up amidst its ruins a more sightly edifice.

The late toleration act of the Sublime Porte, is but of a piece with the past history of Mohammedanism. Though the power of the Moslems is broken, their decaying energies are roused to resist the persecuting spirit of Anti-christ when found in the Roman, Greek, or Armenian church. In the late persecutions by the Armenian Patriarch, the Turks, as usual, espoused the cause of evangelical Christianity, and raised the governmental arm to arrest the madness of the persecutors. It was the arm of Providence. True to its character, Mohammedanism is again a scourge and a judgment on a corrupt Christianity, and a *shield* against anti-christian persecutors. Had not the sword of the crescent been drawn, where, in other times, would the ravages of the Beast and the Dragon have been stayed? The mere chronicler of events asks why the Turks, in 1453, were permitted to take and hold Constantinople, and with such iron severity to hold control over the Eastern church? The Christian historian replies: "This very circumstance arrested the *perversion of the truth* by a corrupt church, and wrested from the hands of persecutors the sword of violence." The Moslems were the watch-dogs of Providence, to protect the flock and to control the wolf. Nothing short of the relentless arm and the iron sinews of the Turk, could arrest the maddening progress of the Beast. In the late Armenian persecution, we again see the stern Moslem interposing the shield against the fiery darts of Antichrist.

And here we have to note another agency, which has been made, providentially, to produce the same result. I mean the movements of England and Prussia to secure the toleration of Protestant Christianity, and to resist the political influence of Russia through the Greek church, and France through the Romish. Without this providential interposition, the palsied arm of Turkey would probably prove too weak to resist the unceasing encroachments of the Beast.

Indeed, throughout their whole history, the Moslems have been true to themselves and to the divine commission which they seem destined to fulfill, *to check and scourge Anti-christ.* In Spain, the oppressed and outraged Jew hailed in secret the approach of the invading Saracens, regarded them as deliverers, and openly co-operated with them in attacking their Christian enemies. And good reason had they to rejoice at their deliverance from Gothic tyranny, as they "lived in peace and plenty under the milder rule of their new masters." Historians speak of the "brilliant age of the kingdoms of Cordova and Grenada as a cheering light amidst the darkness and ignorance which Europe then presented"—of "their liberal toleration granted to all religious sects"—"a wise and beneficent policy long characterized the Moors, and deservedly raised their dominions to a great height of prosperity."

To the Jews, says Milman, "the Moslem crescent was as a star which seemed to soothe to peace the troubled waters on which they had been so long agitated. Throughout the dominions of the Caliphs of the East, in Africa, in Spain and in the Byzantine empire, we behold the Jews not only pursuing their lucrative and enterprising traffick, not merely merchants of splendor and opulence, but suddenly emerging to offices of dignity and trust, administering the finances of Christian and Mohammedan kingdoms, and traveling as embassadors between mighty sovereigns.

Another feature which characterizes the Moslems of the present day, especially the Turks, is a struggling spirit of *reform.* The present Sultan, like his immediate predecessor, has been at much pains to cultivate an acquaintance with the West, and to introduce European improvements, and to encourage European skill. He has effected many useful reforms. And the present Grand Vizier is a liberal and a well educated man, acquainted with European civilization, having been embassador to Paris and

London. He is laboring, and not without success, to modify the laws, and to correct the manners of the Turks. Not long since, we heard of the Sultan presiding in person at a meeting of his council, and himself proposing the abolition of the slave trade in his dominions; a measure which has since been carried into effect.

Innovations of the most encouraging character are daily becoming more and more rife among the Turks, showing a delightful progress of civilized and liberal ideas among the leading minds of the nation, which cannot but meet a response, sooner or later, in the popular mind. Monopolies are abolished; internal improvements made; re strictions removed; a regular system of taxation to take the place of a miserable and oppressive mode of "farming" out a town or province for a fixed sum. But the innovation of the mightiest magnitude, the one which has perhaps done most to break up the stagnations of Turkish orientalism, is the introduction of steam navigation. This has opened a new chapter to the sluggish mind of the East, and portends a revolution, moral, political, social and intellectual, of vast interest to the Christian philanthropist. New elements of improvement are now set to work. Facilities of intercourse and communication are increased an hundred fold—mind is brought in contact with mind. Activity and enterprise in business are promoted—punctuality enforced, and a complete revolution effected on the stereotyped habits of centuries. The whole is told in a word, in the felicitous style of the Rev. Mr. Goodell, of Constantinople: "The Turks have been squatted down here for ages, smoking their pipes with all gravity, and reading the Koran, without being once disturbed. When, lo! a steamer dashes right in among them, and they have to scramble out of the way."

It is, too, quite a new feature in those lands, which have been left to pine so long under the pale light of the crescent, and one indicating the hand of God at work for their redemption, that the Press has at length become no inconsiderable part of the machinery of modern society there. A large imperial printing establishment exists in Constantinople—"new presses are daily set up in the principal towns of the empire, and all desirable facilities granted to writers and journalists." A large number of periodical works and journals are published in the Ottoman empire, among which we find the Ottoman Moniteur or State Gazette, by a Frenchman, at the capital. All sorts of books are distributed through the empire without obstruction; and reading-rooms are established in some of the principal towns, supplied with all works of importance from France, Germany and England. Books of travels are written and published by Turkish functionaries who have resided in Europe; relating to their countrymen the wondrous achievements of science and civilization, and showing the Turks how far they are behind Christian nations.

A complete change has, within a few years, been effected in Turkey, with regard to the periodical press and books. But a short time since, printing was not known there; now it is in great honor. This is an advanced step in that long stagnant empire, presaging a no distant change. With the Sultan at the head of those who wish reform, Turkey is "making prodigious efforts to escape from a state of ignorance and degradation."

We may therefore conclude this chapter with the very pleasant reflection, that the countries occupied by the spiritual seed of the Ishmaelitish branch of the Abrahamic family, are, as never before, providentially prepared to receive the message of the true Prophet, and to act as co-workers with the spiritual seed of Abraham through the Heir of Promise, in the defence and spread of the truth. Already the "crescent is protecting the cross"—the state is throwing its arms around the Armenian converts, and saves them from the fury of their persecutors. And, what is beautifully illustrative of the rich beneficence of Providence, while the Turks have been protecting the persecuted Armenians, they have themselves been brought intimately and effectually in contact with the truth. The late persecution of the evangelical Armenians has presented the truth to the Turkish mind in a more tangible, visible, impressive form than all the preaching of the last century. In the victims of persecution, who have been brought before their tribunals, or been met in private or social life, the Turks have seen living illustrations of the

power of gospel truth, both in sustaining them in the furnace of affliction, and in transforming their characters.
"Witnessing their excellent lives, and hearing them ex-
plain the true nature of the gospel, the Turks are beginning now to feel that they never before had any correct
idea of what constitutes real Christianity." The specimens heretofore before them neither gave any right idea
of what Bible Christianity is, or held out any inducement
to the Turk to change his religion. For the Turks, generally speaking, are, (and always have been,) a better
people, more honest, more virtuous than any nominally
Christian people dispersed among them.

Providence has at length furnished the Turks with ster-
ling examples of Christian character, and of the transforming power of Christianity—living epistles, read and
known of all men.

CHAPTER XVI

HAND OF GOD IN THE TURKISH EMPIRE. The Turkish Government and Christianity.
Mr. Dwight's communication. Change of the last fifty years. Destruction of the
Janizaries. Greek Revolution. Reform. Death of Mahmoud. The Charter of
Gul Khaneh. Religious Liberty. Persecution arrested. Steam Navigation in
Turkey. Providential incidents. Protestant Governments and Turkey. Their pres-
ent Embassadors. Foreign Protestant Residents. Late exemption from the plague.

IT will not be void of interest, we trust, to notice here
a little more particularly some of the providential movements which have brought Mohammedan countries, especially the Turkish Empire, into their present interesting
position. It is but a few years since we could see nothing
in the Turkish empire but an iron despotism, and nothing
in the Turks' religion but a savage intolerance. Late accounts from that quarter have quite astonished us—they
seem almost incredible; and would have been quite incredible in any age but ours. Says Dr. Baird, "the Turkish

Government now favors the spread of the gospel. The Pacha of Egypt and the Sultan of Turkey are disposed to protect missionaries, and the time is at hand when Mussulmen may, with entire impunity, embrace the gospel.' Indeed, such is the construction put on the late act of toleration, that such a time seems fully to have come. No Moslem may now be molested on account of rejecting Mohammed. "The people of Turkey," says another, "are in a wonderful state of preparation for the preaching to them of a pure gospel." And adds the Rev. G. W. Wood, of Constantinople : "It is probably no exaggeration to say that within a year past (1846) more knowledge of the true gospel has been spread among the Turks than all which they had previously obtained since they first crossed the Euphrates."

Such a result is to be attributed very much to the late progress of Christianity among the Armenians of the Turkish empire, and to the recent persecutions among them. Never before has a pure gospel been preached in Turkey so extensively, and certainly have the Turks never before had the excellencies of Christianity so vividly and favorably illustrated before them. The evangelical preaching, and liberal teachings of the missionaries, have of themselves conveyed throughout the whole community an immense amount of Scripture truth ; and, besides, have provoked to jealousy many a priest and bishop to go and do likewise. Hence, gospel truth has been made, in a great degree, to pervade the Turkish nation.

Such changes are attracting the attention of the observers of human affairs. The most unbelieving philosopher will surely be moved to inquire into the reasons of so unwonted and unexpected changes, and will be nothing loth to trace out the steps, as far as he may, by which so great and pleasing a revolution has been brought about. To aid him in such researches is the design of this chapter

The writer would here thankfully acknowledge his indebtedness to the Rev. H. G. O. Dwight, of Constantinople, for the interesting facts found in this chapter, illustrating our general subject. Nor will he be careful to give him credit by quotation marks for his excellent and much valued communication, cheerfully yielding to so valued a

25

friend and excellent missionary, all that is of any ap
preciable worth in the chapter. For the last eighteen or
twenty years Mr. Dwight has been a close and discrim-
inating observer of the hand of God in the Turkish empire. He has observed with the eye of a Christian
philosopher, a philosophic historian, and a zealous, able,
judicious, hoping missionary. He has, as the following
paragraphs show, carefully watched the progressive steps
of Providence as He has been preparing that hitherto
unpropitious soil to receive the good seed of the word.

In a note accompanying his communication, Mr.
Dwight says: " You have given me a mighty subject, and
I feel wholly incompetent to the task of properly presenting it. After having tried to summon all the powers of
my mind, (and also the aid of my brethren here,) to this
deeply interesting investigation, I am sure I have said
very little of what might be said, and what will be un-
folded in eternity to the wondering minds of God's people,
of all his providential interpositions in behalf of his
church here. I pray that the Lord will pardon me that,
in my weakness, I have made so imperfect and unworthy
a record of his doings around us, and that he will grant
unto me, and to all his people, more and more of his
divine aid to enable us to see more clearly his stately
footsteps among the children of men. Let us remember
that we have to do with One who openeth and *no man*
shutteth, and shutteth and no man openeth. According
to my opinion, God is *omnipotent* in his works of *Providence*, as he was in the work of creation."

To introduce the gospel into Turkey fifty years ago,
would have been an enterprise fraught with difficulties
and dangers. Evangelical labors among the Mohammedans, would have been, (as perhaps they are still,) en
tirely out of the question. No Turk could have embraced
the Christian religion, without losing his head, and the
missionary who should have appeared in Turkey for the
avowed purpose of converting the Mohammedans to
Christianity, in those times of the Janizaries, would
probably have shared a similar fate. At any rate, his
presence would not have been tolerated in the country
for an hour. If he had come to labor only among the

nominally Christian sects, he might not so soon have attracted towards him the attention of the Government, but his situation in the country would have been precarious, just in proportion to his success. The Patriarchs of the different Christian communities were then permitted to exercise a very arbitrary and tyrannical power over their own people. They could flog, imprison, and exile whom they liked, by the aid and consent of the Turkish Government, without being required to establish by evidence, any definite charge against the individual. In this way, even as late as the year 1828, the Armenian Patriarch procured the banishment of several thousands of his subjects, (many of them rich and influential,) and their property was confiscated, on a most frivolous pretense,—their only crime being that they were Catholics, and did not, of course, symbolize with the Armenian church in their religious views.

The destruction of the Janizaries must be considered as among the most important providential first-steps towards breaking up this ancient system, and opening the way for missionary efforts. It was, in fact, the death-blow to the power of the Ottoman empire, although not seen to be such by him who inflicted it. From that moment the Turkish government has been growing weaker and weaker, and its only hope of a renewal of its former strength, is an entire abolishment of the old despotic system, and the establishment of just and righteous laws, securing to all its subjects their proper civil and religious rights.

Of course, with the downfall of despotic power in the civil government, the downfall of ecclesiastical power derived from that government, is necessarily involved.

The revolution and independence of Greece is another great event in the history of the Turkish empire, which has been made, providentially, to work so as to favor the introduction of the gospel into the country. Whatever has contributed to weaken the original Turkish system, and render this government dependent on the great nations of Europe, must be considered as a providential instrumentality employed by the great Head of the Church, to prepare for the coming of his kingdom. Of

course, the quasi independence of Egypt, and the frequent
distui bances in Syria, and in other parts of the country,
must be classed under this head.

Whatever providential circumstances of this sort compel the Turks to throw themselves upon their European
allies for assistance or protection, or encourage those
allies in officiously volunteering such assistance, must
always tend to place Turkey more and more under the
influence of the European powers; so that England,
France and Russia, have now come to have a sort of
right to interfere in the internal regulations of this country, and the administration of its government.   And, although these foreign powers sometimes pull in opposite
directions, yet, on the whole, their influence is to advance
civilization, and establish just and righteous laws, and
religious toleration.

Since the overthrow of the Janizaries, *reform* has
been the order of the day in Turkey; and, although the
work has proceeded slowly, yet no one can deny that a
steady progress has been made.   Sultan Mahmoud possessed a clear, liberal, and independent mind, and he
marched on, prudently and steadily, from step to step, in
his efforts to establish the regeneration of his country;
and before his death he had the satisfaction of seeing important changes introduced.   He seems to have been
especially raised up and qualified for the age and country
in which he lived, and the high and arduous work to
which he was called.   The man of faith, who sees God's
finger in every event that transpires in this world, most
readily ascribes to God's special providence the raising
up of such a sovereign as Mahmoud, at such a time.   All
his reforms, though such an effect was probably farthest
possible from his thoughts, tended in a most remarkable
manner, to prepare the way for the coming of Christ's
kingdom in this land.   The peculiar juncture at which
he died, must also attract the attention of a believer in
Providence.

Some Armenians of rank, who were exceedingly hostile to the spread of evangelical sentiments in their community, in the year 1839, through a combination of circumstances, gained direct access to the ear of Mahmoud,

(a very unusual privilege,) and by misrepresentations, procured his active hostility against those of his subjects who had embraced the evangelical religion. He was induced to put forth his mighty power to persecute the true followers of Christ, and several were banished, and others were sorely threatened, and it was determined to make the most vigorous efforts to remove the missionaries from the country. When the persecution was at its height, and the enemies of God seemed to have every thing in their own way, and there were many fears that the garden of the Lord would be completely overrun and devastated by the destroyer, the great Mahmoud suddenly died, and with him, for the time being, passed away all the power of the persecutors to do further injury.

One of those who suffered banishment during this persecution, was Mr. Hohannes, now in America. He was then the leading man among the evangelical Armenians of Constantinople, and he was kept in exile a year after the Sultan's death; and it was the declared intention of his enemies, that this banishment should be perpetual. And they would probably have accomplished their purpose, had not God, in his providence, raised up for him a deliverer, just in the time of need. A humane and friendly English medical man was appointed one of the physicians of the Sultan's palace, and this situation enabled him to speak a good word for the exile, which procured his restoration.

The changes that have taken place since the present Sultan came upon the throne, indicating a providential preparation for the coming of the kingdom of Christ in this land, are still more marked than during the previous reign. Soon after Abdul Medjid succeeded his father, the famous Charter of *Gul Khaneh* (so called,) was granted to the people, in the presence of all the foreign embassadors. This was the more remarkable, since it was not only not called for by the people, but such were the prejudices in favor of the old system, that the new must be introduced with the greatest prudence and caution. The world then witnessed the extraordinary spectacle of a despotic monarch, of his own accord, granting political rights and privileges to a people so wholly un-

25*

prepared for them, as to render the very offer of them dangerous to the peace of the community. The fundamental principle of this charter was, that the liberty, property, and honor of every individual in the community, without reference to religious sentiments, should be sacredly guarded. No one was to be condemned, in any case, without an impartial trial; and no one was to suffer the extreme penalty of the law, without the sanction of the Sultan. Here was a marked providential preparation for the protection of God's people in time of persecution. To the principles of this charter appeals have since been made, by suffering Protestants, hundreds of times, and under its cover they have been protected; while, under the former system, there would have been no help for them.

But by far the most important innovation upon Turkish law and custom, as affecting directly the kingdom of Christ, is that which was effected chiefly through the intervention of His Excellency Sir Stratford Canning; namely, the abolition of the odious law requiring the decapitation of backsliding Mussulmans. The whole history of this movement is interesting in the extreme, and opens one of the most instructive pages in the wonderful book of God's providence. An Armenian young man, of obscure family, and of no personal importance, was understood to have become a Mussulman. This is an event of not unfrequent occurrence in Turkey. The individual in question, before being formally initiated into the Turkish faith, repented of his folly, and made his escape to a neighboring kingdom. After an absence of a year or two, he returned, supposing that there would be no further search for him. He was soon recognized, however, and apprehended, and sentenced to death, according to Mohammedan law. The British Embassador now stepped in, and interceded for his life. The promise was given by the Turkish Government that the young man should not be executed. Turkish fanaticism, however, prevailed, and the renegade was publicly beheaded. And furthermore, a few days after, a renegade Greek was also beheaded, in a village near Broosa. These acts of the Porte being in direct violation of its promise, and par ticularly the second execution, so closely upon the first, very naturally had the effect to render the honorable representative of the British Government more decided and peremptory in his demands. Sir Stratford could, of course, do nothing further for the individual whose case had been the particular cause of his remonstrances, but he demanded, and procured from the Sultan, a written pledge, that from henceforth, no Christian, becoming a Mussulman, and returning to his former religion, shall be put to death in the Turkish dominions. The French Embassador united with the English in making this demand, and both were strongly backed up by their respective governments. The Russian Minister ultimately joined the other two. It was said by some, that the fact of the second person executed being a Greek, was the means of calling the Russian Government into action. The ground assumed by these European powers was, that such executions were a public reproach cast upon the *Christian religion*, which is the religion of Europe.

The promise of the Sultan has since been interpreted by the British Embassador, and the interpretation has, again and again, been admitted by the Porte, that no religious persecution, of whatever kind, is to be allowed in the Turkish empire. This was, in fact, the precise wording of the verbal promise given by the Sultan to the Embassador, though the written pledge was somewhat more restricted in its terms. This new principle, thus introduced, has been successfully appealed to, in numberless instances, by the Protestant Armenians, under the persecutions brought upon them by their ecclesiastics. They would, no doubt, have been banished, and even, in some instances, put to death, under the old Turkish system. It seems as if God, in his providence, permitted the Turkish Government to take the fatal step they did, in regard to that Armenian renegade, in order to call the attention of European governments strongly to the subject, and lead them to procure from the Sultan such a pledge against religious persecution, *just at that time*, when the wrath of the Armenian ecclesiastics was about to be roused up against the true followers of Christ among their flocks ; whom they " would have swallowed

up quick," if they had had the same power as formerly.
The British Minister himself has been heard to express
his admiration at the providence of God in this thing, and
to declare that it was *God alone* who forced this concession from the Turks.

The weakness of the Turkish Government, dependent,
as it is, for its very existence, on the favor and support
of the great European powers, is thus a prominent cause
(ordered and arranged by Providence) of protection and
defence to the infant churches of God, in this land. And
it should be particularly remarked, as a most striking
illustration of that sacred saying, that " The Lord of
Hosts is *wonderful in counsel;*" that, through a sort of
political necessity, not only France, but even *Russia,* was
constrained to join hands with England, in compelling
the Turks, in the instance referred to, to admit the principle of religious liberty into their country.

It is also a striking providential fact, which could not
have been fifty years ago, that the only two *French*
newspapers published in Constantinople, which are under
the protection of the Turkish Government, now come
out, openly and avowedly, in favor of religious liberty ;
and they have repeatedly urged the point in the clearest
terms, that all civil and political power should be taken
from the ecclesiastics, and they be compelled to confine
themselves solely to their ecclesiastical functions.

Among the providences of God in so *timing* things as
to meet the circumstances of his people, and favor the
progress of the gospel in this land, should be mentioned
the following facts. More than once, in the infancy of
the reformation in Turkey, when the ecclesiastical
powers were ready to persecute, cruelly, the few who
had renounced the errors of their church, quarrels have
sprung up in the midst of the Armenian community itself, which have completely diverted attention from the
Protestants, and, for a time, stayed the arm of the persecutor. Sometimes, the quarrel has been about the
Patriarch, and once, at least, it originated in a spirit of
jealousy between the bankers and tradesmen ; and thus
while, for years, nearly the whole attention of the ecclesiastics and chief men of the nation, was absorbed in

these internal disputes the work of God was quietly and constantly gaining ground among the people. At length, these internal troubles were quieted by the election to the patriarchal office, of an obscure old bishop, whose chief recommendation was, that he was a man whom no party cared to claim, and consequently, the only one upon whom they could unite. He held his office much longer than was anticipated, and he was a man of so eccentric a character—bordering on insanity—that almost no one dared to approach him; for no one could possibly divine, beforehand, how he would receive any proposition, or, whether a petition presented would be for the honor or disgrace of him who offered it. During his administration of two or more years, evangelical senti ments gained a firm foothold in the country; and, although there were many and powerful enemies of the truth, who were ready to use all their influence to root it out, yet the peculiar character of their Patriarch discouraged every attempt at a combined effort against the Protestants.

Thus the great persecution, which burst upon the heads of the devoted servants of God in Turkey, early in the year 1846, was stayed, by a series of peculiar providences, until the evangelical party was sufficiently enlarged and strengthened, and the principle of religious liberty was introduced and acknowledged by the Turkish Government, as has been related. At the beginning of his attempts to persecute, the Armenian Patriarch sent to the Porte the names of thirteen individuals whom he considered the leaders among the Protestants, with the request that they might be banished. Formerly, such requests were granted with the greatest readiness, but now, the astonished Patriarch received for answer, that henceforth *no one could be persecuted for religious opinions in Turkey.*

Another striking mark of the special providence of God in this movement, is the fact, that just before the persecution commenced, a change of ministry took place in Turkey; and an anti-liberal and anti-English cabinet was exchanged for one composed of the most intelligent and large-minded men in the country. This cabinet

still remains unchanged.   The Grand Vizier, who is the
leader of it, has long stood at the head of the reforming
party in Turkey, and he is thoroughly opposed to all
fanaticism and bigotry; and the Minister of Foreign
Affairs, who, by a singular coincidence, is also the Minister of Religion, is a man of like spirit.   Both of them
have resided in England, and other parts of Europe.

Under the same general head with the foregoing, that
is, the providential adaptation of things to meet the
wants of the church, the opening of steam navigation in
this country should be mentioned.   When the first missionaries came here from America, not a steamboat was
established on any of these waters.   The first missionary
stations occupied in Turkey, (north of Syria,) were at
Smyrna and Constantinople.   Owing to the current in
the Dardanelles, the upward passage of sailing vessels,
from Smyrna to Constantinople, was frequently thirty days.
This was a serious hindrance to our communications, and
especially to the transmission of the products of our press.
The first steam communication established in the country,
was between these two cities.   Our next missionary stations were at Broosa and Trebizond, and in a short time
lines of steamers were placed upon these routes; and,
although many predicted that they would not succeed,
they have become exceedingly profitable concerns.   The
line to Trebizond also connects us very directly with
our Oroomiah brethren.   At Nicomedia and Ada Bazar,
although we have no missionaries stationed there, yet the
work of God has been such as to render frequent and
easy communication desirable; and, behold, a line of
steamers is placed there also, as if for the very purpose!
Another line has, for some time past, connected Constantinople and Smyrna with Beyroot.   *In every instance* the
missionary has gone first, and after a necessity has been
created for frequent communication, for the purpose of
forwarding the Lord's work, *a line of steamers has been
established!*   The men of the world would no doubt
smile at the intimation that there was a particular providence in these arrangements, and I would that there
were more such *faith* in the world for them to smile at.
It is no doubt true, that those who have brought forward

these enterprises thought only of their own advantage, or of some other mere worldly end ; and it never came into their minds that they were doing any thing to meet the wants of the kingdom of Christ in this world, or to fulfill his purposes. "They meant it not so, neither did their hearts think so," and yet the believer in God's providence, who knows that "God worketh all things after the counsel of his own will," and that worldly men, and even wicked men, are often his tools in carrying forward the purposes of his kingdom, cannot fail to trace all these arrangements directly to the intervention of God, who was thus providing facilities for his servants to spread far and wide the news of salvation. Within the same period of time, also, have those more extensive steam routes been opened, by which missionaries, and friends of the missionary cause, throughout the four quarters of the globe, are now enabled, with great frequency and certainty, to communicate with each other.

I will close this communication with the statement of several facts, illustrating the providence of God in taking care of his people in this land, leaving it with you to arrange these facts as best suits your purpose.

In the year 1845, a young Armenian, in the village of Kurdbeleng, who was led to receive the Scriptures as his only guide, was cruelly beaten, at the instigation of the head priest of the church, and by order of the chief ruler in the Armenian community of that place. The priest and ruler were both present on the occasion, and they procured a Turkish police officer to inflict the punishment, giving him rum to drink that he might lay on the blows with a more unmerciful hand. The poor man suffered dreadfully, having been beaten with a heavy stick, and immediately after he was compelled to leave his shop, his father's house, and his native village, and to wander, an exile, among strangers.

The providence of God soon began to give intimation that the rich and powerful oppressor and persecutor of his people was not to escape unpunished in this world. This ruler began to be odious in the eyes of the people, and they at length found means to remove him from his

office ; although their action was not at all connected
with any religious question or movement among them.

The chief ruler of the Armenians in Nicomedia, who
was himself a persecutor of the church, and a powerful
and notorious oppressor of the people in that part of the
country, went in person to Kurdbeleng, and by his overpowering influence succeeded in reinstating his degraded
friend, against the wishes of the majority of the inhabitants. In returning home, after accomplishing this piece
of iniquity, he fell from his horse, and fractured his
skull, and within a few days, died a miserable death.

Months passed away, when, one day, as the restored
ruler at Kurdbeleng was sitting in his own house, a mus-
ket ball was fired through the window, and, entering at
one of his eyes, passed through his head, and laid him
dead on the spot! The assassin was seized, and he con-
fessed the deed, but declared that he was paid to perpetrate it by an individual whom he named, and was also
urged to it *by the same head priest of the church, who had
procured the cruel beating of the young man for his evangelical sentiments ! That priest is now in prison awaiting
his trial, as a murderer !*

But this is not the end of the story. The individual
who inherited the estate and office of the Nicomedian
ruler, also lent his influence for the persecution of God's
people. Not long ago, some of the leading persecutors
from Constantinople were visitors at his house, from
which they set out in the night, on their return home,
having carelessly left their lighted pipes in their bed-
room. The house took fire, and was entirely consumed,
with a large amount of jewels and other property, taking
away nearly all the man possessed, at a stroke !

My other narrative is of a different kind, though not
less striking as an illustration of the wonderful workings
of Divine Providence. In the year 1839, the reigning
Patriarch, Hagopas by name, was actively engaged in
persecuting the Prosestants. He issued a thundering
bull against them, and several of the leading men among
them he caused to be banished. While employed in this
hateful work, he was also engaged in building for himself
a large house, with money procured, as usual, by exac-

tions from the people. *This house has now become the Protestant Chapel in Constantinople.* Thus, while with one hand he was persecuting the Protestants, and laboring for their complete extermination in 1839, with the other, he was erecting a chapel for them to occupy in 1846; and it is the only building, so far as we know, that is suitable for this purpose, and obtainable by them, in the whole of Constantinople proper ! The Patriarch built the house for himself and brother, and subsequently gave it to the latter as a present. This brother has since become a Protestant, and thus it is that his house has fallen into the hands of the Protestant congregation. It is at present hired for a term of years, as a place of preaching, and we doubt not that it will be held for this purpose, until the providence of God points out to the evangelical Armenians a still more suitable place.

A circumstance of no small moment to those who love to study the doings of Providence, is, that within a few years past Protestant governments in Europe have taken a far deeper interest than ever before, in the prosperity of the Protestant cause in the world, and especially in Turkey. There is no need that I should here introduce the question whether this interest has always led them to the right course of action or not ; or the inquiry, which is still farther back, how far governments, as such, are called upon to meddle with religion. One point I think must be clear to all, namely, that the Protestant governments of the world have a right to use a moral influence in behalf of oppressed and persecuted persons, and especially Protestants, wherever they are found. And who can fail to recognize the finger of God in it, that the cabinets of England and Prussia have, within a few years past, exhibited an interest on this subject, which is altogether new ; and I may add, which is altogether *timely.* Without expressing any thing to the detriment of previous cabinets, and previous embassies, it is to us exceedingly plain in regard to Turkey, that as the work of God's Spirit has gone on here, and the people of God have multiplied in the land, the Lord who is "wonderful in counsel," has put it into the hearts of Protestant sovereigns and their ministers, to sympathize with these

26

people in their trials; and he has also so ordered it, that serious minded men, who feel a personal interest in the spiritual welfare of the world, should be sent here to represent their respective governments. I would, therefore, here record, with gratitude, that during the course of the persecutions that have been waged here against the Protestant Armenians, not only have the British Embassadors, His Excellency Sir Stratford Canning, and the Right Honorable Lord Cowley, who has occupied his place during his absence in England, promptly acted in behalf of the oppressed, but also that Mr. Carr, the Minister of the United States, M. Le Coq, the Prussian Minister, and Count Perponcher, his successor, have always been ready to address to the Porte remonstrances against the persecuting acts of the Armenian ecclesiastics, based upon the promise of the Sultan, that henceforth there shall be no more religious persecution in his dominions. Nor must I omit to mention that, while for a long course of years the representative of the Dutch Government here was a Roman Catholic, a native of this country, during the past year, Baron Mollerus has been sent out from Holland to fill this place, he being not only in name a Protestant, but also evincing a real interest in the establishment and prosperity of Protestantism in this land.

In close connection with this, is the circumstance that foreign Protestant residents have been accumulating here very rapidly within these few years past, forming a community of Protestants, highly important to the interests of religion in the country. A large number of English, Germans and Americans, have come out, by the express call of the Turkish Government, to engage in its service, in the various departments of agriculture, manufactures, medicine, literary instruction, and military tactics. Although the individuals filling these places are not all what they should be, yet many of them would be an honor to any country, and some are very decided religious characters. About eight miles from our residence, an English colony has recently grown up, in connection with some iron and cotton works belonging to the Government, and there will soon be nearly a thousand Englishmen there, including men, women, and children. At present, we supply them with regular preaching every Sabbath, but there is no doubt they will, ere long, have a pastor of their own from England, and also a school-master ; and the influence of such a Protestant colony must be very important in Turkey. A large woolen factory has been established near Nicomedia, and very providentially the gentleman who was first called to take the superintendence of it was an English Christian, of a very decided and consistent character. He with his family resided in Nicomedia for nearly three years, during the whole of the persecution, and from their position they were enabled often to succor the oppressed, and in other ways to exert a very happy influence in that town. When the Protestant Armenians there were driven from every other place of meeting, this gentleman kindly opened a room in his house, where they assembled, unmolested, every Sabbath. When the severity of the persecution was passed, he and his family were called to return to England, where they still remain.

Last of all I would mention, among the providential circumstances which have here combined for the furtherance of the gospel, is the complete cessation of the plague. For many years before the missionaries came to this land, and for several years after their establishment here, the plague was an annual visitor, in a violent epidemic form, and there was scarcely a month in which cases of it were not reported. Its influence on missionary operations was disastrous in the extreme. Our schools had to be disbanded, our congregations broken up, and social intercourse almost entirely interdicted. For ten years past, during which the work of God has been constantly prospering here, and constant meetings, and intercourse with the people have been called for, *we have been entirely exempt from this disease! Not a single case has occurred in this city,* so far as our knowledge extends! Truly "the Lord of Hosts is wonderful in counsel and excellent in working."

CHAPTER XVII.

Africa the land of paradoxes—Hope for Africa. Elements of renovation—Anglo Saxon influence—Colonizing—The Slave Trade and Slavery—Commerce. A moral machinery—education, the Press, a preached Gospel. Free Government. African Education and Civilization Society. The Arabic Press. African languages.

> "*Ethiopia shall soon stretch out her hands unto God.*"
> Ps. lxviii. 31.

AFRICA next demands our attention. Though both Mohammedan and Pagan, it deserves a separate consideration. Ignorant, debased, abused, this continent has lain, till quite recently, hopeless, except to the eye of faith. But is there now hope for poor Africa? Does any morning star, any harbinger of light arise over that dark land? Yes; the angel having the everlasting gospel to preach, is flying, too, over that dark region, with healing in his wings, distilling blessings over the land of Ham. There, too, the hand of God is mightily at work, laying tribe after tribe at the feet of Christian charity, imploring the lamp of life and the full horn of salvation.

The light of Christianity, which, in the early ages of the church, shone in Africa, and numbered among its disciples some of her brightest ornaments, long since set in darkness; and long and deep has been that darkness. Africa has since been given a prey to the fierce rule of the Arabian Prophet, to the sottish dominion of Paganism, and to the cruel ravages of the slave trade. Africa has been cast out by the nations into outer darkness, beyond the furthermost verge of common humanity. But she has once more come into remembrance. *The hand of the Lord is now stretched out for her deliverance.*

A brief survey of some providential movements towards this long forsaken continent, will verify this assertion. Such is the design of the present chapter.

Africa is the land of paradoxes, enigmas, mysteries If we had no other argument to show that our earth has not yet fulfilled its destinies, and, of course, is not ready to be offered, we would present, as such an argument, the past and present condition of Africa. With all her vast natural resources, her fertile soil, unparalleled advantages for commerce, and "infinite variety of physical and national character," she has remained little more than a blank on the map of human development. With the exception of Ethiopia, Egypt, and Carthage, Africa has strangely and mysteriously played no part in the history of man. "She has hung like a dark cloud upon the horizon of history, of which the borders only have been illuminated, and flung their splendors upon the world." Yet to the philosophic historian, there has been acting on that theatre a drama of no common interest. The great Architect has been pleased to make Africa the theatre on which to exhibit the extremes of human elevation and depression, of natural beauty and deformity, of fertility and barrenness, of high mountains and boundless deserts, of burning sands and eternal snows.

Africa has furnished some of the noblest specimens of humanity—plants of renown, delightful examples of civilization, refinement, and advancement in the arts and sciences; in literature and religion; in civil liberty and free government. And the same soil, too, has been loathsomely prolific in ignorance, barbarism, superstition, oppression and despotism. There some of the fairest portions of the globe have, for three thousand years, "been stained with blood and unrevenged wrong; overhung with gloom and every form of human woe and human guilt."

But there is hope for Africa. The Hand that is moving the world is at work in the land of Ham. We are able there to trace the same felicitous combination of circumstances, preparing Africa on the one hand for her regeneration, and on the other, providing facilities and resources for the work. Nearly co-existent with the birth of modern benevolent action in England and America, there commenced a train of providences in Africa, and in respect to Africa, worthy of special remark. The first love and the first sacrifice of the American church was given to Africa. The darling object of Samuel J. Mills, who was, more than any other man, the

26*

father of benevolent enterprise in America, (the object
for which he seems to have been especially raised up,)
was the melioration of the condition of Africa. The
civil, moral and spiritual degradation of that benighted
land, lay with continual weight on his mind. Through
his instrumentality, a seminary for the education of young
men of color, with a view to their becoming missionaries
in their father-land, was established, and went into operation under a Board of Directors appointed by the Synod
of New York and New Jersey, with Mills for their agent.
The last months of the life of this devoted man were
spent on an exploring tour on the Western coast of
Africa; the last energies of his great and comprehensive
mind, and the best affections of his big heart, were devoted to that long neglected land. Yet some years
before Mills explored the wastes of Western Africa, European Christians had begun their work in South Africa.

Our business at present is with the Hand of God, that
has opened the door to this great field, and is now holding out the promise of a great and no distant harvest.

1. We see the Hand of God auspiciously at work for
Africa, in the introduction and increase on that continent of *Anglo-Saxon power and influence.* We have
seen, the world over, that this is a signal of advancement
among barbarous nations. It is the lifting up of the dark
cloud of ignorance and superstition, that light and truth
may enter. It is the harbinger of the gospel; it prepares
the way, and protects the evangelical laborer, and furnishes facilities and resources for the work.

Such a power and influence is now begirting Africa,
and is waxing stronger every year. At Sierra Leone,
Cape Palmas, Liberia and the Cape of Good Hope, the
Anglo-Saxon element is taking deep root, and its widely
extending branches are overshadowing large portions of
those domains of darkness, and dropping over them
golden fruits. In this we discover a divine presage, that
the time to favor this long abused, ill-fated continent, is
at hand. We hazard no conjecture as to the ultimate
destiny of England or America, but we cannot be mistaken that Anglo-Saxondom is now being used as the
right hand of Providence, to civilize, enlighten and Chris-

tianize the Pagan world. Whatever may be the *motives*
of England in extending her empire over Asia and Africa,
or of America in making her power felt, and extending
her commerce, it is not difficult to see what God is
bringing out of such extensions of dominion and power.
But for British power and British sympathy, under the
favor of Heaven, Africa, with scarcely an exception,
might, to the present day, have had the "tri-colored flag
waving on her bosom, bearing the ensigns of the mystery
of Babylon, the crescent of the false Prophet and the emblems of Pagan darkness, from the shores of the Mediterranean to the colony of the Cape of Good Hope."

2. Another providential feature of a kindred character, is the present plan of *colonizing* on the coasts of
Africa. The influence of colonies is not now a matter
of theory but of experience. Carthage was a colony ;
the wealth, power, civilization and magnificence of that
ancient kingdom, was not an indigenous growth of an
African soil. It was an exotic, transplanted thither, and
there made to flourish till it spread its branches far into
the interior, and covered many tribes and nations with
its shadow.

What we are concerned with here, is the influence of
the introduction into a Pagan country of an enlightened,
civilized, thrifty, foreign population. They furnish, first,
a tangible, living example of what skill, industry and intelligence can do. And as the superior and inferior
classes mingle together, this skill and industry will be
communicated and received. It will provoke to imitation ; and the advantages on the part of the inferior class
are immense—immense before we admit into the accoun'
the *moral* element, which we shall see enters largely into
all modern systems of colonizing.

The Carthaginians too well understood the power of a
colonizing policy, not to prosecute it to the extending of
their empire, which, in turn, became a vast benefit to
the adjacent tribes and nations of native Africans. Most
ancient historians have noticed this admirable policy of
the Carthaginians: "It is this way," says Aristotle,
"Carthage preserves the love of her people. She sends
out colonies continually, composed of her citizens, into

the districts around her, and by that means makes them
men of property; assists the poor by accustoming them
to labor." The natives gradually intermingled with the
colonists, and formed the strength of the Carthaginian
state. Herodotus affirms that, beyond the dominions of
the Carthaginian empire, no people could be found in
settled habitations, and engaged in agricultural pursuits.
But no sooner did these same nomadic tribes fall beneath
the transforming process of Carthaginian colonization,
than they became civilized, enlightened and comparatively refined, and were found engaged in "the peaceful
occupations of the field." As examples of this, another
ancient historian (Scylax) describes the country around
the lesser Syrtis and Triton Lake, as "magnificently
fruitful," abounding in tall, fine cattle, and the inhabitants
distinguished for wealth and beauty. Another region,
according to Strabo, between two and three hundred
miles in length, extending southward from Cape Bon, and
one hundred and fifty miles in width, was also distinguished for its fertility and high cultivation. It embraced
the most flourishing sea-ports, and was crowned with
agricultural settlements.

Such was the transforming power of ancient colonization in Africa—a colonization confessedly deficient in
some of the most powerful elements which enter into
modern schemes of colonizing. For of all the transforming elements ever thrown into the confused mass of Paganism, Christianity is the most powerful. Civil and
religious liberty is another mighty element; speculative
science, another; and practical science, yet another.
The first and the mightiest of these, was entirely wanting in the colonizations of Carthage, and the others
scarcely entered into the account.

What, then, may we reasonably expect as the fruit of
modern colonization? The hand of the Lord is in it.
The two great Protestant nations, whose language, literature and science, contain nearly all the truth there is in
the world, and whose churches nearly all the religion,
and whose religion nearly all the benevolence, and whose
governments nearly all the freedom, have, in the wondrous workings of Providence, been moved to colonize in

Africa. The English have colonies at the Cape of Good Hope, and in other portions of South Africa; on the Senegal and the Gambia; at Sierra Leone and Cape Coast Castle; and they are beginning to occupy the mouths of the Niger. And there are American colonies (now an independent government,) at Liberia and Cape Palmas. And these colonies are very much under the auspices of religious and philanthropic influences. Now, with the example of Carthage before us, what have we reason to expect their influence will be on Africa? Certainly nothing less than that they shall furnish tangible illustrations of the religion, the skill, industry and enterprise of the people there colonized; exhibiting the advantages of science, of improvement in the arts and in agriculture, and of a well ordered government; that they shall continue to extend their commerce and other benefits gained, back into the interior, constantly reaching their arms abroad and gathering tribe after tribe within the pale of their influence. Agriculture will be encouraged; a market opened for its avails; the slave trade thereby be effectually discouraged; savage life be abandoned, and the way for the gospel and all its concomitant blessings be opened. The colonist will be seen to possess almost every advantage over the native, and the latter can scarcely do otherwise than to fall in with the new order of things in proportion as he comes in contact with the colony.

Experience gives no hope of success in efforts to *evangelize* Africa, except through Christian colonies. The Moravians, who have yielded to no obstacles, either amidst the snows of the poles or the burning heats of the equator, or from the wrath of man, or the elements, failed in Africa. "Attempts at sixteen different points, made with the heroism of martyrs, to establish schools and missions, they have been forced to abandon, and to retire within the protection of the British colonies. And they now despair of every process, but that of commencing at these radiating points, and proceeding gradually outwards until the work is done."

But there is one peculiar feature in the colonization now going forward in Western Africa, more strikingly

providential and more potent in its bearings on the na
tives than perhaps has been well understood. I mean
the fact that the colonists are of the *same race* or species,
as the natives among whom they are colonized. Any
one acquainted with the habits and modes of reasoning
which prevail on this subject among rude barbarians,
must know that their habits of generalization are very
imperfect. They have no idea that all men are of "one
blood"—the same order of beings—and that what is true
of one people may, under similar circumstances, become
true of another. You may place by the side of a tribe
of native negroes, or native Hindoos, a colony of white
men and women, well educated, well bred, industrious,
intelligent, thrifty, moral and religious, who have, in
every thing, made decided advances beyond the barbarous condition of man, having convincingly demonstrated
the capability and improvability of man, and yet, in
theory, it will exert no influence on the barbarous tribe,
and in practice, but a very slow and partial influence.
And why not? Simply because the barbarian sees the
development (which he may admire and wish he *could*
imitate,) made in what he believes to be another order
of beings. He does not believe it imitable by himself or
his people. It is a development in the white man's nature, not in his.

But no such difficulty impedes the progress of improvement in Africa. The native Ashantee or Foulah, recognizes, in the improved condition and character of the
colonist, his own flesh and blood, his own color and
species ; and he no longer doubts the improvability of
his own tribe.

3. But the thought may be allowed to assume another
shape, and we shall have no less occasion to admire the
wonder-working Hand.

Cordially as every good man is bound by conscience
and by God, to detest and abhor from the innermost recesses of his soul, the slave trade and a wicked system
of slavery, he must admire that gracious Hand in so controlling even man's bitterest wrongs, as to educe from
them a lasting and general good. If God did not bring
good out of evil, and praise out of man's wrath, how little

good would come of this poor world—how little praise accrue to his name.

The slave trade and slavery are giant wrongs—monstrous sins; but let us see what God is bringing out of them. Thousands of wretched beings are yearly forced away from their homes, amidst shrieks, and conflagrations, and blood; submitted to the horrors and deaths of the middle passage; reduced to bondage cruel as death; awful is the sacrifice of liberty, happiness and life; of every thing worth possessing; yet, from this dark and troubled ocean of sin, He, whose ways are not as our ways, deduces a great and lasting good. These wretched victims of man's avarice and cruelty, were benighted Pagans. Their land was the region and shadow of death—the habitations of cruelty. They were brought to a Christian land. In the durance vile, as they toil out their wearisome years, many come in contact with the benign influences of Christianity. To the poor the gospel is preached. This angel of mercy meets them in their wearisome pilgrimage, sheds light about their gloomy path, and brings rest and peace to many a weary and heavy laden soul. Many become Christians, and many more, in spite of the mountain-burdens which crush them to the earth, rise far above their original condition in their native land. Thus God, in the hot furnace of affliction, and in defiance of all human wrong, prepares his materials for the regeneration of Africa. Thousands thus fitted, return to the land of their fathers, to teach and exemplify a pure Christianity; to encourage industry, agriculture and learning among the natives; to create a market for the products of honest industry, and thereby to remove one of the strongest inducements to the slave trade; to exhibit the advantages of a settled life, and of an organized government, and to inclose within the arms of civilization and Christianity, tribe after tribe in the interior; and by these several means, to extinguish, most effectually, slavery and the slave trade.

It is, again, through the wrongs inflicted on Africa, that she has been brought to the distinct and favorable notice of the whole Christian world, and been able to

enlist its profoundest sympathies and prompt compassion.
The heart of Christendom yearns for poor, bleeding
Africa, and it is not too much to expect that her emancipation, and freedom, and evangelization, will become objects of intense interest to all philanthropists and Christians. Recent movements of Providence favor such an
expectation.*

But here we shall need to look for a few moments in
another direction, that we may the better comprehend
what God is working out for Africa. It is always delightful to observe the *timings* of Providence—how one
thing is made to answer to another. With one hand,
God is preparing Africa to receive the richest of Heav-
en's blessings; with the other, he is preparing the materials and instruments by which to carry forward the
ameliorating process. And, at the same time, he is
arousing the energies of philanthropists and Christians,
to enter the field now ripe for the harvest.

During the last twenty years, changes have been taking
place in the slave-holding portion of our country, in reference to slavery and the enslaved, which augurs well for
the work of emancipation at no very distant day. Public sentiment has changed. Slavery is now very extensively regarded as a public burden—an evil. The colored
man is no longer regarded as incapable of holding stations, and pursuing occupations like white men; the laws
which prohibited the education of slaves, have, to a great

* With many good people it has been a subject of profound regret and lamentation,
that the work of emancipation in our country should be retarded, and the cause of
African colonization be maligned and hindered by the strange fanaticism of a large
class of the professed friends of the slave. Why this seeming disaster? The marvel
will cease as we look towards the end. Had the states of Delaware, Maryland, Virginia and Kentucky, freed their slaves, as in all probability they would but for the in-
judicious and provoking agitation of northern abolitionism, our African colonies would
have been inundated by a multitude of emancipated negroes but ill-prepared for self-
government, and before the colonies themselves had become so established, and their
principles so matured, that they should not be overwhelmed in the moral siroccos of
Africa—amalgamated in the heathen tribes about them. Abolitionism came in to retard a ruinous prosperity. A government is now established which is in the hands of
colored men, who have managed their own affairs until they have satisfied themselves
and the world of their ability for republican government. "Schools and churches, and
their necessary organizations, have been operating for years. Society in all its great
departments is organized, opinions formed and principles established." And the way
is now prepared for emancipation and colonization to go on, hand in hand, to almost
any conceivable extent. What would have been the result of *our* experiment at self-
government and religious freedom, had the present immense accessions of European
population poured in upon us fifty years ago, while our institutions were yet in their
infancy?

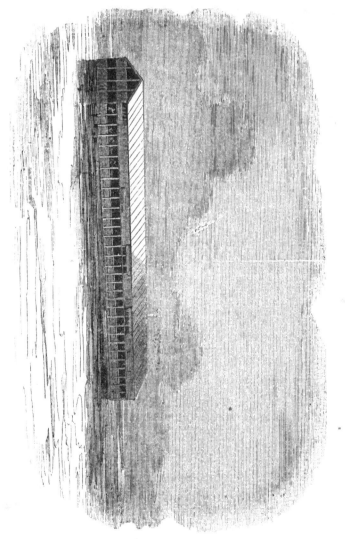

Noah's Ark. Page 313.

extent, become a dead letter; and the idea that slavery is a *necessary* institution at the south, because white men cannot labor in that climate, is quite exploded by the late immigration into that part of the country, of Irishmen and Germans, who have extensively become laborers there. Slave-labor is every year becoming less and less valuable; and, of consequence, *self-interest* is fast eradicating the evil.

Such changes have not only done much to facilitate emancipation, but to prepare a great multitude to emigrate to Africa, and to be useful citizens there: school-masters, preachers, statesmen, and useful members of society in every rank of life. In no respect, perhaps, do we more clearly discern the hand of God, than in the late educational and religious movements among the slaves. God has wonderfully vouchsafed his spirit to this ill-fated class of our countrymen. To the poor the gospel has been preached, and they have received it gladly. "In no period since the existence of slavery," says an intelligent writer, "has there been such attention paid to the religious instruction of the slaves, as in the last ten years; and in no part of the world have there been gathered richer fruits to encourage the laborer." "It is truly surprising and cheering to witness the almost universal feeling and interest on this subject, and the extent to which they have carried out their plans, in establishing schools and churches, and obtaining missionaries and teachers for the sole benefit of the colored people. Some of the church edifices, which are neat and costly, are owned by the slaves themselves, with regular organized churches, and large, orderly congregations, where they enact their own laws, manage their own finances, and take up collections for benevolent purposes. Some of their churches are large, numbering from one to two thousand communicants."

And in connection with these churches, you may meet Sabbath-schools of from one to two hundred children, who are faithfully taught the Bible—and there, the Christian mistress, sitting in the school-room from morning till night, spending her strength in teaching her young slaves, and endeavoring to prepare them for the enjoyment of

27

freedom; and this, month after month; living among
them, not of choice, but because she "dares not run away
from a duty which she feels God, in his mysterious providence has imposed upon her." Says another lady, "I
am living here an exile from my home, on account of my
slaves, which have been entailed upon me, and which I
cannot part with, for they will not consent to be separated from me."

The truth is, the more intelligent and better class of
people at the south regard slavery as a "moral and pecuniary evil," and contemplate the certainty of abolition,
and the importance of educating the mind and elevating
the character, and preparing the slave for that liberty
which they feel sure God designs him one day to enjoy.
Such are topics of not unfrequent discussion at the
south.*

But I am unwilling to dismiss this topic here. The
south is now furnishing delightful indications that God is
there preparing a multitude of men and women for the
high responsibilities of their future destiny, when the time
shall come for their removal to the land of their fathers;
that they may go thither, instructed in the principles of
our blessed religion and of civil liberty, to be instruments
of inestimable good to an ignorant, degraded and barbarous continent. The intelligent writer already quoted,
describes another scene which fell under his observation,
too fitly illustrating the point in hand, not to be tran-
scribed at length. Few at the north may be fully aware
that such things are to be met with on slave-holding territory. Every Christian and philanthropist will rejoice,
and see therein the good hand of the Lord in the execution of his benevolent purposes towards Africa.

Having attended, by invitation, public worship on the
premises of a wealthy slave-holder, in a "commodious
brick church, erected exclusively for the accommodation
of his colored people," where he met a "most orderly,
well-dressed, well-behaved congregation," and a slave in
the pulpit, who delivered a "most sensible, appropriate
sermon," Mr. Sawtell, on returning to the house, took

---

* Rev. E. W. Sawtell, in the New York Observer, April, 1847.

the occasion to learn more of this gentleman's views on the "subject of preparing his servants for liberty in this world, and happiness in the next."

"Why," said he, "we must educate them; we owe it to our slaves, and now we have the power to do it. We must instruct them in the Christian religion, in the mechanic arts, in the principles of free government, or their freedom would prove a curse instead of a blessing.

"I speak not," said he, "theoretically, but from experience. I have already educated about one hundred of mine, who have, of their own choice, gone to Liberia; some of them are merchants, some farmers, and others mechanics. I gave two of them a collegiate education, and the rest I educated myself; and I have the satisfaction of knowing that they are all doing well, are useful and happy. One of them is a missionary, and he writes me that he has nearly two hundred native African children in his school; teaching them our language, our religion, and our laws; and that you may see for yourselves, read these letters." Here he handed a number of letters received from the colony of Liberia, from those that were once his own ignorant slaves; and, to say nothing of the elegance of diction and penmanship, they were so filled with expressions of joy and rejoicing, of love and gratitude to their master, as to make it utterly impossible to read them without weeping—addressing him by such endearing appellations as, "dear father," "dear parent," "dear benefactor," and declaring at the close, that they had but one single wish for ever visiting the United States again, and that was, "that they might see, once more, their dear old father before he died." "Now," said this old gentleman, "this is my idea of our duty and obligation to the slaves, and of God's purposes in sending them here, and what I have done for those in Liberia, I am going to do for all."

On asking him how he managed to teach so many himself, he replied, "I have them divided into four classes: at daylight, on Sabbath morning, I call the first class, and drill them in reading and spelling, till breakfast. After breakfast, the second class is called, and they go through the shorter catechism and the ten command ments. Then comes the hour for public worship, when one of the servants, who is a minister, becomes the teacher, and I the learner. After public service, the other two classes, more advanced, are carried through their respective lessons in the same way as those in the morning. This is the way I spend all my Sabbaths; nor do I suffer any intrusion from my neighbors, unless it be one who is desirous of learning the art of doing good, and of training up his slaves for the high purposes and destiny for which God designs them."

But another peculiarity in this man's system of training his slaves for freemen is, that he allows of no arbitrary control or punishment. In fact, his slaves are organized into a perfect republic, possessing all the elements of a free, legislative government. Their trials for any misdemeanor or crime, are by jury, witnesses examined, and special pleadings, with all the solemnities of a court. In important and difficult cases, the old master is sometimes called in to preside as judge, and decide upon some difficult points of law; but the verdict, the sentence, and its execution, are all in their own hands.

Thus it is in this way they are learning important and practical lessons in the principles of civil polity and jurisprudence. And if we ask this benevolent man for his motive in all this, his answer is worthy of being recorded in golden capitals. "Why," said he, "intelligence, virtue and religion constitute the only sure basis of a republic. I believe Africa is to be a republic, and receive our language, laws and institutions; and I believe the cupidity of England, in first introducing slaves upon this continent, is to be overruled for the furtherance of this cause, and so many of these instruments as God in his providence has placed in my hands, I want to prepare and get them ready to meet their high responsibilities when the time for action shall come."

And so believe I. Monstrous as the curse of slavery is, disgraceful as it is to our country, and cruel as are the dark deeds of those who perpetrate this wrong on humanity, God seems likely to overrule it for a great and general good, and by means the most unexpected. Slaveholders are softened into pity towards their helpless vas-

sals, and have set themselves to prepare them for liberty;
slave-traders, (as the gentleman just referred to once was,)
have personally become their teachers and nursing fathers; famine, pestilence and oppression in the old world,
have driven the vassals of Europe to this new world, to
do the work now done by the African, and thereby to remove the supposed necessity of slavery; and many other
like providential interpositions combine to fit a great multitude of the colored race in America to go forth and
bless the dark continent of Africa. God's thoughts are
not as our thoughts, nor his ways as our ways.

The south possesses the grand lever for raising Africa.
'Let the foot of it be placed at Liberia; let Christian
patriots and philanthropists throw their weight upon this
end of it, making the Bible the fulcrum, and ere long Africa, with her sable millions, will be seen emerging from
the long night of cruel tyranny and barbarism, into the
pure sunlight of civilization, with her churches and
schools, her colleges and legislative halls, her poets and
orators, her statesmen and rulers, taking their position
among the enlightened and civilized nations of the earth.
The Lord hasten it in his time, and to him be the glory."

4. There is another point from which we must contemplate the same mighty Hand. It is in respect to
commerce; a kindred feature with one already named.
Commerce and the colony are working together, and
much in the same way. A legitimate commerce is God's
instrument for the civilization of the world, and the channel through which he brings about its evangelization. It
was commerce which gave to ancient states their renown, and laid the foundation of their greatness. Commerce was the "parent and nurse" of civilization and the
arts in Carthage, in Egypt and Meroe.

Africa has long been without a legitimate commerce;
and now that its white wings, in the revolving wheels of
Providence, are being spread over her, we may take it as
a token for good. This, in connection with the colonizing policy, will do more to annihilate the slave trade
than all that can possibly be effected by the combined
navies of Great Britain and America. Africa has had
wants to be supplied by foreign nations, but with her

past habits she has had nothing to give in exchange for needed supplies, except the flesh and blood of her own sons and daughters.   She is now learning from Christian colonists the worth of the exhaustless resources of her soil, her forests and her mountains, and the yet less developed resources of her own industry.   And we cannot doubt, when she shall have time to accept the substitute which commerce offers, she will sooner take the calicoes and trinkets, and whatever else she may need, in exchange for her cotton, sugar, rice, grain, gums, and gold than for the bones and sinews of her children.

"The emancipation of Africa," says one, "can be effected only from within herself.   Her nations must· be raised to that moral and political power, which shall combine them in firm resistance against oppression.   To do this, the chief points of *commercial* influence upon the coast, and of access to the interior, must be occupied by strong and well regulated *colonies*, from which civilization and religion shall radiate to the surrounding regions." This we hold to be a just sentiment; and in proportion as we see the principal points, and the strong-holds of Africa becoming depots of European arts, science, commerce, and religion, we hail the day as at hand when Christian philanthropy shall realize some of her "divinest wonders," amidst those nations that have so long sat in darkness.

Providential *coincidences*, which we have had occasion more than once to notice, are nowhere more distinctly marked than in the movements in Africa, and in respect to Africa.   The vast and extensive preparations which have been making on that continent for its regeneration, are co-existent with the remarkable waking up of the philanthropic and benevolent engergies of Christendom in its behalf.   As the door is opened on the one hand, the means are provided on the other.

But we shall fail to appreciate the prospective influence of commerce on Africa, if we do not allow a moment's consideration of the *resources* and the commercial *advantages* of that continent.   Few may be aware of the amount of commerce which England and America already carry on with Africa; yet her resources have scarcely begun to be developed, or her advantages to be improved. A single mercantile house in England had a trade with Western Africa, the value of whose imports for the years 1832—33—31, amounted to $1,400,000 annually; and the next year, the importations to England of the single article of *palm oil*, were one thousand two hundred and sixty five tons; worth $1,700,000. But it is rather to the yet unappropriated resources of the country to which we refer, as exhibiting any thing like the due importance to be attached to the providential movement under consideration.

Speaking of Western and Central Africa, a writer, reviewing Mungo Park, says, "there is probably no other equal expanse of territory which has such a portion of its surface capable of easy cultivation. From the base of the Kong Mountains, in every direction to the Atlantic on the one side, and to the deserts on the other, the land slopes off in easy gradations or terraces, presenting luxuriant plains, immense forests, and mountainous or undulating regions of great variety and beauty. It possesses, almost universally, a soil which knows no exhaustion. A perpetual bloom covers the surface, over which reigns the untroubled serenity of a cloudless sky. Aside from the splendors and luxuries of the vegetable world, the great staple of commerce may be produced here in an unlimited abundance. The cotton tree, which, in our southern states, must be planted every spring, grows there for four successive years, yielding four crops of the finest quality. Coffee grows spontaneously in the interior, giving about nine pounds to the plant. Rice, with a little cultivation in some places, equals the fertility of the imperial fields of China; and sugar-cane grows with unrivaled magnificence." Those travelers who have most carefully examined the soil and products, assure us that there is nothing in the glowing climes of the Indies, Eastern or Western, which some parts of Central Africa will not produce with equal richness. "It cannot admit of a doubt," says Park, "that all the rich productions, both of the East and West Indies, might easily be naturalized and *brought to the utmost perfection*, in the tropical parts of this immense continent. Nothing is wanting to this end but example to enlighten the minds of the natives. and instruction to enable them to direct their industry to proper objects. It was not possible for me to behold *the wonderful fertility of the soil*, the vast herds of cattle, proper both for labor and food, and a variety of other circumstances favorable to colonization and agriculture, and reflect withal on the means which presented themselves of a vast inland navigation, without lamenting that a country so abundantly gifted and favored by nature, should remain in its present savage and neglected state."

Her mountains, too, are full of riches—her streams run down on golden sands—her mineral riches seem not inferior to the wealth of her soil. And if we add to all this the facilities which Africa enjoys for navigation and internal communication, we cannot fail to get some just idea of the magnitude of the *commercial* element which is soon to be used, and which Providence has begun to use, for the civilization and the renovation of Africa. To say nothing of the obvious advantages of her immense line of sea-coast, Western, Central and Eastern Africa is drained by numerous large and navigable rivers, down which her gems, and gold, and wealth may flow, to enrich and beautify all lands, while she shall receive, in return, the richer gifts of science, freedom and religion. And the fact that the Niger, which, in its singularly circuitous course, visits a large portion of Central Africa, has already been invaded by the paddle-wheels of European improvement, (English skill and intelligence blessing the hitherto benighted regions of the Niger,) is a pleasing prognostication of what God is about to do for that long forsaken continent.

And God is doing yet more for Africa. The Ottoman Empire has, perhaps, been the most formidable hindrance to the redemption of Africa. By its inhumane policy and intolerant religion ; by the encouragement it has afforded to the slave trade, and its active participation in that inhuman traffick, it has stood as a most formidable barrier to all progress. But that obstacle is, in a great measure, removed. In the sure revolutions of Providence the Ottoman Empire is falling into decay. Its power is gone ; and henceforth, as the tide of knowledge, freedom and religion shall roll on their waves eastward into the centre of Africa, they shall no longer be arrested by the intolerant disciples of Mecca, or be turned back by the withering sirocco of the slave trade.

5. There remains one other point from which I would have you see Africa as a land in which God is preparing his way before him. It is the providential existence of a *moral machinery*, already in successful operation, and increasing every year, which can scarcely fail to work out the redemption of Africa. Education, the press and the preached gospel, are a threefold lever, which, as has been done in so many other lands, will surely raise wretched Africa from the dark vicinity of hell into a delightful proximity with heaven. The introduction, protection and success of recent efforts for the evangelization of Africa, are purely providential. The full amount of this providential agency we can estimate only by bringing before the mind a complete catalogue of all the missionary stations which now begirt Africa—the number of laborers— the means of usefulness, by the press, education, or a preached gospel—their operations—present results, and prospective influence. Such a view, alone, would exhibit the *force* of the moral machinery which Providence has there prepared for the future prosecution of his work. A general idea, sufficiently accurate for our present purpose, may, however, be gained from the following general, though not complete view of evangelical missions in Africa.

Nearly every missionary society, known to the writer, has missions in Africa. Reliable statistics make them, in all, eighteen. These missions are met at Sierra Leone, Liberia, Cape Palmas, Cape Coast Castle; at the Gambia settlement; on the coast of Guinea; on Fernando Po; at various points in South Africa, and a single station on the eastern coast, and one on the northern.

The following may be taken as very nearly the present effective force acting in Africa, as gathered from statistics, which may be relied on.*

---

* Missionary Herald, May, 1847.

	Stations.	Laborers.	Communicants.	Scholars.
South Africa,	115	260	10,725	11,218
West "	53	161	6,323	8,638
North "	1	11	20	234
East "	1	2		
	170	434	17,068	20,090

By laborers, we mean missionaries and assistant missionaries. The above items are, perhaps, all below the reality, on account of the deficiency of reports, but sufficiently accurate to give a general idea of the instrumentality which Providence has made ready for future progress. Much has been done to introduce the gospel into Africa—and yet *how little!* Cut off South Africa, and remove a narrow strip of the western coast, and only two stations will remain.

The Church Missionary Society have thirteen stations in West Africa; the Moravians, seven stations and forty-seven missionaries, and six thousand, eight hundred and forty converts, in South Africa; in four of their congregations five thousand persons are wont to hear the gospel. The Wesleyan Missionary Society has been providentially led, by a train of circumstances which it could neither have foreseen nor controlled, to extend its operations four hundred miles along the coast of Guinea, and two hundred miles interior towards Ashantee.

The instance just alluded to, is too beautifully illustrative of our general position, as well as of the present movements of Providence in Africa, to be passed without a moment's detail. A number of the inhabitants of Badagry, having been sold as slaves, were captured by a British cruiser, and carried into Sierra Leone. There they became acquainted with Christian missionaries and with Christianity. In due time they are returned to Badagry, where they make known the religion of the cross, exemplify Christianity by an improved life, and thus prepare the way for the establishment of a promising mission there under the auspices of the Wesleyans. Mr. Freeman, of the newly established mission, visits Understone, one hundred miles to the north of Badagry, meets there, too, a large number of these Sierra Leone Christians, (or re-captured slaves,) who are overjoyed to see him; he receives a cordial welcome from the King Lodeke, who had become favorably disposed to the English Government, to English missions, and to Christianity, through those of his people who had been so kindly rescued from slavery, and returned, and yet more pleased with the improved *moral condition* in which they had returned. This led to the establishment of another mission under royal auspices, the king himself being the chief patron. Such examples might be multiplied. The re-capture of the Mendians—their being brought to New England—taught Christianity—and their return to their own country, to report what they had learned, and the establishment of a mission in connection with them, is another example of the same character.

Kings and chiefs, not a few, have favored other missions, extending the arms of their protection over them; not only inviting missionaries to reside in their dominions, but offering them houses to live in, and facilities to work with. In the colonies of Cape Palmas, Liberia proper, Sierra Leone, and on the Gambia, are more than one hundred missionaries and assistant missionaries engaged in successful labor; some of them native Africans; five thousand regular communicants, and twelve thousand regular attendants, and tens of thousands perfectly accessible to the preaching of the gospel. The Rev. Mr. Wilson, in late tours to the north and south of the Gaboon, one hundred and fifty miles, and for many miles interior, found "the people generally ready to hear the gospel, and they solicited a missionary" to reside among them. And all this since the settlement at Sierra Leone in 1787. Surely the finger of God is pointing to *colonies* as the medium through which Christian missions are to reach the one hundred and fifty millions of benighted, bleeding Africa.

The colony at Liberia affords a pleasant illustration of this. A population of some seven or eight thousand emigrants and re-captured slaves, has twenty-three churches, embracing a third part of the entire population; fifteen schools, with five hundred and sixty-two pupils; four hundred miles of sea-coast arrested from the slave trade—a civilized and republican government, which extends its sway (beyond the number above named,) over eighty thousand native Africans—one hundred thousand more are in treaty with this government not to engage in the traffick of slaves.

From whatever point we look, we can scarcely fail to see that Providence is accumulating a vast and effective power for the renovation of Africa. His strong arm is now made bare to break the bands that have so long held her in thraldom, and to give her the liberty whereby the gospel makes free. Colonies are opening the way; commerce is giving wings to benevolence; bringing mind in contact with mind; bringing the destitute in proximity with their benefactors, and the Divine agency, through a preached gospel, is furnishing the effective power by which to achieve the desired transformation.

In Western Africa we see the banners of civil liberty unfurled in the creation of a free government in Liberia, which, we hope, is as the little leaven in the meal. An "African Education and Civilization Society" springs into existence, about the same time, in New York, to aid "young persons of color, who desire to devote themselves to God and their kindred according to the flesh," and to promote "the general cause of education in Africa. And, simultaneously with these, there comes an appeal from Syria in behalf of the "Arabic press;" arrangements being made there for the publication of a Christian literature for the "Arab race," including a correct and acceptable translation of the Holy Scriptures in Arabic—a language spoken by a people scattered over Africa from the Red Sea to the Atlantic.

6. Late philological researches in Africa seem to be developing a fact in reference to *languages*, which indicates a most interesting providential arrangement for the encouragement of the missionary, and to facilitate the work of Africa's evangelization. It is the *close affinity of African dialects*. Investigations made by Rev. Mr. Wilson in Western Africa, and by Rev. Dr. Krapf, W. D. Cooley and others, on the Eastern coast, and in the interior of the continent south of the equator, discover a striking affinity among the languages spoken throughout

hat vast territory. So close is this affinity that the na-
ive of Zanzibar, on the Eastern coast, may, with little
difficulty, understand the language of the native of the
Gaboon. Such being the fact, (and a like discovery may
be made in reference to the languages spoken north of
the equator,) we at once surmise that Providence has anticipated one of the most formidable obstacles to the diffusion of the gospel among the unknown millions of that
continent, and prepared the way for its evangelization,
when the fiat shall be given, with an astonishing and
glorious rapidity.

Thus are obstacles vanishing, and means multiplying,
and channels opening through the broad moral wastes of
this great desert, by which the pure waters of salvation
shall course their way, and bear spiritual life and health
to that parched land.

Christian missions are, in a word, following up commercial enterprise, and the laudable efforts to suppress the
slave trade. And, at the same time, Heaven is overruling that nefarious traffick to the great and permanent
good of that long-abused and degraded continent. Thousands of her long-lost sons are returning to bless the land
from which, by the hand of violence, they were so cruelly
torn away. They that were lost are found; they that
were dead are alive. They are acting the part of the
little Israelitish maid. They have brought with them a
good report of the God of Israel, and thousands of their
benighted countrymen are sharing with them the riches,
civil, social, intellectual and spiritual, with which they
have returned laden. Let the present plans of colonization be carried into effect, and the advancement of Africa,
under God, is secured.

It is a delightful feature of our times that a Divine
agency is at work among the nations of the earth, re
moving obstacles, demolishing the strong-holds of Satan,
and gathering resources and providing facilities for the
moral conquest of the world. And in relation to no
country is this agency more visible than in Africa. "And
unless nature's resources must be squandered in vain, and
Christian philanthropy be baffled, and the great movements of the moral and political world come to naught,

28

the period will ere long arrive when she shall be enlightened and powerful, and shall lavish her blessings among the kingdoms of the earth as freely as they have lavished on her chains and ignominy."

Christianity once flourished in Africa. A thousand churches once adorned her northern border. She had her "colleges, her repositories of science and learning, her Cyprians and Bishops of apostolic renown, and her noble army of martyrs." There was light in Africa when there was darkness in all the world beside. Nowhere has learning, and empire, and civilization, and refinement, and Christianity, more prospered. But their light has been extinguished, and no land has been covered with a denser darkness. And as we now see the Sun of Righteousness again beginning to cast its healing beams over that sable land, and the spirit of former years to revivify her moral deserts, we may indulge the pleasing hope that this long neglected, fruitless field, is about to be inclosed within the domains of civil liberty and a pure Christianity.

The view we have now taken of Africa and things pertaining to Africa, supplies an argument in behalf of colonizing our colored population on the coast of Africa. Hundreds—thousands, and many of them emancipated slaves, may now, with their own consent, be transferred to their native land, greatly to the benefit of our own country, and more to their benefit, and most of all to the advantage of Africa. The American Colonization Society is limited in its laudable work only by the want of funds. Africa now holds out every reasonable inducement to colonists; a reward to industry; freedom to all; an abundance of good land; schools and seminaries of learning; the privilege of being *men* and not "goods and chattels." And a free Government—a Republic, opens wide her arms to welcome them to all the prerogatives of citizens and Christians. Perhaps, in the whole range of benevolent enterprise, we shall seek in vain for another cause, which promises more immediate success, or more lasting and extensive good, than the cause of the American Colonization Society.

CHAPTER XVIII.

The Armenians--their history, number, location. Dispersion and preservation of the Armenians. The American Mission ; Asaad Shidiak ; exile of Hohannes. The great Revival. The Persecution, and what God has brought out of it.

"It is a righteous thing with God to recompense tribulation to them that trouble you."—2 Thes. i. 6.

It now only remains to take a survey of some of the *ancient Christian churches*: and should we discover in them, too, the workings of the same Divine Hand, preparing them to receive a pure gospel, it will strengthen the conviction that the dawn of a better day draws near. The simple existence of these churches is a matter of no little interest. They date back to a very early period in the annals of Christianity. They have, each in its day, nobly served the cause of truth—each cast her light over the surrounding darkness ; and each in turn, suffered an eclipse ; and now they seem once more emerging from the cloud which has so long overshadowed them, to send forth the beams of a new day. We shall now attempt to trace the Hand of God as at present engaged to reclaim and revivify those long waste and barren domains of nominal Christianity. We begin with

THE ARMENIANS. The original country of the Armenians lies between the Mediterranean, the Black and the Caspian Seas. The Armenians are a very ancient race ; and as Mount Arrarat occupied a central position in ancient Armenia, and on this notable mount they still, in their dispersion, make their religious centre, (at Eckmiadzin on Mount Arrarat,) we may as well fancy their pedigree to reach back to the first peopling of the earth on the disembarkation from Noah's ark. Amidst all the revolutions of the Assyrian, Persian, Greek, and Roman empires, the Armenians remained a civilized and cultivated people—early embraced Christianity—tradition says

Thaddeus, one of the seventy, introduced the gospel among them, and history responds to its very early introduction. The Armenian Church was found completely organized and established in the beginning of the fourth century. And before the middle of the sixth century it separated from the Greek Church. Though most persevering in their attempts, the Papists have never been able to unite them generally or permanently to Rome, while the Turkish Government has constantly protected them against these wily invaders.

Few nations have so varied a political history as the Armenians. During the respective existence of each of the four great monarchies, Armenia was frequently conquered and re-conquered, ever clinging to her national life with undying tenacity. Since the middle of the sixteenth century, the Armenians have mostly remained subject to the Turks. Armenia has long since ceased to exist as a distinct nation. Like Poland in Europe, she has been divided among her more powerful neighbors, and her people dispersed into almost every part of Turkey and Persia, into Russia and India; and not a few found a refuge and a lucrative business in Amsterdam, Antwerp, London and Marseilles. Wherever found in their dispersion, they are an enterprising, frugal, industrious people. Their number in the Turkish empire is estimated at three millions; one million in Russia; and one hundred and fifty thousand are to be found in Constantinople and its suburbs. They are also numerous at Broosa, Smyrna, Trebizond and Erzeroom, in ancient Armenia; at each of which points the American Board have missions acting in connection with the most important station, which is at Constantinople.

The chief points of interest which demand attention as illustrating our present subject, are the dispersion and preservation of the Armenians; the history of the late mission among them; the late revival, and the consequent persecution.

The Armenians, as I said, have long since ceased to exist as a distinct nation. Driven out from their country by political revolutions, or enticed away by the desire of gain, they are to be found not only in every

Constantinople. Page 328.

part of the Turkish empire, from the Caucassus to the Nile, and from the Danube to the Persian Gulf. but they are found in Koordistan, in different parts of Europe, in Persia and India; and wherever found, they are generally an enterprising, influential and wealthy class of citizens. "In Turkey, they are the great producers, whether they till the land or engage in manufactures. They are the bone and sinew of the land—at once the most useful and peaceful citizens. Were they removed from Turkey, the wealth and productive power of the country would be incalculably diminished."

Already is Providence developing a design to be answered by this singular dispersion of the Armenians, worthy of infinite wisdom; a design in reference to Mohammedan countries, not dissimilar, perhaps, to that to be achieved towards the *whole world* by the dispersion of the Israelitish race. The Armenians are likely to prove the regenerators of the Turkish empire. This is a feature, we shall see, which has been peculiarly developed in the late revival and the recent persecution. In no other way, perhaps, since the rise of Islamism, has the power of Christianity been so directly and effectually brought home to the Mohammedan mind. No accident or blind chance has dispersed the Armenians and preserved them in their scattered condition.

We shall discover more of this design as we proceed to the other particulars which claim our attention.

The unwritten history of the Armenians is full of interest. The last quarter of a century has been to them the season of hope and preparation; the return of spring after a long and dreary winter. We may date the establishment of the American Mission among the Armenians in 1831, and the late spirit of inquiry somewhat earlier. We are unacquainted with the secondary causes which conduced to rouse the Armenian mind into the interesting state of activity which has existed during the last twenty-five years. The time had come for God to work; the time for the great Head of the church to send his embassadors among this people. A mission was established just in time to meet the state of things which the spirit of God had prepared.

28*

It does not fall within the present plan to enter into the history of this interesting mission, but to present certain aspects and features of it, which shall exhibit the Hand of God as engaged to renovate a corrupt and long forsaken church, and, perhaps, to re-establish a long scattered and oppressed nation. The whole history of the mission is a beautiful delineation of Divine Providence.

As early as 1833, the mission at Constantinople report that "many Armenians regard their national church as encumbered with numerous burdensome ceremonies not required by the Scriptures, and of no practical advantage, and sigh for something better, without knowing exactly what they want—as if the Lord were preparing them for a gracious visitation." There was at that period a singular moving of the stagnant waters ; a vague presentiment of a coming change ; a manifest dissatisfaction and restiveness under the yoke of ecclesiastical bondage ; a mental activity that presaged emancipation ; doubt ; skepticism : a spirit of investigation ; some embryo breathings after liberty. The leaven was at work, for the most part secretly, yet, as the event has shown, effectively. For the next three years the work of reform goes on steadily, and for the most part quietly. " There is now a growing spirit of inquiry, not only about the truth as a matter of speculation, but after salvation through the Lord Jesus Christ. No doubt much of this may be referred to the agency of the Holy Spirit." The Armenian mind was roused to seek after truth.

But here we should fail to honor the Hand of God in this extraordinary work, were we not to recur to some incidents of an earlier date.

In the little village of Hardet, five miles from Beyroot, lived a widowed mother with five sons and three daughters. At the age of sixteen the third son enters the college at Ain Waka, passes through the prescribed course of study, and then spends two years in teaching theology to the monks of a convent near Hardet. He afterwards serves the Bishop of Beyroot as Scribe, as he also did at another time the Patriarch. Having occupied these conspicuous stations, he gained still more notoriety by the manner he fell under suspicion and was

dismissed from the Patriarch's service.   But this was the
incident which brought him to the notice of Mr. King,
and in connection with the American Mission, and
finally led to his conviction of the truth and his conversion to God.   His candid, shrewd, powerful, comprehensive mind, could not resist the simple truths of the gospel
when thus presented.   He now became a victim of persecution, merciless and unrelenting, by the Patriarch and
his church.   He is decoyed into the hands of his enemies—thrown into a dungeon, confined in chains, daily
beaten, and here he languishes for years, firm in the faith
and rich in hope, till the kind angel of death set him free.

Thus lived and thus died the well known Asaad Shidiak, a martyr and an ornament to the truth, and a gem
in the diadem of the King.   But he died not in vain.
He was a remarkable illustration of the power of Christianity.   A great mind, once entangled in the meshes of
superstition and error, now broke away, grasped the
truth, and yielded it not with his expiring breath.   His
was a religion that endured in dungeons, chains and
scourgings.   He was a bright and shining light in a dark
place.   Though incarcerated in a dark and filthy prison,
languishing for long and painful years in hopeless con-
finement, his enemies found themselves altogether unable
to suppress the power of his example.   His light shone
over all the countries of the Levant.   An apostolic gospel, and an apostolic piety, had re-appeared on the ground
where apostles and primitive Christians had once trod.
A morning star has risen and cast its mild light over the
dark cloud which had so long hung over all that portion
of Christendom.   The Armenians greatly shared in that
light.   They now saw how strongly the power of vital
godliness, as illustrated in the life and sufferings of Asaad,
contrasted with the dead formalism of their own church ;
and perhaps no one cause has contributed more largely
to rouse their dormant energies than the conversion, the
Christian life and persecution of this eminent saint.   His
connection with the Bishop, and afterwards with the Patriarch, his eminence as a scholar, and his notoriety as a
teacher, all contributed to the same end.   And though his
sun seemed to set prematurely and in a cloud, yet it cast

back a light that illumined those dark lands. And perhaps, too, no one cause has contributed so largely to enlist
the sympathies and prayers, and to secure the co-operation of Christendom on behalf of that portion of the world.

At a later date, (1840,) a similar impression was pro
duced by the exile from their country, for religion's sake,
of Hohannes and others, among the Armenians. This
created a deep sympathy throughout the Turkish empire,
and did much to prepare the way for the separation of
the "Evangelicals" from the national church, a measure
since accomplished, and one fraught with immense good
to the Armenian nation.

The interest of the work continued to deepen, the
leaven was at work; the high ecclesiastical authorities
from time to time interposing the arm of persecution.
The seminary for boys was broken up. Yet this was
but the signal for a wealthy Armenian to come forward
and propose, and himself largely to patronize a school on
a yet more extensive plan. This is but of a piece with
the interpositions of Providence throughout the history
of this mission. Every attempt at persecution (and they
have been neither few nor small) has been overruled for
the furtherance of the gospel.

And we may remark in passing, that perhaps we shall
nowhere find occasion more profoundly to admire the
timely interpositions of Providence, than as they are seen
in the protection afforded to the missions in Western
Asia, or rather the protection afforded to *the development
of the reformation* among the Armenians, as also among
the Nestorians and the Arabs of Syria. It was a tender
germ, sprung up in a forbidding soil, and assailed on every
side by adverse influences. But God has watched over
it as the apple of his eye. Nothing that ecclesiastical
or political power could do, has been left undone, to crush
this rising reformation. Yet it has gone on as surely and
irresistibly as if nothing had attempted to oppose its progress. Its whole history is interesting, but cannot be
dwelt upon at present.

We may date the commencement of what has been
called the Great Revival among the Armenians in 1841.
Yet this seems but the more decided and manifest ad-

vance of a work which had been in progress for some
years previous. Communications dated 1842, speak of
the Hand of God as manifestly at work, preparing the
Armenian mind to receive the gospel. "There is much,
say they, to encourage us in the present aspect of things
among the Armenians. The evidence of the Spirit's
presence becomes more and more distinct." "Until
lately, few could be found among the Armenians who had
any idea other than that all who are baptized, and who
attend to the outward forms of religion, are the true disciples of Christ. Now, multitudes are awake to the distinction between mere nominal Christians and true, and
the solemn inquiry, 'am I a Christian?' is coming home
to many hearts. Many minds are awakened, and some
are on the utmost stretch of inquiry, dissatisfied with all
former views and opinions, and eagerly seeking for something solid to rest upon." And speaking of the *character*
of the converts as affording further evidence of a genuine
work of the Spirit, they say, "There are native brethren
here who are men of prayer and of the Holy Ghost, and
who constitute a living, breathing Christianity in the
midst of their church and community. Among them are
men of influence, boldness and fervor, who would be pillars in any church at home."

Two years later, the same writer says: "There is a
deep and thorough work. Facts are continually coming
to light, showing that the movement on the Armenian
mind is far more general than was supposed. Though
little appears on the surface, it is plain that an undercurrent in favor of the gospel is set in motion. The
Spirit of the Lord is evidently moving on the Armenian
mind." Hundreds and thousands of families would welcome an evangelical teacher. "Many, evidently, are reflecting on the errors of the church. The work is now
pervading all classes of people." It has already been remarked that many of these converts are from the more influential classes—priests, vertabeds, bishops, bankers,
merchants. Others have spoken of the spirituality of
these converts; their eagerness for truth; their zeal in
the work; their solicitude for the spiritual welfare, and
the temporal elevation of their countrymen.

Nor is the work confined to Constantinople and the principal towns, or even the Turkish empire. "Where-ever Armenian mind is found, God has seemed to be speaking to it by his Spirit." Religious books and the Bible, connected oftentimes with little human instru-mentality, have been very prominent means of carrying forward the work. In no other feature, perhaps, has it been more obviously distinguished as a work of God, in-dicating the working of some mighty power on the Ar-menian mind. The avidity for books and the influence they are exerting, will appear in an extract from an ap peal of the Mission to the American Tract Society:

"The call for books increases continually. We can now advantageously dispose of hundreds of tracts, where, formerly, we could tens. A new desire is springing up in the hearts of the people for reading the Scriptures and tracts. Many whole families are furnished with a complete set of our books, and men, women and children read them with great interest, and anxiously wait for ev-ery new work. *Hundreds, who never heard our voice, read them,* and have their minds opened and their hearts impressed.

"Our books are also finding their way to distant places. The good work at Nicomedia, you know, commenced from the reading of a single tract. The present state of the Armenian mind is such that it needs to be fed with spiritual food. God himself has given them the appetite. *God is working here,* and how much better to work with him than to be left to work alone. Never did we need your help as now. Old editions of our books are ex-hausted, new ones should be printed immediately. Many new works of different descriptions are this moment called for. The hopes of inquiring multitudes are defer-red at the very time when this state of mind is most crit-ical. And the danger is, God's spirit will be grieved away, and leave us to toil on alone, unblessed, because we refuse to be co-operators with Him."

When on missionary tours among the Armenians, it is now not uncommon to meet persons for the first time, who have been converted by reading Bibles and books, which have been previously distributed. Little circles of fifteen or twenty are found, who are wont to meet for prayer and the reading of the Scriptures. This is the first notice the missionary has of their existence. The leaven is everywhere at work, and we hope the whole lump will soon be leavened. "I feel confident in the assurance," says Mr. Dwight, "that, with the blessing of God, there will be a certain and speedy triumph of the gospel here."

How the good leaven is at work in different and distant sections of the Armenian population, is beautifully illustrated by an incident which recently came to the knowledge of the mission. Mr. Van Lennep, of Constantinople, was on his way to Aleppo, whither he was going, in answer to an urgent request from certain evangelical Armenians at that place and at 'Aintab, in the same vicinity, for a spiritual teacher. He touched at Cyprus— spending a day at Larnika, where two Armenians were known to reside who had expressed an interest in the gospel, but not openly, for fear of their people. He inquired after them with misgivings, fearing they had fallen back to the world. On finding one of them, he was joyfully surprised to learn that he had not only professed Christ openly and honestly, but through his zeal and labors, *eighteen* others had been brought to Christ. He gladly received the missionary, and took him to his little shop, where, he said, "they had been roused to their duty by the Spirit of God and his word; that they immediately began to hold meetings, to which they invited their friends; that God has most wonderfully blessed their efforts in silencing all objectors, and convincing all that God was among them of a truth."

This solitary disciple, so honored as an instrument, is described as a hard-working, poor man, toiling in his little shop to support a numerous family, with his Bible by his side, which he always kept open while at work, his eye passing constantly from his work to his Bible, and from his Bible to his work. In that little shop, a work of grace was achieved of which angels might covet to be the instruments. Yet *such* are the things now witnessed in many a spot throughout the Armenian nation. The hand of the Lord is there. Of this we should feel a yet

stronger assurance were we to follow Mr. Van Lennep to
Aleppo and 'Aintab.   At the latter place, especially, Mr.
V. L. met a joyful reception from twenty-five praying
souls, who had recently come to a knowledge of the truth.
Two hundred and fifty others were fully convinced that
the superstitions of their church were wrong, and ad-
hered to the gospel only ; and nearly the whole Armenian
population, (fifteen or sixteen hundred heads of families,)
were convinced of the truth of evangelical doctrines.
This work had, up to this time, been begun and carried
forward almost entirely by the reading of the Scriptures
and religious books.

And here we would not avoid noticing a beautiful interposition of Providence in making the wrath and wickedness of man to praise him: "When only a few had
read the Scriptures, and had had their eyes opened to
the errors of their church, a letter came from the Patriarch at Constantinople, stating that, whereas a certain
heresiarch, Vertannes by name, had left the capital to
travel through Armenia, the faithful flock, all over the
country, were warned against listening to his deceitful
words.   He had filled Constantinople with heresy ; a
great many priests and learned men, and the patriarch
himself, had endeavored to convince him of his errors,
but without success.   All people were, therefore, warned
against him.   When this letter was read in the church,
the evangelical men received the first information that
there existed other people besides themselves, who ad-
here to the pure gospel of our Lord Jesus Christ.   And
many people said: 'Why, if the patriarch and learned
men have not succeeded in convincing this heresiarch, as
they call him, how can they expect us to withstand his
reasoning ?   It must be that he is in the right.'   There
is another interesting fact.   There was a certain priest,
of great talents, but a drunkard, who, for reasons best
known to himself, professed to be evangelical.   He went
to 'Aintab, and there preached the truth with such eloquence and boldness that many were convinced by him.
His real character was then discovered, and he was sent
out of the place in disgrace ; but the fruits of his preaching remained."

Jerusalem.   Page 337.

After a lapse of fifteen years from the commencement of his missionary labors in Constantinople, Rev. Mr. Goodell, a time-honored servant in that favored field, looking back on the way the Lord had led them in their work, contrasts the present with the past. "Then every thing, in a moral sense, was without form and void. All direct access to the Armenians was closed. What a change! Now is an open door, which no man is able to shut; although the mightiest ones in the empire had once and again conspired together for the express purpose of closing it forever. Then, there was but one Protestant service in this great city on a Sabbath, and none during the week. Now there are thirteen on the Sabbath, and not less than twenty during the week." An extensive system of education has, during the same time, been brought into active operation—Lancasterian schools, high schools and seminaries; the press has been made largely to subserve the cause of the truth, and an evangelical literature has been created. The elements of growth and progress have been generated and fostered under the benign influences of the mission, and a moral momentum has been created in the form of knowledge diffused; mind enlightened; experience gained; books prepared and published, and souls converted and made the ready and efficient agents for farther progress; which, in the hands of God, cannot fail to work out the regeneration of the nation, and through that nation we may expect the regeneration of the countries about the Levant. May we not hope the Armenians shall become the instruments of restoring the power of the gospel to the regions where, in ancient times, its triumphs were first witnessed?

We can in no way, perhaps, get a juster idea of the glorious rapidity with which God is bringing about a great moral change among the Armenians, and turning the hearts of the powers that be to favor them, than by transcribing a single paragraph of Mr. Schneider's journal, when on a late tour to Ada Bazar, one of the places favored by the recent revival. He contrasts the changes of but a single year, (1845—6,) the time which has elapsed since his previous visit:

"Then, but few of them could call on me, and we could hardly have a prayer meeting; now, they could all assemble without fear. Then, as soon as my arrival was known, a plot was formed for my expulsion, and I was actually driven away, though I had a regular passport and traveling firman; but now, no one even inquired for my passport, or thought of any forcible measure. Then no one dared be seen with me abroad; now, the brethren walk with me in the most frequented part of the city with entire fearlessness. Then they were an unorganized body; now they are gathered into a regularly constituted church, with officers and the regular administration of the ordinances. Then, no one could imagine what would be the destiny of the truth in this place; but now, its foundations are deeply laid, and the prospects of its future extension are truly cheering."

The mission is encouraged to believe that the "whole of the Armenian community are more or less pervaded by a special divine influence." "The door, says Mr. Dwight, "is wide open for the prosecution of missionary labor in its several departments, of training youth, circulating books, and preaching the gospel. At present there is a listening ear. If we are furnished with suitable means for seizing the advantages God is offering us, there is every reason to believe this whole people may soon become truly enlightened and evangelical Christians."

Thus writes a hopeful missionary when he sees the hand of God working mightily to turn a nation from darkness to light. Nor had his far reaching mind overlooked the cloud that was gathering in the dark caverns of the foe. Oft he had heard the distant grumbling thunder, and oft seen the lightnings of wrathful persecution play about him and strike down one and another at his side. The cloud blackened and drew near, and he knew it was the hour and the power of darkness. For long ere this he had expressed himself thus: "We notice the wide-spread alarm and the stern hostility which the slightest success awakens, and we can scarcely be mistaken as to the influence of future and more decided progress. We cannot hide from our eyes the approaching struggle, the gathering storm. We wish not to hasten it prematurely, but we dare not try to avert it. It will come, must come, and ought to come. No one of our plans can be accomplished without it, no one of our prayers heard, no one of our hopes realized. We pray that God may pour out his spirit on this people; but that cannot be without producing instant commotion. We long for the conversion of sinners; but this, soonest of all things, will turn upside down this ecclesiastical world. There is no possible way of avoiding this but by concealing the light of the truth."

But they did not conceal the light of the truth. They prayed—God poured out his spirit—sinners were converted, and the "commotion" did come, fierce, unrelenting, overpowering as the mad billows of the ocean; and, but for the signal interposition of the Almighty Arm, it would have engulfed, in one undistinguished ruin, the whole evangelical effort among the Armenians, the subjects of it, the agents, and all who dared ally themselves with it.

We have less to do with the details of this shameful outrage on all humanity, than with its providential features—the results which were providentially brought out of it. Let it suffice that it was a virulent, religious persecution, a veritable consequence of the gospel truth, which had been diffused among the Armenians, and of the practical results which followed. The design was to suppress the truth, and to crush the rising reformation. For this purpose the Patriarch forces on the evangelical portion of his church an act of conformity; a creed prepared for their signatures, which was as redolent with Popery as any thing could be, not coined at the mint of the vatican itself. Conformity or excommunication was the only alternative. Conform, they could not. They knew the truth; they had felt its power. They had consciences, and they could never again bow their necks to the yoke of spiritual bondage. They saw the storm gathering, and prepared themselves to meet it. The frightful act of excommunication was passed. The fearful and faint hearted went back and followed no more after the Man at Pilate's bar. Others met the thunderbolt like men, and, the first shock passed, they gathered up their

strength, leaning on the arm of their Beloved, and pre
pared for the conflict.

The next day after the act of excommunication and
anathema in the cathedral, began the work of violence
and persecution.   The anathematized were driven out of
their shops and houses, and spoiled of their goods; imprisoned under false pretenses; their debtors prevented
from paying them their demands, and they forced to pay
before the time; permission to trade taken away, and
themselves expelled from the trading companies; cut off
from all intercourse with their people, social, domestic, and
commercial; cast into prison and cruelly bastinadoed;
children turned out of doors by their parents; the sick,
the infirm and the aged dragged from their very beds into
the streets, and left without a shelter; water-carriers, who
are Armenians, will neither bring them water, nor bakers,
bread.   Nothing but the want of power in the Patriarch
was wanting to have consummated this persecution in all
the virulence and madness of the bloodiest days of the
Romish inquisition.

But our business is with the hand of God in this
strange affair.   What has God brought out of it?   Already have we seen enough to regard it as an essential
and active element in the renovation of that rising nation.   Doubtless we shall see more; but already enough
appears to kindle our admiration, and to vindicate the
ways of God in this seemingly mysterious catastrophe.

1. If not the most obvious, perhaps the most far-reaching result of the late persecution, is the practical recognition, the formal embodiment of the great principle of
religious toleration throughout the Turkish empire.   And
this, too, in the very capital, immediately under the eyes
of the Sultan himself, and of the highest dignitaries of the
Mohammedan creed.   We can scarcely attach too much
importance to this event.   It has relations to society, to
the spread of the gospel in those countries, and to the
whole civilized world, which it is scarcely possible for us to
appreciate.   "It is a vast step in the breaking up of the
stagnant pool of Oriental mind and character, and cannot
but be the precursor of great and wide-spread blessings."
Yet how unexpectedly brought about.   The Patriarch

pronounces an anathema on the scripture-readers; a cruel persecution follows; many a good man suffers; yet his faith is tried, he is invigorated for the warfare which must sooner or later come. The Sublime Porte is moved by this unreasonable severity to interpose his mighty arm, and come to the help of the persecuted, suffering Armenians. The crescent protects the cross. Tne power of the state throws its arms around the Armenian converts, and saves them from the fury of their persecutors. The Moslem is still, and he always has been the sworn foe of a corrupt Christianity and a persecuting church.

The Grand Vizier of the Turkish government, Reshed Pasha, and one of the most enlightened and liberal men in the empire, whom Providence had prepared by foreign travel and a residence at the most enlightened courts in Europe, for the part he would now have him act, acts a most important part in the whole affair. The Sultan recognizes the existence of the evangelical Armenians as a protestant church in the Turkish dominions—sends out an edict in favor of religious toleration, and the missionaries and scripture-readers enjoy a measure of freedom unknown to them before.

2. The persecution not only opened the way, but laid a necessity on the evangelical party to seek *a new church organization.* The time had come for God to emancipate his church from a most unnatural alliance, and this Patriarch seemed raised up for this very purpose. Like Pharaoh, he was allowed to persecute just so far, and no farther, than needful to show the impossibility of the evangelical party longer remaining in connection with a corrupt church. Thrust out from their cruel mother, they are now forced to seek an organization of their own, which they may, at once, fix on the New Testament basis; a measure of immense moment to the successful progress of Christianity in the Armenian nation, and perhaps throughout the whole Turkish empire. Nothing could so effectually have brought about an event so much to be desired by the mission, and so much to be dreaded by the Patriarch, as the persecution in question.

Hitherto the mission had avoided all interference with

29*

the church relationships of their converts, laboring to save
souls rather than to sever men from a corrupt church.
The difficulties attending the existing state of things were
thickening upon them daily, and all human sagacity was
found inadequate to devise a mode of relief. The lion
seemed too fierce and mighty to beard, yet the lion himself is left to open the way of escape to the lambs.   The
Patriarch pursues a course which leaves no alternative
to the "evangelicals," but to organize a new church
Henceforward we meet little flocks gathered almost immediately, in Constantinople, Nicomedia, Ada Bazar.
Trebizond, and Erzeroom ; the shield of the Turkish government is around them, and the banners of God's love
is over them. Constantinople is said to contain more
than a hundred converts, who are regarded as suitable
persons for church membership ; ninety-three are already
inclosed in the fold ; one hundred and forty-three in the
four churches.

3. It has served to make evangelical Protestantism and
the gospel *known to the Turks*, and given the world a fresh
illustration of the power and vitality of the Christian religion. Nothing, perhaps, could have brought the work
of evangelism so conspicuously and forcibly home to the
Turkish mind. The Turks had seen Christianity before ;
but it was a Christianity of form—the body, the gilded
corpse, and not the soul. Now the vital godliness of the
persecuted is brought into vivid contrast with the formalism of the oriental churches ; and to whom would not
such a contrast bring conviction ? "The aspect of the
two parties," says an eye witness, "was, and is still one
of great moral sublimity. On the one side all the power,
influence, wealth and numbers of a great nation ; on the
other, fewness, feebleness and poverty. On the one side
were age, wisdom, experience, cunning, craft, dissimula-
tion ; on the other, youth, inexperience, and utter simplicity. On the one side stood up the whole Armenian
hierarchy, excited to the utmost pitch of hate and fury,
and arrayed by all the sacredness of antiquity, and all the
authority of the nation, and with the panoply of civil and
ecclesiastical despotism ; on the other was neither Urim
or Thummim, neither tabernacle nor ark, neither priest-

hood nor church; nothing sacred, nothing venerable, nothing to inspire terror, nothing to attract notice, nothing outward to encourage the least hope of success. On the one side were cunning and falsehood, and blasphemy, the thunder of anathemas, the threatenings of annihilation, the cutting off of bread and water, the driving out of families and individuals from their inheritance and their homes, from their shops and their business; the forcible wresting from them of their necessary protective papers, and thus exposing them, without the possibility of redress, to all the insults and frauds of the most unprincipled and villainous, to a Turkish, filthy prison. On the other side sat patience and meekness, peace and truth. There was joy in tribulation. There was the voice of prayer and praise. The New Testament was in their hands, and all its blessed promises were in their hearts. Their song of praise went up like the sound of many waters, and reminded me of the singing of the ancient Bohemian brethren amidst the raging fires of persecution."*

It was the fire of persecution, but a fire that cast abroad and throughout the whole Turkish empire the bright radiance of divine truth. " I have known many cases," says Mr. Dwight, " in which Turks, high in office, have expressed their sympathy with our brethren, and say that their way was the way of truth." And another says: " The Turks have heard and learnt more of the gospel the last year than in all their lives before."

4. This persecution has served to give the world, after the lapse of eighteen centuries, a fresh example of *apostolic Christianity.* It has shown the spirit of primitive Christians revived in the regions where it had so long appeared to be extinct. Martyrs, bold, meek, enduring to the end, have again periled all things, and not counted their lives dear in defence of the religion of calvary. The thunder and the storm of persecution, while they have left behind some marks of desolation, have been followed by a fresh and luxuriant growth of piety, all the deeper, all the purer for the violence of the tempest. For there was reviving rain and genial heat amidst the strifes of the

---

* Rev. Mr. Goodell, Constantinople.

tornado. It is a resuscitation of primitive piety, fraught
with rich blessings to the Armenian nation, to the Turkish
empire, and to the whole Christian world. It is the spirit
revived, which nerved the soul of Paul, which brought
apostles to a glorious martyrdom, which filled with joy
and praise a noble company of martyrs. It is a delightful presage of better days to the church of the living God.
The spirit of her martyrs shall live again; the souls of
them that were slain for the word of God, shall rise and
flourish again on the earth. It inspires with hope the
awakening energies of the corrupt and formal churches
of the East; it speaks encouragement to the benevolent
enterprise of Christendom. It predicts the day as near
when the kingdom and the greatness of the kingdom shall
be given to the saints of the Most High.

5. The late persecution is a witness to the success of
our mission to the Armenians. The outbreak is but an
expression of hostility to the truth—a fearful apprehension that the truth shall prevail and undermine the colossal fabric of error and superstition, as found embodied
in a formal, corrupt church. The Patriarch and the high
dignitaries of the church see their craft to be in danger,
and they have made one desperate struggle to save the
falling Babylon. It is an unwilling concession that truth
is mighty—that it is very generally diffused—that it has
taken deep hold of the Armenian mind, and that it is
likely to prevail—a stone from the sling of David against
the head of Goliath.

It has done much, too, to create a *native agency* among
the Armenians, and thus to favor the work of evangelization. It has given character, and vigor, and zeal to the
native converts. It has greatly increased their moral
power. It has assured them that God is at work with
them and for them. It has inspired the mission with
fresh confidence and courage. It has, as in the days of the
persecution about Stephen, scattered abroad many who
go everywhere preaching the gospel. It has disburdened
the rising seminary at Bebeck of a class of ungodly youth,
from whom the mission had little hope of future usefulness, and has filled their places with a greater number of
pious, promising young men, who, being by the persecu-

tion thrown out of the secular employments to which they seemed destined, were at once brought into the seminary, where they are now preparing to be the pastors of the newly organized churches, or missionaries to their benighted countrymen.

6. It has created a common sympathy among the evangelical Armenians themselves, binding them together by the ties of a common brotherhood; and it has created a common sympathy in their behalf throughout Christendom. And not only so, but *locality* and *definiteness* are now given to the prayers and benefactions of those who may come to their aid in this time of need.

And it would here be overlooking a very essential providential feature in this wonderful work, not to allude, at least, to the care and skill with which God has provided his agents wherewith to carry it forward. To say nothing of the peculiar fitness of the missionaries whom he has, with much care and training, raised up and stationed there for such a time as this, (and we should, perhaps, in vain look the world over to find the same number of men elsewhere, so beautifully adapted to act in such circumstances,) we cannot too profoundly admire the providence that brought together in the Turkish empire, at that particular time, such men as Sir Stratford Canning, English embassador, Mr. Le Coq, Prussian embassador, Mr. Carr, American minister, and Mr. Brown, American Charge d' Affaires in the absence of Mr. Carr; and perhaps more especially than all others, Reshid Pasha, the liberal and enlightened Prime Minister of the Turkish Government. Rarely do we meet a happier combination of talent, firmness, Christian decision, and enlightened tolerance, than Providence had thus concentrated in the capital of the Turkish empire, to be used at this very crisis. And the Hand that provided them and placed them there, has not failed, effectually, to use them for the protection and establishment of his cause.

We may now dismiss the Armenians, with the delightful reflection that the hand of the Lord is engaged on their behalf. He has, in a remarkable manner, prepared them to receive the gospel. He has raised up a strong native agency by which to carry forward among them the work

of evangelization—has created an evangelical literature—
accumulated vast resources in the form of printed matter.
Bibles and religious books—brought into being an efficient
system of education—provided an active mass of intelligent, sanctified mind for the future progress of the work
and given them protection under the strong arm of the
Turkish Government, endorsed and guaranteed by the
organs of the three principal Protestant nations.

With such elements of progress—with such preparations for advancement, have we not the most substantial
grounds for the expectation that the work of Christianiza-
tion in that land shall advance, till not only the Armenian
nation, but many tribes and kindreds in Western Asia
shall be inclosed in the fold of the Great Shepherd.

CHAPTER XIX.

THE JEWS.   Providential features of their present condition, indicating their preparedness to receive the Gospel.

" *And as I prophecied, there was a noise, and behold a shaking.*"—
Ezekiel, xxxvii. 7.

WE shall next turn to the JEWS, and see what an ever
active Providence is doing to prepare them for restoration to the land of their fathers, but more especially for a
return to them of the favor of their God.   The Jews have
a history of intense interest.   God honored them from
their beginning—granted them a rich and beautiful country—conducted them thither by his own strong arm, signalizing the whole way by monuments of his goodness—
preserved them two thousand years amidst the commotions of a most revolutionary period—made them the de-
positaries of his grace for the world—Zion, his earthly
temple, the place of the promises, the covenants, the living

oracles. And he has made Israel the *key* to empire. Kingdoms rose and fell, prospered and decayed, according to the good pleasure of God as touching Israel.

And the great drama is yet in progress. The prelude and some preliminary scenes have been acted ; a long and melancholy interlude has interposed, and now the shadows, which coming events cast before them, indicate the termination of Israel's afflictions, and the opening of another scene more resplendent in promised glory and Divine munificence than any preceding one.

The day of Israel's visitation came. The crown is taken from his head; the priestly robes fall from his shoulders; the sceptre departs from Judah, and he becomes as ignominious, weak and poor, as he had been honored, rich and powerful. Not a jot or tittle of all the evil spoken against Israel shall go unfulfilled. Their miseries begun with their rejection and crucifixion of the Messiah. When they signed his death-warrant, they signed the death-warrant of their nation. When the earth quaked, and the sun hid his head, their nation was shaken to its centre, and the sun of their political existence was covered in sackcloth. When they cried, "His blood be on us and on our children," they put to their lips the cup of the wine of the wrath of God, poured out without mixture.

But a brighter day is dawning. The page of Providence is at this moment sublimely interesting in reference to the seed of Abraham. Every year brightens the signs that the time to favor Zion is near. The spirit of God is moving on the face of her dark waters. An angel of mercy is seen walking on the troubled sea of Israel's afflictions, saying, "peace, be still."

" *These bones* are the whole house of Israel." "They are very many and very dry"—indicating the extremely depressed and hopeless state of Israel ; hopeless in the estimation of those who would come to their relief, and hopeless in their own estimation. The "noise," I apprehend, means the two-fold proclamation of the Christian church and of Christian nations, the one proclaiming the truth *as it is in Jesus*, the other proclaiming by various legislative acts and movements, the removal of their

civil disabilities, thus creating an interest and sympathy
on their behalf. While "the shaking," on the other hand,
refers to a movement among the Jews themselves—a stir
in their own camp. The "noise" *and* the "shaking" are
related as cause and effect. For the civil disabilities of
the Jews, and the neglect and contempt of nominal
Christianity, have been the most formidable obstacles to
their reception of the gospel.

I may range what I shall say on the providential
features of the present condition of the Jews, as indicating a preparation on their part to receive the religion of
the Cross under the following heads:

1. There is much at present in their *civil condition*,
that indicates the returning favor of Heaven. Nothing
decisive or permanent was done to remove the disabilities of the Jews till the beginning of the present century.
The first recognition that the Jews *had* rights, was made
in 1806, by Napoleon Bonaparte.* The German states,
however, led the way in actually conferring on them the
rights of citizens, and disenthralling them from the untold,
unpitied wrongs of eighteen centuries. Other states of
continental Europe begun to extend to them the reluctant hand of fellowship. In England, a single ray of light
darted above their horizon, but was soon extinguished.
An act passed in Parliament, (1753,) in favor of Jewish
emancipation, but was repealed the next year; and not
till the year 1830, was the question renewed, and then
only to be lost. Yet in the same year a bill in their favor
was carried in France.

Within the last few years, indeed, successful attempts
have, from time to time, been made to bring relief to the
wronged and oppressed Jew. Amid recent commotions
in the East, the Jews in Turkey, Egypt, Arabia and

* We may take the following as a specimen of the cruel intolerance of the Romish
Church against the Jews: Speaking of the Jews in the twelfth century, Berk says, they
were special objects of hatred during the ceremonies of Easter week. The misguided
multitude thought they were doing a service to the Redeemer, whose sufferings they
then commemorated, by persecuting the descendants of those who had nailed him to
the cross. Thus, at Beziers, every year, on Palm Sunday, the Bishop mounted the pulpit of the Cathedral, and addressed the people to the following effect: "You have
among you, my brethren, the descendants of the impious wretches who crucified the
Lord Jesus Christ, whose passion we are to commemorate. Show yourselves animated with the spirit of your ancestors; arm yourselves with stones; assail the Jews
with them; and thus, as far as in you lies, revenge the sufferings of that Saviour who
redeemed you with his own blood."

Algiers, have been recognized as citizens, and their life, property and honor protected. In Greece, in the islands of the Indian Archipelago—in South America and the United States, they have flourishing synagogues and schools enjoying governmental protection. In Norway, the prohibition that Jews enter the kingdom is removed. In Denmark a bill has been lately introduced in favor of Jewish emancipation. In England and Holland, the Jews are exciting unwonted interest. In France, Prussia, Austria and the German States, restrictions have been taken off; Jews are allowed to purchase estates, invest funds, prosecute education ; are eligible to office, and allowed the rights of citizens. The Senate and Council of Hamburg have recently passed an act in favor of the Jews. And even in the Pope's domains, and in Russia, the Jews have hope. Throughout Tuscany, they enjoy perfect liberty, and partially so in Piedmont.

Political changes are every year taking place in the East, which augur well for the Jews ; and present appearances favor the expectation that further changes will soon so dispose of the nations about Palestine, that the scattered remnants of Israel may be restored to their native land.

The late projects of two eminent European Jews, Rothschild and Sir Moses Montefiore, the first to *purchase Jerusalem* and its environs, as a refuge and home to all Jews, wishing to return to a land consecrated by a thousand sacred associations ; and the other to secure by a sort of lease, the possession of several towns and villages, held sacred by the Jews, for the purpose of *colonizing* there the children of Israel, may indicate one means by which Israel may be reinstated into more than his original civil privileges. Sir Moses is at this time on a mission to St. Petersburgh, to negotiate with the great Autocrat of the North, that the Jews of Russia, against whom a barbarous edict had been issued, should be permitted peaceably to emigrate. Sir Moses writes that "he has been graciously received by the Emperor," who has favored his wishes to visit his brethren of the dispersion in Russia, and consented to the emigration of ten thousand to Palestine, or some other settlement which Sir

Moses may fix upon. The British Government recently appointed a Consular Agent to be stationed at Jerusalem, with instructions that he should, to the utmost of his power, afford protection to the Jews. The Emperor of Austria has recently issued two ordinances in favor of the Israelites, conferring on them unwonted privileges.

2. Corresponding with the great political movement in behalf of the Jews, is *an interest and sympathy on the part of the Christian church.* Nothing, perhaps, more than this, has quickened into life, in many a Jewish bosom, a generous feeling towards Christianity. The time was, and not remote, when the poor Jew was kept without the pale of Christian sympathy. He was despised and abhorred of all men—had no home among the nations, no pity from the church. In his miserable wanderings he had strayed into those dark and frigid regions of humanity on which the genial rays of human kindness never shine. But they that were afar off are brought near. The partition wall is broken down—the alienations of centuries removed. A generous warmth in the heart of the Christian church is winning back the long exiled sons of Israel.

It is but a few years since the church evinced any distinctive interest in behalf of the Jews. Prayers were offered of old, but they were prayers without charity. There was faith, but it was faith without works. It is a matter of just marvel that the early Christians, in their laudable zeal to spread the gospel, so soon overlooked the Jews. After the death of the apostles and their immediate disciples, the poor Jew could say, "no one careth for my soul." Nor did the glorious revival of the sixteenth century bring pity or relief to afflicted Israel.

But we live in a day of better promises. The daughter —the daughter-in-law rather, the *adopted* child, is beckoning the exiled mother to return to the bosom of their common father's love, that they may sit together in heavenly places, the first last, and the last first.

Ecclesiastical bodies now discuss and pass resolutions in behalf of the Jews. The press espouses their cause. Kings, and high dignitaries of the church, lend their great influence. The royal patronage of the King of Prussia deserves particular regard. The Archbishop of Canterbury, is Patron of the London Society, and the Bishops of London and York, Vice Patrons. "No meetings in England are more crowded, or excite more interest, than meetings in behalf of the Jews."

It is this feeling which has called into existence *societies* for the evangelization of the Jews. The most efficient is the London Society. This has been in operation near forty years; has thirty stations, in France, England, Holland, Germany, Poland, Prussia, and among the Spanish Jews about the Mediterranean; employs eighty missionaries, forty-five of whom are of the house of Israel.

An interesting result of this society is the establishment of a mission on Mount Zion. This mission has done much to direct the attention of the Jews in all parts of the world towards Jerusalem and their own best interest. "The church and bishop at Jerusalem, says one, kindles the hope of the approaching revival of the Jewish church."

Jerusalem may now, again, be regarded as the centre of the Jewish nation. Any influence exerted here will tell on the whole Jewish world. For here are Jews, resident or visitors, "out of every nation under heaven." And not only this, but the *Jewish Rabbis of Jerusalem maintain a constant communication with their brethren in all parts of the world.* These two facts deserve regard in all our plans for the conversion of Israel.

Another fact worthy of notice is, that, for the first time since the Babylonish captivity, the Hebrew language, in its ancient purity, is again a language of conversation in Jerusalem.

However manifested, the fact is obvious, that Christendom, now as by a common impulse, is beginning to feel a deep and solemn interest and sympathy for her elder and long exiled sister. We have seen how this *interest* is manifested. A few other facts will show how readily the *sympathy* of Christian nations can be drawn out, if the arm of persecution be stretched out against the Jew.

I refer to the late barbarous persecution of the Jews at Rhodes and Damascus, (1840.) The details of this atrocious outrage I need not repeat. It was as if a demon of the dark ages, suddenly roused from his long slumber, had re-appeared on the earth, and, unmindful of the age, boldly and bloodily recommenced his old work. Scarcely has the black history of persecution a blacker page than the brief one to which I here allude. Atrocities hardly paralleled in the foulest days of the Inquisition, are perpetrated in the nineteenth century—in the light of this enlightened age—in the presence and in spite of the predominant influence of Europe and America.

Those tragic scenes here supply, to all who love to watch the varying star of Jacob, an instructive lesson, and one much to our present purpose, as auguring well for Israel: It is *the simultaneous and deep* SYMPATHY *excited in behalf of the sufferers of Rhodes and Damascus.* Fifty years ago every Jew in the Turkish empire might have been slaughtered, and no great sensation produced anywhere. But now, so changed is public feeling towards the Jews, let the foot of oppression attempt to crush them, or the bloody mouth of persecution to devour them, and ten thousand voices are raised in one general remonstrance. Meetings are held in London, Liverpool, New York, Philadelphia, Constantinople; the most cordial sympathy expressed, prayers offered to Israel's God for their relief, and petitions sent to the several governments of Europe and the United States, that these governments would make it the duty of their respective Consular Agents in the East, to urge on the Pacha of Egypt the necessity of treating the Jews in Damascus and throughout his dominions as men who have rights like his other subjects. And what is more, these governments listened to such petitions, and instructed their agents accordingly; and so promptly, as to indicate a public sentiment against persecution, strong enough to prevent the recurrence in our world of another such scene.

Thus are the Jews learning, for the first time since apostolic Christianity, that the Christian church has a *heart,* which can be touched in pity for the poor exiles of Israel; yea, that the world, too, feel *its* cold heart begin to warm with indignation, if, in these latter days, upstart vandalism dare lay its uncircumcised hand on earth's

nobility. Too long has the poor Jew had but too much
reason to regard Christianity either as idolatry towards
God, or contempt, cruelty and outrage towards the house
of Israel. The "pillar of cloud and of fire," has long
turned its *dark* side towards them, and God has treated
them as aliens and enemies; and now that the light side
is beginning to shine on them, we may indulge the delightful hope that God's former love is about to return.

There is a " noise," a sound like the low murmuring of
many waters, distant, distinct, and gathering strength
with every new commotion, now pervading the whole
Gentile world, in behalf of the seed of Abraham. It is
the precursor—it is to a considerable extent the cause of
the present movement on the Jewish mind. Though itself not a feature, directly, of the Jewish mind, it is a
feature of our times, which has had much to do in *making*
the Jewish mind what it now is in its favorable disposi-
tions towards Christianity.

3. The "shaking" among the Jews themselves. Recent religious and intellectual movements among them
indicate that the day of their redemption is near. The
Jewish mind is everywhere awake. Never was there
among them such a spirit of inquiry. A few facts will
illustrate :

From a communication by the Rev. Mr. Goodell, Constantinople, it appears that the Jews in the metropolis of
the Turkish empire are agitated by an unusual spirit of
religious inquiry. Some are anxiously looking for the
speedy restoration of their nation to their beloved Palestine ; others expect the immediate advent of the Messiah ;
others doubt whether he be not already come. " The
chief Rabbis had led them to expect that, according to
their books, the Messiah must absolutely appear during
the year 1840. A learned Jew occasionally visits me,
and almost the first, and sometimes the very first question I ask him is, *Has he come ?*" "Not yet," has always
been his reply, till his last visit, when, laying his hand on
his heart, he said, in a low and solemn tone, " If you ask
me, I say he *has* come ; and if you will show me a *safe
place*, I will bring you ten thousand Jews to-morrow who
will make the same confession." I replied, " the apostles

30*

and prophets had no safe place shown them to confess truth in, but they made the confession in the face of stripes, imprisonments, and death."

But what more particularly demands attention here, as a proof of the awakening energies of the Jews, are the PUBLIC DISCUSSIONS among them in regard to the Talmud and Rabbinical traditions.

The Talmud is a medley of traditions, claimed by the Rabbins, (the modern Pharisees,) to be the *oral law*, given through Moses, and of equal authority with the written law, not unlike the traditions of the Romish Church. Bating a sparse sprinkling of good throughout, the Talmud is a mass of crude fables, superstitions, and absurdities. From the bondage of this yoke the Jewish mind is laboring to be free. A large class of Jews, principally in Germany, called the Reformed, have taken strong ground against the Talmud. Conventions of Rabbis and learned men have from time to time been held, to discuss the authority of the Talmud, the expediency of an alteration of the liturgy, a reform of the ritual, and a new translation of the Scriptures.

Convince the Jews that the oral law is only of human authority, and the colossus of modern Judaism will fall to the ground. The question, therefore, before the Jewish mind is nothing less than this: *What is the basis of our religion*, the word of God, or the commandments of men? Precisely the question which divides the Protestant and the Romish churches.

British Jews have already adopted a Prayer Book which is free from all references to the oral law.

Leading Jewish writers, also, freely discuss topics like these: *the present position, character, and privileges of the Jews, past and present, their degradation, hopes, and fears.*

Another question of much practical importance, and much discussed, is, *Is it necessary that Israelitish worship should be conducted in the Hebrew language?*

In some places, the Reformed Jews have organized societies, binding themselves to the non-observance of Rabbinical rites and injunctions. They regard circumcision as non-essential, and the promise of the Messiah as fulfilled. In Gallicia, there is a secret society, the object of which is to undermine the authority of the Talmud, and the whole fabric of Judaism. The Scottish deputation to Palestine found the influence of this society to be working a secret, though powerful influence, among the Jews in the southern provinces of Russia. "The field," they say, "in Moldavia and Walachia, is ripe for the harvest. The Jews are in a most interesting state. Many here have their confidence in the Talmud completely shaken." Of their interview with the Jews of Jassy, the capital of Moldavia, they say: "All had an open ear to our statements of the truth."

In France, Germany, and Poland, there is a very general abandonment of Rabbinism. In England and Holland the Jews are catching the spirit of life which is abroad on the stagnant waters of Judaism. In Berlin, the capital of Prussia, a writer says, "there is an extraordinary stir among the dry bones of Israel. The time has come when they themselves feel dissatisfied with the Rabbinical and fanatical systems of Judaism." A Jewish preacher recently said in a public discourse: "It is, alas! too true, that our religion does not answer what God had in view—which is not, however," says he, "the fault of Judaism, but of the Jews. Our state is certainly lamentable." "Within the last few years," says another, "every event connected with the Jewish people has assumed an intense interest and importance."

We may, then, well credit the preacher in a Jewish synagogue in London, who recently said: "We are happily emerging from the darkness into which persecutions of unparalleled intensity and duration had banished us. Our domestic, social, and political life is assuming a brightness, which we feel assured will become more and more cheering." Or, Lord Ashley, who in a late meeting of the Jews' Society in London, said: "At no time has the horizon been so bright for the Jewish people. At no time prophecy so near its fulfillment. A year ago no imagination was lively enough to conceive one-tenth of what we have heard this day."

In Smyrna, "there is great freedom of inquiry among the Jews." Many families admit Jesus of Nazareth to

be the Messiah, yet retain some national rites. They
read the New Testament, are weary of the bondage of
the Rabbis, and give an intellectual assent to Christianity.
Pointing to a Romish priest, a Jew says: "Our Rabbis
and these priests are alike impostors." The late Prussian
Embassador at the court of Rome, declared that "throughout the vast dominions of Germany and Poland, *there is
a general movement of inquiry, and a longing expectation
abroad, that something will take place to restore them to the
lana of their fathers.*" Rev. T. Grimshawe says, " A
vast number of Jews are preparing to emigrate from
Germany and Poland to settle in Palestine; while
throughout the whole of Europe and Asia, a general expectation is raised among them that the time of their
deliverance is drawing near. Throughout Italy, the
same uneasiness and expectation may be observed."

This *movement* of the Jews towards *Palestine*, whatever
may be thought of it as an evidence of a literal restoration, is at least indicative of a *state of mind* not to be
overlooked in our present discussion.

In Prussian Poland, especially in the Grand Duchy of
Posen, the Scottish deputation found everywhere "an
open door for preaching the word to the Jews;" "the
state of the Jewish mind decidedly favorable to missionary efforts;" "patient to listen to the exposition of the
word;" and "parents manifesting an extraordinary, un-
suspecting readiness to send their children to Christian
schools." " Twelve years ago," say two indefatigable
missionaries in this province, " the Jews would not come
near a Christian church, nor converse on matters pertaining to salvation; now they seem rationally convinced that Judaism is false, and that Christianity may
be true."

Indeed, a spirit of inquiry is abroad; and multitudes
who have all their lives long lain buried beneath the rubbish of modern Judaism, are beginning to emerge. The
long and dreary winter of Jacob's captivity seems to be
nearly passed. The genial sun of the divine favor is
beginning again to shine, and to melt from their hearts
the ice of ages. And soon we may expect the sons and

daughters of Judah will take their harps from the willows,
 nd in the sweet lays of their own poet, sing,

> " Lo, the winter is passed, and the rain is over and gone,
>   The flowers appear on the earth,
>   The time of the singing of birds is come,
> And the voice of the turtle is heard in the land."

Symptoms of ever-welcome spring appear—marks of
resuscitation among the dry bones of Judah. And each
revolving year shall witness new developments of the
rising star of Jacob, till the kingdom shall be restored to
David, and Judah shall again wear the crown, and bear
the sceptre, and Jerusalem become a joy and praise in
all the earth.

But it must not be supposed that this mental and
moral revolution has been the work of a day. The
leaven of reform has been at work at least for a century.
Moses Mendelsohn gave the first impulse to Jewish mind
in modern days. Himself an eminent proficient in literature and science, he infused his spirit into the minds of
his countrymen. He sapped the foundations of Jewish
bigotry ; and what is more, struck the death-blow to that
corrupt, tyrannical system of Talmudism, the Popery of
Judaism, which has done more than all other causes to
debase the Jewish mind.

Nothing, perhaps, more distinctly betokens the dawn
of a brighter day for Israel, than the late efforts and improvements in the education of their youth.

In concluding this head I cannot forbear quoting the
very valuable testimony of the Rev. Mr. Bellson, a converted Jew and missionary in Posen, and late candidate
for the Bishopric in Jerusalem :

"I am more than ever," says he, "impressed, that the
Jews are hastening to a great crisis. It must be evident
to any common observer, there is a great movement
among them. This wonderful people, who for eighteen
hundred years remained unaltered, have undergone a
marvelous revolution within the last forty years, especially within the last twenty. They are in a transition
state. Thousands, convicted of the hollowness and rot-
tenness of Rabbinism, and, therefore, thrown it off, feel a

vacuum in their souls, which Christian truth alone can
fill. The Talmud is sinking fast, and its giving up the
ghost cannot be far off."

Or, in the words of another intelligent writer, "the
Jews are entering upon a new era in their history; their
position is becoming every day more interesting to the
missionary, the student of prophecy, and the politician."
There is, indeed, a "shaking" among the dry bones, and
the sinews and flesh come upon them and the skin. And,
moreover, the spirit from the four winds is breathing on
these slain, and they are beginning to live.

4. Hence our next position: the Jews as disposed to
receive the Gospel, and the success of Christian missions
among them.

A few facts here will confirm what has been said
already, and show the present condition of the Jews to
be one of delightful interest.

"A surprising change," says another resident in Constantinople, "has taken place among the Jews of this
city. Instead of persecuting or slaying those who show
inclination to Christianity, or giving them a *hint* to remove from the city, the chief Rabbi receives visits from
Mr. Schaffeler, the Jewish missionary, corresponds with
him; commends his translation of the Old Testament into
Hebrew Spanish, and urges it on the people. Constantinople contains from sixty to eighty thousand Jews.

In Germany the movement is mighty and onward; the
Lord seems everywhere making way to execute his work
among his people Israel—stirring up the hearts of many
to search the Scriptures and seek salvation. The young
men in the universities speak publicly and boldly on
Jewish subjects. Whereas, twenty years ago, they were
ashamed to be *even known as Jews*. In Frankfort, the
missionaries are surrounded from morning till evening by
multitudes of Jews, opening to them the Scriptures, and
alledging that Christ must needs have suffered and risen
again from the dead. A Jew in Russia came with his
wife four hundred miles to receive baptism. Two different deputations come to the mission at Warsaw to inquire and get an "exact account of Christianity." Missionaries at Bagdad, and other places in the East, speak

oi many hundreds of Jews opening their houses for instruction, and still a greater number who are prosecuting their inquiries more privately.

"In Hungary are hundreds of villages where half the Jewish population would ask baptism if they might have regular Protestant preaching." A missionary writes: 'I nowhere find so much work and so kind a reception as in Hungary." "In *Prussia* the spirit of inquiry is still more general and intense. At Comitz, Posen and Zempal, the Jews hear the missionary gladly; his room is crowded all day with Jews and Jewesses, to whom a great number of Scriptures is distributed, and Christ crucified preached with no bitter opposition. They come in crowds, old and young, eager for books on Christianity."

"In Berlin the progress of Christianity among the ancient people of God is extraordinary, and the opposition of the Rabbis cannot stop it. The Jews join us by dozens, by scores, and I hope they will soon come by hundreds." There is, in the single city of Berlin, one thousand Christian Jews—one hundred baptized in a single year. Within a few years, three hundred have been baptized in the Hebrew Episcopal Chapel in London; one thousand eight hundred and eighty-eight in Prussia; five hundred and eighteen in Selisia; three hundred and sixty-four in Warsaw and Kiningburg; three thousand and four hundred Jews are in communion with the Christian Church. There is no considerable town in Germany where there are not found baptized Jews.

In Prussia, too, as also in many parts of Germany, thousands of Jewish children attend Christian schools, and are instructed in Christianity. "The present state of the Jewish mind," writes one, "is favorable to missionary abor. Throwing off Jewish prejudices and the trammels of the Talmud, they are anxiously inquiring after something new—something more satisfactory than the puerillities and outward observances of the Rabbis. The field is ripe."

In Cracow, it is said, that if the means of *support* for proselytes could be obtained, one half of the Jewish population would become Christians. Indeed, not only here,

but in many other places, it costs the Jew his very live-
lihood to embrace Christianity.

Many Jewish fathers in Vienna, and also in Gallicia,
are bringing their children up Christians, though they
prefer themselves to die Jews.

"Inquirers from foreign countries not unfrequently come
over to England, for the express purpose of investigating
the truth of the Gospel."

Rev. R. H. Hershell, by birth and honor a Jew, having
extensively visited his brethren in Europe and Asia, and
heard, in their synagogues, their confessions of sin and
their earnest cries unto the Lord in the land of their dispersion, says : "I found a mighty change in their minds
and feelings in regard to the nearness of the time of their
deliverance. Some assigned one reason, some another,
but all agreed in thinking the time is at hand." While
dining, on one occasion, with the Elders of the Synagogue,
and conversing on the present condition of the Jews, one
said : "Ah, we need a Jewish *Luther* to come among us
and stir us up." When he declared that Jesus of Nazareth
is the Messiah, it excited little astonishment or opposition.

Indeed, I may here quote the declaration of Professor
Tholock, of Germany, that "more Jews have been converted to Christianity, during the last twenty-five years,
than during the seventeen centuries preceding."

And, what is particularly encouraging to Christian
effort, not a few converted Jews, and others not converted,
are filling places of influence and trust, both in the world
of letters and of politics, both in Church and State. Five
Professors in the University of Halle are Jews; three in
Breslau. The celebrated Neander, Wehl and Brenary
are Jews—ten professors in Berlin alone. Drs. Lee,
Stahl and Capadose are Jews. So is a medical professor
in St. Petersburg, and eight clergymen in the Church of
England.

Whether it be in pecuniary ability and financial tack,
or in the higher walks of learning, or in military prowess,
or in political or diplomatic skill, the Jews are not wanting in men thoroughly furnished for every exigency. The
Minister of Finance in Russia is a Jew. The Minister,
Senor Mandezabel, of Spain, is a Jew. The late Presi-

dent of the French Council, Marshal Soult, is a Jew.
So are several French marshals. The first Jesuits were
Jews. No great intellectual movement in Europe, remarks one, has taken place in which Jews have not
greatly participated. Indeed, not a small share of human
activity is this day kept in motion by Jews. That mysterious Russian diplomacy, which so alarms western
Europe, is organized and chiefly carried on by Jews.
The mighty reformation now preparing in Germany is
developing itself under the auspices of Jews. It is
strongly surmised that the celebrated *John Ronge* is a
Jew.

The daily political press in Europe, is very much under
the dominion of the Jews. As literary contributors, they
influence almost every leading continental newspaper.
In Germany alone they have the exclusive control of
fifteen public journals. An intelligent writer speaks of the
"magic power" of their present intellectual influence in
Europe. "For better or for worse, they are on the move.
Every month brings tidings of a change. Old chains are
being severed. Old opinions, associations and observances
are being broken up. The harbor of Rabbinical Judaism
is left. They must now either be piloted to the haven of
truth, or, borne along for a time by every wind that blows,
be at length stranded on the shore of Infidelity."

We cannot but regard the Jews as on the eve—yea, in
the midst of some mighty movement. There is, on their
part, a singular preparedness for some great change. They
are in a transition state—now being *schooled* in every nation on the face of the earth, and in every branch of practical, profound, and useful learning, and in the various
functions of office—prepared in lessons of rich and varied
wisdom and experience, to construct a more perfect civil
and church polity than the world has yet seen.

There is, doubtless, Jewish *material* enough, at the
present time, to form a strong body politic. They have
numbers, wealth, intelligence, industry, enterprise. Should
certain Jewish families in Europe suddenly withdraw
their capital, they would cripple kingdoms.

These are encouraging features to Christian efforts in
behalf of the Jews. Such material, if once converted to

31

God, would be mighty to the pulling down of the strong-holds of Satan in the Gentile world.   Large portions of the Mohammedan and Papal world are accessible only through the Jews resident among them.   In Egypt, Pal-estine and Turkey, you find the followers of the Arabian Prophet almost inaccessible to the Gospel ; yet you may preach to the Jew.   In Wallachia and Moldavia, in Hun-gary, Austria and Italy, the attempt to evangelize the blind votaries of Rome, or of the Greek Church, would, till very recently, bring instant vengeance on the head of the missionary ; yet he may, without let or hinderance, preach to the thousands of Jews scattered there, and *through them*, introduce the gospel throughout all those wide realms of death.

Finally, in contemplating the Jew, as he appears in the now passing scene of Israel's grand drama, we have before us a pilgrim and a sojourner, with staff in hand and loins girt—a man *from home*, with little to attach him to the soil of his adopted country, and his heart as warmly sigh-ing for the hills and valleys of his beloved Palestine, and for the Holy Hill of Zion, as the Jew who had wandered from the fold in the days of David ; and his expectation of returning thither, as sanguine as were those of the waiting captives of Babylon.

Whether or not such expectations shall be literally realized, none, I think, will question that the Jews *are* on the threshold of a great revolution, and, with the page of prophecy before us, we cannot doubt this revolution shall be a return to the favor of God within the pale of Christianity.

Such are some of the facts connected with the present condition of the Jews.   Do they not warrant the expec-tation that the time draws near when the Father of Jacob will again smile on his wayward, wandering children, and accept their services in their beloved Zion ?   The bowels of his love, the energies of his Almighty arm, are once more engaged for his ancient people, to restore them to his favor, and make them a praise in all the earth.   God has not cast off his people.   He has engraven them on the palms of his hand.   He is kindly visiting Jacob in his dis-persion, and is calling his chosen from the ends of the earth The Lord will arise and have mercy on Zion, for the time to favor her has come.

In bringing to a close a chapter already protracted much beyond the original design, the importance of the subject seems to urge on us a few brief reflections.

1. The question now so vigorously discussed by tne Jews, assumes a double importance, from the fact, that it is *the great question of the age.* It is the Bible question. Shall the church take the Bible for her text book, her only and infallible guide in all matters of faith and practice, or shall the traditions of the elders, the commandments of men, the decrees of councils, be her authority? The "shaking" among the Jews is but a kindred movement with the present shaking in the whole religious world. It is the great question that divides Rome and Geneva. And this momentous question is likely to be first settled on Jewish ground. And have we not here a clue to the *manner* in which the Jews shall exercise so prominent an agency in the conversion of the world to Christianity? Having themselves settled the great question of the age, broken down the last great, and perhaps the most formidable strong-hold of the adversary, they will come up to the great moral conflict as experienced, skillful, valiant men and successful warriors.

2. What *lesson of duty* is here taught to all who revere the Messiah, and look and pray for the speedy coming of his kingdom; and look for it, too, as to come especially *through the agency of the Jews.* They are to be as "life from the dead" to the slumbering nations. Consequently, an intellectual and religious movement among no other people can possess so much interest to the Christian. The destinies of the world are bound up in the destiny of Israel. And as we see this destiny developing, and sublimer scenes in the great Jewish drama transpiring, we can hardly mistake that a new dispensation is unfolding itself, more extensive, more sublime, than the world has yet witnessed. Every feeling of piety will, therefore, respond, with unfeigned gratitude, to what God is now doing to recover the house of Israel; every pious effort be put forth to bring Israel again into the pale of the divine favor, and of the visible church of God The

Jewish mind is ripe either for the messenger of the gospel, or for the teacher of infidelity. If we do not sow the good seed, while we sleep the enemy will sow tares.

3. *What kind of efforts* will be found more effectual to the conversion of the Jew? Whether for Jew or Gentile, it must be in substance the preaching of *Christ crucified;* but to the Jew, not precisely in the same way. To him it is not a new presentation of Christ, but an *identification* of the Messiah already come, with his *expected* Messiah. He is ready to believe, if he can identify Jesus of Nazareth as the foretold Christ. Hence these "dry bones" must be "prophesied" to. Correct expositions of the prophecies must constitute the burden of the labors of the missionary to the Jews. He must preach Christ the end of the Jewish law; Christ, the reality of all their types, the substance of all their shadows, the thing signified by all their signs, the great sacrifice and sin-offering, the Lamb of God, the Messiah so long looked for. They cannot believe till they see Jesus the prophet like unto Moses; the spirit of prophecy, a testimony concerning Jesus. Already much has occurred to force the Jewish mind to the study of their prophetic writings. The word of God is becoming more and more the only authority in religious controversy.

4. All things are preparing for, and approaching *a crisis of intense interest to our entire race.* This is an inference from a survey of the present condition of the Jews, as connected with their *providential* relation to the whole world. Any divine purpose fulfilled towards Israel, or any movement in their camp, *involves in it a series* of purposes and movements towards the whole Gentile world. Every leaf that stirs on the mountains of Israel, is a signal of a mighty commotion among the nations; every ripple on the waters of Judah, a precursor of a storm that shall shake the foundations of the great deep. When God shall deign to smile again on his ancient people, and restore them to their promised inheritance, all that have opposed his purposes shall be taken out of the way; all that have wronged and oppressed Israel shall drink of the cup of his indignation It shall be the overturning of the world; shall bring peace

to them who love the Prince of Peace, but destruction
to them who have fought against the Lord's anointed
ones.

Are you prepared, reader, for the coming of such
events : laboring, watching, praying, waiting, hoping, till
the Son of Man come in his glory, restore his people to
his favor, avenge himself on their enemies, convert the
world, and take the kingdom to himself?

CHAPTER XX.

THE NESTORIANS—their country, number, history. The Ten lost Tribes. Early conversion to Christianity. Their missionary character. The American Mission
among them. Dr. Grant and the Koordish mountains. The massacre. The great
Revival—extends into the mountains. The untamed mountaineer. A bright day
dawning.

*" They shall build the old wastes ; they shall raise up the former
desolations."*—Isa. lxi. 4.

WE shall pass over the Syrian, Coptic, and Greek
churches without any particular notice, not being aware
of any thing in their present condition especially encouraging to the labors of the evangelist. That a renovating process has begun among them—that the hand of
God is at work, preparing the way for the recovery, at
no very distant day, of those lapsed portions of the one
great fold, we do not doubt. Already facts indicate such
a process. Yet the lines of Providence are not distinct;
the point of their convergence not certain. Nor need
we speak immaturely. It is quite sufficient that we take
a cursory survey of but one other of these ancient
churches.

THE NESTORIANS. This ancient people occupy the
border country between the Turkish and Persian empires. They are found mostly among the mountains of

31*

Koordistan, (the ancient Assyria,) and in the province of Ooroomiah, in western Persia. The western portion of this territory is subject to the Turks, the eastern to the Persians, while the central portion, among the wild ranges of almost inaccessible mountains, is nearly independent—ignorant and barbarous.

The Nestorians, computed now at 150,000, are the remnant of a noble race. They have a history of thrilling interest; a history not yet written, and perhaps never can be. The antiquity of the Nestorians, their location, their preservation as a distinct people, and a Christian church; their doctrinal and Christian purity and spirituality, compared with all other oriental churches; their entire exemption from idolatry, and their remarkable missionary character, are facts which bespeak an attentive perusal of their history, and which can scarcely fail to suggest to every reflecting mind, that a people who have so long been the objects of an ever-watchful Providence, are reserved for some signal display of his grace.

An intelligent traveler, the late Rev. Dr. Grant, who recently visited them among their mountain fastnesses, has, with much plausibility, claimed for the Nestorians a *Hebrew origin*. They are, he believes, the remnant of the Ten Tribes, which Shalmaneser, King of Assyria, carried captive into Assyria 721 years before Christ. They are found in the very same spot where, twenty-five centuries before, God put the Ten Tribes. They resemble the Jews in features, manners, dress, and language. Their names are Jewish; and tradition, both among themselves, and the nominal Jews that reside among them, as also among the Koords, assigns to them an Israelitish descent. And another species of evidence is produced. It is of the character of circumstantial testimony. Dr. Grant finds in this ancient Christian church certain relics of Judaism; remains of sacrificial customs; traces of religious vows, especially that of the Nazarites; of first fruits brought to the sanctuary; of Jewish purifications and washings; of the Passover; of the prohibition of eating unclean animals; of the cities of refuge and the avenging of blood; the extraordinary sanctification of the Sabbath; the appointment of a High Priest, and the peculiar structure of their places of worship, in which the "Holy of holies' is still to be seen.

Though these "beggarly elements," the relics of a by-gone dispensation, but ill become the simplicity of a Christian church, they are just what we should expect to find on the hypothesis that these Nestorians were converted to Christianity *at a very early period*, and that they were *Jews* before their conversion. That the Ten Tribes, wherever they were at the time of the first promulgation of Christianity, did very early receive the gospel, admits of little doubt. For the gospel was, in the order of appointment, first of all to be preached to the "lost sheep of the house of Israel." The work of evangelization among the Gentiles was deferred till this preliminary work was done. Both the Twelve and the Seventy were especially charged with a commission to the seed of Abraham. And it must further be borne in mind, that a full eight years elapsed from the Resurrection to the calling of the first Gentile; an eight years of unusual Christian activity and missionary zeal, yet not a suspicion seems to have been breathed, during this time, that this activity and zeal had the slightest concern for any one beyond the seed of Abraham. At the beginning of these eight years occurred the notable Pentecost, in which three thousand *Jews* were converted, Jews "out of every nation under heaven." In this remarkable assembly were Jews from the very regions into which the Ten Tribes were carried, and where Josephus and other historians affirm they still were in the first century of the Christian era;* and these, the Parthians and Medes of Peter's assembly, were no doubt the first to bring the gospel to the notice of their brethren among the mountains of Assyria, to meet, perhaps, a ready reception. Perchance they had already heard of Jesus, the King of the Jews, and the long looked for Messiah. Perchance the "wise

---

* Josephus says : "The Ten Tribes are beyond the Euphrates till now."—Antiq. B. XI. Ch. V. King Agrippa, in a speech to the Jews, alludes, as to a well-known fact, to their "fellow tribes" dwelling in Adiabene beyond the Euphrates. Adiabene was a name given to the central part of Assyria, where these tribes were placed by their royal captor, and where the Nestorians are still found. And Jerome, the most learned of the Latin fathers, very expressly and repeatedly states, that the Ten Tribes were to be found in that region in the fifth century.

men from the East" had gone out from those very se-
cluded glens, and returned with the joyful news that they
had seen and worshiped this King of the Jews.   Indeed,
the Nestorians have a tradition, supported by the predictions of Zoroaster, that the Magi who visited our Saviour,
went from Ooroomiah.

The work of evangelization, begun by the converts of
Pentecost, seems to have been carried forward by certain
of the immediate disciples of our Lord.   Most historians
name the Apostles Thomas and Thaddeus, as embassadors
to the Parthians and the Medes, while the disciples Matthew, Simon, and Bartholomew, together with Mares,
Adeus, and Agheus, appear among the number who, at
this early period, preached the gospel among the mountains of Assyria.

Admitting Christianity to have been established among
the Nestorians as early as I have supposed, *by Jews*, before they were themselves more than half emancipated
from the yoke of Judaism, and *among* Jews who were
still subject to the yoke, we should expect to find, as the
result, a sort of Jewish Christianity, a mongrel of Judaism
and Christianity, a cross nearer to Judaism than the
Christianity of the Apostles before the vision of Peter.
And the existence of *such* a Christianity there, is in turn
an argument that it was introduced at the time, and
among such a people, as I have supposed.

The Nestorian Christians compare very favorably with
every other oriental church, in doctrine, form, and spirituality.   They have the greatest abhorrence of all image
worship, of auricular confession, purgatory, and many
other of the corrupt dogmas and practices of the Papal,
Greek, and Armenian churches, and may with propriety
be called the " Protestants of Asia."

The preservation and local position of this people, for
the last twenty-five centuries, is a matter of intense interest.   Shut up in the midst of the munitions of the
rocks, in the place God had prepared for them, they have
been preserved from destruction, while thrones and
dominions were falling to decay about them, and the
world was shaken by the heavings of a thousand revolutions.   And especially during the last twelve centuries,

have they been invaded on all sides by the emissaries of Rome, and hunted, like the hart on the mountains, by their Moslem neighbors. During this whole protracted period they have been a little flock surrounded by ravening wolves, yet the Great Shepherd has provided a fold for them, and nothing has been permitted to hurt them.

Standing on the summit of a mountain that overlooked the vast amphitheatre of the wild, precipitous mountains, amidst whose deep defiles and narrow glens are found the abodes of the Nestorians, our late traveler thus eloquently describes the protecting hand of God in the preservation of this people: "Here was the home of one hundred thousand Christians, around whom the arm of Omnipotence had reared the adamantine ramparts, whose lofty, snow-capped summits seemed to blend with the skies in the distant horizon. Here, in their munitions of rocks, has God preserved, as if for some great end in the economy of his grace, a chosen remnant of his ancient church, secure from the Beast and the False Prophet, safe from the flames of persecution and the clangor of war."

We can scarcely resist the conviction, if we would, that these dwellers among the mountains and in the vales, have been kept, as the special objects of providential care, for some great and special end; and what this end is we are now beginning to see.

But before proceeding to notice the present providential indications of the returning favor of God on the Nestorian church, we must allude at least to one other feature of this ancient church—*its missionary character*. This is a remarkable feature, especially when contemplated in connection with the persecuted and oppressed condition of that church during the period of her most laudable missionary zeal. From the third to the sixteenth century, her missions spread over the whole vast regions of central and eastern Asia, amidst the wilds of Tartary, and through the vast empire of China. Persia, India, and all the intermediate countries, from the mountains of Assyria to the Chinese Sea, had, to some extent at least, been made acquainted with the gospel through these zealous missionaries from the mountains of Koordistan; while Arabia and Syria, and the western part of Asia, shared in

their indefatigable and self-denying labors.* As early as
the fifth century, the Patriarch had sent out no less than
twelve Metropolitans, and a corresponding number of
Archbishops, to the very borders of China; which implies
the existence in those places of bishops, priests, and
churches. In the seventh century we find them propagating their faith " from Persia, India, and Syria, among
the barbarous and savage nations inhabiting the deserts and the remotest shores of Asia;" and especially
in this century did they carry the gospel into China.
The Emperor Coacum, (from 650 to 684,) commanded
Christian churches to be erected in all the provinces of
China. The gospel was propagated in ten of the provinces of the empire, and all the cities were supplied with
churches. Even in the tenth century, the very midnight
of Christianity, when the light of the gospel seemed
scarcely to disturb the universal darkness, except as it
faintly gleamed out from the mountains of Koordistan and
of the Alps, these intrepid disciples were penetrating the
wilds of Tartary, and lighting there the fires of Christianity. During the darkest portion of the dark ages,
from the seventh to the middle of the thirteenth century,
the Nestorians were in Asia what the Waldenses were in
Europe.

Such a providential feature is full of encouragement to
all our endeavors to resuscitate the dormant energies of
the Nestorian church. This church has been signally
marked as a missionary church; and she was, especially
in the dark ages, a signal instrument for the carrying forward the work of redemption. Is not, then, every indication of the return of God's favor to this people, full of hope
for the whole Eastern world? If once reanimated with
their former missionary zeal, what have we not reason to
hope from their undaunted courage and untiring zeal,
when the power of the press and all the increasing means
of modern times are brought to their aid? Long since
did the burning tide of Mohammedanism sweep over the
fair fabrics of their missionary toils in Asia, and seemingly prostrate them in the dust, yet we may hope a rem-

* See a Sketch of Nestorian Missions, drawn up for the Missionary Herald for August
1838, on the authority of Mosheim, Assemane, Gibbon, &c.

nant may remain, who, even in those new idolatrous lands, shall be roused from their long slumbers by the trump which seems about to shake the mountains of Assyria, and who, risen again, shall once more stand in their lot, witnesses for the truth, which they once so fearlessly professed and beautifully adorned in the days of their first espousals. Through them we may renew their missions in all Central Asia and China. Let the present Patriarch feel as Patriarch Tamotheus did a thousand years ago, and we should need to send very few men from the West to evangelize Asia. We should find men nearer the field of action, oriental men, with oriental habits, and better fitted to win their way to oriental hearts. And as the returning fire of Christianity shall again warm the centre, may we not expect its benign heat shall extend to the ancient extremities, and China and Tartary again become, through their instrumentality, vocal with the praises of our God?

But let us take a cursory glance of the present condition of the Nestorian Christians, and see what the hand of God is now doing for them, and what prognostics there may be that their winter is passed and their spring cometh.

The American mission was commenced at Ooroomiah in 1835; just in time to frustrate the nefarious schemes of the Jesuits to entangle the Nestorians in the subtle folds of Rome. A Jesuit offered the Patriarch ten thousand dollars on condition that he would acknowledge allegiance to the Pope; to whom the Patriarch replied, "Thy money perish with thee." And later still the assurance has been tendered him, that if he would so far become a Catholic as to recognize the supremacy of the Pope, he should not only be Patriarch of the Nestorians, but all the Christians of the East should be added to his jurisdiction. To this the Patriarch replied: "Get thee hence, Satan."* The providential interposition of the American Board saved this lapsed, yet interesting branch of the Christian church from a catastrophe so disastrous.

From this time forward the providential history of this

------

* Dr. J. Perkins of Ooroomiah, in the Bible Repository.

mission is full of interest. When God would send thither
his servants, he sent before them to prepare the way such
men as Sir John Campbell, Lord Ponsonby, Commodore
Porter Dr. Riach, and Colonel Sheil, not to mention others of like noble character and expansive philanthropy, to
whom Providence had, at this time, given power and influence at the courts of Persia, and of the Sublime Porte.
It was through the very timely instrumentality of these
men, that our mission found so ready access to the Nestorians in Persia and among the Koordish mountains.
Nooroolah Bey, the fierce Koordish chief of the independent Hakary, who had put to death the German traveler Shultz, the only European who had ventured in his
territories, is disarmed and made a friend by the professional skill of Dr. Grant.   Being seized with a severe illness of which Dr. G. restores him, he is made ever afterwards his friend.   Who does not discern the hand of
God in this ?   The raising up and qualifying such a man
as Dr. Grant, and the protection afforded him throughout
his hazardous excursions among the barbarous Koords, is
sufficiently providential to excite our admiration.   Such
travelers are few and far between, and such excursions
are under the guidance of a specially protecting Providence.   Again, the general favor our mission met from
the ecclesiastics of the Nestorian church, is to be regarded in the same light.   The missionaries were received as fellow laborers, to resuscitate a lapsed and dormant church.   The mission schools were welcomed as a
public blessing; priests and bishops put themselves under
the tuition of the mission, and at the same time became
efficient helpers; their places of public worship were
thrown open to the preaching of the missionaries, and all
strove together to give to the Nestorian nation the Bible
in their venacular tongue.

   All seemed prosperous, and a brighter day dawning;
when, suddenly, the heavens were overcast and portended
a storm.   The Koords rise on the mountain Nestorian
massacre a great number, and drive others from their
homes.   The mission in the mountains, which had already
cost much in life and treasure, is broken up.   The Patriarch and the higher ecclesiastics, acted on, no doubt,

The Emperor leaving Vienna.   Page 372.

by the emissaries of Rome and of Oxford, allow their influence to go against the mission. The village schools, forty-three in number, are disbanded; the two boarding-schools broken up; all looks dark. But it was the darkness that precedes the dawn. There was a bow on that cloud. God was about to appear for his down-cast people, and to prosper the labors of his faithful servants.

A delightful presage of what God was now about to do, had been given in the beginning of the year 1844. While assembled on the first Monday of January, there appeared an unusual seriousness, betokening the presence of the Spirit. The result was the conversion of a few individuals, mostly young men from the seminary. During the next two years the mission was not left without tokens, from time to time, of a work of grace. But the year 1846, was the year of the right hand of the Lord. While the little church were again assembled on the first Monday of January, praying for the descent of the Spirit, the windows of heaven were opened, and a copious blessing came down. The first cases of inquiry appeared in Miss Fisk's school. Almost simultaneously, similar scenes were witnessed in Mr. Stoddard's seminary. From that good hour the work extended through the year, and over the plains of Ooroomiah, and among the mountains of Koordistan, till, in the judgment of charity, it has numbered near two hundred hopeful conversions. Indeed, no number can safely be named. The effect is well nigh *national.* The common mind has been moved. While a large number have been converted, a vastly larger number have been brought under the influence of evangelical truth, and may be said to be in a state of inquiry. It has never been the writer's privilege to be made acquainted with a revival of religion which bears more marks of a genuine work of grace. If deep and pungent convictions—abasing, self-loathing views of sin—if stillness and solemnity, prayers and tears, be an indication of a work of the Spirit; if ecstatic views of pardoning love and joy in sins forgiven; zeal for the honor of Christ; tenderness of conscience, and ardent solicitude for the salvation of others, be evidence of a gracious work, such a work was witnessed among the Nestorians.

32

But it does not fall within the limits of our present plan to go into the details of the work, truly interesting as they are. We are to contemplate it only as a *providential measure preparatory to future progress.*

And the first thing which demands our attention is, the *moral power* for the evangelization of the Nestorian nation, which Providence created and secured by this revival. Mind is hereby sanctified and prepared for moral activity. But it is not the amount of mind now brought into the work, so much as its character, which develops the providential bearing of the revival. The same number of souls might have been converted, and yet no great moral result follow to the church and nation at large. But when we recur to the character of the converts— bishops, priests, deacons, members of the Patriarch's family; the most influential part of the nation; nearly all that portion of the youth of the nation who are in the process of receiving an education, and, of consequence, being prepared to exercise a controlling influence in time to come, we discover the finger of God at work there in reference to some great, prospective good. Here are provided mental and moral resources, which we may confidently expect shall be employed for an adequate end. Does God design to convert this ancient people, and revive this ancient church, that he may again employ them as they were nobly employed a thousand years ago in the work of evangelizing Asia, he has provided himself with just such instruments as we should expect.

Another providential feature of this revival is, its *diffusive character,* and *the long time of its continuance.* These two features blended, exhibit a beautiful providence. It was widely extended because it was long continued. It was continued till the seminaries should have their vacations, and a large number of the recently converted should be scattered through the villages and among the mountains, everywhere carrying with them the light and love of the gospel, and kindling a flame in the bosom of their several family circles, and in their neighborhoods; and, till the inhabitants of the mountains should witness the wonderful power of God, and many of the mountaineers become vitally interested in the work. The most interesting sea-

son was in the *winter*, when thousands of the poor mountaineers are forced down to the plain of Ooroomiah to
seek food. They now found the bread of life, and returned rejoicing in the fullness of Christ. But there is at
this point a yet more remarkable providence to be noticed. The unprovoked and shocking massacre by the
Koords, had now driven thousands more from their
mountain recesses, where there seemed little hope the
missionary could reach them, and forced them down upon
the plain, and thus brought them in contact with evangelical influences. Their children were unexpectedly
brought into the schools, their priests enlightened and
converted, and the people brought to hear a pure gospel.

And not only so, but the revival extended into the
mountains. In this, too, the hand of God was signally
manifested. An instance or two will illustrate : A little
girl from Hakkie, in a mountain district, joins Miss Fisk's
school, and, during the progress of the revival, becomes a
Christian. Her father, an untamed mountaineer, soon
visits her. The silken cords of a daughter's love are
thrown about him, and these young disciples point him to
the cross of Christ. He hears with indifference, then
with wonder. Light increases ; conviction presses on
him that he is a sinner, and his heart rises in opposition.
He struggles with his feelings. The strong man bows and
weeps like a child—the trembling sinner becomes a peaceful Christian. This man was deacon Guergis. Having
consecrated himself to the cause of Christ, he returns
home to make known the more excellent way to his
friends and neighbors. The light thus kindled, spreads,
till evangelical doctrines are promulgated from village to
village over the whole district. Many inquire the way
of life—many are converted. And when, after some
months, the missionaries visit Tergarwer, the district in
question, they meet a hearty welcome, find the people
everywhere waiting to receive the word ; deacon Guergis, who had been a principal instrument in the work, laboring with great zeal, prudence and efficiency, and the
good work widely extended and extending.

The position of this district, and the character of its inhabitants, are represented as giving this religious move-

ment a peculiar interest. "Familiar as they are from infancy with the Koords, accustomed to mountain life and
its attendant hardships, they will be able, if truly converted to God, to carry the gospel into the districts of Koor
distan under more favorable circumstances than our helpers in Ooroomiah can command for some time to come."

The commencement of the work in Gawar, another
mountain district, fifty miles still further among the
mountains, and more especially in the heart of the mountain population, is not the less worthy of note as a providential movement.

A rough mountaineer from Gawar, comes to Ooroomiah on business; is persuaded to remain a few days in
the hope he may be led to attend to the concerns of his
soul. He is immediately made the subject of prayer and
exhortation; is soon effected by the truth, which, in turn,
increases the anxieties of others for him, and the fervor
of their prayers for his salvation. He is deeply and pun-
gently convicted as a sinner, and soon hopefully a new
creature, sitting at the feet of Jesus. He returns to his
mountain home, with no one to instruct him, sympathize
with, or encourage him, and himself unable to read.
Months pass, and nothing is heard from Gawar, or the
mountain convert. The vacation of the seminary comes,
when a younger brother of the convert returns home and
finds there a blessed work of grace in progress, which he
does not a little to advance. The mountain convert had
gone in the fullness of the Spirit and in the power of his
Master, told the simple tale of the Lord's doings for his
soul, exemplified the truth in a life of prayer and simple
faith and holy zeal, and it was the mighty power of God
to the pulling down of strong-holds. His honest labors
had been signally owned, and he had prepared the way
for the labors of other converts, who now followed, and
who were more perfectly instructed in the way of life.
A glorious work of the Spirit was the result, which spread
throughout the district.

Thus, before the missionaries had made their first
visit, an extensive work was in progress, commenced
without any direct agency of theirs, and in a district of
country hitherto inaccessible, and where, too, the preva-

lence of pure religion must be peculiarly salutary and
efficient on the neighboring population, and bring the
gospel in contact with the barbarous Kôords. It is,
probably, in this manner that the gospel is to make its
way, without observation or display, into the mountain
districts, independent of human government or protection.

All opposition seems hushed, and a conviction to pervade the common mind, that the hand of the Lord is at
work to revive the Nestorian church. There is almost
a universal readiness to listen to a preached gospel—a
general spirit of inquiry pervading the nation.   And
there is, too, an efficient and suitable instrumentality
prepared, to advance the work till the whole nation shall
be regenerated. It has never been the policy of the mission to organize a new church, but to resuscitate the old
one. And present appearances indicate that what has
proved impracticable among the Armenians, may be
achieved for the Nestorians.

Already an extensive native agency is in the field.
Ecclesiastics have generally shown themselves the friends
of reform, and are the principal instruments in advancing
the work. Four bishops are pupils and helpers to the
mission, and a large number of priests and deacons ; and
successors to bishops and priests are pupils in the Mission Seminary, and converts of the late revival.

Says the Rev. Dr. Perkins of Ooroomiah : "The light
of true piety, kindled at various points on the plain of
Ooroomiah, and in the neighboring mountain districts, is
brightening and extending, and we have more and more
evidence of the power and extent of the revival of last
year. Indeed, in its blessed effects, this revival has never
yet ceased, but has been, and is still, constantly advancing ; and where it has taken the strongest hold, the entire
mass seem to be pervaded by its influences. Some of
our native evangelists are itinerating in remote districts
of this province, and with encouraging success."

Reference has already been made to the character of
the converts. No feature of the late revival, perhaps, is
more strikingly providential, or possesses a higher interest to the pious mind, than the activity and zeal of the
converts, to extend the work throughout the nation—
32*

especially that the gospel be preached to their brethren
in the mountains of Koordistan. District after district of
those almost inaccessible regions has been visited, and
the gospel preached, as one door after another has been
providentially opened, with a zeal and self-denial worthy
the days of the apostles; and soon we may expect to
hear that those hills and valleys have become vocal with
the praises of our God. The hand of the Lord is in the
thing for good, to that long forsaken but truly interesting people.

But Providence has provided other resources there for
carrying forward his work, in the form of the press, of
education, and the preparation and publication of the
Scriptures. Three millions of pages of printed matter
have been scattered among the Nestorians, within
scarcely more than twice that number of years; and
an efficient system of Christian education is preparing
the mind of a large class of youth to act for the further
regeneration of their nation.

Do not these things indicate that the night, which has
so long covered the Nestorians, is far spent, and the day
is at hand? And have we not some pleasing indications
that the Lord of the harvest has important purposes to
accomplish through the Nestorians—a conspicuous part
to act by them in bringing in the latter-day glory?
"What position could be more important and advan-
tageous, in its bearing on the conversion of the world,
than that occupied by the Nestorians, situated as they
are in the centre of Mohammedan dominion? And is it
too much to believe that this ancient church, once so renowned for its missionary efforts, and still possessing such
capabilities, as well as such facility of location for the
renewal of like missionary labors, will again awake from
the slumber of ages, and become bright as the sun, fair as
the moon, and terrible as an army with banners! that it
will again diffuse such floods of light as shall forever put
to shame the corrupt abominations of Mohammedanism,
roll back the tide of Papal influence which is now setting
in so strongly and threatening to overwhelm it, and send
forth faithful missionaries of the cross in such numbers
and with such holy zeal as shall bear the tidings of sal-

vation to every corner of benighted Asia. We confidently look for such results, and that at no very distant period. The signs of the times in this eastern world betoken the speedy approach of mighty political revolutions. The Mohammedan powers are crumbling to ruin. Christian nations are soon to rule over all the followers of the false prophet. Turkey and Persia are tottering, and would fall at once by their own weight, were they not upheld by rival European governments. The universal catastrophe of Mohammedan dominion cannot, in all human probability, be much longer postponed."[*] They that take the *sword* shall perish with the sword—when the sword shall be taken from them.

We look, perhaps, in vain over the whole face of the earth for a spot where the arm of the Lord is more manifestly revealed; and we wait with increasing interest to see what shall be the future developments of Providence, concerning this ancient and interesting people

---

CHAPTER XXI.

EUROPE IN 1848. The Mission of Puritanism— in Europe. The failure of the Reformation. Divorce of Church and State. The *moral* element in Government. Progress of liberty in Europe; religious Liberty. Causes of the late European movement. The downfall of Louis Phillippe. What the end shall be.

"*I will overturn, overturn, overturn—till he come whose right it is.*"—Ez. xxi. 27.

THE time has not come to write, in the annals of the world's history, the Chapter on Europe in 1848. Yet the time has come to *begin* to write such a chapter. This, however, does not fall within the province of the

---

[*] Rev. Dr. J. Perkins, in the Biblical Repository for 1841.

present treatise. It is ours to take history as we find it,
and in its ever interesting evolutions, to watch the Hand
of God as He reigns in all its events. Since the foregoing chapters were prepared for the press, revolutions and
changes have transpired in Europe, which beautifully
sustain our main position. Precisely what will come of
these revolutions, we have not yet seen enough to predict. But we are quite sure God is in them, and that He
will, in due time, educe results which shall honor himself,
and signally advance the kingdom of truth and righteousness.

We took occasion in a foregoing chapter, to speak of
the Hand of God in the discovery of America, and of the
controlling influence here given to the Puritan element;
how it has given existence, form and character to our
government, been the main spring of our national prosperity, formed our social relations, entered largely into
all our commercial, educational and industrial enterprises, and set religion free from the trammels which
fettered her in the old world, disrobing her of senseless
rites and more senseless trappings, and giving her a new
vitality : and how this same controlling influence has
followed, wave after wave, the tide of population westward, fulfilling its mission none the less effectually in the
remotest settlements of the West, by incorporating itself
with the heterogeneous materials collected there from
every nation, tongue and kindred, softening, melting,
fusing and running them into the New England mould.

The Puritan seems the true type and representative of
the Anglo-Saxon race, a race which seems destined to
be a chief instrument in the rapid progress and elevation
of man. New England is at once the nursery, the repository and the school-master of the whole nation. The
Puritan element is everywhere the motive power. It has
set in motion the wheel of the manufacturer ; opened the
mine of precious and useful metals and minerals ; projected our canals, railways and telegraphs ; spread our
canvas on every sea ; covered our rivers and coasts
with steamers ; built our colleges, and given existence,
character and efficiency to our common schools, and
published our books. Go West or South, and you will

People in the Throne Room of the Tuileries. Page 381.

find this same Puritan character telling on the industry and enterprise, the thrift and prosperity of the people. Ask who teaches this school, who the president and professors of this college, the cashier of this bank; who your lawyers, physicians, preachers, statesmen; who your most thriving farmers, mechanics, merchants, manufacturers?

Such having been the *domestic fruits* of Puritanism, we are prepared to inquire whether there be any *foreign* fruits which at all correspond. Nations have within a few years been brought into a strange proximity; and if, as has been affirmed, our civil and religious institutions are more nearly, than those of any other nation, in harmony with the religion of the New Testament, are we to expect their renovating influence will be confined to America? Truth is mighty; and institutions which harmonize with truth, shall extend. Oceans cannot hinder them; national boundaries form scarcely an obstacle to their progress; the iron gates of despotism cannot shut them out. Truth is a strong leaven, and though it work unseen, it is sure to leaven the whole lump.

We hesitate not, therefore, to assume, that the present condition of Europe—the condition since the 23d of February, 1848, is but the carrying out and maturing of the magnificent scheme of Providence, begun in the discovery of America, and yet more ostensibly begun in the safe landing of the Mayflower at the Rock of Plymouth In support of this assumption, the following considera tions deserve attention.

1. The Reformation of the sixteenth century, both in respect to civil government and religion, was arrested before it had completed half its work. Luther left un touched some odious features of Romanism. The Re formed religion needed to be immediately reformed. But we allude at present to a single feature, which, it is believed, contributed vastly to check the hopeful progress of the Reformation. We mean the neglect of the early reformers *to effect a separation of Church and State.* The Christian church was but half emancipated. Like her great Apostle, she sighed for deliverance: "O wretched man that I am, who shall deliver me from the body of this death"—from this dead body, the State? Puritan-

ism cut the cord, and the church began to be free. The Reformation did not reach the depths of religious freedom. Next to the usurpation and tyranny of Rome, this miserable union with the state has inflicted the severest blow. Puritanism proclaims a divorce; and so universally and successfully has the "voluntary system" been adopted in this country, that no sect would for a moment consent to such an alliance, if it were proffered. It would be regarded as death to the vitality of religion. It is under the voluntary system, that personal piety has so far pervaded the public mind, revivals prospered, our charitable enterprises originated and sent the gospel over the whole earth, and made Christianity so beautifully aggressive. This is essentially American—an advanced step under the favoring auspices of Puritanism—but not confined to America. It has found its way back across the Atlantic. The little leaven, which was not allowed room to work in England, was transported to America. Here it worked successfully, and has returned, with the accumulated power of two centuries, to do its destined work in Europe, and thence to fulfill its mission round the world.

How this work is advancing in England, the present struggle, indicated in the term Church Reform, is ample voucher. The mass of the English nation has willed the severance of the Church and State, and Church and State must be severed. It is but the sure consequence of principles which have taken deep root in the English mind— an *effect* so imperative, that neither the power of the throne, nor the pride of the aristocracy, nor the piteous remonstrances of church dignitaries can long hinder it. What the Reformation unfortunately left undone for England, is likely soon to be done; and once done there, where will this miserable relic of Romanism much longer find a foothold?

The late secession from the establishment of the Hon. and Rev. Baptist Noel, of London, is at this time ominous of coming change. It has undoubtedly struck a blow at this unhappy alliance, which will be felt throughout the English Church. Mr. Noel has sent through the press an explanation of the bold step he has taken, and a defence of his present position, which, if we may judge from the obvious merits of the book itself, and from the eagerness with which it is sought by thousands of all denominations in Great Britain, is destined to exert a no insignificant influence in the final emancipation of the Church from the incubus of the State.

But we have, perhaps, a more forcible illustration of the progress of this feature of American Christianity, in the present religious condition of the continent. So accustomed had European Christians become to see Christianity dwindle under the shadow of the State, that they scarcely knew she could survive the open sunshine of heaven—stand by her own native strength, and grow and expand as the plant of heaven, unpropped, unaided, unfed by the beggarly elements of the world. Yet, within a few years, and especially during the present year, an astonishing change has been wrought there. The union of Church and State has become irksome and offensive in proportion to the progress of civil and religious liberty. Persons well informed in the affairs of France, say that faith in the "voluntary system," and the disunion of State and Church, is making great progress among Catholics as well as Protestants; and there is, in the Catholic church, a great disposition to throw off the supremacy of Rome. And such a sentiment, it is confidently believed, is pervading most of the European states. The public mind is very generally agitated on this question. Societies are formed for the purpose of realizing such a result, and the spirit of the age favors it.

2. To Puritanism we must accord the honor, under God, of developing a new element in the science of civil government—the *moral* element. Heretofore, bayonets and cannon had formed the substratum of governmental authority. Might gives right, was the motto of kings. Certain men were born to rule; and certain others were as undoubtedly born to regale themselves in the royal sunshine; and vastly larger classes of men, the masses, were as surely born *for* the king and his nobility, to live and toil for his profit, to be ruled for his pleasure, or to be "flesh for his cannon." Such is government by one man or by the few, who rule irrespectively of the suffrage or

the good of the people. It is a government of force as
opposed to a government of choice. The one requires
implicit obedience, the other rational obedience. Under
one, men worship gods they know not whom, and obey
laws they know not what. Under the other, reason
guides, and an enlightened private judgment decides. One
is the self-government of rational and moral beings ; the
other, the application, by a few, of brute force, to keep in
subjection the mass. The one makes freemen, the other
slaves.

Liberty was born in America. Long had she travailed
in birth in the Old World. Many a throe had convulsed
Europe to the very centre, till, in this fair land, liberty
first saw the light. There had been before much in the
world called liberty, but it was the mere glimmering of
star-light, or the meteor's blaze, compared with the full-
orbed luminary which now arose. Puritanism gave birth,
form and ascendency to the moral element in government. From time to time nations had given signs of woe,
and sent up their aspirations for deliverance, vindicated
their high claims to freedom, and gained a temporary relief. But it was in America the great experiment was
first fairly tried, whether self-government is yet practicable. And, though our ship has not steered clear of
rocks and quicksands, nor shunned the storm and tempest,
yet we have found our vessel sea-worthy, able to ride on
the crested wave, and to breast the roaring storm. A
result has already been gained, which has demolished
thrones, and sent disease and decay into every system of
absolutism in Europe.

The Declaration of American Independence passed
over Europe, yet it was as the voice of distant thunder.
It was an ominous sound, starting from his throne the too
long quiescent monarch. Yet the danger seemed distant.
He hoped that that cloud, which turned so dark and
threatening a face towards the kingly estates of Europe,
yet a face so bright and promising towards the free-born
sons of America, would scatter with a brief outburst of
popular indignation. But the *establishment* of American
Independence came like a thunder-bolt, or like the shock
of an earthquake, and made thrones tremble. France first

received the shock, and, unprepared as she was, what a shock!

The French Revolution was a premature birth, and the birth of a monster, conceived in America, but gestated and brought forth under auspices altogether unfavorable to the beauty and proper development of the offspring—a monster-birth, whose history is written in violence, crime and blood. Yet it indicated the *power* of the new element which had been cast among the nations. It was a burning star cast into a stagnant sea. France was unprepared, yet her mercurial sons, driven into a phrensy by the first gleam of liberty that flashed across the western main, kindled a fire, soon to be quenched in blood. Though smothered and quenched for a time, it burnt unseen—its internal fires ever and anon finding vent in some outburst for liberty. We need not trace its several steps. Liberty was not extinct in France from the day of the return from America of young La Fayette to the eventful twenty-third of February; nor did she ever cease her struggle against the incubus of royalty when a befitting occasion offered.

France has lived half a century within the last year. What she so long struggled for, she obtained in a day. Year after year the unseen Hand had been preparing men, means and resources, yet all things seemed to remain as they were; but the moment of consummation came, and all was done. And, what may well astonish the unbeliever in Divine Providence, all was done at the very moment when human sagacity, and diplomacy, and skill, and perseverance, were the most diligently employed to prevent such a result. Louis Phillippe is driven from his throne, the monarchy demolished, and a republic formed, just at the time, and in the manner, which seemed the most unrelentingly to mock all the efforts he had made, all the alliances he had formed, and all the precautions he had taken to ward off just such a disaster. With Paris so admirably fortified; and a rich, numerous and influential priesthood for his allies; and the Pope as the right arm of his strength; and a cringing alliance with England and Russia, there seemed—there *was* no human power that could molest him. Yet we see him fleeing from his

33

palace and his throne, as helpless and unresisting, as if all
human powers were in league against him.   Providence
had done with him and with his throne, and where is he?

But what progress has liberty made in other States of
Europe?   On the outbreak of the late French Revolution,
the people of *Holland* demanded a larger liberty.   The
king is made to feel the necessity of granting it.   He
chooses new ministers—proposes important reforms in the
constitution, and promises to govern agreeably to the national will.   The King of Belgium yields to the liberals,
and on this condition keeps his crown.   The kingdom of
Prussia is shaken to its centre, and its republican tendencies are gaining the ascendency.   Poland is agitated and
ripe for revolt.   Venice is a republic.

But more remarkable than all, the stagnant waters of
Austria are all at once thrown into a foam.   The tide of
revolution came rushing into Austria like a cataract.
The Austrians had seemed completely under the yoke.
Yet, in a moment, as unexpected to Prince Metternich as
if the tenants of the grave-yard had awaked, the people
aroused from their long sleep, and proclaimed democratic
principles.   Prince Metternich, who had, for more than
forty years, ruled Austria with a rod of iron, flees before
the vengeance of an indignant people—an idiot monarch
quits his throne—despotism is struck to the heart, never
to recover.

All Germany, in a word, is on fire—insurrection is
everywhere triumphant.   Germany was the land of Martin Luther, the land of reforms, in whose rich soil lie
deeply planted the seeds of liberty.   The waiting friends
of freedom throughout Germany had felt the electric
shock from Paris, and saw that their hour had come.
Consternation and dismay seize the heart of every absolute power.   The people seem rising over the continent
like the waves of the ocean, and kings and ministers feel
that their hour is come.   The people are ripe for liberty,
and now is the time to strike the blow for rights too long
delayed.   A German Parliament is convened, elected by
universal suffrage, and composed of delegates from the
kingdoms of Austria, Prussia, Hanover, Bavaria, and the
smaller principalities.   The objects of this parliament are

to unite all Germany into one confederation—to relieve the different states from the oppressions and exactions of their present rulers, and the more effectually to establish free institutions. This parliament is truly a strange feature in European politics, and a more sure index of the real progress of free principles than any thing we have yet seen. A promising feature, not of this parliament only, but of the French republic, is, that they have proclaimed the true American doctrine of *non-interference*— a delightful pledge that when the moral element shall predominate in the construction of governments, nations shall learn war no more.

In *Italy*, too, liberal principles have made gigantic strides. Constitutional laws are universally promulgated. To say nothing of Sardinia and Florence, Naples and Milan, where the moral element is allowed to take the lead in the formation of their new governments, Pope Pius IX. was compelled to concede a constitutional government to the long-oppressed and priest-ridden people of the Papal states. The press is made free—laymen are admitted to a participation in civil affairs—an independent judiciary is organized—a Chamber of Deputies is appointed by the people, and free schools for the poor are established in every district in Rome. An act was passed, April, 1848, to provide means for the better education of the people. Yet the battle in Italy is still to be fought. Here are the strong-holds of despotism. The grim giant, though bearded in his den, and lying prostrate with his deadly wound, fearfully growls, and rouses to the encounter. Rome is divided against herself—a pitiable anarchy. Two great conflicting parties have been contending for the mastery. On the one side, the Pope and his adherents; on the other, the political councils and the legislative assemblies of the people. The irritation became more and more violent. The Pope had granted much; the people demanded more. The Pope at length becomes virtually a prisoner in his own palace; the cardinals dare not appear in the streets; many of the priests are ill-treated and even beaten, and the liberals openly declare that Pius IX. will be the last of the Popes. But the popular indignation against the ghostly tyranny of the

Vatican remained unappeased. Unwittingly had the people been allowed to taste the sweets of liberty. The
clarion of freedom had sounded from afar. Crushed in
the dust by the foot of the Beast, the poor, oppressed
Italians start to their feet, awaked from a thousand years'
slumber. The bow, too far bent, rebounds with a vengeance. The Pope is driven from his palace, glad to
wrap up his marvelous infallibility in a footman's coat,
and to coil his once dreaded supremacy in a footman's
hat. Democracy is in the ascendant; the temporal power
of the Pope is at present suspended. How the struggle
shall end, remains to be seen. A coalition of Catholic
powers may restore the Pope to his throne, and the power
of the bayonet may, for a little time, keep him there. And
this may be the occasion that shall light the torch of war,
and set all Europe in a blaze. All this may be; but that
liberty will be again suppressed in Italy for any great
length of time, and the Italians be made to bow again to
the yoke, is less problematical.

Cold murmurs of discontent are heard, too, from the
hyperborean regions of the Muscovite Czar. The tocsin
of liberty has been heard over Russia, and many a brave
heart echoes back the sound. The Revolution of France
came on Nicholas like a thunderbolt. His alliances with
Austria and Prussia were disturbed, his plans defeated, or,
at least, retarded. Nicholas received the dispatches announcing the events of February with amazement. A
deadly paleness came over his face as he read, and the
paper trembled in his hand. A Republic in France! A
new appeal to the nations against tyranny! A dangerous experiment for kings. A death-blow to tyrants.
How this Anglo-Saxon element mocks the divine rights
of kings, and proclaims the people the only legitimate
sovereigns!

Nor have wretched Spain and Portugal escaped the
shock. A suppressed but deep indignation rankles beneath the surface of those ill-fated nations—an ominous
calm that precedes the irruption of a volcano.

All Europe is in motion—all Europe has entered on a
new course of action. Altogether a new principle of
government is in successful operation; and though we

may expect commotions, and anarchies, and re-actions—disorderly progress, and seemingly disastrous retrogressions, yet we may confidently await the establishment of a new order of things, which shall more beautifully harmonize with the present advanced state of Christianity, knowledge, and civilization.

3. The progress of *religious* liberty in Europe still more directly illustrates the extended and the extending progress of the Puritan leaven ; and indicates, too, the steady workings of a sleepless Providence.

The progress of religious liberty has, within a few months, been truly astonishing. Since the breaking out of the late French Revolution, the severe laws against Protestants have been relaxed in every country in Europe. In some of these countries full religious toleration is already enjoyed. The revolutionary tide spared not even the seven hills, demolishing dungeons and extinguishing the fires of persecution. The right of private judgment seems virtually conceded, even in Rome. The ancient Waldensian church, the true link between the apostolic age and ours, has at length been allowed liberty of conscience and of worship. Austria, despotic Austria, "whose frowning ramparts presented no chink through which even one ray of light might penetrate to the darkness within," is now open to the Bible and the missionary. In Germany all restraints to the spread of the gospel are removed. The Press is free, and never was its power more manifest than at the present moment. Full freedom of religious profession is enjoyed. The exercise of religious rights no longer depend on the profession of the Romish faith.

And yet more astonishing has been the progress of religious liberty in France.

The zeal and prompt unanimity with which the *Jesuits* have been expelled from nearly every state in Europe, not excepting Rome, is an undoubted index of the progress of religious liberty. The Jesuits are but too well known, the world over, as the implacable enemies of liberty, equality, and civilization—the sworn allies of absolutism—always ready to use the rod and the sword, to stifle the first symptoms of liberty, making religion the cruelest weapon of oppression. This general and simulta-

33*

neous rising against the Jesuits, and a growing aversion to
religious orders, is an unmistakable symptom of the progress of free principles.   The people of Europe have been
brought to feel that liberty and the society of Ignatius can
never prosper together.   Their expulsion at this time is
significant.   Pius IX. had declared the Jesuits *the strong
and experienced oarsmen that keep from shipwreck the bark
of St. Peter,* yet he was obliged, *in obedience to the de
mands of the people,* to expel them from the Papal states.
The concession, significantly, bespeaks the weakness of
Rome.   The power of the Papacy is terribly shaken.
Though still claiming infallibility in *doctrine,* the Pope
very prudently concedes that "*the Church must follow the
necessary requirements of the age.*"

The opinion of a Romanist is worth something here.
The Tablet, a Romish paper, says : "The rising persecu
tion is not confined to the Jesuits, but is directed against
every religious community.   The Dominicans, the Capu-
chins, the Augustinians, have all received unequivocal
notices of their approaching fate."   And he might add
the "Sisters of the Sacred Heart."   While on the other
hand it is now not uncommon to meet Romish ecclesiastics, who, disgusted with the mummeries of Rome,
boldly expose her errors—"earnestly advocating the
abolition of compulsory celibacy of the clergy, the abro-
gation of fasts and abstinences, and other Popish observances."

Thus is God moving on in the might and majesty of
his providence, overturning and overturning, till his
church shall be disenthralled from the bondage of the
world, and established on the everlasting foundation of
truth and righteousness.

4. Or do we inquire after the *causes* of the great European movement, we are again brought to the same conclusion.   These causes had been in secret and active
operation, at least, since the American Revolution, and
only waited a favorable opportunity.   Intensely did the
internal fires burn, and an irruption was inevitable.
Liberal principles were daily gaining strength.   All
classes of the people were feeling their burdens more and
more grievous, and their growing discontent gave no

doubtful signs of an outbreak. Radicalism had given birth to numerous societies throughout Europe—many of them secret associations, all animated by one spirit, a determination to throw off the shackles of despotism. The death of Louis Phillippe should be the signal to strike the blow. The French Revolution, however, indicated that the hour had come. They arose by one common impulse, and despotism quailed before them.

Again, *facility of communication* greatly hastened such a result. Books, journals, newspapers, travelers, reach the remotest parts of Europe in a few days, give timely notice of change, and communicate every new opinion. And all the vigilance and precautions of an argus-eyed absolutism cannot shut them out. The nations, as never before, flow together; a common sentiment pervades them. An electric spark thrilled Austria, Russia, Italy Poland, the moment an explosion took place in France.

We discover another cause in the fact, (instructive to kings,) that the potentates of Europe *turned a deaf ear to the cries of their oppressed subjects.* They had neither listened to their wants nor been careful to keep their engagements with them. Napoleon had done much to prepare Europe for liberty, and when the people of Europe were called on by the allied powers to take up arms against him, they did it with the promise that their rights should be respected, and liberal laws granted. The rulers promised, and the people freely shed their blood. But the danger past, the "scourge of Europe" put down, kings forgot their promises. "Austria did not grant to the Italians the institutions she promised. The king of Prussia conceded to his subjects only some petty reforms. Germany was held under a slavish yoke." Poland was crushed. Italy was left the miserable dupe of tyranny— the prey of every unclean bird. Nowhere was there respect for law, or security against arbitrary power. The rights of conscience were systematically invaded. The judiciary was a mere tool for kings. "The nations bowed their necks, but they meditated the hour of deliverance. That hour is come; they have seized it; they have risen .ike one man, and the well-trained armies of kings have scarcely opposed an obstacle to the realization of their wishes."

The day of retribution has come. Kings tremble, and their thrones crumble. The haughtiest monarchs, who could once insolently put their foot on the neck of nations, now in vain sue for mercy at the hands of their revolted subjects. Deeply, indeed, do they drink to the dregs the cup of their debasement. The last was a hard year for kings. Late have they learned the humiliating lesson that kings are made for the people, not the people for kings; that the rights of the people are as sacred as those of princes, and that their only chance for quiet and safety, is to live in good understanding with their subjects.

The downfall of Louis Phillippe is here ominously instructive. What would a serious observer of Providence expect would be the end of a powerful prince in the nineteenth century, who should pursue the course Louis Phillippe pursued? Did he so demean himself in the high and responsible station to which Providence exalted him—especially when we bring into the account the *manner* and *condition* of his taking the crown—did he so demean himself as to guarantee the continued smiles of Heaven? In many respects Louis Phillippe was a very worthy man. He possessed many excellent traits of character. But in his regal life, when weighed in the balance, he was found wanting. He did more than to commit fatal political blunders. His sceptre was stained with palpable injustice and outrage, both towards man and God. He came to the throne as a liberal prince. Heaven and earth heard his vows, that he would reign as a republican king; would surround the monarchy with republican institutions. The people, whose voice called him to the throne, hailed him as a father and a friend—the deliverer of an oppressed people from the thraldom of Bourbon despotism. And the Protestant world had reason to expect he would reign, at least, as a liberal Catholic prince. France and the world too well know how he has cringed to the most miserable system of absolutism. Had Louis Phillippe been half so ambitious to retain the good opinion of his people as he was to main tain his throne and to vindicate his legitimacy; at least, had he been half so ambitious to render stipulated *justice* to his people, he might still have been the king of a prosperous and affectionate people. Or had he been half so careful to act the liberal Catholic prince, extending the arms of his regal influence to promote, wherever French interests exist, education, civilization and Christianity, as he was to impose, by his strong arm, on an unoffending people just emerging from heathenism, corps after corps of Romish priests, who, he could not but know, would, if they acted in character, cripple, and, if possible, destroy every Protestant mission within their influence, he might still have been the head of a great and noble nation, on whom should come the blessing of many. That dark page in the history of Tahiti, will ever remain a darker page—an indelible disgrace, in the history of Louis Phillippe. When he directed his cannon against that newly Christian island, he directed them against his own throne. Those missions live and prosper, while Louis Phillippe has gone into an inglorious exile. An influence exerted in Greece, flowing from the throne of France, drove Dr. King from Athens and from his mission, a temporary wanderer; Dr. King has returned to his work, and Louis Phillippe has bid farewell to his throne forever!*

We may subjoin as subordinate causes of his downfall, regal extravagance, heavy taxation, a monstrous army, the fortifications of Paris, opposition to electoral reforms, the press subjected to vexatious embarrassments, money and other favors lavished on the priesthood, with a hypocritical attachment to Popery, hoping thereby to strengthen his dynasty at the expense of the people. Like Saul, who, in his troubles, had recourse to the witch of Endor, Louis Phillippe sought the favor of the Romish clergy, flattered the bishops, and favored the establishment of monasteries. But this resource failed him, and did but hasten his downfall. Such are some of the causes which irrepressibly irritated the public mind, and

---

* The very law which had been so often, of late years, applied by Louis Phillippe and his government to impede the spread of the gospel, and suppress free discussion, became, at length, the occasion of his own downfall. Discern ye not the Hand of God?

made the revolution inevitable. The Lord was depaited from Saul, and he was sore distressed.

And, finally, the *Bible* has had much to do in producing the late religious and political convulsions in Europe. The Bible is a revolutionary book, meaning by revolution, an advance of right opinions, manners and constitutions; a resistance of oppression and monopolies; a demand for liberty and natural rights. The word of God is a great leveler, which is upturning and overturning this wicked, distracted world, and preparing it for a complete civil and religious renovation. It is not too much to believe that the million of Bibles, which have been circulated in France during the last five years, have been a powerful element in the present downfall of despotism; the breaking up of old foundations to make way for better. And, what is prospectively encouraging for France and the nations that easily adopt her opinions, the late revolution has, in a remarkable manner, opened the door for a more abundant and effectual introduction of the Bible.

Through the admirable system of Bible colportage, the Sacred Scriptures are being distributed throughout France, in every condition of society. The cottage, the palace, the soldier, the sailor, the school, are, without let or hinderance, visited by the indefatigable colporteur, and blessings follow in his track. Here lies our brightest anticipation for France.

The revolution has brought to light an amount of Protestantism in France, which was not before supposed to exist. Villages, where a Protestant could not find a congregation, if allowed to preach at all, have dismissed their Catholic cure, and called in evangelical ministers. All the religious societies find large fields open to their efforts, which they are prevented from occupying only by the want of the pecuniary resources.

Thus has the great idea, so happily conceived—divinely suggested—in the Mayflower, been steadily and gradually developing, and never more gloriously than at the present moment. God may be seen in its progress at every step. The Lion of the tribe of Judah has been steadily opening the unsealed Book; the eternal decrees have been unfolding, and being executed by an Almighty

Providence, and nothing has been able to retard their
progress. The kings of the earth have set themselves,
and the rulers taken counsel against the Lord, and
against his anointed. But all their counsel and wisdom
have been brought to naught. He that sitteth in the
heavens has had them in derision. He has spoken to
them in his wrath, and vexed them in his sore displeasure.
Never was the skill, sagacity and power of man more
signally foiled; never the wisdom and power of God
more illustriously magnified. Austria, France, Italy, had
done all that human sagacity and forecast could do, to
save their thrones and their despotisms from the invading
tide of popular reform. But it came, rolling over the
troubled billows of the Atlantic, and all the strong-built
fortresses of despotism, and triple lines of restrictions to
shut out liberal opinions, and an unholy coalition with a
corrupt priesthood, and the well taught doctrines of absolutism, and the profoundest skill of man and the power
of the bayonet were but cobwebs.

Europe has been swept over as by a tornado; yet we
confidently look that when this desolating tornado shall
have passed by—desolating only to the towering fabrics
of aristocratic pride and regal tyranny, and a grasping,
ambitious priestcraft, we shall see a fairer temple arise,
the temple of universal liberty, adorned with intelligence
and virtue, where men, politically and socially free, shall
rest from the turmoils of revolution—the temple of a
pure religion, too, of a free and ennobling Christianity,
all radiant with the wisdom and purity and glory of
heaven.

Such we anticipate as the glorious consummation of the
present desolating revolutions in Europe. Anarchy may
for a time prevail; darkness and confusion, for a time,
cover those lands which have so long been covered with
darkness and confusion, but we look for the time, as not
distant, when the great hammer of Revolution shall
have done its work; when the huge, confused mass of
broken materials shall have been cast into the great crucible of the Almighty Hand, and fused, and a new order
of things shall follow; a remodeling of the nations; of
their governments; an establishment of universal liberty

and a re-installment of Christianity on the simplicity and purity of her ancient foundation, disenthralled from her present cumbrous trappings and carnal armor; when she shall renew her youth, and "rejoice as a young man to run a race."

The little ripple, produced in the great waters of human activity by the Puritan fathers, two hundred years ago, and which, to all human sagacity, seemed likely to die away almost as soon as produced, or to be merged in the billows of the ocean, becomes itself a mighty wave, rolling over the whole continent westward, and seeming to renew its strength as it crosses the Atlantic, and sweeps, like an overwhelming surge, over every nation in Europe. Roll on, ye heaven-sent billows, till despotism, and bigotry, and priestcraft, and every thing that opposes an heaven-born religion and a divine liberty, shall be crushed beneath your power. May the Lord hasten it in his time.

CHAPTER XXII.

Remarkable providences—small beginnings, and great results. Abraham. Joseph. Moses. David. Ruth. Ptolemy's map. Printing. The Mayflower. Bunyan. John Newton. The old marine. The poor Choctaw boy. The linen seller. Russian Bible Society. The little girl's tears, and Bible Societies. Conclusion.

"*Behold, how great a matter a little fire kindleth.*"

AFTER having completed the task originally contemplated, there still remained in our repository, slips, memoranda, a budget of unappropriated items; not a few instances of remarkable providential interpositions, which did not find a place in the general illustration of our subject, but which all go to illustrate it. We shall, therefore, give some of these a place in a concluding chapter.

It cannot but interest the pious mind, and confirm the

waveiing, doubting soul, and quell the rising fears of un-
belief, and give confidence in God's purposes and promises,
and foster a delightful anticipation of the certain triumph
of Christ's kingdom on earth, to see how, out of small beginnings, God is wont often to bring the most stupendous
results; setting at naught the wisdom of man; ordering
strength out of weakness, and making the most wonderful effects follow the most unlikely and insignificant
causes.   The following instances will farther illustrate
the mode of providential agency in carrying out the great
work of human salvation:

Scripture history is full of illustrations of this sort.   It
seemed a small matter that *Abram* should emigrate from
his country, an adventurer into some strange land, he
knows not where.   Thousands might have done the
same; and the fact of his departure seemed an affair
likely to concern few beyond his own particular family.
But what did God bring out of this small matter?   Abram,
the chosen progenitor of a great nation, should take possession of the promised land—be the father of the faithful—
his numerous seed be the people with whom God should
enter into covenant; with whom, deposit his revealed
will; with whom were the promises, and through whom,
all nations should be blessed.   That quiet, unpretending
departure of the son of Terah from Chaldea, was the
humble beginning of the most remarkable series of events
which go to make up the history of our world.   It was
the preliminary step to the founding of the Jewish commonwealth; a civil polity which has exerted a more controlling influence among the nations of the earth, than
any empire that ever existed; and the preliminary step,
too, to the founding of the Jewish church, which was a
remarkable advance on any prior dispensation of grace,
as well as an efficient instrument in the progress of human redemption.   As long as the world stands, the influence of that act shall be felt.   As long as heaven en-
dures, the spirit of just men made perfect shall bless God
for the call of Abraham, and angels shall join in the cho-
rus of thanksgiving to the Lamb.

It was a small matter that *Joseph* should dream a
dream; or, that the daughter of Pharaoh should discever,

while bathing in the Nile, an ark of rushes, floating on
the river; or, that the same casualty should befall Daniel, which fell to the lot of many a noble youth of that
day, to be transported from his native hills of Palestine to
an unwelcome captivity in Babylon.   Each of these
seemingly unimportant incidents was the first link in a
chain of stupendous events.   Great and noble purposes
were answered by the captivity of Joseph in Egypt, and
of Daniel in Babylon; and, perhaps, to no mere man that
ever lived, has the church and the world been so much indebted as to Moses.   He was a signal instrument in the
hands of God for civil, social and moral advancement.
In that little rush bark lay the germ of the most extraordinary reform and advancement in every thing that pertains to the best interests of man, both in this world and
the world to come.

Or, we might speak of *David*—the trivial circumstance
of his being sent, when a mere lad, with supplies for his
brethren, who were serving in Saul's army, leads, very
unexpectedly, to his successful encounter with the giant;
to his signalizing himself in the sight of all Israel, and to
the illustrious course which he afterwards pursued as the
head of the chosen nation, and the guide and teacher of
the church.   He was an illustrious type of Christ, and an
extraordinary instrument in forwarding the great work of
human salvation.   No one can trace up, step by step, the
history of the son of Jesse, from the time that, in obscurity
and in his childish simplicity, he watched his father's
flocks in Bethlehem, till, with a "perfect heart," he sat on
the throne of Israel, and wielded the destinies of the
chosen tribes, and not admire the wonder-working hand
of God, in so controlling human events as to bring the
most extraordinary and far-reaching results out of the
most simple, and, aparently, insignificant causes.

Or, we might, ere this, have spoken of *Ruth*.   It was a
little matter that Abimelech, of Bethlehem-Judah, goes to
sojourn in the country of Moab, he and his wife and two
sons, because of a famine.   Many others do the same.
Abimelech dies; the sons take wives of the daughters of
Moab, and soon die.   The widowed mother turns her
eyes longingly towards her native land, and resolves to

return. Her daughters-in-law propose tc accompany
her. One relents, and returns to her people and her
idols ; the other perseveres, and casts in her lot with Na-
omi and the people of God. By a felicitous train of circumstances, all beautifully providential, Ruth becomes
the wife of Boaz, who was the father of Obed, who was
the father of Jesse, the father of David. We trace back
to that little Moabitess girl the lineage of the most illustrious race of kings, of which was David, the sweet singer
of Israel, and Solomon, the great and the wise, who raised
Israel to the acme of national glory ; yea, the lineage of
the King of kings, the Prince and Saviour of the world.
A glorious issue from a most insignificant source !

Profane history furnishes illustrations scarcely less interesting, of the same overruling Hand, so controlling all
the events of this lower world, as best to subserve the
great scheme of redemption.

A little mistake, (probably a mishap of ignorance,) is
made by Ptolemy in drawing up a map of the world.
He extended the eastern parts of the continent of Asia so
enormously as to bring it round almost in contact with
the western parts of Europe and Africa, of course making
the distance across the Atlantic ocean to Asia but trifling.
Consulting this map, Columbus conceived the idea of effecting a passage to India by a westerly route. Hence
the discovery of America. And though he must first discover Ptolemy's mistake, and encounter difficulties of
which in the outset he had no conception, yet his mind
having become fired with ardor for discovery, his preparations being made, and his zeal not easily abated, he
pressed forward, not over a sea of a few *hundred* miles,
but of thousands, till the expected land appeared. "A
little fire" was kindled in his ardent soul for discovery,
the result was an immensely "great matter," the discovery of a new world, the magnitude of which we have yet
scarcely more than begun to see, and which we can
never estimate, till we shall see the end of the magnificent plans which God has to accomplish in connection
with the American continent.

So it was a little matter that a Dutchman should *cut a
few letters of the alphabet on the bark of a tree,* and then,

by means of ink, transfer an impression of them on paper. But here was the rude idea of *printing*. Nor did it
seem a much greater matter that he should, (as the first
improvement of the art,) cut letters in blocks of wood,
which he used for types, to print whole pages for the
amusement of his children. This was the day of "small
things." But if you have a mind far-reaching enough to
measure the present power of the press; its power to
perpetuate the arts and sciences; to control *mind*; to instruct and reform men, and, by a thousand ways, contribute to the advancement of our race, you can tell *how*
"great a matter" this art of printing is.

Again, a vessel of a hundred and eighty tons is a
small affair. Had you seen her afar off on the bosom of
the broad Atlantic, a mere speck in the horizon, tossed
like a feather on the huge waves, nearing the rock-bound
coast of New England, you would not have suspected *her*
laden with aught that should particularly effect the destinies of the American continent. The *Mayflower* was
laden with about one hundred persons, men, women and
children, with their implements of husbandry and trade,
with their books and Bibles, their preachers and teachers.
A somewhat singular freighting! yet even curiosity
would have dismissed any raised hope of signal good to
come from such an enterprise when they were seen to
land on *Plymouth Rock;* to cast their destinies, at the
very commencement of a stern New England winter, on
that wild, inhospitable shore. To all human sagacity,
they must perish amidst the frosts and snows; or, should
they escape the severity of the climate, die with hunger,
or fall by savage hands. Many did die; all suffered se-
verely; and many a hard year's toil, trial and suffering,
passed by before the world could see that the arrival and
settlement in this country of our Pilgrim fathers was
more than a quixotic expedition of a few refugees from
Europe.

But what has God brought out of it? There was hid in
that little nut-shell of a vessel, the germ of our free institutions, of our present advanced condition of knowledge
and virtue. Wrapped up in the bosoms of the men that
occupied the cabin of the Mayflower, were the principles

and ideas which, when developed and clothed in real
acts and institutions, presented to the world a form of
government, and a pure, evangelical, free Christianity,
and a system of popular education and of morals, and an
industry and enterprise, and inventive genius, which, under God, have made our country what she is. And if
any one can estimate the influence on our country and on
the world, of the practical working of the principles imported in the Mayflower, he can tell us how great a matter has sprung from so small a beginning.

Puritanism, wherever found, embodies the elements of
progress and improvement. It is this that has given
character to our nation; developed the resources of our
country; penetrated our mountains and brought out their
wealth; made our rivers highways; secured our water-
power; filled our land with books and schools and teachers, and made us a great, noble and prosperous nation.
It is Puritanism that has given new form and power to
the church; that has clothed Christianity in a more beautiful garment, and breathed into her the breath of life.

A few individual instances may be adduced to illustrate
the same truth.

A sturdy Puritan is serving in the parliamentary army
under Oliver Cromwell. At the siege of Leicester, in 1645,
he is drawn out to stand sentinel; a comrade, by his own
consent, takes his place, and is shot through the head at his
post. Thus was *John Bunyan*, whose life had already
twice been saved from the most imminent danger of
drowning, again spared an untimely death. Though long
since dead, he yet speaketh to millions in his own language, and to as many millions in other tongues; one of
the most signal instruments for good that ever lived.
John Newton was another chosen vessel; and how did
God watch over him when calamity, pestilence or disease was near, and shield him from danger, while yet his
heart was enmity to God. We quote a single instance:
"Though remarkable for his punctuality, one day some
business so detained him that he came to his boat much
later than usual, much to the surprise of those who had
observed his former punctuality. He went out in his
boat, as heretofore, to inspect a ship, but the ship blew up
34*

just before he reached her." Had he arrived a few min-
utes sooner, he must have perished with those on board.

Again, an obscure Highlander boy is taught the first
principles of our religion by his humble parents amidst
the glens of Scotland. He early learns to revere the Bible, and to honor God and the religion of his fathers.
We next hear of him, in mature years, a marine on board
a British man-of-war. A battle rages. The deck is
swept by a tremendous broadside from the enemy. Captain Haldane orders another company to be "piped up"
from below to take the place of the dead. On coming up
they are seized with a sudden and irresistible panic at
the mangled remains of their companions strewed on the
deck. On seeing this, the Captain swore a horrid oath,
wishing them all in hell. A pious old marine, (our High-
land boy,) stepped up to him, and very respectfully touching his hat, said, "Captain, I believe God hears prayer,
and if he had heard your prayer just now, what would
have become of us?" Having spoke this, he made a respectful bow and retired to his place. After the engage-
ment, the Captain calmly reflected on the words of the
old marine, which so affected him that he devoted his attention to the claims of religion, and became a pious
man.

Through his instrumentality his brother, Robert Haldane, though at first contemptuously rejecting his kind attentions, was brought to reflection, and became a decided
Christian.

James Haldane, (the Captain,) became a preacher, and
is pastor of a church in Edingburgh. Robert subsequently
settled in Geneva, and being much affected by the low
spiritual condition of the Protestant church there, and
the neological views of the clergy, he sought an acquaintance with the students of the theological school, invited
them to his house, gained their confidence, and finally became the means of the conversion of ten or twelve,
among whom were Felix Neff, Henry Pyt, and J. H.
Merle D'Aubigné. Few men have so honorably and
successfully served their Divine Master as Neff and Pyt;
and few fill so large a sphere in the world of usefulness as
the President of the theological school at Geneva, and the

author of the immortal History of the Reformation; and
few spots on earth are so precious to the truth, as the city
of Geneva. It was a "little fire" that kindled these great
lights, and made the ancient and honorable city of Calvin
once more worthy of that great name; it was a little
spark, struck from the luminous soul of a poor Highlander,
and well lodged in the soul of his unpretending boy.

After preaching successively and successfully in Berlin,
Hamburgh and Brussels, D'Aubigné was, providentially,
brought back to Geneva, his native city, which event led
to the establishment there of the present evangelical
"school of the prophets," with D'Aubigné at its head.
This seminary is the hope of piety in Germany; the cit-
adel of the doctrines of the ever blessed Reformation; a
fountain sending out the healing streams of salvation to
all Europe, and to the waste places of the Gentiles.

A poor Choctaw boy, (Dixon W. Lewis,) is seen wandering in the streets of Mobile; is taken into the house of
a kind Christian lady, and fed at her table. The blessing
she piously asked before eating, impressed him deeply,
though he understood not a word of it. He is sent to a
Sabbath-school, learns to read, and is converted. The
Juvenile Missionary Society of Mobile send him to the
Alabama Centenary Institute, and thence to Emory College, Georgia. In 1846, he is licensed to preach, and appointed to labor among a remnant of his own tribe, in
Kember County, Mississippi. His people, though not a
Christian among them, build him a school-house and a
church. His school opens with thirty-six scholars, from
the child of five years old, to the adult of thirty-eight.
He instructs them, prays with them, and in three months
thirty-two of them are converted. At the close of his
conference year, he reports one hundred and three conversions, and a church organized among the Choctaws,
ninety-eight strong. His father was among the converts,
and many of his relations, and an old man of more than a
hundred years old.

A young man from the highlands of Averné, in France,
is selling linen in a neighboring department; is met by a
Protestant; taken to a place of evangelical worship; he
hears, believes, embraces the truth—exchanges his wares

for Bibles and tracts, which he widely distributes at his own expense. He writes to his parents and friends—the declaration of his new sentiments excites a general inquiry, and the curate forbids his letters to be read. The young man in due time returns; his neighbors and friends gather about him. The curate attempts to convince him in the presence of his father; but failing, the father and the whole family, and many others, are led to forsake Rome; a good work begins in the neighborhood, a missionary is sent for, with the prospect that the whole region will be evangelized.

Many have been the instances of late in France, where the slightest, apparently the most insignificant circumstance, has thus been the occasion not only of introducing the gospel to a certain spot, but of diffusing it till the whole province be turned from Rome, and evangelized.

In the latter years of Alexander, Emperor of Russia, there existed in that vast and semi-barbarous country, a Russian Bible Society, which distributed, under the favoring auspices of the Emperor, a vast many copies of the Sacred Scriptures, and accomplished much good. In 1818, it had one hundred and twenty-eight branch societies, and had printed the Bible in twenty-eight languages. But where, among the mountains of that desert clime, shall we look for the little rill that gave rise to this fertilizing river? I see it in the far-off region of Moscovia; and its incipient streamlet sparkles in the light of the flames of that ancient capital. The Rev. Mr. P. is passing through Moscow on his way to England; is invited to the house of the Russian Princess M., who had just returned from the exile into which she had been driven on the invasion of Napoleon, and finally becomes the teacher of her children. He employs the influence of his station for the spiritual interests of benighted Russia. And especially did he, through the influence of the Princess, obtain a rescript for the formation of the first Russian Bible Society. It arose amidst the ashes of the ancient capital; another of those lights which gleamed up from the confused darkness and the fiery upheavings of the career of Napoleon Bonaparte.

This brings to our recollection the case of a yet larger

river which arose from a still smaller rill : A Welch cler
gyman asks a little girl for the text of his last sermon
The child gave no answer—she only wept. He ascertained that she had no Bible in which to look for the text.
And this led him to inquire whether her parents or neighbors had a Bible ; and this led to that meeting in London
in 1804, of a few devoted Christians, to devise means to
supply the poor in Wales with the Bible, the grand issue of
which was the formation of the British and Foreign Bible
Society—a society which has already distributed more
than 15,000,000 copies of the Bible—its issues now reaching nearly a million and a half annually. And this, in
turn, led to the formation of the American Bible Society,
and to the whole beautiful cluster of sister institutions
throughout the world, which are so many trees of life,
bearing the golden fruits of immortality among all the nations of the earth. This mighty river, so deep, so broad,
so far-reaching in its many branches, we may trace back
to the tears of that little girl. Behold, what a great fire
a little matter kindleth.

But it is time that the subject of this volume be brought
to a conclusion. And to what conclusion shall we come ?
We can scarcely trace the footsteps of Providence through
so long a period of time, and over so varied a field,
without being impressed with the majesty, and wisdom,
and power of Him who directs every wheel of the great
providential scheme, and brings to pass his own predes-
tined results. In the review of our subject, we are brought,
at least, to the following conclusions :

1. That, in working out the stupendous problem of the
redemption of men and of nations, *God takes time*. Moral
revolutions are of slow development. The works of
Providence, more especially, perhaps, than those of creation, have a direct reference to the display of the Divine
character, and to the exhibition of man's character. It
was needful, therefore, that these works be prolonged—
that the book of Providence lie open continually for perusal. It had been easy for God to speak the heavens
and the earth and all therein, into existence in a moment
of time—instantaneously to give form, fertility and beauty
to the earth, and matured perfection to the animal, min-

eral, and vegetable worlds. But God chose to lay open
his works to inspection, that they might be examined
piece by piece. It had been easy for God to have brought
his Son to die a sacrifice for sin, immediately on the fall
of man. But a thousand sublime purposes had then failed—
God's glory had been eclipsed, and man's redemption been
another thing. Four thousand years should be filled up
in preparation—not a change or a revolution should
transpire which was not tributary to the one great purpose. The Hand of God was all this time busy in well-
directed efforts—not an abortive movement, not a mistake, not a retrograde motion, did he make. All was
onward, and onward as rapidly as the nature of the work
permitted. There was neither hurry nor delay.

God, as a perfect Architect, is rearing, in this world of
ours, a perfect building. We believe the golden age of
the earth is to return, when Christianity shall be glorified
as one complete and perfect Temple. But this Temple
shall be constructed of pre-existing materials. All sorts
of systems, religions, politics, and ethics, have been permitted to exist, the perfect with the imperfect, the good
with the bad. And it has, in all past time, been the work
of the Hand of Providence, to overrule, select, reject, and
out of the good and acceptable, to rear the perfect building. Our present civilization, and systems of free government, and of morals, are *results* of former facts, systems and experiences—structures formed from the ruins
of former edifices—*compounds*, from various gone-by in-
gredients; all thrown into the crucible of human progress, fused, and run in a new mould. And may we not,
philosophically speaking, say the same of our religion?
Shall not the perfect building be reared in the same manner?—be wrought out of materials selected and brought
together by the ever-busy Hand of Providence, from every
system, organization, form of government and religion,
which ever existed?—the eternal mind so overruling the
whole as to bring good out of all? If so, we see reason
enough why God should *take time* to consummate his one
great final purpose.

Again, it had been easy for God to settle his people at
once in the goodly land, without the migratory life of the

Patriarchs, or the bondage of Egypt, or deliverance from the hand of Pharaoh, or the forty years' wanderings, hardships and temptations of the wilderness ; yet their settlement in Palestine would, then, have been no more than the making stationary any other wandering tribes from the desert. The history of that whole eventful period was full of God and his grace, full of man and his rebellion. Or the Reformation of the sixteenth century might have been the work of a day, instead of a result of three centuries' preparation. Or the teeming millions of Asia might have received the gospel without a train of preparatory events running through several centuries, exhibiting the wickedness and the withering influences of idolatry ; the inefficacy of every conceivable form of error and false religion, to ameliorate the civil, social and religious condition of a nation ; and finally producing the conviction that nothing short of a pure Christianity can do it. Or the dark continent of Africa might have been evangelized in a single generation, instead of the protracted, mysterious process, which Providence has pursued, administering a burning rebuke on Africa for her long-protracted sins, as a grossly wicked abettor of the slave-trade, yet visiting the captives in their cruel bondage, and by his converting grace preparing thousands to return to that ill-fated land, laden with the best of Heaven's blessings for poor, forsaken Africa. Had the shorter process been pursued, God's glory and his abounding, condescending grace had been but sparingly developed, and man's sin but partially exposed. God takes time.

2. We may infer, from facts stated, that often the *original* and *direct* object which men have in view in their endeavors to do good, or to benefit themselves, is of less importance than the *incidental* and *indirect* objects which Providence brings out of it. We may be doing the greatest good where we least suspect it. The original and direct object for which *Columbus* entered upon the adventurous voyage across the Atlantic, was to find a shorter passage to India. The incidental advantage which was gained by the prosecution of the enterprise, was the discovery of the New World. The *alchemists* toiled for generations, in pursuit of the philosopher's stone : their

original and direct object was of no value. Yet their researches incidently led to the discovery of facts, in connection with the properties and composition of bodies, which served as the foundation of the science of modern chemistry. The *inventor of printing* had no object in view beyond the amusement of his children or of himself; or, at farthest, his own emolument. The incidental benefits are world-wide, and past all human calculation. *Luther* buckles on the harness as a Reformer, simply to oppose an *abuse* in the sale of indulgences; at first, perhaps, incited only by the fact that that sale was likely to be monopolized by the Dominican monks. The incidental advantage which grew out of the original controversy, was the ever glorious Reformation. Some men toil all their life long to accumulate wealth, a penny of which they will not give to the Lord, yet the Lord takes the whole in the end. Others, like Saul of Tarsus, toil for years to perfect themselves in learning for some selfish end; God frustrates them in that, yet makes them accomplish an infinitely more worthy end in the building up of the Redeemer's kingdom. Nations engage in expensive, bloody wars, for most unworthy, trifling purposes; He that sitteth King of the nations brings out of such wars incidental advantages of a noble and enduring character. One nation is thereby opened to receive the gospel, and, in another, mountain-like obstacles to the setting up of the kingdom of Christ, are removed. Man, in his schemes and operations, means one thing; God, in his plans and agencies, means quite another thing. Hence,

3. We may with perfect confidence leave *results* with God. God will complete what he has begun. Not one of his purposes can fail. Man sees but a little way; God sees to the end. Examples already referred to will illustrate the thought. Little did the young Chaldean adventurer anticipate the illustrious race of kings that should descend from his loins, or his more illustrious spiritual seed. Little did he conceive that his departure from Chaldea was the first link of a most brilliant series of events. Little conscious were the brethren of Joseph, when they nefariously sold their brother into slavery; or Pharaoh's daughter, when she drew the babe Moses from

the rush cradle; or the captors of Daniel, when they forced him into exile, that theirs were preliminary steps to the establishment of a power which has again and again revolutionized the world, and shall continue to revolu tionize it till the kingdoms of this world shall become the kingdom of our Lord. Little did Columbus think of the amazing consequences which have resulted to mankind from his adventures; or the Pilgrim fathers, the grand and truly astonishing effects of their zeal, and faith, and love of liberty, in their consequences on the history of mankind; or Faust, in his invention of the art of printing; or Luther, in his bold essays to reform a corrupt church. And that little band of Christians met in London to devise means of supplying the poor in Wales with the Bible, were as far from foreseeing that their deliberations should result in the formation of the British and Foreign Bible Society, which, with affiliated societies, (all her own legitimate daughters,) should so soon enter on the work of giving the sacred volume to the entire world. And as little did Robert Raikes think what an instrument for the renovation of the world he had originated, when, having gathered about him a few beggarly children in the by-ways of London, he embodied the idea suggested by a benignant Providence into the form of a Sabbath-school. A child may set a stone rolling which the mightiest man cannot stop.

We look back through nearly sixty centuries, and see with what a steady, irresistible step God has carried forward the great work. Not a failure has occurred—not a mistake—not an obstacle that could stand in the way. The mountain has been made a plain when He would pass over. Kingdoms and dominions—the stateliest fabrics of human power and skill have been as nothing before him—as the cobweb in the path of the giant. What perfect confidence may we then have that God will complete what he has begun; and especially as we now see he is, as never before, bringing all things into subserviency to the one great end. Learning, skill, inventions, improvements, discoveries, governments, all human activity is so shaped, or such a tendency given to it, that

35

it is made, in an unwonted manner, to subserve the work of human salvation.

4. Another conclusion to which we arrive is, that the *church is safe.* No opposition has ever prevailed, no weapon formed against her, prospered. Ten heathen persecutions raged, and their fire was hot enough to dissolve any thing but God's Church. In the last, her enemies boasted that "now they had done the business for the Christians, and overthrown the Christian Church." Yet, in the midst of their triumph, the church prevails, while the persecuting power, the great Roman Empire, is brought to nought. Again, the Arian heresy threatens to swallow up the church; or the beast on the seven hills makes war on the saints, and seems to overcome them; or the unnumbered hosts of the Saracens spread like locusts over the Christian world, and seem for a time commissioned to annihilate it; or Protestantism is assailed by an Invincible Armada; or likely to be blown up by the Gunpowder Plot in a Protestant Parliament. Yet all these mad endeavors avail nothing. God signally appeared for the deliverance of his people, and turned the machinations of the wicked against themselves.

And so it has been in every age of the Church. She has outrode every storm, though shaken by the thunderbolt and scathed by the lightning. No confederation has been half so much assailed or opposed with half so much power and virulence; none has stood so firm, none withstood so long. And, as it has been, so it shall be. "Judgment shall return unto righteousness"—the seeming darkness and disorders of Providence shall issue in the furtherance of the cause of righteousness—the progress of truth. All shall be so overruled that the right and the good shall triumph. The righteous shall see it and be glad. The arm of Omnipotence is engaged to carry forward his cause—to make every one feel that if he be on the side with God, on the side of truth and righteousness, *he is safe.* The stars in their courses may fight against him—all may appear dark, and confused, and adverse—the tempests may beat, the floods come, yet his foundation standeth sure. It is the rock. His house will not fall. All his earthly interests may fail, the earth be burned up, the elements be dissolved, yet the man who has God for his portion can suffer no loss. His treasure lies too high—his home beyond these temporary turmoils of time —his interests are all in the safe keeping of One who never allows a single purpose of his to fail.

But on the other hand, how different is the condition of the ungodly man? He may seem to prosper for a while; but his prosperity is as the "baseless fabric of a dream." It has no foundation. Be it riches, honors, pleasures, any thing in which God and eternity do not enter, it will change with the changes of time. It hath no permanence.

5. Again, we are led to conclude that all human affairs, and the great work of redemption, are approaching a *crisis.* The lines of Providence seem fast converging to some great point of consummation. Great events thicken upon us. Events which were wont to occupy centuries, are now crowded into less decades of years. The wheels of Providence run swift and high, far outstripping in their magnificent consummations any thing that a few years ago imagination could conceive or faith realize. We now see the whole world in motion, animated by a common soul; and that soul is Providence. All is gloriously moving forward to a destined point; and that point the next great step of advancement in the sublime economy of grace. There is commotion among the hosts of Rome. The waters of the mystic Euphrates are glimmering for the last time in the rays of the setting sun. The Pagan world is shaken to its very centre—its temples crumbling, its idols falling, its darkness dissipating, and, as never before, it is prepared to receive the gospel. And the spirit of life is passing over the face of the stagnant Christianity of the East, and preparing those lapsed and corrupt churches once more to arise and let their light shine. And there is discovered, too, a shaking among the dry bones of Israel, a spirit of renovation and life, betokening the long night of their dispersion and affliction to be nearly passed, and the day of their redemption at hand.

In correspondence, too, with all this, there is a movement in the sacramental host, and a counter movement in the camp of the enemy, both heralding **the** approach of the same crisis. This heaving of the lungs of a new spiritual life in the Church—this recent movement of the moral muscles of the body of Christ, has given birth to a delightful progeny of benevolent associations, brought into being just in time to meet the demand created by the movements of Providence in opening the field. The Church has at length roused from her deep sleep of apathy over the Pagan world, and is extending the arms of her compassion to the ends of the earth, and reaching the bread of life to waiting millions. While, on the other hand, the enemies of the truth are on the alert, ready to contest with the saints the last inch of ground. The adherents of infidelity, error and Anti-christ, are gathering up their strength, combining their forces, and preparing to come up to the last great battle. "Satan is driven from one strong hold to another and foiled at every turn. Expedients are failing him. He stirs up war, and it becomes the occasion of spreading the kingdom of peace. He excites persecution, but instead of exterminating the saints of God, it brings about full liberty of conscience, and favors the organization of independent Christian churches. He panders to superstitions, by devices so successful in the dark ages, but only provokes another reformation in the land of Luther. His old arts will not serve him now." All things betoken the approach of another great crisis in the work of human redemption.

6. Another conclusion, therefore, to which we are brought, is, that although the world is soon to be given to Christ, yet there shall come a *dark day first*. The enemy has usurped the dominion of this world. He is the god of this world; the prince of the power of the air. Though overcome, he is not yet dispossessed of his usurped inheritance. The strong man armed is still spoiling the goods. Often he is made to feel the weight of a stronger arm, and, like a chafed lion, is roused in his wrath. Truth is mighty. He fears its invading footsteps as he sees its irresistible progress. Yet he will not yield the possession of six thousand years without a last desperate conflict. Nothing so soon brings on this conflict as the progress of truth. It is but the legitimate effect of

the diffusion of the gospel. And as the probability increases, that Christianity shall fill the whole earth, that
all shall be brought into subjection to Christ, all learning,
wealth, earthly power, manners, maxims, habits, human
governments, and whatever belongs to man—the rage of
the enemy becomes more and more rampant ; and as he
sees his territory diminishing, and his last foothold threatened, he will make his last grand rally, and never yield
while there remains a forlorn hope. The friends and the
enemies of the truth are no doubt fast bringing things to
a grand and dreadful issue, which shall for a little time
cover Zion with a cloud, but which shall soon bring her
out fair as the moon, clear as the sun, and terrible as an
army with banners.

7. The missionary work is *the* great work of the age.
It is the work to which God by his providence is espe
cially calling his church at the present day. Our age is
not characterized by wars and rumors of wars, nor even
by great political revolutions. In nothing is it so remarkable as for increased facilities for the spread of the
gospel, and the actual diffusion of civilization and Christianity by means of Christian missions. Few are fully
aware what has been the progress of evangelization since
the world was hushed into peace on the plains of Waterloo. But a single generation has passed, yet the moral
changes which the world has undergone during this short
period, are truly astonishing. The historian who shall
write the history of this period, will needs fix on the work
of evangelizing the heathen, as the great work of the age.
Infidelity and fanaticism concede this, when they so
carefully hold up the amelioration of the condition of
man and the conversion of the world, as the Ultima
Thule of all their systems, and of all their wild or wicked
devices. No one would now think to hazard a new
scheme, which should not hold up the spread of civilization, knowledge, and Christianity, as the consummation
to be reached.

8. The present is the *harvest age* of the world. A busy
and all-controlling Providence has been preparing the
ground for centuries past, and sowing the seed, and
watering it with the heavenly dew, and warming it with

35*

the rays of the Sun of Righteousness.   He has, too, been preparing laborers for such a harvest, and now he is gathering in the sheaves.   Indeed, for the last thousand years, all things have been preparing for this very age. Midnight darkness then covered the earth.   That was the crisis of spiritual night.   From that gloomy epoch causes have been at work ; revolutions taking place ; instruments, resources, facilities accumulating, which have all been employed to bring about just such a day as the present.   The lines of Providence seem converging here. The labors of Wicklif, Huss, and Jerome, the ever-glorious Reformation of the sixteenth century, prepared agencies, established principles, recovered, from the rubbish of a corrupt church, doctrines, and restored to the church vitality and spiritual vigor, all of which seem to have been looking forward to the present age.   The revolutions and activities, and the great and good men of the seventeenth century, were especially contributing to this same end. Baxter, Bunyan, Doddridge, Flavel, and the hosts of giants of those days, were laboring for our times.   Great and good men are always as the tree of life which bare twelve manner of fruits, and yielded her fruit every month, whose leaves were for the healing of the nations; yet those men seemed more especially to have been raised up for our age.   Never more than now, perhaps, were the writings of those men fulfilling their divine commission.

And, in like manner, the wars and political movements of the eighteenth century, with all its intellectual and moral advances, were contributing to the same consummation. The American Revolution ; the conquests of the English in the East ; and the career of Napoleon Bonaparte, were all far-reaching events, and immensely influential in bringing in the present harvest season of the church. By these means modern liberty found habitation and rest ; the territories of Paganism were thrown open to the benevolent action of the church ; and many a formidable obstacle was broken down by that hammer of Providence, the hero of Corsica.   Before him quailed the despotisms of Europe ; Rome shook on her seven hills, and the internal weakness of the Turkish empire was revealed, and from that time Mohammedanism began to decline.

9. Finally, if such be the indications on the part of Providence, such the facilities and resources secured for evangelizing the world, and such the preparedness of the world to receive the gospel, WHAT IS THE DUTY OF THE CHURCH, *what the duty of every individual Christian* at such a time, and under such circumstances?

This was announced as the THIRD general topic of the present treatise. But our volume has already swollen to its prescribed dimensions. We may not, therefore, enter upon any discussion of this topic, but we leave it with the pious mind to *infer* his duty in the solemn and interesting circumstances in which, at the present moment, he finds himself providentially placed.

We possess advantages which neither the apostolic age, nor any subsequent age ever yet enjoyed. Such improvements, inventions, discoveries, facilities of communication and intercourse with all parts of the world, have been the heritage of no preceding age. The Printing Press, the Mariner's Compass, modern improvements in Navigation, and Magnetic Telegraphs, were equally unknown in the early ages of Christianity. Different portions of the world were estranged, one portion not even knowing of the existence of the other. Commerce was restricted to a small portion of the earth's population, and education was confined to a few individuals of a few nations. Science had scarcely been made to favor Christianity at all, and governmental power was generally opposed to it. Liberty, the only political atmosphere in which Christianity can flourish, scarcely existed, even in name. The literature of the world, too, and its philosophy, were opposed to the progress of Christianity.

But in the revolutions of Providence, how different it is now! What immense advantages does Christianity now enjoy for its universal propagation and establishment over the whole earth. The mighty power of God is everywhere at work, accomplishing the one great end for which the earth was made. All things are being brought into subserviency to this one purpose. God has risen up, and by the strong arm of his providence, is pre-

paring to give the kingdoms of this world to his Son
The church has never before been brought into a position
so favorable for the conquest of the world.

What, then, is the duty of the church? and of the
individual Christian? She should work when and where
God works. She should follow the leadings of Providence; take possession of every inch of territory open
for her occupancy; send a missionary, plant a mission,
wherever she may; erect a school wherever pupils may
be found, and give the Bible and the religious book where-
ever she may meet the reader. The harvest of the world
is at hand; the fields are ripe; every disciple of Jesus
Christ is a reaper. Each has his own sphere, and befitting capacities, and opportunities for using his capacities.
He must, therefore, serve his Divine Master in *his own
sphere;* which, if he do with fidelity, his reward is as
sure, and he may feel as delightful a confidence that he
is performing a useful and important work, as the man
who may be laboring in a very different sphere. Causes
may be at work, or instruments be preparing, in some
obscure corner, which we may help mature; and which
when matured, become potent engines to build up truth
or demolish error. Duties are ours; events, God's.

The work to be done is as varied as it is vast and important. None can be idle for the want of an appropriate
work; none, whether high or low, rich or poor, can be
idle innocently. God now, as never before, is calling
every professed disciple of the Lord Jesus to stand in his
lot; to do his duty as, in providence, it now devolves
upon him. The Great Captain is rallying his forces for
the great battle. He expects every man to do his duty.

Ride on, victorious King, conquering and to conquer,
till the kingdoms of this world shall be thine, and thou
shalt reign forever and ever.

Printed in the USA
CPSIA information can be obtained
at www.ICGtesting.com
LVHW010227260624
784030LV00022B/256